The Economic Growth Engine

The International Institute for Applied Systems Analysis

is an interdisciplinary, nongovernmental research institution founded in 1972 by leading scientific organizations in 12 countries. Situated near Vienna, in the center of Europe, IIASA has been producing valuable scientific research on economic, technological and environmental issues for over three decades.

IIASA was one of the first international institutes to systematically study global issues of environment, technology and development. IIASA's Governing Council states that the Institute's goal is: 'to conduct international and interdisciplinary scientific studies to provide timely and relevant information and options, addressing critical issues of global environmental, economic and social change, for the benefit of the public, the scientific community and national and international institutions'. Research is organized around three central themes:

- Energy and Technology
- Environment and Natural Resources
- Population and Society

IIASA is funded and supported by scientific institutions and organizations in the following countries: Austria, China, Egypt, Estonia, Finland, Germany, India, Japan, Netherlands, Norway, Pakistan, Poland, Republic of Korea, Russian Federation, South Africa, Sweden, Ukraine, United States of America.

Further information: <http://www.iiasa.ac.at>

The Economic Growth Engine

How Energy and Work Drive Material Prosperity

Robert U. Ayres

Novartis Professor (Emeritus) of Management and the Environment, INSEAD, France and Institute Scholar, International Institute for Applied Systems Analysis (IIASA), Austria

and

Benjamin Warr

PhD, Senior Research Fellow, Social Innovation Centre, INSEAD, France

PUBLISHED IN ASSOCIATION WITH THE INTERNATIONAL INSTITUTE FOR APPLIED SYSTEMS ANALYSIS (IIASA)

IIASA

Edward Elgar
Cheltenham, UK • Northampton, MA, USA

Published by
Edward Elgar Publishing Limited
The Lypiatts
15 Lansdown Road
Cheltenham
Glos GL50 2JA
UK

Edward Elgar Publishing, Inc.
William Pratt House
9 Dewey Court
Northampton
Massachusetts 01060
USA

Paperback edition 2010

A catalogue record for this book
is available from the British Library

Library of Congress Control Number: 2008939767

Mixed Sources
Product group from well-managed
forests and other controlled sources
www.fsc.org Cert no. SA-COC-1565
© 1996 Forest Stewardship Council

ISBN 978 1 84844 182 8 (cased)
ISBN 978 1 84980 435 6 (paperback)

Printed and bound by MPG Books Group, UK

Contents

Figures

Tables

Preface and acknowledgments

This book has had a very long gestation. The senior author (R.U.A.) has spent much of his time during the last 40 years or more – amidst numerous distractions – trying to understand the fundamental relationship between technology and economics. Some of that history is recapitulated in the book. However, the author's learning experience during a year at Resources for the Future, Inc. (RFF) during 1967–8 was crucial. In particular, it was a line of research initiated by Allen V. Kneese at RFF that has led us finally to this point. It was during that period that the senior author began to see that the economy is truly a physical system that converts raw materials into goods and services, subject to the laws of thermodynamics. It has taken most of the rest of the time since 1968 to understand how and why our conceptualization is inconsistent with standard neoclassical economic theory. Enlightenment has been very slow in coming, and even now it would be foolish to claim 'Eureka!' But since the two of us joined forces in 2001, we have made some progress – enough, we think, to warrant publication of some results.

During the past decade we have received valuable intellectual stimulation from discussions with a number of persons deserving special thanks, including (in alphabetical order) Kenneth Arrow, Christian Azar, Jeroen van den Bergh, Jonathan Cave, Paul David, Nina Eisenmenger, Karl-Erik Erickson, Marina Fischer-Kowalski, Arnulf Gruebler, Andrey Krasovskii, Reiner Kuemmel, Katalin Martinàs, Nebojsa Nakicenovic, Shunsuke Mori, Adam Rose, Warren Sanderson, Heinz Schandl, Leo Schrattenholzer, Gerry Silverberg, David Simpson, Alexander Tarasyev, David Toman, Chihiro Watanabe and Eric Williams. None of them is responsible for any errors or misunderstandings on our part.

The collection, compilation (and occasional correction) of the US and Japanese exergy/work database that underlies Chapters 3, 4 and 7 is primarily due to Leslie W. Ayres. Ms Ayres has also provided a great deal of personal support to one of us, not to mention computer expertise when needed.

Chapter 9 is partly the work of Jie Li, a Ph.D. student at Princeton, who was a member of the Young Scientists Summer Program at IIASA, in 2005. It was she who (under the direction of Robert Ayres) carried out the statistical analysis in the published paper that finally resulted (Li and Ayres 2007) and which is the basis for the results presented in this book.

We also gratefully acknowledge financial support for one or both of us from the European Commission (project TERRA), the European Science Foundation (ESF) and the Austrian Central Bank (through the University of Klagenfurt, Center for Social Ecology), INSEAD, and especially the International Institute for Applied Systems Analysis (IIASA) in Laxenburg, Austria. If any single institution can be regarded as the 'foster parent' of this book, it is IIASA.

Introduction

In the year 2000 at the end of the Clinton Administration the US federal budget had a surplus of 1 percent of GDP. By 2007 the surplus had become a deficit of over 6 percent of GDP, a figure more usually associated with Latin America. Part of the swing from surplus to deficit was due to the military spending to finance the war in Iraq. Another part was due to the huge new 'homeland security' program. A third part was due to the continued outsourcing of manufactured products (and exodus of manufacturing jobs) from East Asia. The Bush Administration's tax cuts for the wealthy was another major cause. The overvalued US dollar, propped up by its role as the major reserve currency of the world, has played a role. The budgetary deficit has been compensated in part – but only a small part – by the anti-recession policy of the Federal Reserve Bank, resulting in extraordinarily low domestic interest rates for several years (2001–04). That policy permitted (indeed encouraged) excessive consumer spending, which, in turn, generated steady growth in the US GDP (and kept tax returns from collapsing) until the end of 2007.

But the low interest rates, together with lax, or lack of, regulation, permitted some clever financial operators to create a real estate boom that soon became a 'bubble'. This was driven by huge numbers of sub-prime 'teaser' mortgages, which were sold by predatory lenders to unqualified people who should not have been buying houses in the first place. There were two results, clear in retrospect, but somehow neither predicted nor expected. One was a five-year boom in US house prices that persuaded even 'sensible' investors to take on variable rate mortgages in the expectation of selling out at higher prices before the rate adjustments came into force. Many real estate investors will now lose both their homes and their savings. Real estate prices are falling and the 'wealth effect' on spending has gone into reverse. The US economy is now in recession.

The other result of the cheap money policy was that many of the variable rate mortgages that had been sold to people with poor credit ratings were packaged with other mortgages in the form of 'mortgage-based securities' and sold by brokers to insurance companies and pension funds. These securities were treated, for a while, like AAA or AA rated bonds, because the rating agencies never examined the credit ratings of the individual borrowers. As a result, many financial institutions now have 'assets' based on assumed revenue streams that have suddenly become very uncertain. These securities have uncertain values. The financial institutions that own such securities are now (Winter 2009) in varying degrees of trouble. A further consequence of that fact, in turn, is that banks are suddenly reluctant to lend. It looks like a global repetition of the collapse of the Japanese 'bubble economy' in 1989–90. The dollar is weak. The US government seems incapable of doing anything to prevent this. How far will it go? Nobody knows.

What point are we making? Simply that economic theory has lagged rather far behind reality. However, we hasten to add that our focus is on the longer term; we have relatively little to say about short-term fluctuations.

According to most professional economists, the post-2000 acceleration in labor productivity – literally, output per (non-farm) man-hour – is very good news for the economy in the long run. The reason for this rosy assumption, at bottom, is that long-term historical trends suggest a correlation between productivity, growth and wealth creation. But sadly, whereas employment did increase slowly in the past few decades, the recent dramatic increase in US labor productivity (before 2008) has yielded very little increase in employment whereas the downturn has increased unemployment drastically. The French experience since the official 35-hour week was instituted (supposedly to create more jobs) has been similarly discouraging.

For some reason the historic link between output (GDP) growth and employment has been weakened, if not broken. We think that the historical 'engine' of economic growth has (so to speak) run out of steam. It is getting harder and harder to create jobs, outside of the import/retail trade area. The unwelcome implication of this is that 'raw' human labor, on average, is no longer a scarce or essential resource, except perhaps in some types of agriculture. Nor, it seems, is capital a scarce resource in the modern world. Capital has become cheap because capital accumulated in the past can be used as collateral for new loans, while still being productive in the present. Moreover, in recent years, institutions have been created that permit borrowing well in advance of hypothetical future earnings that are projected to flow from both current and past investments. In short, financial capital can, and does, increase much faster than savings from current income. Is this flood of capital being invested in wealth creation through new technology? Or are we exploring for oil (as it were) on Wall Street? Is the new capital being invested mainly in financial instruments, mergers and acquisitions, private equity and hedge funds?

Most people nowadays believe in economic growth for much the same reason they believe in God or in the power of prayer: it is politically proper. US currency is imprinted with the phrase 'In God we Trust'. Faith is widely regarded as a moral virtue. Faith is a cousin of confidence, and consumer confidence is said to be growth-friendly, at least in the short term. But in economic affairs clear sight, sensible policies and a bit of luck are needed too. Let us start with clarity. The key point to understand is that government (and private sector) economists assume that future economic growth will continue indefinitely at something like historical rates.

What justifies this assumption that growth is automatic? The answer is, simply, that the easiest assumption about the future, *ceteris paribus,* is that it will be like the past. Given a 200-plus year history of steady economic growth, it is fairly natural to assume that the historical trend will continue. Governments, businesses and institutions are now, and have been for several decades, effectively addicted to the presumption of perpetual and inevitable economic growth. Any suggestions that growth might not continue indefinitely (or that it might not be a good thing for society) are ignored or disparaged. Periods of turmoil, such as the recent past, are invariably regarded as exceptional. Analysts and pundits of all stripes speak of 'recovery' as though the US economic experience from 1999 through 2007 was merely like suffering from a cold, or perhaps, a mild case of the flu. We think, on the contrary, that it was (and is) symptomatic of a deeper disease.

It is important to recognize that there is no quantitatively verifiable economic theory to explain past growth. This is a fairly shocking statement, so it is worthy of repetition for emphasis. To be sure, we can say quite a lot about growth stoppers. But there is no theory, based on general behavioral laws, to explain quantitatively why some economies grow, but some grow faster than others and some do not grow at all.

To be sure there is a qualitative theory, widely accepted and rarely challenged. It goes like this: consumers save part of their current incomes in order to invest. Investment creates productive capacity. The purpose of saving and investment is partly to provide a safety net against times of trouble and partly to enjoy increased consumption (higher income) in the future. There is a well-established tradeoff between the desire to enjoy income in the present and greater income in the future. It is called the discount rate, because most people will discount future income that they might not be alive to enjoy or that might be wiped out by events beyond their control or because of simple short-sightedness. In order to induce society as a whole to save and invest, the prospects for future economic growth must be attractive enough to compensate for the loss of current consumption. But if growth is assumed to be automatic, then the incentive to save and invest disappears. The Chinese now save almost 45 percent of current income, in order to assure that they will be better off in the future. The US savings rate is zero or negative, because most Americans seem to be convinced that economic growth happens without effort, and (thanks to a lot of 'shop until you drop' urging by politicians and economists) that saving is negative for growth whereas current consumption favors growth. Besides, if one can simply borrow and spend the savings of others, as the US has been doing for decades, why save?

Energy

Apart from lack of savings other factors are at work. There have been fairly major departures from the overall growth trend, during wars, the Great Depression, and the oil embargo of 1973–74. The problem is to understand how they interact.

In contrast to the neoclassical economic model, the real economic system depends on physical material and energy inputs, as well as labor and capital. The real economic system can be viewed as a complex process that converts raw materials (and energy) into useful materials and final services. Evidently materials and energy do play a central role in this model of economic growth. This process has stages, of which the first stage is to convert raw materials into finished materials and raw fuels into finished fuels and electricity. In fact, this book argues that over the past two centuries, successive improvements in the efficiency of these various conversion stages have accounted for most of the economic growth our Western civilization has experienced. Just as many durable goods markets are approaching saturation, there is evidence that opportunities for further technological improvements in the energy- and materials-conversion stages of the economic system are simultaneously approaching exhaustion.

We said earlier that the 'engine' of growth is running out of steam. To explain that statement we need to characterize the 'engine' in potentially quantifiable terms. The growth engine is a kind of positive feedback system. Demand growth for any product or service, and hence for raw materials and energy services, is stimulated by declining prices. Lower prices enable present consumers to buy more, and marginal consumers to enter the market. (Higher prices have the opposite effect: they induce consumers to buy less or seek cheaper alternatives.) Increased demand induces suppliers to add new capacity (that is, new factories), which also tends to result in greater economies of scale, and savings from 'learning by doing', thus enabling further decreases in prices. Production experience also cuts costs by stimulating technological improvements in the production process itself. Finally, firms may invest in R&D to cut manufacturing costs or to increase product quality, which also helps sales. Evidently the system feeds on itself, which is why it can be described as a positive feedback loop or cycle. The details are discussed at length in subsequent chapters of this book.

However a significant share of the cost reductions since the early 19th century has occurred at the second stage of production, where crude fossil fuels are converted into a more highly processed form of energy, which we can call 'useful work'. Work, in the technical sense, is the service obtained from raw energy by first-order conversion. Power, a slightly less misleading term, is simply the rate at which work is performed, or work done per unit time.

In any case, fossil hydrocarbon prices are more likely to increase than to fall in the future. Emission controls are becoming a significant element of costs to electric power producers, refiners and other industrial fuel users. Another more urgent problem is the approaching 'peak oil', that is, the time when global output peaks and begins to decline. To be sure, the age of oil is not yet ended. Still, several independent lines of argument suggest that global peak production will occur between 2010 and 2020 (for example, Campbell 2004; Deffeyes 2001; Strahan 2007). As production drops, prices may fluctuate but the long-term trend will be likely up rather than down.

Of course rising prices will eventually bring some new 'unconventional' sources into production, such as bio-fuels, Greenland Shelf oil, Venezuelan heavy oil, Athabaska tar sands and Green River oil shale. But bio-fuels compete with food production. Demand for ethanol, created by government actions, is – together with rising demand for meat consumption from China – already driving up corn and wheat prices dramatically. The other unconventional sources are said to be potentially larger than the global stock of liquid petroleum. But the costs of recovery are likely to be much higher than current costs and the energy-return-on-investment (EROI) will be much lower. Extremely large amounts of capital (and energy) will be required. This creates a potential supply bottleneck; it may take a number of decades before new sources could reach the output levels of today. And higher oil prices will soon be accompanied by higher prices for gas and coal, since oil will have to be replaced by other fuels wherever feasible.

To summarize: In this book, we attempt to characterize economic variables, where appropriate, in terms of primary physical properties, namely *mass* and *exergy*. The term 'exergy' is used here, and throughout the book, rather than energy, because it is what most people really mean when they speak of energy. (We explain the terminology below.) We specifically address the economic implications of the First and Second Laws of Thermodynamics. The First Law, says that mass/energy are conserved quantities. It is primarily useful as an accounting tool, closely analogous to double entry bookkeeping, but it has powerful implications as well. On earth, where nuclear reactions are insignificant in mass terms, the First

Law says that all the mass that flows into any transformation process – including any economic process – must end up either as a useful product, a stock change or a waste. In fact most materials extracted from the earth's surface end up as wastes. *Wastes, both material and energy, are a pervasive accompaniment of all economic activity.*

The Second Law, sometimes called the entropy law, says that the availability of energy to do useful work is reduced by every transformation process, whereas the non-useful component increases. *Entropy* is a measure of that increasing non-useful component. The technical term for the useful component is *exergy*. But, according to the First Law, energy is a conserved quantity, which means that it doesn't increase or decrease. The energy content of a physical entity or system does not change during a transformation process, such as production or consumption. However exergy is the useful component of energy; it is the component that can perform useful work. Exergy is not conserved. In fact, it is partially 'used up' in every transformation or process.

It follows that *every production process is dissipative*. A continuous process requires a continuing flow of exergy to keep going. Capital equipment without an activating flow of exergy is inert and unproductive. In the eighteenth century, the main product of every economy was agricultural: food or animal feed. The primary exergy input was sunlight, which was free. At that time productive capital consisted mainly of land, tools and animals, apart from a few smelters, water mills and windmills. So the exergy flow at the time was mostly invisible, being embodied in human or animal labor. It was natural for the early economists to consider capital (including land and animals) and labor to be the primary factors of production.

However, since the industrial revolution, mechanization – beginning with the steam engine – has increased enormously. Machines have largely replaced humans and animals as power sources. These machines required coal, at first, and more recently petroleum, natural gas or electric power. In short, the mechanized industrial economy depends upon inputs of exergy. Without exergy inputs, there can be no production. It follows, then that *exergy should be considered as an independent factor of production, along with capital and labor.*

The standard economic theory of growth, developed since the 1950s, retains the two traditional factors of production but does not include exergy. However this standard theory, based on increasing capital stock and increasing labor inputs, does not actually explain the growth that has occurred. To remedy the deficiency, economist have introduced an exogenous multiplier called 'technical process' or, more recently 'total factor productivity'. In fact, most of the growth seems to be due to this exogenous multiplier.

One theoretical innovation in this book is the explicit introduction of *exergy efficiency* as an economic variable. We noted above that exergy is defined as potential useful work, that is, the amount of useful work that could be performed, in principle, by a given amount of energy. A moment's thought suggests that there can be a big difference between the amount of work actually performed and the amount that could theoretically be performed. The difference is lost work, mainly as waste heat. The ratio between actual work done and the potential amount of work that could be done in theory, is the *exergy efficiency*. We have estimated the work done by the US economy since 1900, and the exergy efficiency of that work. Not surprisingly the efficiency has increased fairly dramatically, corresponding to a significant reduction in the waste as a fraction of the total.

The final innovation discussed in this book is the introduction of useful work actually performed, instead of exergy input, as the third factor of production. The justification for this is simply that the input exergy is mostly unproductive (that is, waste heat), whereas the work actually performed by the economy is the productive component. It turns out that with this innovation, past US economic growth can be explained very well by the three factors, capital, labor and energy without needing to invoke exogenous 'technical progress' or 'total factor productivity'.

The question is: what will be the impact of rising energy (exergy) prices on economic growth? Standard theory says that there is little or no link between energy costs and growth. We disagree. Our results suggest that the link is much stronger than conventional theory admits. We think that economic growth in the past has been driven primarily not by 'technological progress' in some general and undefined sense, but specifically by the availability of ever cheaper energy – and useful work – from coal, petroleum (or gas). These energy-related price declines can no longer be expected to drive economic growth in the future. Clearly higher energy prices will – other things being equal – result in reduced demand for energy and therefore for energy services and all the other goods and services that depend on energy inputs.

As Alvin Weinberg once said, energy is the ultimate resource. It is essential. It is needed for every economic sector and activity, and there is no substitute. The implications of non-substitutability will be discussed extensively in this book.

1. Background

1.1 GROWTH AND THE NEOCLASSICAL PARADIGM

This book is about technological change and economic growth. It is generally acknowledged that the latter is driven mainly by the former. But the motor mechanism is surprisingly obscure and the nature of technological change itself is poorly understood. Part of the problem is that neoclassical microeconomic theory cannot account for key features of technological change. In this chapter we briefly review and summarize some of the difficulties and their origins, beginning with the neoclassical economic paradigm. It has been informally characterized by Paul Krugman as follows:

> At base, mainstream economic theory rests on two observations: obvious opportunities are rarely left unexploited and things add up. When one sets out to make a formal mathematical model, these rough principles usually become the more exact ideas of maximization (of something) and equilibrium (in some sense) . . . (Krugman 1995)

This characterization is drastically oversimplified, of course, but it conveys the right flavor.[1]

At a deeper level, the neoclassical paradigm of economics is a collection of assumptions and common understandings, going back to the so-called 'marginalist' revolution in the 19th century. Again, to convey a rough sense of the change without most of the details, the classical theory of Smith, Ricardo, Marx and Mill conceptualized *value* as a kind of 'substance' produced by nature, enhanced by labor and embodied in goods. Prices in the classical theory were assumed to be simple reflections of intrinsic value and the labor cost of production. The newer approach, led by Leon Walras, Stanley Jevons, Vilfredo Pareto, and especially Irving Fisher, conceptualized value as a situational attribute (utility) determined only by relative preferences on the part of consumers. This change in viewpoint brought with it the notion of prices, and hence of supply–demand equilibrium, into the picture. It also defined equilibrium as the balance point where marginal utility of additional supply is equal to the marginal disutility of added cost. Thus calculus was introduced into economics.

Neoclassical theory has been increasingly formalized since the 19th century. But, because the economic analogies with physical concepts are imperfect, this has been done in a number of different and occasionally somewhat inconsistent ways. The most popular textbook version of the modern theory has been formulated by Paul Samuelson (1966) and characterized by Robert Solow as the 'trinity': namely, *greed, rationality*, and *equilibrium*. 'Greed' means selfish behavior; rationality means utility maximization – skating over the unresolved question of utility measurement – and equilibrium refers to the Walrasian hypothesis that there exists a stationary state with a unique set of prices such that all markets 'clear', that is, supply and demand are balanced for every commodity.

We recognize, of course, that the above assumptions can be (and have been) relaxed, without losing everything. For instance, utility maximization can be replaced by 'bounded rationality' (Simon 1955) and 'prospect theory' (Tversky and Kahneman 1974). Equilibrium can be approached but not achieved. The notion of utility, itself, can be modified to extend to non-equilibrium and dynamic situations (for example, Ayres 2006).

There are, of course, other features of the standard neoclassical paradigm. One of them is that production and consumption are abstractions, linked only by money flows, payments for labor, payments for products and services, savings and investment. These abstract flows are supposedly governed by equilibrium-seeking market forces (the 'invisible hand'). The standard model assumes perfect competition, perfect information, and Pareto optimality, which is the 'zero-sum' situation in a multi-player game (or market) where gains for any player can only be achieved at the expense of others.

The origins of physical production in this paradigm remain unexplained, since the only explanatory variables are abstract labor and capital services. In the closed economic system described by Walras, Cassel, von Neumann, Koopmans, and Sraffa, every material product is produced from other products made *within* the system, plus exogenous capital and labor services (Walras 1874; Cassel 1932 [1918]; von Neumann 1945 [1932]; Koopmans 1951; Sraffa 1960). The unrealistic neglect of materials (and energy) flows in the economic system was pointed out emphatically by Georgescu-Roegen (Georgescu-Roegen 1971), although his criticism has been largely ignored by mainstream theory. Indeed, a recent best-selling textbook by Professor N. Gregory Mankiw of Harvard describes a simple economy consisting of many small bakeries producing 'bread' from capital and labor (Mankiw 1997 pp. 30 ff.). The importance of this fundamental contradiction seems to have escaped his notice.

This book is not intended as a critique of neoclassical economics, except insofar as it pertains to the theory of economic growth. In several areas we depart significantly from the neoclassical paradigm. The most important of these departures are (1) in regard to the nature and role of technological change, (2) the assumption that growth follows an optimal path and dependence on optimization algorithms and (3) in regard to the role of materials and energy in the theory. But there are some other minor departures as well. We have begun, so to speak, at the beginning, so as to be able to clarify and justify these various departures as they come up in the discussion that follows.

1.2 THE RAMSEY THEORY OF OPTIMAL GROWTH

In 1920 Arthur Pigou, suggested that – thanks to congenital myopia – people discount future utility; that is, they don't save enough to provide for their later wants or, in a different context, people in every generation consume too much, leaving too little for their successors (Pigou 1920). This left an unanswered question: namely what is the optimal rate of savings? Frank Ramsey tackled this problem by means of the calculus of variations (Ramsey 1928).[2] He did not believe in discounting – in fact, he thought it unethical – so he devised a clever way to avoid the problem of comparing infinities. He assumed that there is a utility due to consumption but that there is a disutility arising from the need to work (labor) and a maximum utility, called 'bliss'. He also assumed that the maximum social utility for every generation would be achieved when that generation achieved bliss. The problem, then, is to minimize the distance between present utility and bliss, by choosing the best possible tradeoff between savings (investment) and loss of consumption in the early generations.

The mathematics of the Ramsey model have been extensively discussed in textbooks and need not be recapitulated here. Since there are two controls in the model (labor and capital), there are just two Euler-Lagrange equations. The first equation yields the result that the marginal disutility of labor must always be equal to the product of the marginal utility of consumption times the marginal product of labor. The second equation – as interpreted by Keynes – says (in words) that the optimum investment times the utility of consumption is equal to the distance from bliss or, more intuitively, the marginal benefit to later generations of faster approach to bliss must be balanced by the marginal loss of consumption benefits by the earliest generations. This became known as the Keynes-Ramsey rule. Ramsey's analysis confirmed Pigou's conjecture that the optimal savings rate is higher than the rate chosen by myopic agents in a market economy.

For various reasons, largely due to discomfort with Ramsey's social utility function and his unfamiliar mathematics, the notion of optimality was neglected for nearly 30 years. Jan Tinbergen and Richard Goodwin were the first to revive the idea, as applied to the Harrod-Domar growth models (Tinbergen 1956, 1960; Goodwin 1961). These attempts were criticized early on for obvious difficulties, notably that they imply an authoritarian 'social planner' which was an idea already past its time (Bauer 1957). In any case, the Harrod-Domar model was soon replaced by the Solow-Swan model.

There was one other early application of the calculus of variations by Harold Hotelling, not to growth but to the optimal extraction of exhaustible resources (Hotelling 1931). The problem, posed by Hotelling, was to maximize the total cumulative benefits from an exhaustible resource. The control variable, in this case, is the stock R of the resource. The consumption benefit can be defined as the product of the price $P(t)$ multiplied by dR/dt, discounted by the factor $\exp(-\delta t)$. Hotelling assumed that extraction would cease after a finite period $t = z$, when some 'backstop' technology would become available at a lower price. The simple integral can be integrated by parts, yielding the well-known result that (in equilibrium) prices will increase at the rate of discount, that is, $P(t) = P(0)\exp(-\delta t)$. Extraction costs can be introduced explicitly as a function of the remaining stock R, and the resulting integral can be solved by use of the Euler-Lagrange equations. The results in this case are similar. Hotelling's result has been the foundation of the field of resource economics. Hotelling's simple model has been elaborated in recent decades to deal with a variety of technological and geological complexities and uncertainties. However, these complications have made it difficult to verify the fundamental theory.

1.3   THE SOLOW-SWAN MODEL OF ECONOMIC GROWTH

Until the 1950s growth theory remained primitive and qualitative because it lacked any empirical base. (Some will argue that it is still primitive.) However, thanks to the development of the system of national accounts (SNA) in the 1930s and 1940s, it became possible for the first time to construct historical GDP figures for the US and some other countries for a number of prior decades. Economists had previously assumed that economic growth was determined by the accumulation of capital stock per worker. The availability of SNA data and quantitative estimates of historical GDP enabled economists to test this assumption for the first time.

Capital stock in the neoclassical paradigm is measured strictly in monetary terms.[3] Capital stock is normally estimated – 'constructed' might be a better word – by a procedure called the 'perpetual inventory method' or

PIM. In brief, net investment is accumulated from a convenient historical starting point. Net investment in a period can be estimated as the product of total investment expenditure (often equated with savings) allocated among capital types – as given in the system of national accounts – times useful service life. Or it can be equated with gross expenditure for capital less depreciation. Service lives can be determined by survey, or using a mortality function. Depreciation rates can be determined by tax rules, company accounts or surveys.[4] It is important to note that there is no adjustment in the PIM method for increasing productivity (or quality) of capital in use.

Using the PIM construct, it was discovered in the early 1950s that historical growth of the US economy could not be explained by the accumulation of capital stock, or the increase in capital per worker, as most economists had previously assumed (for example, Fabricant 1954; Abramovitz 1956). The key innovation in growth theory at that time was the explicit use of an aggregate *production function* of capital and labor services which enabled economists to account for the relative importance of the two factors of production and sources of productivity growth (Solow 1956, 1957; Swan 1956). Though not all economists are happy with the use of production functions, their limitations have been relegated in recent years to footnotes or ignored altogether.

It has also been convenient, although somewhat inconsistent with observed scale economies at the micro-scale, to assume constant 'returns to scale' at the macro-scale. This is tantamount to assuming that if the inputs of capital and labor are doubled (or multiplied by any constant), then the output (GDP) will be larger by the same factor. Mathematically, this implies that the production function should be a homogeneous first-order function of the input variables (the so-called Euler condition), together with a time-dependent multiplier.[5] With this analytic machinery it is easy to calculate the marginal productivities of each input factor, namely as the respective logarithmic partial derivatives of the production function with respect to the input variables. The simplest functional form satisfying the Euler condition is the so-called Cobb-Douglas function, which is widely used in growth models. (However that function also implies that the marginal productivities are constants, independent of time, which is not necessarily realistic.) It also seemed natural, based on a simple theory of income allocation, to equate these calculated marginal productivities with corresponding payment shares in the national accounts, as Solow did (Solow 1956). Thus, returns to capital stock can then be equated to payments to capital (interest, dividends, rents and royalties) in the national accounts. Similarly, returns to labor can be equated with payments to labor, consisting of wages and salaries. Solow observed that the capital share of payments in the SNA had indeed remained relatively constant at about 30 percent throughout the period covered by his analysis (1909–49), with the labor share relatively constant at about 70 percent. This appears to justify the choice of Cobb-Douglas production functions. However, we reconsider the use of production functions later in this book.

Solow was surprised to discover that the capital/labor ratio, as determined by the perpetual inventory method (PIM), could not account for nearly 90 percent of observed growth in US GDP, per capita, between those same years, 1909–49 (Solow 1957). The difference had to be explained by 'something else'. That something could have been time-dependent multipliers of capital and/or labor, respectively (interpreted as quality improvements), or a 'neutral' time-dependent multiplier for the capital-labor combination as a whole. Statistical tests, admittedly not conclusive, originally suggested that the latter scheme was best. Solow called this overall multiplier 'technological progress', although he admitted that it was simply 'a measure of our ignorance'. Others have called this multiplier the 'Solow residual'. More recently the annual increments of Solow's progress multiplier have been termed as increases in total factor productivity (TFP). One of our objectives in this book is to offer a plausible explanation of TFP in terms of measurable changes in real technology as related to the use of energy (or, to be more precise, *exergy*).

Of course, thanks to technological change, older capital is normally less productive than more recent vintage capital. Similarly, labor becomes more productive, thanks to education and training. Hence time-dependent augmentation multipliers can be introduced to explain part of the Solow residual, mentioned above. But, in this case, the apparent returns to capital and labor inputs, as such, are reduced by the inverse of the augmentation factors. Neither augmented capital stock nor returns to capital can be measured independently of the other. The same is true for labor. This has been a source of controversy and confusion. Indeed, some have argued that aggregate capital cannot logically be measured independently of its rate of return, and – for this and other reasons – that the concept of production function itself is faulty (Robinson 1953–4; Pasinetti 1959; Sraffa 1960; Sylos Labini 1995).

On the other hand, there is a statistical way out of the difficulty, if one is willing to assume that the augmentation functions are smooth and mathematically tractable; for example, simple exponentials. Inserting such functions into the production function previously introduced – commonly of the Cobb-Douglas type – it is possible to carry out a statistical fitting procedure to determine the 'best fit' parameters of the augmentation functions. In principle, this might eliminate the TFP multiplier, though in practice it does not appear to do so.[6]

Given a population of perfectly competitive producers of a single all-purpose good in a simple single-sector model of income allocation, in equilibrium, it follows that the demand for capital and labor services will be proportional to their respective marginal productivities.[7] The two factor Cobb-Douglas production function with constant returns is particularly convenient because it provides an immediate economic interpretation for the parameters of the function, which (as noted above) are set equal to the marginal productivities.

The annual increments of total factor productivity or TFP tend to fluctuate around a long-term trend. The fluctuations have some regularities. Enormous effort has been expended on identifying 'business cycles' with various periodicities, from four years to 50 years and attempting to explain them. Productivity calculations and projections have become a mini-industry. Nevertheless, it is important to realize that the (presumed) trend itself is assumed to be exogenously determined. The so-called 'endogenous theory' introduced by Romer and others (discussed in Chapter 5) offers various qualitative explanations, but nothing quantitative.

1.4 OPTIMAL GROWTH THEORIES, BACK IN VOGUE

For the sake of completeness, it should be mentioned that the advent of the Solow-Swan model did trigger a number of applications of Ramsey-like optimal growth models, again focusing on the question of optimal savings. At least six economists independently derived something called the 'golden rule' of economic growth: namely, that the optimal rate of investment (hence savings) should be such as to make the return on capital equal to the natural rate of population growth. None of these derivations required an assumption of intergenerational social utility in the Ramsey sense. The first to publish this interesting result was Phelps, followed by Desrousseaux, Allais, Robinson, von Weizsaecker and Swan (Phelps 1961; Desrousseaux 1961; Allais 1962; Robinson 1962; von Weizsaecker 1962; Swan 1963). Of course, the same objections raised earlier with respect to the efforts of Tinbergen and Goodwin remain applicable (for example, Bauer 1957).

But meanwhile, Koopmans and others found a way to make the intertemporal utility notion more palatable (Koopmans 1960; Koopmans et al. 1964). Along with others, including Cass, Malinvaud, Mirrlees and Shell, the Ramsey model was re-created as a formal Cass-Koopmans model of optimal growth in a single sector model (for example, Koopmans 1965; Cass 1965, 1966; Malinvaud 1965; Mirrlees 1967; Shell 1967). Once again, however, the underlying notion of an all-powerful (however altruistic) social planner seemed increasingly anachronistic and irrelevant. Moreover, the models themselves exhibited a peculiar mathematical 'saddle point' property, with stable and unstable branches. This left a residue of doubts as to why the real economy should 'choose' an optimal trajectory.

That problem was apparently resolved in the 1980s by the advent of 'rational expectations', which seemed to provide the missing mechanism by which the economy would select a stable – rather than an unstable – trajectory from a saddle point (for example, Lucas and Stokey 1984). The fact that the economic growth trajectory seemed to be stable prior to 2008 was regarded as indirect evidence of the operation of the mechanism. As a result, optimal growth exercises are no longer considered to be normative, in the sense of explaining how things *should* work, but rather, as exercises in explaining how the economy really does work, as in modern business cycle theory.

1.5 BUT DOUBTS REMAIN

As a point of departure for rigorous, if simplistic, mathematical analysis of various subsidiary topics, the neoclassical theory of growth sketched – much too briefly – above has undoubted virtues. However, the underlying assumption of optimal growth in equilibrium is very troubling. In this context, it is important to note a number of difficulties, as follows: (1) the real multi-sector, multi-product economy is never actually in equilibrium and (2) if it were, there would be no opportunity or incentives for entrepreneurs to innovate. In an equilibrium world, technology would stagnate. The traditional solution to this problem, since von Neumann (1945 [1932]), has been to regard technological progress as exogenous, like the biblical 'manna from heaven'. As it happens, we adopt a modified version of this view, for reasons discussed in Chapters 2 and 3.

Furthermore, the notion of growth and development along an optimum path is problematic. For instance, (3) the real economy is a complex non-linear system, and non-linear systems do not exhibit equilibrium states. Moreover (4) while entrepreneurs at the micro-scale undoubtedly try to optimize their own activities at least within the limits of bounded rationality (for example, Conlisk 1996), the aggregate results of many micro-optimizations virtually guarantee a non-optimal result at the macro-scale.[8] Moreover, (5) even if the complex non-linear economic system could be optimized by a hypothetical social planner, a dynamic optimum is not the same as a static optimum. (In other simpler words, notwithstanding Koopmans' ingenious effort (Koopmans 1960; Koopmans et al. 1964) one cannot simultaneously optimize for the present, and for a later time.)

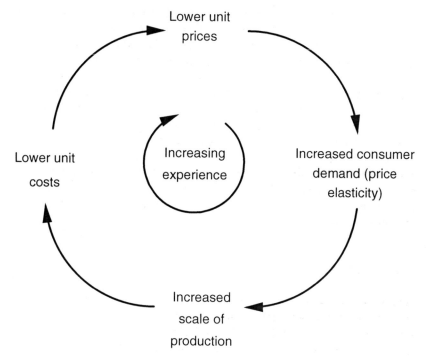

Figure 1.1   Simple Salter cycle

Finally, and most important, (6) notwithstanding Georgescu-Roegen's contributions (1966, 1984) – especially with regard to insisting on the fundamental distinction between 'funds' (which are unchanged) and 'flows' (which are consumed) – the lack of any general theory to explain physical production in physical terms (that is, in terms of energy and materials) is extremely troubling. It is the latter problem, more than any other, that has motivated this book.

While technical progress is normally treated as an exogenous driving force, there is an endogenous mechanism that can explain some aggregate economic growth in equilibrium – beyond that which is accounted for by labor and capital accumulation – *without* radical (structure-changing) technological innovations. The mechanism in question is a simple positive feedback between increasing consumption, investment, increasing scale and 'learning-by-doing'. These result in declining costs and declining prices, stimulating further increases in demand and investment to increase supply (Figure 1.1). The phenomenon of feedback is addressed later (Chapter 5) in greater detail.

However, if learning and economies of scale are the only types of technological change allowed by the model, there must be declining returns and an eventual limit to growth as the potential for incremental improvements in existing products and production technologies are exhausted. However, neoclassical economic theory cannot explain radical (Schumpeterian) innovations, insofar as many, if not most, radical innovations are not the outcome of rational investment projects. For every big winner there may be many losers, and the eventual big winners are often just lucky beneficiaries of the work of others. In fact, the early risk-takers rarely see a positive return. To put it another way, the expectation value of most risky investments in radical innovation is negative, and to that extent inconsistent with the rationality and 'greed' (profit maximization) axioms. Hence, though radical innovation is essential for long-term economic growth, and the social rate of return is clearly positive, the closed neoclassical economic model does not explain the radical innovations that change the structure of the economy.

Finally, there is no essential role in the Solow model for energy or materials, except as a consequence (not a cause) of economic growth. This is significant, because if resource consumption is *not* needed to explain growth, then 'decoupling' growth from resource consumption – a popular notion in some current discussions of sustainability[9] – is conceptually easy: From the theoretical perspective, it seems, they were never coupled in the first place. There is also no role for wastes and pollutants in the closed Walrasian equilibrium system, where all products are abstractions. The neoclassical conceptualization implies that wastes and emissions – if they exist at all – do no economic harm and can be disposed of at no cost. It is unclear how much of the neoclassical apparatus can survive when this simplification is abandoned.

1.6   THE DISEQUILIBRIUM PARADIGM

In contrast, the disequilibrium (quasi-evolutionary) approach characterizes the economy at the macro-level as an open multi-sector materials/ energy processing system. The system is characterized by a sequence of value-added stages, beginning with extraction of crude resources and ending with consumption and disposal of material and energy wastes, which can do harm if not eliminated. Referring again to Figure 1.1, if the system is open, then the causal link between materials and energy consumption and economic growth implied by this mechanism must be *mutual*. In other words, it must be bi-directional, not uni-directional.

This means, *ceteris paribus,* that a two-factor production function involving only labor and capital services as inputs cannot reflect this mechanism. A third factor representing resource flows (in some way) is minimally necessary to reflect the feedback between increasing resource consumption and declining production costs. This is needed, for example, to explain the long-term decline of resource prices (Barnett and Morse 1963; Barnett 1979; Potter and Christy 1968).

However, the simple positive feedback mechanism sketched in Section 1.2 allows for only one type of technological change; namely, the combined effects of scale economies and experience or learning-by-doing *at the societal level*. However these forces do not distinguish between sectors. Hence they cannot explain structural change. But, in reality, there is not one single aggregate technology of production for a single composite universal product, nor even a single technology for each product as assumed by activity analysis. The real world exhibits multiple competing technologies for each product and in each sector.[10]

The qualitative evolutionary change mechanism at the firm level (assuming abstract products) has been described by Nelson and Winter (1974, 1982). It applies in a multi-product, multi-sector system. As the rate of improvement of the existing dominant technology for one product slows down, the incentives to search for, and find, a new technology (or a new material or even a new product) grow in parallel. If the demand for continued improvement is sufficiently powerful, there will be enough R&D investment to achieve a 'breakthrough' enabling some radically new innovations capable of displacing the older techniques (Ayres 1988a). Schumpeter's evocative word for this process was 'creative destruction' (Schumpeter 1934).

Spillovers from radical innovations since the industrial revolution, especially in the field of energy conversion technology, have probably been the most potent driver of past economic growth. However, in contrast to some evolutionary models, we insist that breakthroughs and radical innovations do *not* occur at random, and do not necessarily affect productivity in other sectors or stimulate the creation of new products and industries. Finally, we note that there is a natural order of major discoveries in the material domain, depending on the physical properties of materials and the physical capabilities of tools. For this reason, technological progress is extremely uneven and its effects are inhomogeneous.

Nelson and Winter are not the only economists who have developed evolutionary models with self-organizing features. Since the early 1980s there has been an explosion of interest in evolutionary models, mainly focusing on non-linear dynamics and innovation.[11] It must be said, however, that most of these contributions are purely theoretical. Empirical studies in this area are scarce.

The disequilibrium evolutionary resource-conversion perspective elaborated in this book depends less upon theory than on empirical data. We cite relevant theory only where and when necessary. Our work implies that long-term growth, and progress towards sustainability, will require more than the gradual efficiency gains resulting from economies of scale and social learning. Radical Schumpeterian innovations (resulting in new products and services and structural change) are also necessary, and – as it happens – not as easy to explain as Schumpeter originally suggested (1934, 1912). We touch on this point later in this chapter.

1.7   EMPIRICAL 'LAWS' OF PROGRESS

Technological progress (as distinguished from knowledge) is normally understood, as above, in terms of the performance of some activity or function, however generic (for example, transportation, communications, life expectancy). Functional capability typically grows according to a different 'covering law', namely the 'law of constrained growth'. The idea of such a law was originally suggested by the biologist Raymond Pearl, who applied it (for example) to the growth of a colony of fruit flies in a bottle or yeast cells in a dish (Pearl 1925; Lotka 1956 [1924]). Growth is constrained by natural limits.

It is worth mentioning here that two important empirical regularities have been put forward, by different authors, as quasi-general laws. The first pseudo-law is the so-called 'experience curve' – or 'progress function' – which treats direct labor input, or costs, as a characteristic function of cumulative production experience, where the parameters of the curve vary from technology to technology. This regularity was first noted in aircraft manufacturing (Wright 1936) and subsequently observed in a variety of other cases (namely, Hirsch 1956; Conway and Schultz 1959; Rapping 1965; Argote and Epple 1990; David 1970).

The good news is that once a trajectory as characterized by a rate of progress in relation to experience has been established, it is likely to continue for some time, perhaps as in the case of microelectronics even for many doublings of cumulative production experience (see Table 1.1). Unfortunately, however, the progress function or learning curve has never become a reliable basis for forecasting *a priori*. There have been many efforts to 'explain' the observed regularity in terms of economic theory, but so far the results are mixed. One of the crucial difficulties is that empirical progress functions may change direction unexpectedly (Ayres and Martinás 1990). In many cases, it appears that there are limits to learning, in any given situation. The earliest and most noteworthy effort to explain

Table 1.1 Examples of productivity improvements from experience

Example	Improving Parameter	Cumulative Parameter	Learn. Curve Slope	Time Frame	No of vol. doublings
Model-T Ford Production	Price	Units produced	86%	1910–1926	10
Aircraft Assembly	Direct man-hrs per unit	Units produced	80%	1925–1957	3
Catalytic cracking units for petroleum	Days needed per 100 million bbls	Million bbls run	90%	1946–1958	10
Cost of fluid cracking units	Cost per bbl of capacity	Installed design capacity of plants	94% 80%*	1942–1958	5
Equipment maintenance in electric plant	Avg. time to replace a group of parts during a shutdown	No of replacements	76%	circa 1957	4
Man-hrs per barrel in petroleum industry	Avg. direct man-hrs per bbl refined	Millions of bbls refined in US	84%	1860–1962	15
Electric-power generation	Mils per kW-hour	Millions of kW-hrs	95%*	1910–1955	5
Steel production	Production worker man-hrs per unit produced	Units produced	79%	1920–1955	3
Integrated circuit prices	Avg. price per unit	Units produced	72%*	1964–1972	10
MOS/LSI prices	Avg. price per unit	Units produced	80%	1970–1976	10
Electronic digital watch prices	Avg. factory selling price	Units produced	74%	1975–1978	4
Hand-held calculator prices	Avg. factory selling price	Units produced	74%	1975–1978	2
MOS dynamic RAM prices	Avg. factory selling price per bit	No of bits	68%	1973–1978	6

13

Table 1.1 (*continued*)

Example	Improving Parameter	Cumulative Parameter	Learn. Curve Slope	Time Frame	No of vol. doublings
Disk memory drives	Avg. price per bit	No of bits	76%	1975–1978	3
Price of minimum active electronic function in semiconductor products	Price of minimum semiconductor function	No of functions produced by semiconductor industry	60%	1960–1977 (early products)	13

Note: * Constant Dollars.

Source: Cunningham (1980).

14

the phenomenon was by Arrow (Arrow 1962). Other efforts include Oyi (1967), Preston and Keachie (1964), Sahal (1979, 1981). The subject has not been discussed intensively in recent years, however.

The second pseudo-law is the 'logistic', or S-shaped, curve, often modeled on a simple biological process such as yeast cells reproducing in a constrained medium (Pearl 1925).[12] The logistic function takes values between zero and unity. It increases slowly at first, then more rapidly until the slope reaches an inflection point, after which the slope gradually falls again to zero as the function approaches unity. The simplest form of this function is the solution to a differential equation

$$\frac{df}{dt} = kf(1 - f) \qquad (1.1)$$

where f is symmetric about the origin on the time axis and symmetric, with an inflection point, at $f = 0.5$ on the vertical axis.

Quite a number of adoption or diffusion phenomena seem to have fit this pattern, or a closely related one. One of the early economic studies invoking this law was on the adoption of hybrid corn (Griliches 1957). Edwin Mansfield used the logistic function to describe the rate of adoption of an innovation in a firm (Mansfield 1961, 1963). Others have applied it to a variety of adoption and diffusion phenomena (for example, Fisher and Pry 1971).[13] Early applications to technological change were noted especially by Ayres (1969) and later by Linstone and Sahal (1976). Market researchers, such as Mahajan and colleagues have also adopted the logistic form and simple variants to explain market penetration (Easingwood et al. 1983; Mahajan and Schoeman 1977; Mahajan and Peterson 1985).

The form of the function can be varied by modifying the above differential equation, mainly by adjusting parameters or adding terms on the right-hand side. For instance, the inflection point can be in the lower-left quadrant, or in the upper-right quadrant, depending on parameters (for example, Blackman 1972; Skiadas 1985). In recent years double logistics and other complexities have been suggested (Meyer and Ausubel 1999; Meyer et al. 1999).

Why is the pattern of acceleration followed by deceleration so general? Recall Schumpeter's description of a radical innovation as the implementation of 'new combinations' such as new goods (or services), new methods of production, new markets, new sources of supply and new forms of organization (Schumpeter 1934, p. 66). Schumpeter was not only referring to innovations in the realm of products or processes. Examples of important social inventions with economic implications include laws and courts-of-law, taxes, professional armies, insurance, public schools, universities, churches, and various forms of governance, both corporate and political.

But notwithstanding Marchetti's many examples, and others, the S-curve tool has proven to be unreliable as a 'law', for quantitative forecasting. There are too many exceptions and alternative shapes for the S-shaped diffusion curve. Historical examples developed for various biological and epidemiological cases include those of Gompertz (1832), Pearl (1925), Bailey (1957) and von Bertalanffy (1957). But the bottom line is that the range of possible variations is extremely large and there is no way to predict *a priori* which shape the curve will take in any given case.

1.8   ON TECHNOLOGICAL PROGRESS AS PROBLEM SOLVING

One of the problems associated with the study of technological change at the macro-scale arises from the fact that it is inherently a result of many different search processes that occur in response to problems and challenges that appear only at the micro-scale. More often than not, the successful innovations are attributable to individuals or very small groups responding to very specific problems. A few historical examples may convey the idea.

One of the most interesting historical examples was the deliberate search for a technique to determine longitudes accurately at sea. Latitude could be determined quite accurately from astronomical observations, but longitude was much more difficult to ascertain because it required very precise timekeepers. The method of longitude determination by chronometer was known (and published) as early as 1530. Christian Huygens was the first to attempt to build such a timepiece (1662–79), but the necessary accuracy in metal-cutting was not achievable at that time. As a response to a naval disaster in 1714 in which several warships were driven aground in the Scilly Isles (off Cornwall) and hundreds of sailors died, the British Parliament offered a large reward (£20,000) for any practical solution to the problem. The final solution (until satellites came along) required very accurate time-keeping by some method that did not rely on a pendulum (the pendulum is only reliable on a very stable base). A chronometer with the necessary accuracy was finally achieved by a carpenter and self-taught inventor, John Harrison.[14]

Other more recent examples include the search for better sources of illumination, starting with oil lamps and candles, followed by gaslight, the incandescent lamp, fluorescent lights and finally the light-emitting diodes (LED); the search for better methods of refining iron and making steel that culminated in the basic oxygen process (BOP); and the long search for a practical method of 'fixing' atmospheric nitrogen, which culminated in 1913 with the successful Haber-Bosch process for ammonia synthesis. The main point here is that such searches are triggered by needs and/or barriers, but they are *not* explained by human curiosity. Nor are they random events. In fact, radical innovations in technology or business practices are not explained either by learning or adjustment.

In recent times, the problems, and the solutions, have become progressively more complex. Breakthroughs increasingly result from a deliberate, wide-ranging, and usually costly, search process prompted by a 'barrier' of some sort. When the barrier has been overcome by a 'breakthrough', the subsequent search process is much more narrowly focused and, typically, much more productive (at first) than the search process which led to the breakthrough itself. This topic is explored in more detail in Chapter 2.

Some conceptual and terminological distinctions are needed to facilitate the discussion that follows. Gradual changes at the product or process level, within a sector, are sometimes characterized as 'Usherian', in honor of the historian of technology who (properly) emphasized their cumulative importance (Usher 1929). The more radical innovations are sometimes characterized as 'Schumpeterian' for a similar reason (Ruttan 1959; Schumpeter 1912). The difference between them is crucial, because only radical Schumpeterian innovations (in general) result in structural change to the economy. We argue subsequently that Schumpeterian innovations are, by far, the dominant creators of new technologies and new products or services that, in turn, induce new demands and new sectors. It is the creation of new products and services that drives economic growth, even though gradual incremental (Usherian) improvement processes dominate the short and intermediate time frames. Unfortunately much of the economic literature fails to distinguish clearly between the two kinds of innovation.

1.9 MACROECONOMIC THEORY OF CHANGE AND INNOVATION

From the 'standard' macro-perspective, the core theory of technological change in the aggregate is usually termed 'induced innovation'. This theory has been elaborated qualitatively in several books by Rosenberg (for example, Rosenberg 1969a, 1976, 1982a) and, in more mathematical modeling terms, by Binswanger and Ruttan (Binswanger and Ruttan 1978). Here the fundamental idea is that scarcity induces innovation. For example, economic historians have argued persuasively that the US was short of labor (compared to Europe), but had plenty of good land and fodder for horses in the 19th century. This combination made horse-drawn harvesters and other kinds of agricultural mechanization more profitable to farmers in the US than in Europe. This seems to explain why many innovations in the area of agricultural mechanization, such as the combine harvester (and later the tractor), were innovated – but not necessarily invented – in the land-rich but labor-scarce US.

The theory of induced innovation applies especially to the impact of natural resource scarcity – real or perceived – on economic growth. This topic is so important for this book that we discuss it in a separate section at the end of this chapter.

We note, here, that the induced innovation framework sketched above does not actually explain technological progress or economic growth at the macro-scale. This is because, while the 'bottom up' formulation of micro-economics allows for learning-by-doing and incremental improvement along an established trajectory, it offers no actual mechanism to explain systematic discovery, invention and radical innovation by economic agents. Economists have generally been content to assume that invention occurs spontaneously, perhaps as a consequence of 'monkey curiosity' or something of the kind, and that adoption follows automatically. This issue must be addressed first at the micro-scale before it can be extended to the macro-scale.

At the microeconomic level, one main strand of theory in the literature concerns selection, adoption/diffusion and/or substitution.[15] A different strand of theorizing concerns the phenomenon that has been called 'path dependence'. In brief, this can be regarded as an outgrowth of interest in 'chaos' or more particularly the 'butterfly effect' associated with non-linear models. The underlying idea is that infinitesimally different starting conditions can lead to dramatically different outcomes. It follows that many different outcomes are almost equally possible, but that whatever happens depends on what has happened in the immediate past, not on the 'gravitational attraction' of some distant goal. In short, the conventional picture of the economy as a system always traveling along an optimal path, while simultaneously remaining in equilibrium, is false and misleading. As evidence, there are a number of examples of technological choices that have been made in the past, presumably satisfying short-term benefit-cost criteria, but which would not be made the same way today if the original choice set had not been 'locked in' by economies of scale or returns to adoption.

To return to the question of driving forces, the mechanism that drives this knowledge accumulation, including R&D and innovation, is the expectation of increasing financial wealth, via increasing asset values. (Welfare presumably follows wealth, although it is by no means equivalent and the relationship is unclear and certainly non-linear.)

1.10 TECHNOLOGICAL PROGRESS AS IMPEDED BY 'LOCK-OUT' AND 'LOCK-IN'

Notwithstanding the growth-driving mechanisms noted above, there are contrary forces. An important aspect of the technology selection process that follows a breakthrough, in practice, is that one candidate configuration is selected and 'locked in' before all (or even many) of the possible combinations have been tested. Experience suggests that the first two or three combinations that 'work' reasonably well tend to lock out the others. The economics of 'lock-in' have been described in some detail by Brian Arthur (1994). Lock-out/lock-in is another way of saying that once a technology has become established, it is extremely difficult to displace – thanks to various advantages accruing to scale, experience or network linkages – even if an alternative emerges that is intrinsically superior but not fully developed.

Favorite examples of this phenomenon include the QWERTY keyboard (David 1985), the English system of weights and measures, and the Microsoft Windows operating system for PCs. At the aggregate national level, a number of studies have indicated that, if the US economic system operated on a 'least cost' basis (that is, by assuming the most efficient solutions were utilized everywhere), energy consumption and carbon emissions would both be reduced by something like 20 percent and costs would also be lower by a similar amount (Carhart 1979; Sant 1979; Sant and Carhart 1981; Berndt et al. 1981; Lovins and Lovins 1991, 1981; Lovins et al. 1981; Morris et al. 1990; Casten and Collins 2002, 2003). In effect, the argument is that the economy has been 'locked in' to sub-optimal patterns by some combination of positive returns to scale, and inappropriate or obsolete regulations.[16]

For example, Casten and Collins (2002) argues that a technology known as decentralized combined heat and power (DCHP) would displace a significant fraction of the demand for centralized electric power, as well as fuel for domestic and commercial space heating and water heating, if not for regulatory restrictions. (DCHP is a system in which many small electric power plants utilizing natural or manufactured gas and small gas turbines can provide both heat and power to industrial sites and apartment buildings). To be sure, many economists deny that alternatives (like DCHP) would in fact cut costs, usually by introducing the notion of 'hidden costs' of change. But the undeniable existence of some (hidden and unquantified) costs of moving from one local minimum to another in a multi-equilibria system does not contradict the possibility that another minimum may be lower than the one we currently occupy. The basic reason this 'opportunity' has been neglected is that regulation introduced three-quarters of a century ago still favors centralized power generation. This point is important for what follows, because it weakens the argument for using so-called 'computable general equilibrium' (CGE) models, much favored by mainstream economists for forecasting purposes. We elaborate the arguments against equilibrium models subsequently.

An established technology cannot be displaced without also displacing a host of associated technologies and investments. Another name for this phenomenon is 'path-dependence'. Path-dependence has an enormous influence on technological evolution. There are several mechanisms involved in the selection and lock-in process. One is learning-by-doing, which creates specialized skills and favors the producers and/or service providers with the greatest experience. Economies of scale favor the largest producers, which are often the earliest entries ('first movers') in a new market. Returns to adoption are important in some technologies with the property that the more they are used, the more useful they are. The telephone is an obvious example of this. The internet is another example.

In fact, the qualitative pattern of conception, birth, childhood, adolescence, maturity and senility so resembles the life cycle of an organism, that the analogy has established itself in the literature of techno-economic change.[17] This process is known as the life-cycle model of technology (Abernathy and Utterback 1975, 1978). The model says that when a new product moves from the 'childhood' stage (when several different configurations are competing on the basis of performance) to the 'adolescent stage' (when manufacturing costs and prices become the main basis for competition), the market leader is very hard to displace (Ayres 1987). Experience enables a manufacturer to take advantage of 'learning-by-doing' as well as economies of scale, and thus to minimize costs. The Boston Consulting Group (BCG) advised many large corporations on competitive strategy based on exploiting the experience curve (Cunningham 1980). It is well-known that Texas Instruments and several of the large Japanese electronics companies used the curve (together with Moore's Law) to plan for growth and price policy. The market leader automatically has more production experience than its smaller rivals. This gives the market leader a built-in competitive advantage in the market for a standardized product.

However, standardization is not necessarily an advantage in a market where many designs are competing freely. Needless to say, an established market leader, with much to lose, is actually less likely to innovate than a new entry with everything to gain. This makes market leaders conservative and inhibits technological change. But it also ensures that market leaders in a rapidly changing field are likely to be replaced by others on a regular basis as the technology evolves.

1.11 RESOURCE SCARCITY AS A DRIVER OF INNOVATION

Until the mid-19th century land was virtually the only economic 'resource', with a few minor exceptions, mainly metals. The idea of resource (land) as a factor of production originated with the French physiocrats, especially Quesnay, and of course the Scotsman, Adam Smith (Smith 1976 [1776]; Kuczynski 1971). Quesnay and Smith were disputing Locke's assertion that land only generates welfare through the application of labor and tools (Locke 1998 [1689]). He regarded tools as a 'store' of labor. Locke's view was the intellectual precursor of the so-called labor theory of value, as refined by Marx and others (Weissmahr 2000).

The notion of land scarcity as a constraint on economic growth goes back to Thomas Malthus (Malthus 1946 [1798]). In the 18th century, when capital primarily meant land, and when most arable land in Europe was already being tilled, it was not clear how a growing population could be fed from a finite supply of land. This was the conundrum that motivated Malthus to write his pessimistic assessment of the consequences of population growth in 1798 (Malthus 1946 [1798]).

Natural resource scarcities, actual or anticipated, have kicked off major efforts to find substitutes or alternatives. There have been a number of cases of actual resource scarcity – or even exhaustion – usually limited to a particular resource or country. To name a few historical examples: charcoal became scarce in western Europe, especially England, by the 17th century, due to land clearing, a building boom and ship-building for the navy.[18] Coal came into general use in Britain as a substitute for charcoal in the 18th century. The availability of fossil fuels has been a subject of controversy since 1865 when W.S. Jevons predicted that British coal reserves would be exhausted within a few decades (Jevons 1974 [1865]). Later, other natural resources – and especially exhaustible resources – began to be seen as 'factors of production' in their own right.

Sperm whales, the preferred source of lamp oil and tallow for candles in the early 19th century, were becoming scarce by mid-century. Whaling ships in those days were often away for as long as three years. The increasing scarcity of whales and the high price of sperm whale oil ($2.50 per gallon by the early 1850s, equivalent to $25–50 per gallon today) induced an intensive search for alternatives. Camphene, derived from turpentine, was the early leader. Kerosine derived from 'rock oil' seepages or from asphalt or tar pits (available in a number of places, such as Trinidad) was also in the market, as was animal fat from meat-processing plants. But the combination of ancient Chinese salt-drilling techniques and refining methods already available, prompted the search for, and discovery of, liquid petroleum at moderate depths in northwestern Pennsylvania in 1859 (Yergin 1991). Kerosine, derived from 'rock oil' (petroleum), was the eventual choice from among several possibilities, including lard oil, turpentine and camphene (Williamson and Daum 1959). It remained so until it was overtaken by electric light a generation later. Gasoline was originally a low-value by-product of kerosine (illuminating oil) refining and remained so until about 1910.

Kerosine, derived from petroleum ('rock oil') became the main source of light for the world after 1870. But the loss of its original prime market was just in time to allow petroleum-based fuels to propel automobiles and aircraft. (The year gasoline sales exceeded kerosine sales for the first time was 1911.) Meanwhile petroleum-based lubricants had become essential to the operation of all kinds of machines. In short, the creation of the oil industry was a Schumpeterian innovation in that it spawned or enabled many new industries far beyond its original use.

Acute worries about scarcity arose with respect to petroleum reserves in 1919 and the early 1920s, thanks to the conversion of naval ships from coal to oil and the spectacular rise in US gasoline consumption. The director of the US geological survey even warned that known US reserves would be exhausted in nine years and three months (Yergin 1991, p. 194). New discoveries, especially in east Texas and Oklahoma, converted the anticipated scarcity of the 1920s into a glut in the 1930s. Many petroleum analysts cite that experience to support the thesis that there is still plenty of oil in the world waiting to be discovered.

The Japanese invasion of the Dutch East Indies was prompted by its need for access to oil, for which Japan had been previously dependent on the US (California) as a source. The US cut off oil exports to Japan a few months before Pearl Harbor, probably triggering that event. The German invasion of southern Russia was aimed at the oil resources of the Caspian region. Petroleum became very scarce in German-controlled Europe during 1943–5. In response, the Germans produced synthetic liquid fuels on a large scale by hydrogenation of coal via the Bergius and Fischer-Tropsch processes (Yergin 1991, p. 330). In early 1944 German aviation gasoline was 92 percent synthetic (Bergius) and over half of German oil production through the war period was derived from coal (Yergin 1991, p. 344).

The potential scarcity issue (as applied to oil) was reviewed again in the aftermath of World War II, when the so-called Paley Commission, appointed by President Truman, took up the question in the US.[19] It was revived yet again in the early 1970s, even before the Arab oil embargo in 1973–4 led to a brief shortage and a radical price increase that transferred enormous sums from the industrialized consumers into the hands of petroleum-producing countries.[20] Major efforts were undertaken in the late 1970s and early 1980s to develop oil shales and tar sands as substitutes for Middle Eastern petroleum. Nuclear power was seen as the other long-term substitute for soon-to-be-scarce fossil fuels until the accident at Three Mile Island, Pennsylvania, in 1979 and the worse one at Chernobyl in the USSR in 1987.

One last example is worthy of mention. The rapid population growth in Europe during the early 19th century that had alarmed Malthus outstripped European agriculture and threatened food shortages.[21] A German chemist, Justus Leibig, called attention to the need for fertilizers in agriculture, both to replace nutrient elements (especially nitrogen and phosphorus) removed from the soil by harvesting, and to supplement natural stocks in the soil and thus increase agricultural productivity (Leibig 1876).

Natural fertilizers – notably guano and nitrate deposits from the west coast of South America – were exploited at first, but supplies were very limited. Super-phosphates were made from bones, and later from mineral apatites (phosphate rock). Germans also began to extract ammonia from coke oven gas to manufacture synthetic nitrates. But more was needed. An international race to develop practical means of 'fixing' atmospheric nitrogen led to the development of three processes early in the 20th century. The first was the Birkeland-Eyde electric arc process to manufacture nitrogen oxides. It was successfully commercialized in Norway (1904) where hydro-electric power was cheap. Next came the calcium cyanamide process, based on a high temperature reaction between calcium carbide and nitrogen. The cyanamide subsequently hydrolyzes to yield ammonia and urea. Finally, the Haber-Bosch catalytic process to synthesize ammonia from hydrogen was developed circa 1914. This process soon displaced the others and remains the dominant source of fixed nitrogen for agriculture – and military explosives (Smil 2001).

Modern resource economics began with a famous paper on the economics of exhaustible resources by Harold Hotelling (Hotelling 1931). However, the possible contribution of natural resource inputs to economic growth (or to technical progress) was not considered seriously by economists until the 1960s, especially due to the study by Barnett and Morse (1963) sponsored by Resources for the Future (RFF). The message of that study, which relied heavily on long-term price trends for exhaustible resources, was that scarcity was not an immediate problem, nor likely to be one in the near future, thanks to technological progress.

This conclusion was seemingly challenged by events of the early 1970s, including the 'energy crisis', the rise of OPEC and partly in response to the Club of Rome's 'Limits to Growth' report (Meadows et al. 1972). Neoclassical economists responded immediately with a number of papers disputing the 'Limits' conclusions (for example, Solow 1974a and b; Stiglitz

1974; Dasgupta and Heal 1974). It follows that, in more recent applications of the standard theory (as articulated primarily by RFF and Solow), resource consumption has been treated as a consequence of growth and not as a factor of production (Solow 1986, 1992; Smith and Krutilla 1979). This assumption is built into virtually all textbooks and most of the large-scale models used for policy guidance by governments. We argue *a priori* that the assumption is unjustified and that energy (exergy) consumption is as much a driver of growth as a consequence.

One of us has argued that a key feature of any satisfactory economic theory should be that it treats materials – extraction, conversion, and use – as essential core activities, not incidental consequences of market functions involving abstract 'resources' (for example, Ayres and Kneese 1969; Ayres et al. 1970; Ayres 1978, 1998; Ayres and Ayres 1999; Ayres and Warr 2002, 2005). Hence resource scarcity is potentially a major concern for us in this book. However, we do not discuss it at length hereafter.

1.12 SUMMARY

The standard neoclassical model of the world assumes growth in perpetual equilibrium driven by an external driving force called 'technological progress'. The latter is assumed to be exogenous, rather like 'manna from heaven'. Goods and services in this model are abstractions. When there is excess demand for goods, prices rise, profits increase, there is more competition for labor, and wages rise. Higher wages result in increased demand, which accelerates the economy still further. However, higher wages induce producers to become more efficient. They increase labor productivity by investing in new capital equipment incorporating new technology. The creation of new technology is not really explained by the model.

These new investments take some time to come on stream. When they do, wages stop rising and demand stops increasing. The result is excess supply, such as the present situation in the industrialized world for most products. In a competitive 'free market' prices start to fall, but in a world of oligopoly and cartels, prices do not fall, or very little. Nevertheless, older factories become less profitable, or unprofitable, and eventually they close (unless governments step in to prevent it). In the ideal competitive world supply finally declines and demand increases due to falling prices, unless fear of unemployment causes consumers to stop spending, thus making the problem worse. Both expansion and contraction tend to feed on themselves, to some extent. Note that this idealized description does not depend in any way on natural resources, as such, except insofar as they are supplied like other goods subject to market demand.

Needless to say, the real world is not much like the idealized free market world where there are no unions, no cartels, no regulators, no taxes and no subsidies. However, even in the neoclassical paradigm the microeconomic role of new technology is straightforward, provided the incentives for investment and the sources of profits to re-invest are not questioned: Progress results from investment aimed at cutting costs so as to reduce prices or to increase the performance or consumer appeal of products or services. Either way, the purpose is to hold or increase market share, which is the surest way to increase the profits of the firm.

The macroeconomic role of R&D in the neoclassical model is much less clear. As mentioned before, the majority of simple models assume that technological progress occurs automatically, in equilibrium, and that its effect is to increase productivity at a steady rate. Some recent models equate technology with knowledge and call it 'human capital' or (equivalently) 'knowledge capital'. But these models cannot be quantified or used for forecasting purposes, lacking a reliable measure of knowledge/human capital. As we have said before, the neoclassical model has no convincing explanation of why technological progress should not be uniform or continuous (in fact it isn't), or why R&D and radical innovation should occur at all.

In the alternative disequilibrium paradigm the macroeconomic role of technology is still straightforward: When products become cheaper (due to technological improvements in production) or more attractive to consumers by virtue of improved performance, the result is to increase aggregate demand. Increased demand leads to increased output, higher wages, lower costs (thanks to economies of scale and learning), increased capital investment and more R&D. All of these combine in a positive feedback cycle that drives overall economic growth.

More important, new technology in any given sector may have unexpected spillover effects on others. We could mention a number of examples. For instance, cheap electricity made a number of new materials available for the first time (for example, synthetic abrasives, chlorine, aluminum, stainless steel, tungsten). These, in turn, opened the door to other important innovations, such as high speed grinders, chlorinated water, PVC, incandescent lamps, X-rays and the aircraft industry. These spillovers are difficult to predict, and they have uneven impacts across the spectrum. Thus, not only is new technology created as an essential part of the positive feedback cycle, it is far from uniform in its impacts.

These differential impacts result in significant departures from equilibrium. For instance, when a new technology creates a demand for some product that displaces another older one, there is an automatic imbalance: demand for motor vehicles left buggy-whip manufacturers and wooden wheel manufacturers with excess capacity and declining markets. Electric lighting left candle and kerosine lamp manufacturers with excess capacity, while demand for electric light bulbs grew explosively. The role of technology is (in effect) to create a perpetual *disequilibrium*.

The other key conclusions of this chapter can be summarized in several related propositions.

1. The process of invention, including (but not limited to) formal R&D is usually (but not always) driven by economic incentives. These incentives may be as simple as the Schumpeterian desire to obtain a temporary monopoly (by means of patents, secrecy or 'first mover' advantages) in some growing field. The fields where opportunities for such gains exist tend to be relatively new ones, often resulting from a scientific 'breakthrough' of some sort. However, resource scarcity (or anticipated scarcity) also provides a major incentive for innovation. Military conflict provides a powerful but non-economic incentive that has triggered a number of important innovations in the past.

2. Technological breakthroughs presuppose barriers. Barriers may be absolute physical limits, but much more often they result from limits of a particular configuration or 'trajectory' consisting of a sequence of modifications of an original basic idea. Barriers can also arise from a variety of causes, ranging from wars to geo-political developments, to problems arising from the adoption of a pervasive technology (such as motor vehicles), including resource scarcity or environmental harms. Radical innovations overcome these barriers by opening new 'morphological neighborhoods' to exploration. Breakthroughs can rarely be predicted in advance, either as to timing or direction. The probability of a breakthrough is essentially proportional only to the intensity of the search for it. If the need is great, the problem will be solved sooner rather than later.

3. Once a barrier has been breached, gradual improvements, based on investment in R&D, are relatively smooth and predictable in the short run. Indeed, they tend to follow a standard pattern that is common to many processes, including diffusion, namely the elongated S-shaped curve. The parameters of the curve can be determined from its history and from a forecast of the ultimate limits of the particular technological trajectory.

4. Breakthroughs tend to have unexpected impacts in fields (sectors) other than the one where the barrier originally existed. The greater the range and scope of the spillovers, the greater the growth-promoting impact. The most important breakthroughs have impacts far beyond the original objective, resulting in new opportunities in other sectors. Breakthroughs

tend to create imbalances and disequilibrium. These 'spillover effects' are major contributors to long-term economic growth.

We still lack a useful measure of the past and current state of technology as a whole. We also lack a quantifiable link between past technological change and future resource consumption. These topics will be considered in the next several chapters.

NOTES

1. The first of his two observations is not strictly true: there are numerous counter-examples. We can agree (based on intuition rather than analysis) that his assertion is probably valid in a competitive free market, where market entry costs are non-existent or very low. Otherwise, it is a dubious generalization. At the firm level, there are numerous well-documented counter-examples that need not be recapitulated here. Interested readers can dig further in sources such as Nelson (1989), Lovins (1988, 1996), Romm (1993). As regards the second of Krugman's observations, namely that 'things add up', it actually follows from accounting identities that are even more fundamental than so-called 'laws of nature' (which are occasionally shown to be false or incomplete) and far more powerful than mere 'observations'. The accounting identity for money has undoubtedly had a powerful impact on economics in a variety of ways, from double-entry bookkeeping and auditing to trade theory and monetary theory. In physics the accounting identities are expressed as conservation laws, especially for mass, energy and momentum. The first two of these conservation laws, which is really a single law (the first law of thermodynamics), have major implications for economics, as noted later in this book.
2. Possibly the first use of variational methods in economics.
3. This seems natural, since capital stock is so heterogeneous that there is no other obvious unit of measurement. We accept this point for the present. Nevertheless, the issue has been controversial.
4. For a survey of the methods in common use see Blades (1991).
5. In recent years (since the work of Romer (1986)), the possibility of non-constant (increasing) returns received a good deal of attention from theorists. However, the empirical evidence for this idea is weak and the long-term implications are very awkward (Solow 1994). Hence we do not consider the possibility further in this book.
6. Kendrick reports that Dale Jorgenson and Zvi Griliches claimed to have eliminated the Solow residual altogether by this procedure, using a multi-sector model. However they were forced to retreat after an exchange with Edward Denison (Kendrick 1991). A recent and detailed example of this approach, as applied to the US economy between the years 1948 and 1979, is exhibited by Jorgenson et al. (1987). The apparent contribution of TFP to growth in that period was reduced from 46 percent to 24 percent. For a recent application see McKibben and Wilcoxen (1995).
7. The mathematical derivation is straightforward, but not worth reproducing here. See, for example, Kuemmel (1980, pp. 41–4).
8. There is a well-known theorem to the effect that with rare exceptions one cannot simultaneously optimize two different objective functions. This means that optimization at the task or work unit level, or at the branch or subsidiary level, cannot be optimal for the parent firm. Similarly, what is optimal for a firm or industry sector is very unlikely to be optimal for a nation.
9. As regards the future, it is clear that environmental constraints (arising from material extraction, processing and consumption) will become increasingly important. Continued

economic growth, in the sense of welfare gains, will probably require multiple radical technological innovations, resulting in dramatic ('Factor Four', 'Factor Ten') reductions in raw materials and energy consumption as well as more gradual improvements such as more recycling and end-of-pipe waste treatment (Schmidt-Bleek 1992; von Weizsaecker et al. 1998; Ayres 1996). All of this can be regarded as 'decoupling'.

10. Sectors are ultimately defined in terms of product families which have gradually become increasingly differentiated over time. The sectoral structure of the economy has evolved as a consequence of a large number of micro-mutations (so to speak) at the product and process level.

11. Major edited volumes on the topic include, for example, Dosi et al. (1988), Day and Eliason (1986). Other pertinent papers are by Day (1984, 1987, 1989), Dosi (1982, 1988), Silverberg et al. (1988); Silverberg (1988); Silverberg and Lehnert (1993); Silverberg and Verspagen (1994); Silverberg and Verspagen (1996), and Kwasnicki (1996).

12. At least one respected scientist has tried to elevate the logistic function to the status of a law of nature Marchetti and Nakicenovic (1979); Marchetti (1981). Two other well-known growth laws Gompertz (1832) and von Bertalanffy (1957) and some less well-known ones have been suggested in the past. For a detailed comparison see Kenney and Keeping (1962, part 1) or Ayres (1969, chapter 7).

13. The logistic model, or variants of it, has become a mainstay of theoretical marketing analysis Easingwood et al. (1983); Mahajan and Schoeman (1977); Mahajan and Peterson (1985); Mahajan and Wind (1986).

14. Harrison finally received the prize for his fourth, and last, in a series of time-pieces ('chronometers') built from 1729–60 (Sobel 1996). One of Harrison's chronometers was used by Captain Cook.

15. This topic has been explored at considerable length and depth by Griliches (1957, 1958), Mansfield (1961), David (1975), Nabseth and Ray (1974), Davies (1979), Stoneman (1976) and Metcalfe (Metcalfe and Hall 1983). More recently an evolutionary perspective has come to the fore. Important contributions since the pioneering work of Nelson and Winter (mentioned previously) include works by Iwai (1984a, 1984b), Winter (1984), Silverberg (Silverberg et al. 1988) and Metcalfe (1992).

16. The theory of 'lock-in' (also known as 'path-dependence') has been developed mainly by Brian Arthur (1983, 1988).

17. Authors who have utilized this idea include Levitt (1965), Vernon (1966), Abernathy and Utterback (1975, 1978), Polli and Cook (1969), Nelson (1962), Ayres (1987, 1992, 1989a).

18. A reviewer has added an interesting sidelight. In Britain (and probably elsewhere) 'royal' oaks were reserved for the crown (that is, for ships), and farmers were not allowed to cut them. As a probable consequence, farmers fed the acorns to pigs and otherwise discouraged the growth of seedlings, thus contributing to the ultimate shortage.

19. The first major postwar assessment of resource needs and availabilities was sponsored by the Twentieth Century Fund, namely *America's Needs and Resources* by J. Frederick Dewhurst (Dewhurst 1947, 1955). President Truman created the Materials Policy Commission, chaired by William Paley. The Commission's report, entitled *Resources for Freedom*, was published in 1952 (Paley 1952). To continue the work of the Commission, Resources For the Future Inc. (RFF) was created and funded by the Ford Foundation, also in 1952. RFF sponsored its first major conference in 1953, resulting in a book, *A Nation Looks at its Resources* (Resources for the Future 1954), and many others since then.

20. A partial list of studies carried out in the US alone during the years 1972 and 1973 includes the following: 'Patterns of Energy Consumption in the United States', Office of Science and Technology, Executive Office of the President, January 1972 (Stanford Research Institute 1972); 'The Potential for Energy Conservation', Office of Emergency Preparedness, Executive Office of the President, October 1972 (United States Office of Science and Technology (OST) 1972); (National Petroleum Council Committee on US Energy Outlook 1972); 'US Energy Outlook', Committee on US Energy Outlook, National Petroleum Council, December 1972; 'Understanding the National Energy

Dilemma', Livermore National Laboratory, for the Joint Committee on Atomic Energy, US Congress, Fall 1973 (Bridges 1973), later updated and republished as 'Energy: A National Issue', F.X. Murray, Center for Strategic and International Studies, Georgetown University, 1976 (Murray 1976); 'Energy Facts' prepared by the Congressional Research Service for Subcommittee on Energy, Committee on Science and Astronautics, US House of Representatives, November 1973 (Congressional Research Service (CRS) 1973); 'The Nation's Energy Future', A Report to Richard M. Nixon, President of the United States, submitted by Dixy Lee Ray, Chairman of the United States Atomic Energy Commission, December 1973 (Ray 1973). The multi-volume Ford Foundation Energy Policy Study (Ford Foundation Energy Policy Study 1974) was also commissioned in 1971, although publication did not occur until 1974.

21. The food shortage became most acute in Ireland in the late 1840s, although the immediate cause was a disease, the potato blight. Hundreds of thousands of starving Irish peasants emigrated to the US at that time. Scandinavia and Germany also experienced serious food shortages in that period.

2. Technical progress

2.1 INTRODUCTION

In the previous chapter we focused primarily on macroeconomic theories relevant to growth, and secondarily on the role of technology in those theories. In this chapter we reverse the emphasis, focusing on technology and technical progress *as such*. It must be acknowledged that, although we by no means exclude social technologies and institutional changes from consideration, our discussion hereafter is almost exclusively focused on physical technologies. This bias is due to the fact that it is far more difficult to define a social technology precisely, still less measure its performance in quantitative terms, than it is for a physical technology. However, we assume that most of the general conclusions of this chapter are equally applicable to social technologies as well as to the physical technologies presented here from which most of our examples are taken.

2.2 TECHNOLOGICAL TRAJECTORIES

The gradual evolution of a constrained upward-tending knowledge search and acquisition process over decades has been described as a *technological trajectory* (Perez-Perez 1983; Freeman 1989). We would modify the definition slightly. For us, a technological trajectory is a sequence of developments starting from a distinct functional configuration utilizing a basic principle. For instance, the 'atmospheric' reciprocating steam engine beginning with Newcomen can be regarded as the starting point of a trajectory. The trajectory changed direction and was accelerated by James Watt's condensing engine. This was followed by his double-acting valve system, the 'sun and planet' gearing, and the crank and flywheel scheme for converting reciprocating motion into rotary motion. Trevithick's and Evans' high pressure engines (circa 1800), the double and triple compound engines and other later innovations, such as the monotube boiler, continued the same basic trajectory by making reciprocating steam engines bigger, more efficient and more powerful.

A new trajectory arguably started with Charles Parson's steam turbine (1884). This was followed by de Laval's innovation (high speed helical gear, 1890), which facilitated applications at low speeds, and Curtiss' velocity compounding (1898), which permitted still smaller sizes (Forbes and Dijksterhuis 1963, p. 462). The internal combustion piston engine of Nikolaus Otto started a different trajectory, as did the gas turbine.

Similarly, the whale oil lamp and the kerosine lamp were arguably a continuation of the prior trajectory (open flames) that went back to torches in pre-Roman times. The gas light started a new trajectory early in the 19th century. The electric arc light began another new trajectory, replacing gas light. That trajectory was accelerated by the advent of incandescent lamps, fluorescent lights, and so on. The newer light-emitting diodes (LEDs) appear to be the natural end of the sequence.

In this case, and many others, the performance and efficiency of the new technology increased dramatically along the trajectory, from first introduction to maturity – and presumably to eventual phase-out and replacement. In the case of electric power generation by steam turbines the efficiency gain from 1900 to 1970 was a factor of ten (from 3.5 to 35 percent). In fact, the rate of progress along an established trajectory is relatively predictable, at least for some time. As noted already in Chapter 1, Section 1.5, performance improvement along a trajectory is partly the result of learning (or experience) and partly due to the level of continuing R&D investment. The latter (in the private sector, at least) is likely to be dependent on the recent rates of return on R&D (Foster 1986; Mansfield 1965; Mansfield et al. 1977).

A pattern of crisis-driven innovation has recurred a number of times. The crisis may arise because of war, blockade, resource scarcity or even from the extraordinary success of a new technology. The latter may result in an imbalance between supply of some essential component and demand for the service or 'functionality' of the technology. Or a crisis may arise when increasing demand for a product or service cannot be met by the older technology due to the approach of a physical limit. Any of these cases can be regarded as a barrier. It is worthwhile giving examples of each as a way of introducing a general pattern.

2.3 MILITARY NEEDS AS DRIVERS OF INNOVATION

The importance of war and threats of war in this context is well-known. Many technologies were invented, innovated or adopted in response to military exigencies. Harrison's development of the spring-driven chronometer, for navigational purposes, was noted in Chapter 1. The trigger was a navigational error resulting in the loss of scores of ships and hundreds of sailors, and the British need to maintain naval superiority over its continental neighbors. New weapons, from the musket to the machine gun, the bomber, and the atomic bomb, obviously had military origins. Wilkinson's boring machine for cannon served a double purpose by boring the cylinders for Watt's steam engines. The use of metal cans for food preservation arose at first from the needs of Napoleon's armies, and later the US Civil War. Breakthroughs in nursing and sterilization, antiseptics, anesthetics, antibiotics and surgical techniques came about in response to wartime casualties.

New metal-working technologies were often first applied to gun manufacturing, as in the case of the boring machine mentioned above. Another example was Eli Whitney's machine tool innovations (notably the milling machine), the French-inspired goal of interchangeable parts, and the so-called 'American system of manufacturing' later refined by Colt, Remington and Winchester. These innovations were originally intended to make guns cheaper and more reliable, but were soon adopted throughout the metal-working industries (Rosenberg 1969b; Woodbury 1972; Carlsson 1984; Hounshell 1984). Significant improvements in steel casting and forming in Germany were driven by the race to build bigger and longer-range guns, especially for battleships ('dreadnoughts').

Arguably the most important chemical technology in history, the Haber-Bosch process to synthesize ammonia (more generally, to 'fix' nitrogen), was driven in part by the German desire to break the British monopoly of natural nitrate deposits found in the Atacama desert in northern Chile (Smil 2001). This was strategically important not only because of the importance for agriculture in a Germany whose population and demand for food were rapidly increasing, but also because its leader wanted Germany to be a Great Power which – at the time – meant a strong army and navy, requiring munitions. All chemical explosives still depend in some way upon nitro-compounds, either nitrates or amines. The two main coal gasification processes were also developed in Germany, starting in World War I, to substitute coal for petroleum, and in World War II these processes accounted for half of the gasoline consumption of the country and most of the aviation fuel (Yergin 1991). Meanwhile synthetic rubber technology, originally developed in Germany during the 1920s, was developed rapidly in the US to compensate for the Japanese capture of the Malaysian and Indo-Chinese rubber plantations in 1942.[1]

The substitution of oil-burning ships for coal-burning ships before and during World War I is yet another example of war as a driver of change. The British Navy had long resisted any change (on the grounds that coal was available everywhere while oil was not), but the advantages of higher speed, achievable thanks to greater power-to-weight, together with less manpower required for stoking coal – especially in battle – proved decisive (Yergin 1991). Oil was used at first to drive conventional steam turbines[2] but diesel oil powered German submarines nearly cut off allied shipping in 1916–17. The British Navy's conversion from coal-burning steam turbines to oil-burning diesel engines was completed by the war's end.

The development of the aircraft industry during 1914–18 was even more accelerated by war. Prior to 1914, aircraft were not much more than toys for rich young adventurers. Top speeds were around 60 mph (96 kph). By war's end speeds were up to 125 mph (200 kph) and altitudes of 27,000 feet (8000 meters) had been reached. The first practical all-metal aircraft (Junkers J.1) was a wartime German development. Large-scale production was perhaps the most important development: Germany produced 48,000 planes during the war, while the allies, altogether, produced 158,000 planes (55,000 by Britain, 68,000 by France, 20,000 by Italy and 15,000 by the US in just the last 18 months (Yergin 1991, pp. 171–3)).

Demand lapsed after the war, and progress in aeronautical engineering slowed down considerably, despite great public interest, especially thanks to a series of highly publicized flights culminating in Charles Lindbergh's epic flight from New York to Paris. The first all-metal (aluminum) fuselage for civil aircraft did not appear until Ford's Tri-motor in 1927. True commercial service emerged (slowly) in the early 1930s. But it was World War II and the need for long-distance bombers that really provided the airport infrastructure and further technological developments in engine power, instrumentation, communications and manufacturing capability. It was the latter that, in turn, enabled the civil air transport industry to expand rapidly after the war.

World War II produced synthetic rubber, synthetic gasoline, RADAR, SONAR, aircraft jet engines, rocketry, decryption computers and nuclear reactors. Missile technology – especially the V2 rocket – was developed in Nazi Germany during World War II in the vain hope of converting a losing cause into a last-minute victory. The nuclear fission bomb used by the US to end World War II was developed in response to a well-founded fear that Germany was also trying to develop such a weapon (Rhodes 1988). But this innovation led to nuclear power. Radar was developed in both Germany and Britain, in the late 1930s for military (defense) purposes, and it was eventually crucial to the outcome of the Battle of Britain in 1940 (Jewkes et al. 1958). Now it is an essential feature of civil air travel, not to mention traffic control and microwave ovens. Jet engines were another pre-World War II invention, whose development and application were vastly accelerated by wartime needs. Jets were converted to civilian purposes in the 1960s, but rockets are still primarily military in application, although they will be the primary enabling technology for space travel.

2.4   OTHER BARRIERS AND BREAKTHROUGHS

The rise of the Ottoman power in the 15th century after the fall of Constantinople (1453) created a geo-political barrier to trade and ended the dominance of Venice and Genoa. It reduced the importance of the so-called 'silk road' that had been 'opened' by Venetian traders like Marco Polo, and somewhat inhibited overland access between Europe and Asia. The Ottoman rise, together with the Venetian-Genoese monopoly on the spice trade, created a demand for alternative sea routes. This improved navigational techniques (notably the invention of the astrolabe, for calculating latitudes) which Portugal, under its Prince (later King) Henry the Navigator, and (later) Spain, under Ferdinand and Isabella, developed and exploited. Much of the global exploration by sea in the following years by Portuguese, Spanish and later British and Dutch ships, including the discovery and colonization of the Americas, was triggered by this geo-political change. European rivalry in the Indian Ocean, and the eventual 'opening' of China and Japan to seaborne European traders, were other consequences. Similarly, the British-French search for the non-existent 'Northwest Passage' led to the exploration of Canada.

The wartime or war-related examples already mentioned (nitrogen fixation, synthetic gasoline, synthetic rubber) could also be attributed to blockades. Finally, the Arab oil embargo of 1973–4 had downstream consequences, not all of which are obvious, but among them a panoply of studies and government and industry technological and regulatory responses, mostly short-lived, but nevertheless – taken together – significant early steps towards the development of renewable energy options, including solar power, wind power, biomass (and fuel cells).

One of the most interesting examples of a barrier resulting from unexpected success arose when the spectacular growth of the automobile industry after 1900 created an unexpected but urgent demand for gasoline. The number of cars registered in the US increased 100-fold, from 1900, when only 8000 cars were registered, to 1910 when 902,000 vehicles were on the road. The number of cars in service increased ten-fold again to 9.2 million by 1920.

Gasoline in the 1880s and 1890s was an unwanted by-product of kerosine ('illuminating oil'), which had been the main product of the petroleum industry since the 1860s. The volatile liquid fraction, known as 'natural gasoline' accounted for only 15 to 20 percent, by weight, of the distillation products. Natural gasoline had sold for as little as 2 or 3 cents per gallon in the 1890s and was used only for dry-cleaning. But the spark-ignition internal combustion engine developed by Nikolaus Otto (1876) opened the door. Otto's assistant, Gottlieb Daimler, invented the carburetor to vaporize and utilize cheap natural gasoline. The size and weight of Otto's engine was cut drastically by adding a cylinder (and soon, more cylinders) to balance the forces and reduce the need for a heavy flywheel. Higher speeds permitted still lighter weights. This was the key to the development by Daimler, Maybach and Benz of the self-powered vehicle, or 'automobile' (Field 1958; Ayres 1989c).

After 1900 the demand for gasoline naturally increased in proportion to the number of vehicles. Gasoline outsold kerosine for the first time in 1910 and in October 1911 the price had risen to 9.5 cents per gallon. Sixteen months later, in January 1913, the price had jumped to 17 cents per gallon in the US. People in London and Paris were paying 50 cents per gallon and even higher prices in some cases (Yergin 1991, p. 112).

Luckily the prospect of a gasoline shortage had been foreseen years earlier by chemist William Burton, who worked for the Standard Oil Co. at the time. Starting in 1909 he began laboratory experiments on 'cracking' heavy petroleum fractions to increase the yield of gasoline. The thermal cracking process was operational in 1910. He applied to the firm's headquarters in New York for permission to build 100 cracking stills, but his request was turned down. However the Standard Oil monopoly was formally broken up by court order in mid-1911 and Indiana Standard, Burton's employer, became independent of the parent firm. Burton's cracking stills were built, and Indiana Standard began licensing the Burton (batch) process in 1914. The licensing was extremely profitable because there was no alternative.

But the high cost of licensing naturally induced other oil companies to try to develop alternative processes. Continuous versions of the thermal process soon emerged from several laboratories. This was followed by batch catalytic cracking and reforming processes in the 1930s and 1940s, and finally a continuous version in the 1940s and 1950s (Enos 1962; Yergin 1991). Thanks to the cracking processes and new discoveries, the price of gasoline fell steadily after a peak of 22 cents per gallon in the early 1920s. In 1927 it had fallen to 13 cents per gallon in San Francisco and 11 cents per gallon in Los Angeles.

Another barrier emerged in the second decade of the 20th century. Gasoline engines could be 'miniaturized' by increasing the compression ratio to about 4:1, but after that the engine suffered from pre-ignition, known as 'knocking' during the compression stroke. Knocking was not only annoying; it cut the power and the efficiency. There was an industry-wide search for an effective additive that could eliminate knocking. The successful anti-knock product, tetraethyl lead, was discovered by a chemist at a small laboratory called Dayton Engineering Laboratories Inc. (Jewkes et al. 1958). That laboratory, along with its leader, Charles Kettering, was later acquired by General Motors, where it became the Delco division.

This breakthrough enabled the auto manufacturers to increase the allowable compression ratio above the previous limit of 4:1 in order to increase engine power-to-weight and fuel efficiency for automobiles.[3] The anti-knock additive was commercialized in the 1930s as 'ethyl' gasoline. It significantly increased the so-called 'octane' level of the fuel. This was particularly important for aviation gasoline, where high compression engines were essential to maximize efficiency and minimize the weight of the engine. This development arose directly from a 'need' created by the success of the automobile.

Other examples of success-driven innovations are numerous. Some of the most interesting examples have arisen out of the information technology revolution we find ourselves in today. Perhaps the first of these was the development of the transistor, which came about as a result of a deliberate search, at Bell Telephone Laboratories, for a solid-state technology to permit telephone switching equipment to consume far less electricity than the electro-mechanical equipment in use in the 1940s (Jewkes et al. 1958; Evans 1979). It is said that a senior Bell Labs executive initiated the project after noticing that the projected future use of electricity for telephone switching, allowing for continued growth in demand, would eventually outstrip the nation's electricity supply. True or not, the transistor was born out of problems arising from the success of telephone technology.

A similar story explains the development of the integrated circuit (IC). It had been noticed that the complexity of computers was growing rapidly and that as computers became increasingly complex the number of individual components and interconnections was growing even faster. Industry technology leaders, such as Jack Morton, vice-president of Bell Labs, worried about the 'tyranny of large numbers' (Reid 1985). Some speculated that the maximum size of computers would soon be reached. However, Jack Kilby of Texas Instruments and Robert Noyce of Fairchild independently solved the problem. They simultaneously invented the integrated circuit (IC) or 'chip', using slightly different approaches, for which they later shared the Nobel Prize.

Physical barriers, too, sometimes induce a search for breakthroughs. At one level the barrier may be simple ignorance. The progress of medicine and public health was long inhibited by wrong (and fundamentally harmful) assumptions, especially as regards the nature and cause of infection. The discoveries of Jenner, Pasteur, Koch and others had an enormous impact on medical practice. More often the barrier is technological, for example, the absence of some necessary input or capability, such as microscopes capable of seeing micro-organisms, very precise measuring devices, means of achieving very high (or low) temperatures, pressure, vacuum or very hard metals for cutting tools. The ancient problem of determining time accurately on a ship at sea, where a pendulum will not function, has been mentioned already.

The history of metallurgy is a long search for ways of achieving temperatures in a confined space high enough to melt pure iron and make steel (Schubert 1958; Wertime 1962). Steel melts at a temperature of about 1500 degrees C. whereas 'pig' iron from a blast furnace (6 percent carbon) melts at less than 1100 degrees C. The additional 400 degrees C was a huge barrier, until the mid-19th century when two inventors, independently, William Kelly in the US and Henry Bessemer in the UK, conceived the idea of blowing air through the molten iron to oxidize the excess carbon and raise the temperature simultaneously.[4] Prior to this breakthrough such temperatures were previously only achievable, by Benjamin Huntsman's so-called 'crucible process', in very small externally heated volumes at very great cost. Before 1750 such temperatures were not achievable by any known process.

Important materials, such as stainless steel and the so-called refractory metals (nickel, chromium, cobalt, molybdenum, tungsten), could not be melted or refined until William Siemens and Henri Moissan's electric furnaces became available in the last two decades of the 19th century, thanks to the new availability of electric power on a large scale. The same was true of the tungsten filaments introduced in electric light bulbs around 1910. A less well-known example was synthetic abrasives, starting with silicon carbide, that led to high speed drills and grinding machines, essential for mass production of crankshafts and camshafts for automobile engines, among other products.

The internal combustion engine (ICE) had been sought since the first steam engines, mainly to avoid the need for bulky and dangerous boilers and condenser systems. But such an engine required (among other things) a gaseous or liquid fuel. Experiments began when synthetic 'town gas' became available at the beginning of the 19th century. The French engineer, Philippe Lebon, was among the first to consider the possibility circa 1801. Potential advantages of a stationary gas engine were obvious: no boiler or condenser, the ability to stop and start at will, and no need for on-site fuel storage, assuming a gas pipe was available. By 1860 a hundred versions of ICEs had been proposed and a dozen had been built (Bryant 1967). In 1860 Etienne Lenoir and Pierre Hugon, in France, (independently) built the first semi-practical ICEs, utilizing coal gas from coke ovens as a fuel. But the early prototypes could not really compete with well-developed steam engines at that point in time. They still suffered from a significant drawback; inability to control the shocks from explosive combustion inside the cylinder.

However, Lenoir's example inspired others. In 1867 Nikolaus Otto solved the shock problem by disconnecting the piston from the load (a direct imitation of Newcomen's steam engine) driving the 'free' piston up against gravity in a vertical cylinder and letting its weight and atmospheric pressure do the work on the return trip. Later, he found that the shock problem could be solved in another way, by increasing the number of explosions per minute to 80 or 90. Between 1868 and 1875 some 5000 Otto and Langen engines were built and sold in sizes up to 3 hp, as a power source for small factories and workshops, using 'town' gas as fuel – as an alternative to steam engines. This version of the engine was severely power limited, however. To allow more power, Otto introduced a four-stroke cycle with compressed fuel-air mixture, using the return stroke of the non-working intake stroke for compression and a flywheel. Even though the 1876 'Otto silent' engine weighed over 500 kg/hp, it was the primary breakthrough that finally enabled automotive transportation (as noted above) and (after 1900) heavier-than-air craft.

The shift from reciprocating steam engines to steam turbines was already mentioned. It came about because reciprocating piston engines had reached a size limit, exemplified by the famous 1400 hp Corliss triple-expansion engine at the Century of Progress exhibition in Philadelphia in 1876. That engine – the star of the show – was as big as a house. In 1899 a 10,000 hp unit 40 feet high was built for the New York City subway system. But it was scrapped only three years later, in 1902, and replaced by a steam turbine only one-tenth of the size (Forbes and Dijksterhuis 1963, p. 453).

The diesel engine was conceived on the basis of theory, and subsequently developed by Rudolph Diesel in the 1890s. The original motivation was to find a way of avoiding the 'knocking' problem in gasoline engines, mentioned above, by using heavier fuel oil that would not pre-ignite. The essential feature of Diesel's invention was 'compression ignition', which means that if an air fuel mixture is compressed sufficiently, the heat of compression will cause it to ignite spontaneously. It takes a compression ratio of around 15:1 to achieve this result reliably. The higher compression ratio also results in significantly higher efficiency than the gasoline engine could (or can) achieve, but at the cost of greater weight. The technical challenges of achieving such high compression in practice, without blowing the engine apart, were formidable, and the difficulty was compounded by problems of cold starting. However the operational advantages, especially for ships (where a large and heavy engine could run continuously), were great. The first significant applications of diesel were marine: diesel engines replaced coal-burning reciprocating steam engines on naval ships during World War I, followed by diesel-electric railroad locomotives in the 1930s, then heavy off-road equipment and large trucks. Applications in passenger automobiles (thanks to turbo compressors) has grown explosively since the 1960s, especially in Europe. The diesel-powered car is now superior in most respects to its spark-ignition competitor.

The history of physical science is replete with continuing efforts to approach limits of temperature (high and low), high pressure, high vacuum, particle beam energy, wavelength, bandwidth, and so on (Ayres 1994b). The first practical mercury vacuum pump was invented by Hermann Sprengel in 1865. Without vacuum pumps there would have been no incandescent lamps (1875–8) or so-called 'vacuum tubes' (circa 1910). J. A. Fleming patented the 'thermionic valve', a two-electrode diode, in 1904. Lee De Forest patented the three-electrode triode in 1908. Without these vacuum tubes there would have been no radios, no television, no radar, no electronic computers. Semiconductor technology may have replaced vacuum tubes, but the extremely high purity of silicon 'chips' requires even higher vacua and correspondingly more sophisticated vacuum pumps.[5]

Chemistry offers a number of examples of targeted searches. The search for cheap substitutes for expensive natural dyestuffs (such as indigo) was the impetus to find practical uses of aniline – a by-product of coal tar – that virtually created the German chemical industry. The search for cheap artificial substitutes for expensive natural silk, by means of chemical modifications of natural cellulose, led to the discovery of cellulose nitrate (used for photographic film) and later of rayon by Hilaire de Chardonnay (1885). This eventually kicked off a general search for ways of polymerizing small molecules available from hydrocarbons. The first commercial success was a polymer of formaldehyde and phenol that resulted in the first thermosetting plastic 'Bakelite'. The German chemical industry, followed by others, began to research polymer chemistry in earnest in the 1920s, which finally led to the whole range of modern synthetics and plastics (Mark 1984).

There are also some interesting examples of searches that were carried out by amateurs with little or no scientific knowledge. The development of the chronometer, mentioned at the beginning of this section, was one such. The breakthrough discovery of hot vulcanization of natural rubber by Charles Goodyear (1839) was another. The discovery of xerography and the discovery of self-developing film (and Polaroid cameras) were others. The long search for means of flying in heavier-than-air craft, accurately conceived in the early 19th century by Sir George Cayley, but finally achieved by the Wright brothers, is perhaps the most dramatic example of a successful search by amateurs.

2.5   THE DISCONTINUITY HYPOTHESIS: IS THERE A PATTERN?

The question is whether technological progress tends to be discontinuous. The short answer is clearly 'yes' (Ayres 1987, 1988a). While the motivations of inventors and researchers vary considerably – as we have indicated above – there are significant common features. The most important common feature, we suggest, is *discontinuity*. Most institutions are resistant to change, because change makes planning difficult and uncertain. The general attitude of established management in government and industry, including the military, is characterized by the phrase 'If it ain't broke, don't fix it!' Moreover, in most cases, this is probably reasonably good advice. The assumption underlying most demographic and economic models, too, is that change will occur very smoothly and gradually, and this is to some extent a self-justifying assumption. It is also a fairly accurate characterization of past history *provided* a sufficiently long-term and aggregated viewpoint is adopted.

The situation changes when the viewpoint is more localized and myopic. Continuity in many spheres, including technology, is the exception rather than the rule. Discontinuity is the rule. The discontinuity may be due to the fact that a conflict – violent or otherwise – must be resolved one way or the other (one side wins, the other loses). It may be due to geo-political power shifts, as in the Ottoman case mentioned above, the Protestant Reformation and the wars of religion, the failure of the Spanish Armada, the French Revolution and its aftermath, the rise and fall of the British Empire, the rise and fall of Marxism and the end of the Cold War. Some people think that the world is now embarking on a fundamental clash of civilizations (for example, Huntington 1993). Or a discontinuity may arise from a change in regulation, as for instance the electricity supply crisis that erupted in California in 2001–2 after the partial (and ill-designed) deregulation of the electric utilities.

A discontinuity may result from a sudden resource scarcity. Such a scarcity may be temporary and artificial, as in the case of the Arab oil boycott of 1973–4; yet that resulted in a sharp (albeit temporary) change in prices and patterns of capital investment. Or it may be due to an unexpected decline in new discoveries and reserves, as happened in the US in 1970–71, when domestic oil production peaked and the balance of power in the world oil industry suddenly moved from the Texas Railroad Commission, which regulated output, to the Persian Gulf and OPEC. Scarcity can arise from natural causes such as a famine or drought. People sometimes forget that fresh water and benign climate are fundamental resources. Cultures have been wiped out in the past due to natural events, such as Noah's Flood which seems to have occurred in the Black Sea due to the rising of the water level of the Mediterranean, due – in turn – to the melting of the glacial ice. The Atlantis myth may have originated from such a flood. More gradual climate change can also lead to catastrophic results. Such was the fate of the inhabitants of Easter Island, the Viking colony in Greenland, the

Anasazi Indians in the American West and to the formerly great Buddhist cities of central Asia, now buried under sand in Xinjiang, western China.[6]

Man-made discontinuities, apart from wars, have included ethnic cleansing in various countries and religious conflicts (the Reformation, the Counter-reformation, Islamic fundamentalism). Economic discontinuities worth mentioning include 'bubbles' and 'crashes' ranging from the Dutch tulip craze, the Mississippi bubble and the South Sea bubbles circa 1720 in France and England respectively, up to the Wall Street speculative bubble of 1927–9, the Tokyo land bubble of the late 1980s and the US 'dot-com' bubble of the late 1990s. The sub-prime mortgage market, which is working itself out as we write, may be another example. All of these bubbles were followed by crashes. Financial problems also include hyper-inflation, as in Germany in the early 1920s, and in a number of other countries, especially in Eastern Europe and Latin America, since then.

Finally, and most importantly from our perspective, a discontinuity may arise from a rapid substitution of one technology for another, with consequent disruptions, gains for some and losses – called 'creative destruction' by Schumpeter – for others. The rather sudden replacement of gas light and kerosine lamps by electric light, the replacement of steam power in factories by electric motors fed from central generators, and the rather sudden replacement of horse-drawn vehicles by automobiles are just a few examples. All of these, and others, created unexpected supply–demand imbalances, which led to still further technological innovations, as the decline of kerosine lamps and the spread of the automobile forced a radical transition of the global petroleum industry from producing kerosine to producing gasoline.[7] The concurrent transition to an 'information society' has already created significant imbalances, and will likely create more.[8]

Finally, a crisis in technology may be due to the approach to some intermediate physical barrier. One of the first such barriers to be recognized was that heat engines are subject to a maximum thermal efficiency (known as the Carnot limit).[9] Another famous example is the so-called 'sound barrier' (known as Mach 1), which is a discontinuity in the speed–power relationship: the power required to overcome air resistance suddenly increases non-linearly at Mach 1 and constitutes an effective limit to the speed of civil airliners. Other intermediate physical limits include the maximum current-carrying capacity of a wire, the maximum electrical resistance of an insulator, the maximum information-carrying capacity of a channel, the maximum tensile strength of steel plates, beams or wires, and the maximum temperature that a turbine alloy can withstand without losing its strength. All of these examples, and many others, have had significant impacts on the rate and direction of technological progress during the past several centuries.

One common feature of any impending shortage is a rising price of one or more 'bottleneck' commodities. The rising price of oil since 2006 is a good example. Where the barrier is a physical limit of some sort, the returns to R&D along the current trajectory begin to fall. This, too, constitutes a useful signal – albeit one that is typically only available to a narrow group of executives within the firm or industry (Mansfield 1965; Foster 1986).

To conclude this section, we see the history of technology, and the economy, as examples of 'punctuated equilibrium', appropriate terms introduced some years ago in the context of biological evolution and speciation (Eldredge and Gould 1972; Gould 1982; Rhodes 1983). While the analogy between biological evolution and human history is far from perfect, it seems to us that the key point is that, in both cases, relatively sudden changes – whether endogenous or exogenously caused – play a crucial role in the evolutionary process. But one difference is important: in the biological case, both the external change agents (such as tectonic processes, glaciation or asteroid collisions) and the internal change agents (mutations) are essentially unpredictable, if not random. In the human case, the opposite is now increasingly true. Some important discoveries are accidental, or quasi-accidental, as the discovery of penicillin is reputed to have been, but most are intentional.

2.6   IMPLICATIONS FOR ECONOMIC GROWTH

The history of technology clearly demonstrates that crisis-driven radical innovations, as distinct from incremental changes and adjustments, do *not* often occur at random, as assumed by most economists[10] and in some evolutionary economic models (for example, Nelson and Winter 1977, 1982). It is also important to recognize that radical innovations are not costless, even at the societal level. Apart from the costs of research, development and commercialization, such innovations may cause the demise of competing and obsolescent technologies and the businesses dependent on them. Schumpeter coined the phrase 'creative destruction' to characterize this phenomenon.

It is worth adding here that radical innovations typically provide solutions to particular problems that are obvious to industry leaders and sometimes even to the general public. In fact, we argue that experts can, and do, know the likely direction of change, because they – unlike the general public – can foresee the most plausible avenues to search for breakthroughs. Some are temporary: we already know that they can be surmounted by approaches that are easily identifiable and require finite investment along well-defined lines. The space program, culminating with the moon landing in 1969, was an example of this sort of barrier and breakthrough.

An important barrier to progress in some fields is the lack of a market for a technology that is 'needed' but unprofitable to the private sector. Needs of this kind may arise from threats to health and safety, for instance. One historical example was water pollution by sewage, an obvious health (and aesthetic) urban problem since the first cities. Sewer pipes separated well-water from sewage but only transferred the wastes into the rivers. The first practical solution to the water contamination problem arrived in the late 19th century, partly by accident. An electrolytic process had been developed and quickly adopted to produce caustic soda (sodium hydroxide) from salt. Caustic soda was essential for the soap, petroleum-refining, pulp and paper, rayon, aluminum and other growing industries. Chlorine was a by-product of electrolytic alkali production, with few uses at first. But it worked well as a way of decontaminating water. This lucky coincidence prompted the development of chlorination of water, and subsequently of sewage treatment systems.

The carnage of the Crimean War and the US Civil War in the mid-19th century generated public pressure to attack other infectious diseases, and injuries from war. Moreover, increasing wealth prompted the expansion of hospitals, medical services and medical education. These eventually prompted the successful search for causes of infection (especially by Pasteur), and a growing collection of medical innovations, from vaccination to antiseptics, anesthetics and antibiotics. The discovery of the anesthetic properties of nitrous oxide ('laughing gas') was probably accidental, but the subsequent search for more efficient and effective alternatives has never ceased.

Health and safety are now accepted government responsibilities. The bans on DDT and other dangerous pesticides, tetraethyl lead in gasoline and chlorofluorocarbons, due to their role in destruction of the ozone layer, are examples of regulatory barriers. However, up to now, creative responses to regulatory barriers are still comparatively scarce. Institutional barriers are much subtler and more widespread. An example might be the prevalence of building codes prescribing what materials may, or may not, be used in house construction.

Other barriers are more fundamental in nature and may be surmountable by means that cannot yet be described, but which involve no violation of physical laws. An example of this sort might be the unsolved problem of removing trace quantities of copper from recycled steel and recycled aluminum. Until this problem is solved, unwanted copper will accumulate in the recycled steel and aluminum, significantly reducing the quality of recycled metals *vis-à-vis* virgin metal. There is no existing process for accomplishing this objective at reasonable cost, so it is clearly a barrier. But it is one that will almost certainly be overcome at reasonable cost some day. Only the timing is uncertain.

Some barriers appear to be real, even imminent, but cannot be characterized very precisely. The current example is micro-miniaturization. Almost every electronics expert is convinced that miniaturization has its limits, and there have been many attempts to quantify the limits of silicon-based chips. But for nearly four decades the limits have kept receding into the future. At this point, nobody in the industry is very sure what the limits of silicon technology really are, and consequently, the industry is unsure in what directions it should focus its research.[11] But, scientists already know that there are no limits to information technology *in principle*, until at least the molecular level has been reached. Meanwhile, the composition and design of a microprocessor to be produced in – say 2020 – cannot be forecast with any confidence.

Finally, of course, there are fundamental limits that simply cannot be overcome within the constraints imposed by the basic laws of physics as we know them. Laser swords (as in *Star Wars*) or 'phaser' pistols, teleportation ('Beam me up, Scotty'), anti-gravity, or faster-than-light travel – technologies imaginatively illustrated in the TV series *Star Trek* – are physically impossible, according to our current understanding of the laws of nature.

Reverting to the question of predictability, it is only the details (including timing and costs) that are essentially unpredictable, in the sense of throwing dice. But even there, the process of technical development only appears random to outsiders. It follows that radical innovations can often (but not always) be forecast as to functionality and occasionally as to sources, though rarely as to particulars.[12]

What cannot be forecast with any confidence at all is the *'spillover'* potential of a future technological breakthrough. The term spillover is used by endogenous growth theorists in reference to benefits (or costs) not captured by the innovator, but available to 'free riders' (that is, the rest of the world). For example, the technology of cheap electric power delivered to a user was initially developed by Thomas Edison to facilitate electric lighting. But this innovation soon found a host of other uses from trams and elevators to electric furnaces and electrolytic processes that created new industries and jobs totally unrelated to illumination. Cheap aluminum was one of them. Aluminum, in turn, helped facilitate the modern passenger aircraft and airline industry. None of these downstream impacts was anticipated by Edison or his backers. It is, however, the spillover potential that determines the overall long-run impact of a technological innovation on economic growth.

The 'bottom line' of the discussion in this section is that there is an important difference between *technology* at the aggregate level, as modeled in neoclassical economic theory, and *technological change*, as it actually occurs in localized fits and starts. Technology in the theory is a smooth increase in factor productivity. It is often regarded as a stock of useful knowledge, homogeneous, uniform and fungible. The reality is that the most important technological advances are radical breakthroughs that occur initially in a particular sector and subsequently find applications (creating new products and services) in other sectors. But virtually all incremental improvements of existing technologies, and even most break-throughs, have little or no spillover impact. This point is very important for what follows later in this book.

2.7 TECHNOLOGY AS KNOWLEDGE, IN THEORY

Returning to the economic domain, technological knowledge can be regarded as a valuable asset, insofar as it is embodied in, or 'owned' by, a firm. A few inventor-entrepreneurs in the past, such as James Watt, used patents effectively to restrain competition and enforce a profitable monopoly. Later, Eli Whitney, Samuel Morse, Alexander Bell, Thomas Edison and others used patents and, occasionally, government contracts as collateral for loans or equity stock issues to private investors. The inves-tors, being greedy and risk-averse, typically expected large returns in terms of immediate dividends. However, the sort of market where a group of university scientists can form themselves into a firm – a legal entity – and raise money from professional investors based only on ideas and abilities, leading to *potentially* valuable future products, is a phenomenon of the late 20th century. It is still limited to a very few advanced countries.

With rare exceptions (mainly patents), technological knowledge is not marketed or even marketable, *as such*. There are very few examples of firms that survived and prospered by developing and selling technologies as such, without exploiting them. In most cases, new knowledge is utilized internally to increase the productivity of the labor and capital assets of the firm, or to improve the product(s) being sold. In short, it increases the *competitiveness* of the firm and the quality and performance of its products, but it cannot be traded off in the short term against stocks of other assets of the firm (goods and/or money) (Ayres 2006). Thus, it plays no part in immediate decisions to buy or sell goods, or to produce or not to produce.

Many economists, reflecting on the role of specific (firm-level) knowl-edge in economics, have focused their attention on the interesting and important fact that formal knowledge, such as a design or a program, is hard to monopolize. Agent A can pass useful productive knowledge to agent B without losing ownership of, or access to, that same knowledge. Teaching people to read, solve equations, speak foreign languages, drive cars or how to use computers are examples of this sort. In short, many knowledge transfers are clearly not 'zero sum': it is possible to 'have one's cake and eat it, too'.[13] For some reason this characteristic has been given a special name by economists: knowledge is called a 'non-rival' good, in contrast to physical products. This 'non-rival' characteristic might seem at first glance to be entirely beneficial to economic growth, since knowledge and its benefits can be transferred to others without being lost to the donors. But from an entrepreneurial perspective, there is an unfortunate consequence: the incentives to increase 'non-rival' wealth-creating knowledge by investing in R&D are lacking. If the discoverer of a new law of nature or the inventor of a new product or process cannot 'own', and thereby profit from, the rights to it, there is no obvious incentive to allocate scarce resources to do the research and development. Since knowledge cannot be monopolized indefinitely, there is no certainty of earning 'extraordinary' (that is, monopoly) profits from it. Nor is there any need to do research to defend against the possibility that a rival will acquire the knowledge first and achieve an insurmountable lead in the competitive race.

In short, R&D pays off for a sponsoring firm if, and only if, the resulting knowledge can be licensed or monopolized for a significant period of time. To create economic incentives for research and invention, patent and copyright laws have been introduced in all Western countries. In principle, such laws provide temporary monopoly benefits to owners of intellectual property, namely, inventors, composers and writers, by allowing them to demand license fees or royalties from users of the new knowledge. Indeed, the acceleration of technological progress that accompanied and followed the industrial revolution coincided with the introduction of this legal and institutional innovation. The coincidence was probably not accidental.

It is clearly beneficial to society as a whole to encourage the spread of new technical knowledge, either by licensing or other means of diffusion (via 'spillovers'), since the whole knowledge-creation activity is essentially cumulative. One invention or discovery begets others, and every cutting-edge researcher stands figuratively on the shoulders of many predecessors. It is therefore socially desirable to minimize the costs of knowledge dissemination and adoption throughout the economy. This provides the justification for limiting the life of monopoly rights on inventions to a few years, normally 17 years after the issuance of a patent, and beyond that, for providing public subsidies to education and scientific research. Understanding the complex tradeoffs involved in devising optimal public policy in this area has preoccupied many economists over the past half century.

Scientific and technical knowledge related to specific processes, products and markets is one kind of 'core' asset of firms (provided that it is not limited to a few individuals or embodied in a specific patent or piece of software). As regards material products, gains in this knowledge base are typically reflected in terms of costs and/or product or process performance measures, such as speed, power output, or power per unit of weight, fuel consumption or electric power consumption, thermodynamic efficiency, or average time-to-failure. Knowledge accumulation from exploration in the physical domain is an important aspect of the extraction industries, especially mining, oil and gas. But exploration in a different domain is no less important for other firms. Chemistry and metallurgy have created new products and processes from exploratory research. Market research is a systematic exploration of the parameters of demand for products and services. R&D can then be regarded as exploration of the possibilities for supply of products and services, whether by changing the characteristics of the product or service, or by improving the production method. Today the creation, storage and transmission of knowledge is a major human activity that comprises several sectors of the economy, employs a large number of people and generates a large fraction of the GDP.

Some kinds of knowledge, such as skills, are strictly individual. Transfer occurs, if at all, by imitation and repetition. 'Expert systems', so-called, have attempted to duplicate mechanical skills in machines, but with limited success up to now.[14] Other kinds of formal knowledge are transferable between individuals, via lectures, classrooms, tutors or books. Still other kinds of knowledge are embodied in groups (or firms) rather than individuals. Social skills, like language skills, are partly informal. They cannot be taught exclusively in a classroom; such skills evolve over time, mostly through observation, imitation, learning-by-doing and experience.

Social and cultural knowledge are not easily transferred across group (or firm) boundaries, still less across national boundaries (language and culture are a big problem in this case). This sort of knowledge has both internal and external dimensions. The internal dimension is organizational and managerial, and depends on the organizational structure. It may be strictly top-down (as in a military organization) or it may incorporate a bottom-up component. Either way, it facilitates essential communication, both vertical and horizontal, shared values, shared goals and effective actions. It enables the group, whether a family, a tribe, a firm or a nation, to function efficiently and effectively as a group. The external aspect enables an organization or firm to communicate effectively and to induce fear, respect, admiration or trust, depending on circumstances; that is, to function in 'the marketplace' and in society, in a broad sense.

This social knowledge, which tends to be specific to ethnic groups, religious groups and regions, is essential for interacting successfully with others, whether in religion, regulatory functions, commerce, diplomacy or war. Although some of it can be taught, both types of knowledge – like skills – are largely the result of learning from experience. In the economic domain, the 'culture' of a firm may differentiate one firm, even firms in the same business, from another. There has been much discussion of this intangible factor among business scholars in recent years, due in part to the otherwise inexplicable fact that the majority of mergers – whether of equals or not – are unsuccessful and do not create any wealth (except for the top managers and their investment bankers).

Individuals are not always involved in production, exchange or consumption of goods or services. They have multiple non-economic roles as consumers, family members, members of groups and citizens of a country. In such roles, knowledge of neighbors, family relationships, religion, culture, history, art and literature – for instance – may constitute a significant element of personal welfare without contributing to economic productivity. Moreover, knowledge accumulation in the social sphere – for example, knowledge of how to avoid unnecessary conflicts with people from different social or cultural or religious backgrounds – contributes enormously to social welfare. Similarly, knowledge gained by experience of the successful, as well as the unsuccessful, mechanisms for achieving agreement and political stability in a multi-ethnic or multi-racial society are essential in the modern world, while contributing very little to economic productivity in the immediate sense. The economic value of this kind of knowledge lies mainly in avoiding or eliminating institutional political or social barriers to progress. By the same token, one of the challenges we face as a society is how to accelerate economic growth and increasing productivity of labor or capital without undermining established social relationships and religious beliefs in traditional societies.

Returning to economics, once again, the recognition that technical progress is a major factor in explaining economic growth is now well over a century old. Marx understood it, though he seems not to have understood the incentive structure. However, explanations of this factor are still scarce and unsatisfying. The so-called 'endogenous growth' theories that have become fashionable in recent years, starting with Romer (1986, 1987b) conceived of knowledge as a kind of unspecific, self-reproducing and ever-growing currency, applicable to the whole domain of human activity (that is, uniformly applicable across all sectors). In fact 'knowledge', in most economic models, is regarded as *homogeneous*, and *fungible*. In this branch of neoclassical growth theory, knowledge is not precisely defined or quantified, but it is implicitly attributed to society as a whole.

The theory of growth is then endogenized by postulating investment in generalized knowledge creation by entrepreneurs and by allowing for 'spill-overs' from those same entrepreneurs to 'free riders' who put the new knowledge to work, creating new markets and jobs. The existence of spillovers is treated analytically in some aggregated models as positive returns to societal investment in knowledge. (Anticipating the later discussion, we argue that to explain the pattern of punctuated, structure-changing growth as it occurs in the real economy, something more is needed, namely occasional radical innovation at the sectoral or sub-sectoral level.)

2.8 TECHNICAL PROGRESS AS KNOWLEDGE ACCUMULATION

Technical knowledge of this kind has several important characteristics that differentiate it from the other elements of wealth, such as stocks of goods and money or securities. In the first place, 'know-how', as reflected by quantitative measures, seems to increase almost automatically over time. This phenomenon has been called 'learning-by-doing' (Arrow 1962) or 'learning by using' (Rosenberg 1982a). It has been observed and quantified in a wide range of industrial activities, from cigar-rolling to aircraft and ship manufacturing. In some cases, learning is combined with increased scale of output, and in such instances the term 'experience' is preferred to 'learning' (Argote and Epple 1990; Andress 1954; Baloff 1966; Wene 2000; Yelle 1979; Cunningham 1980).[15] But in some attempts to endogenize technical change, it has been attributed to 'experience' (for example, Rowthorn 1975; Verdoorn 1951, 1956; McCombie and de Ridder 1984; Rayment 1981; Ayres and Martinás 1992).[16]

Experience, as well as learning, clearly does have economic value to firms and individuals, though the value is rarely quantifiable except as it applies to easily measurable skills such as typing or brick-laying. More commonly, the economic value of experience (for employees) is attributed to time-in-service or seniority.

From the perspective of this book, knowledge is productive and therefore worth investing in, either for purposes of increasing skills and 'know-how' or – as R&D – in order to promote discovery and invention. Knowledge tends to increase the market value of so-called 'brain workers' but only in an average sense. Knowledge embodied in procedures, protocols, software and designs is productive and therefore adds to the potential profitability, competitiveness and market value of firms. However the knowledge base of any given firm is of little value to others, except possibly a very close competitor in the same business. But knowledge is not an element of economic wealth *per se*, except to the extent that it can be protected, like patents or copyrights, and exchanged.

The idea that knowledge, in the broad sense, is the driver of human evolutionary progress is quite an old one. We cannot undertake a review of this intellectual history. The biological background is simple enough: knowledge is derived initially from exploration. Humans, like all the higher animals – as well as firms (which are structured groups of humans) – deliberately explore their environments to locate potential sources of food, shelter and danger, that is, to maximize their chances to survive and grow. Animals rely only on memory or observation and imitation of others of their species or social group. Knowledge accumulation among animals, as populations or species, is extremely slow and inefficient by human standards.[17]

However, while curiosity plays a role and undoubtedly accounted for some of the earliest human discoveries and inventions such as the deliberate use of fire for cooking and for hardening bits of wet clay to make pottery, curiosity alone cannot account for the deliberate and systematic search for new combinations and configurations, to overcome a barrier and solve a specific problem. The same incentives to explore are applicable, although the environment is different and mostly non-physical. Humans and human organizations have steadily improved on this quasi-random process of exploration, especially (in the beginning) by learning to communicate and record information, so that later explorers need not rediscover everything anew. In prehistoric hunter-gatherer times, knowledge was passed from generation to generation by word-of-mouth, using simple sounds and gestures. These gradually became words and sentences. Since then, knowledge has been increasingly codified in language, both verbal and subsequently as pictographs, hieroglyphics, cuneiform and finally alphabets and icons. It has been stored and accumulated in written and physical form, in inscriptions, books, pictures, formulae, blueprints, libraries and computer programs.

Most economic macro-models still assume, for convenience, that knowledge growth is effectively autonomous and self-reproducing – hence *exogenous* – because knowledge permits the creation of more effective tools for research and discovery. The justification for this assumption is that 'knowledge begets more knowledge'. Telescopes have multiplied our knowledge of astronomy. Microscopes have vastly increased our ability to observe and understand microscopic phenomena. Computers enable us to calculate faster and retrieve archival data faster and test theories more quickly. And so on. From this perspective it is reasonable to assume, as some have done, that knowledge grows exponentially, and without limit (Adams 1918; Sorokin 1957 [1937]; Price 1963; Ayres 1944).

Scholars focusing on knowledge accumulation, as such, have suggested output measures such as the number of publications, journals, patents, or PhDs (for example, Lotka 1939). Other scholars have focused on generic functional capabilities, such as energy conversion, information-carrier capacity, information-processing speed, strength of materials, thermodynamic efficiency or power/weight ratio of engines.[18] Some of these measures appear to grow exponentially, over a long period of time, because the upper limits are far away or even unknown. However, in most cases the period of exponential growth eventually comes to an end.

2.9 TECHNOLOGICAL CHANGE IN THE FUTURE

It has been clear since the mid-1950s, if not longer, that economic growth is largely driven by technological change, at least in a broadly defined sense. Economic forecasting – a very important activity – concerns the understanding and extrapolation of economic growth from the past to the present and into the future. This consequently implies a need for technological forecasting. Yet economists have largely avoided this topic, although there is a very large literature (already cited) on the closely related subjects of innovation, diffusion, imitation, substitution, returns to R&D, returns to adoption ('lock-in') and evolution. Most of this literature, except that subset which deals with R&D and diffusion case histories, is essentially theoretical, dealing with change processes as such. Few economists have considered technological change in terms of the specific technologies that characterize and enable various economic sectors – as defined by products and service outputs – still less their inherent limits and changing functional capabilities over time.

This persistent avoidance of the specifics has its obvious justification, in terms of the need to find or create broadly defined variables with explanatory power. Examples of such variables include capital stock, labor supply, money supply, agriculture and forestry, industry, commerce, transportation, energy services (electricity, gas, etc.), communication services, production, trade, and consumption. Each of these, and many other standard variables used by economists, are really an aggregation of heterogeneous elements, each one of which is likely – on inspection – to be revealed as an aggregation of subsidiary elements. The disaggregation process can be continued to lower and lower levels, with further proliferation of elements at each level. The similarity to biological classification into phyla, sub-phylae, families, genera, and species is obvious (and intentional).

Thus, industry can be subdivided into mining (extraction), manufacturing, construction, transport, and so forth. Manufacturing can be further subdivided into primary processing of raw materials (agricultural products, forest products, metal ores, fossil fuels, etc.), secondary refining and processing into finished materials and finished fuels, tertiary processing into shapes and simple components, combination and assembly into subsystems, assembly of subsystems into structures, vehicles, etc. Similarly, transport can be subdivided by modes (air, sea, road, etc.) and each mode can be further subdivided into components, like vehicles, guide-ways (if appropriate), terminals, fuel distribution, traffic control, and so forth. Systems can also be defined by attributes such as distance, speed, load, schedule, route structure, propulsion system, fuel economy and others.

Evidently each level and branch of this 'tree' structure is characterized by its corresponding technology. Many of these technologies – but not all – can be assigned to a specific economic sector. Thus underground mining is essentially a generic technology that differs only in minor respects from coal mines to silver mines, but has little relevance elsewhere. Surface mining is also generic, but utilizes different earth-moving and physical concentration techniques. Drilling through earth and rock is recognizably similar, whether the object is water, oil, gas or to build a tunnel. Furnaces converting fuel to heat are similar; they differ only in minor ways depending on the fuel, the ignition, and the way in which the heat of combustion is utilized. Carbo-thermic reduction of metal ores is essentially the same whether the ore (concentrate) is an oxide of iron, copper, lead, zinc, phosphorus, silicon or some other metal. The same holds for electrolytic reduction: the technology is very similar for aluminum, chlorine, phosphorus or magnesium, although electrolytes and voltages differ. Grinding mills are similar whether the material being ground is limestone, iron ore or wheat. Rolling mills are quite similar, whether the material being rolled is metal (hot or cold), paper pulp or some plastic. Pumps and compressors are similar, except for size and power, whether they are used to pump water, crude oil, natural gas, air or refrigerants.

Prime movers (engines) differ in terms of power output and on whether the fuel combustion is external (that is, steam engines) or internal, whether ignition is by spark (Otto cycle) or by compression (diesel), whether the working fluid is steam, some other working fluid (like helium) or exhaust gases, or whether they utilize pistons and cranks or turbines. But most prime movers convert heat from combustion (or nuclear reactors) into rotary mechanical work. Electric motors differ in detail depending on the configuration of windings, load patterns and whether the electric power supply is AC or DC, but they all convert electric power into mechanical work, usually in the form of rotary motion.

It is important for what follows to emphasize that, while all of these different technologies depend on design, the possibilities for design, in the case of physical systems, depend upon, and are limited by the specific properties of materials. As already mentioned, some technologies, such as prime movers and many metallurgical reduction and synthesis processes, depend on the temperatures, and in some cases, pressures, achievable in a confined space. These are limited by the strength and corrosion resistance (chemical inertness) of structural materials at elevated temperatures. The performance of engines, whether turbines or piston, also depends upon the pressure gradients that can be utilized and the rotational speeds that can be sustained – also limited by the tensile strength of metals. Turbine efficiency also depends, in turn, on the precision with which turbine blades, piston rings, gears and bearings can be manufactured, which depends – again – on the properties of the materials being shaped and the properties of the ultra-hard materials used in the cutting and shaping of tools.

In short, the limiting efficiency of all metallurgical, chemical and electronic processes depends essentially on the properties of structural materials. Some technologies are limited by the precision of metal cutting and shaping, as noted above. Some technologies are limited by the properties of hard materials, others by ferromagnetic materials, diamagnetic materials, superconductors, semiconductors, photo-conductors, photo-electrics, photo-voltaics, thermal conductors, thermal insulators, electrical insulators, optical conductors, optical reflectors, elastomers, long-chain polymers, chemical solvents, catalysts, lubricants, surfactants, flotation agents, adhesives, . . . the list is nearly endless.

Evidently materials have become more and more specialized over the years. This trend has enabled machines of all kinds to become more efficient and functional. But increased functionality almost always entails more complicated processing and more complex, and costly, capital equipment. The apparent and highly touted trend toward 'dematerialization' is an illusion. (We discuss the material requirements of industrial society in greater detail in Chapter 3.)

While it is true that high strength alloys may reduce the weight of aircraft or trucks – plastic containers weigh less than glass containers, modern raincoats are lighter than their rubberized predecessors, and so on – lightweight products based on light metals or composites invariably require much more complex pre-processing than the materials used in similar products a century ago. An extreme case, perhaps, but nonetheless suggestive, is the transistor. A silicon computer chip of today may only weigh a gram or two, while embodying the capabilities of literally millions of the vacuum tube triodes that were employed in the early electronic computers. However, precisely because of their power, today's ultra-advanced chips are produced by the billions and employed in hundreds of millions of products each year. Moreover, the weight of materials embodied in the chips is but a tiny fraction of the mass of materials that must be processed (and almost entirely discarded) in the manufacturing process.

However the key implication of the points already made is that specific processes depend upon the properties of specific materials. It follows that the capabilities of virtually every technology utilized by our industrial society is also limited by the properties of existing materials. As technologies approach these limits, it is occasionally possible to find or develop a substitute material that will enable superior performance and surpass the prior limitations. For example, all kinds of turbo-machinery effectively reached the temperature and pressure performance limits allowed by alloy-steel turbine blades nearly half a century ago. Super-alloys have permitted gas turbines to reach somewhat higher performance, but at much higher prices. For several decades, researchers have attempted to surpass these limits by substituting ceramics for metals, but – up to now – ceramics have proven to be too difficult to manufacture with sufficient purity and to shape with sufficient accuracy. In effect, turbine design is up against a materials-based limit that it may, or may not, be possible to overcome.

The point is that particular technologies – as contrasted with technology in general – always have limits. When a limit is approached, it can be characterized as a *barrier*. When the barrier is overcome, it is a *breakthrough*. Technological change in the past can be characterized quite accurately as a sequence of barriers and breakthroughs. But not every material has a viable substitute and not every process can be replaced by another, cheaper one. This is also an illusion fostered by oversimplified economics.

2.10   REVISITING THE ROLE OF TECHNOLOGY IN ECONOMICS

The standard neoclassical model assumes growth in a fluctuating but never-far-from equilibrium, driven by an exogenous force called 'technological progress' or 'total factor productivity' (TFP). Goods and services are abstractions. When there is excess demand for goods, prices rise, profits increase, there is competition for labor, and wages rise. Higher wages result in increased demand, which pushes up demand still further. However, higher wages induce producers to become more efficient. They increase labor productivity by investing in new capital equipment incorporating new technology.

These investments naturally take some time to come on stream. When they do, wages stop rising and demand stops increasing. The result is excess supply, such as the present situation in the world for most products. In a competitive 'free market', prices then start to fall, but in a world of oligopoly and cartels, prices do not fall, or fall very little. Nevertheless, older factories become less profitable, or unprofitable, and eventually they close (unless governments step in to prevent this). In the ideal competitive world, supply finally declines and demand increases due to falling prices, unless fear of unemployment causes consumers to stop spending, thus making the problem worse. Both expansion and contraction tend to feed on themselves, to some extent. Note that this idealized description does not depend in any way on natural resources, as such, except insofar as they are supplied like other goods subject to market demand.

Needless to say, the real world is not much like the idealized free market world where there are no essential resources (other than labor and capital), no wastes, no unions, no cartels, no regulators, no taxes, no subsidies and no crime or corruption. However, even in the neoclassical paradigm the *microeconomic* role of new technology is straightforward, provided the incentives for investment and the sources of profits to re-invest are not questioned: it results from investment aimed at cutting costs so as to reduce prices or to increase the performance or consumer appeal of products or services. Either way, the purpose of R&D for the firm is to hold or increase market share, which is the surest way to increase the profits of the firm.

The macroeconomic role of R&D in the neoclassical model is much less clear. As mentioned already, the majority of simple models assume that technological progress occurs automatically, in equilibrium, and that its effect is to increase productivity at a steady rate. Some recent models equate technology with knowledge and call it 'human capital'. But these models cannot be quantified or used for forecasting purposes, lacking a reliable measure of knowledge/human capital. As we have noted, the neoclassical paradigm has no convincing explanation of why technological progress should be uniform or continuous (since it isn't), or why generic R&D or innovation should occur at all in the assumed equilibrium state.

In the disequilibrium paradigm the macroeconomic role of technology is more straightforward: when products become cheaper due to technological improvements in production, or more attractive to consumers by virtue of improved performance, the result is to increase demand. Increased demand leads to increased output, higher wages, lower costs (thanks to economies of scale and learning), increased capital investment and more R&D. All of these combine in a positive feedback cycle that drives overall economic growth, insofar as saturation of demand allows.

Technology may be equated (in some sense) with a stock of knowledge, or 'human capital'. But we assert strongly that the stock is not homogeneous, nor is it fungible. It is simply not true that innovations in every field are equally productive. The stock is not homogeneous, as Romer's theory, for instance, implies (Romer 1994). In reality some technologies are much more productive – by means of spillovers – than others, and economic growth depends on continued innovation in productive technologies, rather than innovation in general. We will come back to this point later, especially in Chapter 6. We still lack a useful measure of the past and current state of technology. We also lack a quantifiable link between past technological change and resource consumption. These topics will be considered later. What we still need for macroeconomic modeling is a viable quantitative measure of the state of technology (knowledge, skills, etc.) at the national level. Later in this book we propose a new measure to serve this function by focusing on the impact of accumulating knowledge as applied specifically to aggregated materials-conversion processes in the economy. We suggest hereafter that a quantifiable thermodynamic measure, namely *exergy conversion efficiency*, can be regarded as a plausible surrogate for technical progress, at least in the past. This measure is defined and estimated subsequently, in Chapter 4.

2.11 SUMMARY

The key conclusions of this chapter can be summarized in several related propositions.

1. It is clear that the mobilization of scientific and engineering talent and resources to solve a problem is virtually never accidental; it is usually a response to a perceived opportunity (arising from a perceived need or challenge) of some sort.
2. Need or potential demand are not always enough. Needs may not be sufficiently clearly articulated to generate a private-sector 'market' for solutions. Or the scope of the problem may be too great for the resources of the private sector. When – and only when – the need is well articulated and can be met by producing more of what is already being produced, or by improving the existing technology along well-established lines, the 'free market' will normally respond.
3. Under modern conditions, the resource mobilization process is formally characterized as R&D. It almost always begins with an allocation of funds for a particular goal or mission. The goal or mission is normally very specific indeed. If the goal is to achieve a modest improvement in a product or process, the basic principles are well known and the only problem is to apply them systematically at the right scale. The outcome is subject to very little uncertainty. Reducing the weight of an automobile body, or determining the optimal method of welding aluminum, designing a faster microprocessor or a larger

civil aircraft, scaling up an industrial process – even sending a man to the moon – are also examples of the 'normal' process in operation.

4. But when a need becomes acute because the free market cannot respond for some reason, there is a crisis. A crisis arises from a *disequilibrium* that cannot be resolved by 'normal' means. In a crisis there is a possibility of *radical* 'outside the box' (Schumpeterian) innovation. Examples of normal means at the macro-level include investments (or disinvestments) in existing means of production, political compromises or engineering adjustments of existing systems – in short, by doing more (or less) of what is already being done.

5. At the micro-level, demand and supply often refer to *functionality* and the analog of resource exhaustion is the approach to a physical or physical-economic limit. Every technology is subject to physical limits, resulting from properties of physical materials or laws of nature (that is, of thermodynamics). As performance limits are approached, the cost of further improvement rises without limit.

6. Radical 'Schumpeterian' innovations involve some departure from known principles, or at least, from conventional wisdom, and correspondingly much less certainty of cost, elapsed time or ultimate success. This is sometimes called 'thinking outside the box'. Where the departure from the established technological trajectory is significant, costs can become too burdensome and failure is a real possibility. Examples from the recent past include the AT&T picture-phone, the Wankel engine, Philips Stirling cycle engine and the video disk. Numerous single technology 'startups' have failed and disappeared. Needless to say, the risks of developing totally new materials, new types of machines or instruments, new industrial processes or new business models are greater still. The ongoing search for a viable broadband internet business model, or an alternative to the use of hydrocarbon fuels for internal combustion engines for automobiles are two current examples.

7. Differential impacts of a new technology can result in significant *disequilibria* – a fancy word for supply–demand imbalances. For instance, when a new technology creates a demand for some product that displaces another older one, there is an automatic imbalance. To take a somewhat trivial example, demand for motor vehicles left buggy-whip manufacturers and horse breeders with excess capacity and declining markets. Electric lighting left candle and kerosine lamp manufacturers with excess capacity, while demand for electric light bulbs exploded. Disequilibria may arise from sudden military needs (in war), sharp increases in demand confronting limited supply, or sharp decreases in supply due to blockades, sanctions, regulation or

resource exhaustion. The greater the disequilibrium the stronger the economic (and social) incentives to resolve it. However, the incentives operate mostly at the micro-level. Major innovations occur in response to particular problems, even though they may (rarely) have significant applications in other areas.

8. Technological breakthroughs presuppose barriers. Barriers may be absolute physical limits, but much more often they result from exogenous factors or interactions between economics, institutions and physical characteristics of a technological configuration or 'trajectory' (as explained in the text). Barriers can also arise from a variety of causes, ranging from wars to geo-political developments, to problems arising from the adoption of a pervasive technology, such as motor vehicles, including resource scarcity or environmental harms such as climate warming. Radical innovations may overcome these barriers by opening new 'morphological neighborhoods' to exploration (see Zwicky 1951). Breakthroughs in functionality can sometimes be predicted in advance, once a barrier has been clearly identified, although timing and details cannot. The probability of a breakthrough within a given time period is essentially proportional to the intensity of the search for it. If the need is great, the problem will probably be solved sooner rather than later.

9. Once a major barrier has been breached, gradual improvements, based on investment in R&D, are relatively smooth and predictable in the short run. Indeed, they tend to follow a standard pattern that is common to many processes, including diffusion, namely the elongated S-shaped curve (discussed in Chapter 1). The parameters of the curve cannot be predicted *a priori*, but sometimes the curve can be projected once it is established, from its history and from a forecast of the ultimate limits of the particular technological trajectory.

10. Breakthroughs may have unexpected impacts (spillovers) in fields (sectors) other than the one where the barrier originally existed. The greater the range and scope of the spillovers, the greater the growth-promoting impact (and the harder it is to predict). The most important breakthroughs have impacts far beyond the original objective, resulting in new opportunities in other sectors. The role of technology is, in effect, to create a perpetual *disequilibrium*. We have mentioned a number of examples. For instance, cheap electricity made a number of new materials available for the first time (for example, synthetic abrasives, chlorine, aluminum, stainless steel, tungsten), which, in turn, opened the door to other important innovations, such as high-speed grinders and mass production of automobile engines. Aluminum was an essential prerequisite to the development of the aircraft industry.

In more recent times, computers and digital communications may be having comparable cross-border impacts. These spillovers are often difficult to predict, however, and they have uneven impacts across the spectrum. Thus, not only is new technology created as an essential part of the positive feedback cycle, it is non-uniform in its impacts.

NOTES

1. Standard Oil, the US licensee, had to be compelled to release the licenses to allow other US firms to participate.
2. An oil-burning ship could save 78 percent in fuel and gain 30 percent in cargo space, as compared to a steamship (Yergin 1991, p. 155).
3. Automobile engines reached average compression ratios of more than 11:1 in the early 1960s, but the elimination of lead (in the US) starting around 1970 has forced a regression to around 8:1 or 9:1 today, despite significant use of other additives, such as alcohols and aromatics (benzene, toluene, xylene). The difference has resulted in a fuel economy reduction in the neighborhood of 10 percent.
4. Because of the importance of steel, the Bessemer process (so-called) was designated by historian Elting Morrison as 'almost the greatest invention' (Morrison 1966).
5. Meanwhile vacuum technology itself has progressed, largely thanks to another technology, cryogenics, which was initiated in the 19th century in response to a practical need to keep meat from spoiling during long sea voyages, and later in households. But subsequently cryogenic technology found a host of new industrial applications requiring lower and lower temperatures, including the liquefaction of air and the separation of oxygen and nitrogen. Still later, liquid hydrogen was produced in large quantities for military and space purposes (rockets). When liquid helium temperatures first became achievable in laboratory apparatus, in the 1950s, serious research on the phenomenon of superconductivity began. This research has already led to significant developments in magnet engineering and may eventually pay off in electric power transmission and high speed rail systems utilizing magnetic levitation.
6. In both of these cases the probable cause was the disappearance of the glaciers and the glacial meltwater that had formerly irrigated the land. The remains of that water constitute the Ogallala aquifer underlying much of the US high plains, from Montana to Texas. This water is being rapidly pumped out and is not being replaced.
7. Some experts foresee that the industry will soon be forced to shift once again, from gasoline from oil to hydrogen from natural gas or coal. Such a transition will inevitably be extremely difficult and traumatic.
8. We cannot help mentioning the crisis that was widely expected (and expensively guarded against) but did not occur, namely the so-called Y2K computer glitch problem. One well-known financial economist, Edward Yardeni of Deutsche Bank, predicted a 5 percent drop in the US economy, while others forecast increases in growth due to heavy investment. What actually happened was that US growth did accelerate in the late 1990s, peaked with the stock market in early 2001, and fell into recession thereafter for reasons unrelated to Y2K.
9. This is actually an absolute limit for any heat engine that extracts work from the heat in a high temperature reservoir and rejects heat into a low temperature reservoir (Carnot 1826). Real heat engines, such as the Rankine (steam) cycle, the Otto cycle and so on, have lower limits. However the Carnot cycle does not apply to fuel cells, for instance.
10. The following quote exemplifies the standard view: 'Technical knowledge, being the product of a production process in which scarce resources are allocated, can be produced. *We do not know exactly what will be produced, but we are certain that we will know*

more after an uncertain period' (Heertje 1983; emphasis added). While we agree with the statement, we disagree with the implication.

11. As far back as 1980, *Science* published a gloomy assessment in its Research News section, entitled 'Are VLSI Microcircuits too Hard to Design?' (Robinson 1980). Many other gloomy assessments since then have proven to be wrong as every problem identified by a pessimist was quickly solved. Moore's Law, which has been restated a couple of times since it was first promulgated in 1965 by Gordon Moore, then at Fairchild, subsequently CEO of Intel, who predicted that the complexity of computer chips would double every 18 months. This trend has continued unabated to the present time. However, the concerns being raised nowadays; for example, by Intel engineer Paul Packan (also in *Science*), involve fundamental physical limits, such as the limiting concentration of dopants (impurities) in the silicon wafers, the increasing variability of dopant concentrations as circuits get smaller, and the increasing propensity to peculiar quantum effects (for example, electron 'tunneling') as semiconductor gates become smaller (Mann 2000). A further difficulty is the disposal of excess heat from very dense circuitry. Nevertheless, optimists still predict that progress will continue at past rates for another decade or two.

12. The assertion that technological progress can be forecast as to general direction hardly needs elaborate justification. For instance there is wide agreement that the 'hot' fields at present are bio-technology (including genetic engineering), information technology and nano-technology. At the next level, of course, the forecasts become more uncertain, and it is important to recall that some past 'near certainties' – such as the development of nuclear fusion technology and space technology – have become much less so as major difficulties were encountered. But there is a massive technical literature on the use of specialized forecasting methodologies to reduce uncertainty. The journal *Technological Forecasting and Social Change* is perhaps the best source of this literature.

13. There is another sense, or perhaps another kind of knowledge, for which this is not the case. Some kinds of knowledge are only valuable to particular users who have the means to profit from it, at particular times and places. For example, when the London branch of the Rothschild bank learned the outcome of the Battle of Waterloo 24 hours in advance of the rest of the London financial community (thanks to some clever use of signals), it first spread rumors that the battle had been lost, and took advantage of the immediate market crash to buy shares that subsequently rose sharply in value when the true results of the battle were reported. Tens of thousands of others who had the same information were unable to make any use of it, either because they were still in Belgium or France, or because they had no access to funds. Others lost money because they were taken in by the false rumors. The point is that knowledge is not valuable in itself, but only to those with other necessary attributes.

14. There are two reasons. First, human arms, hands and fingers have many more degrees of freedom than any machine yet conceived. Second, and more important, up to now computerized motion controls are exclusively deterministic, which requires simultaneous solution of non-linear equations of motion with as many interdependent variables as there are degrees of freedom. It is obvious that the human brain does not control the motions of the body by solving simultaneous non-linear equations. Similarly, a chess-playing computer does not decide on a move in the same way a human player does. However, nobody has yet figured out how the human brain solves problems, still less succeeded in teaching a computer to solve problems the same way. Artificial intelligence is still a long way off.

15. The rate at which this improvement occurs is typically expressed as a number representing the percentage decline in costs resulting from a doubling of experience, measured in terms of cumulative output. This number is usually taken from the slope of a curve representing the logarithm of unit cost (or price) versus the logarithm of cumulative production, also in units. The steepness of the slope is a quantitative measure of the rate of the learning, which depends on a firm's investment in R&D.

16. The economic literature is comprehensively reviewed in Argote and Epple (1990). For a more technological approach, see Ayres and Martinás (1992).

17. A behavioral characteristic that also certainly plays some role is human curiosity (sometimes called 'monkey curiosity'). The desire to learn about the world one lives in may, or may not, need explanation in economic terms, but human curiosity certainly preceded economic relationships. It is a behavioral characteristic common to most higher species of animals. A propensity to explore (provided it can be done safely) has obvious evolutionary survival benefits: the more an individual organism knows about its environment, the more easily it can avoid dangers and find shelter or food.

18. The list of names is very long. Early writers include Ridenour (1951), Holton (1962) and Price (1963). More recent examples include Ayres (1994b, 1998c), Gruebler (1998) and Smil (2001, 2003).

3. Industrial metabolism: mass/energy flows

3.1 INTRODUCTION

For practical purposes it is fair to say that wealth, which underlies welfare, is based on stocks of material goods (including land).[1] From an economic perspective, welfare is a consequence of *consumption*, which is essentially that part of economic activity that is not productive of more wealth or simply destructive (such as warfare). The productive component of wealth is known as (industrial) *capital*, whereas the consumption-related part, consisting of residential housing and durable consumer goods, is not usually counted as part of capital stock, even though some have argued that it should be so counted. What matters for this chapter is that both production and consumption require flows of material goods, as well as energy (or at least energy carriers) such as fuels and electricity. These flows can be characterized as *industrial metabolism*.

Technology (or knowledge) is not an element of wealth *per se* except to the extent that it can be protected and exchanged. Technology may be productive and therefore worth investing in, either for purposes of increasing skills and 'know-how' or – as R&D – in order to promote discovery, invention and innovation. But the knowledge base of an individual, or a firm, is rarely transferable or usable by others, except by means of a cooperative effort of teaching and learning. Hence it is not a component of wealth.

On the other hand, material goods that are either portable or transferable to different owners by exchange of title are certainly a component of wealth as the term is understood. Evidently the raw materials from which economically valuable goods are produced (by the systematic application of knowledge and useful work) must be extracted directly from the earth or from biomass, sorted into separable components, refined, converted, recombined into useful intermediate substances, formed, in the case of solids, into useful shapes and assembled into useful devices or structures. From the first law of thermodynamics, better known as the law of conservation of mass,[2] it follows that all materials extracted from the earth or atmosphere must ultimately return to the natural environment as fertilizers, wastes or accumulate in the human-built environment, or anthroposphere (Ayres et al. 1970; Ayres and Kneese 1969). This yields the *mass-balance principle*, which is a very useful accounting tool with more applications than most people realize.

To form a coherent picture of all of these separation, conversion and recombination relationships, it is helpful to view the flow of materials through a sequence of processes as a 'life cycle', sometimes characterized as 'cradle to grave'. Energy carriers (fuels, electricity) must have an original material basis. Similarly material goods, in turn, constitute the basis of most final services (even haircuts require scissors). It is only the final services themselves that are immaterial.

Waste flows quantitatively approximate extraction flows, inasmuch as only a small fraction of the total mass of materials extracted from the earth is ultimately embodied in the anthroposphere (mostly in structures). Not all wastes are captured or treated. In fact the greater part overall consists of carbon dioxide and water vapor from combustion processes, which are currently discharged directly into the atmosphere. Wastes that are not treated can cause harm to the environment, health damage to humans or directly to other goods (for example, via corrosion). Those wastes that are captured and treated (in the industrialized countries), including sewage, municipal refuse, toxic industrial wastes and combustion wastes such as fly-ash, sulfur oxides (SOX), nitrogen oxides (NOX), and particulates, nevertheless require a considerable application of capital, labor, knowledge and thermodynamic work which could otherwise be utilized productively.

Consequently, waste flows can be characterized as 'bads' from an economic perspective (in contrast with 'goods') and the costs of treatment or the unpaid costs of harm done must be regarded as 'value-subtracted' (in contrast to 'value-added'). The costs or value subtractions associated with materials extraction, processing and use are – in a very broad sense – proportional to the overall quantities of material flows. On the other hand, it is also true that the waste flows associated with the material economy are reflections of the inefficiencies in the system. The more efficient the conversion (especially energy conversion) processes the less the waste flows and the environmental harm, other things being equal.

Thus aggregate material flows are also related to long-run sustainability. It is in this context that the notion of 'dematerialization' has become a topic of some interest in recent years. This chapter addresses several of these topics, beginning with mass flows.

3.2   PHYSICAL CONSTRAINTS: THE FIRST LAW OF THERMODYNAMICS

The laws of physics most constraining to technology (and therefore to economics) are the first and second laws of thermodynamics. The first law of thermodynamics is the law of conservation of mass/energy. Since mass and energy are equivalent in the sense of interconvertibility (Einstein's equation, $E = mc^2$), this law actually implies that mass and energy are *separately* conserved in every process or transformation except nuclear fission or fusion. Putting it another way, any process or transformation that violates this fundamental condition is impossible. In more familiar language, it is impossible to create something from nothing. Tjalling Koopmans expressed this principle as 'the impossibility of the land of Cockaigne', and made use of the theorem in developing his mathematical treatment of 'activity analysis', an extension of input-output analysis and one of the first serious attempts, after Leontief, to model technological dynamics in a multi-sector world (Koopmans 1951).

The impossibility of creating something from nothing and its converse, the impossibility of converting something, such as a waste into nothing, have surprisingly non-trivial consequences for neoclassical economics. Contrary to the more superficial versions of standard theory, where goods and services are mere abstractions, production of real goods from raw materials inevitably results in the creation of waste residuals. In standard economic theory 'consumption' is a metaphor and wastes are not considered at all. In reality, since waste residuals have no positive market value to anyone – in fact, they have negative value – but do *not* disappear by themselves, they tend to be disposed of in non-optimal ways.

The most common approach to waste disposal in the past, and still normal in most parts of the world, is dumping into waterways or burning. Either method of disposal involves using common-property environmental resources as sinks. This causes harm, ranging from serious illness to dirty collars, to people who obtained no benefit from the original economic use of the material before it became a waste. But standard economic theory does not allow for damages to third parties; it presupposes transactions only between mutual beneficiaries. Disposal of harmful wastes to common property environmental resources by dumping or burning creates a built-in market failure, or externality. In fact, this externality is not rare or exceptional, as earlier theorists sometimes claimed. On the contrary, it is pervasive because it is an automatic consequence of the fact that the economy has a material basis (Ayres and Kneese 1969).

As hinted above, the quantity of waste materials associated with raw material extraction approximates the total quantity extracted. On the other hand, it far exceeds the amount of useful product. For instance, about 160 tonnes of copper ore must be processed to yield a tonne of virgin copper. For scarcer metals, like silver, gold, platinum and uranium, the quantities of waste material per unit of product are enormously large. Even in agriculture, the quantity of biomass needed to support a human population, especially if a significant part of the diet consists of animal products, is many times the actual quantity of food consumed.

The materials-balance principle, derived from the first law of thermodynamics, is evidently a useful tool for estimating waste residuals from industrial processes, since the outputs of one sector become the inputs to another. Comparing inputs and outputs it can be seen that substantial mass is 'missing' at each stage. Even where the process technology is unknown, it may be sufficient to obtain data on purchased inputs and marketed outputs.

The first law of thermodynamics – conservation of mass-energy – is directly applicable to every process and every process network. It is therefore applicable to every firm. This means, in words, that, over the life of the process-chain, the mass of inputs (including any unpriced materials from the environment) must exactly equal the mass of outputs, including wastes. For a continuous process, this balance condition must hold for any arbitrary time period.[3] The materials-balance condition is much more powerful than it appears at first glance, since chemical elements do not transmute into other chemical elements under normal terrestrial conditions. (The alchemists were on the wrong track; there is no practical terrestrial process for converting base metal into gold.) Taking this into account, *the mass-balance condition holds independently for each chemical element.* Moreover, in many processes, non-reactive chemical components, such as process water and atmospheric nitrogen, can also be independently balanced. Thus half a dozen, or more, independent materials-balance constraints may have to be satisfied for each steady-state process.[4] This fact provides a powerful tool for imputing missing data.

3.3   MASS FLOWS AND THE LIFE CYCLE

The materials 'life cycle' can be characterized schematically as shown in Figure 3.1. It is obvious that the stages of the life cycle correspond to familiar economic activities, already defined as 'sectors'. At the beginning are the extractive industries, consisting of agriculture, fishing, forestry, mining, quarrying and drilling for oil and gas. Substantial quantities of waste are generated at this stage, but mostly these are left behind at or near the place where the extraction occurs, whether the farm, forest or mine.

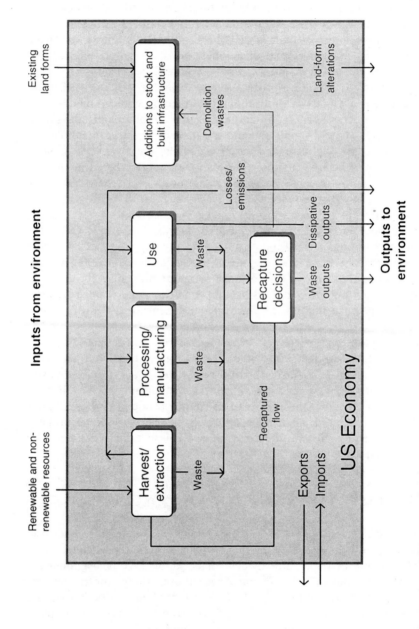

Figure 3.1 The materials life cycle

The next stage consists of primary conversion, where 'raw' materials are cleaned, sorted, separated, upgraded (or 'beneficiated', in the case of metal ores), refined and purified into finished materials. Fuels are also cleaned, refined and converted into higher quality forms of energy-carriers, ranging from clean natural gas to coke, gasoline, diesel oil and other hydrocarbon fuels, as well as petrochemical feed-stocks. Fuels are finally converted by combustion, through the agency of so-called 'prime movers' (that is, heat engines) into mechanical power. Or they produce heat that is used directly as such, either in industrial processes – such as metal ore reduction or petroleum refining – or by final consumers. A further conversion, mainly from mechanical power, generates electric power. Primary conversion processes, including combustion, account for the vast majority of material wastes.

As we will explain subsequently (Section 3.4), both the raw material inputs to, and the finished outputs of, primary conversion processes, whether material or energy carriers, can all be measured and quantified in terms of a common physical unit, namely *exergy*. Outputs of energy (actually exergy) conversion can all be characterized and measured as *useful work* – in the physical sense, not to be confused with human labor. We discuss this in more detail in Sections 3.4 through 3.6.

The third stage of the life cycle is another conversion, from finished materials and useful work – outputs of the primary conversion stage – to finished products, including infrastructure and capital goods. Wastes at this stage arise mostly from intermediate recombination, especially in the chemical industry, where many intermediate materials, such as solvents, acids and alkalis, are consumed in the conversion process and not embodied in final products. Most toxic and hazardous wastes arise from intermediate processing. The final stage, where finished products produce services, also generates wastes as the so-called final products are consumed, wear out or become obsolete in the course of providing their services to humans. This may happen almost instantly, as in the case of food and beverages, cleaning agents, paper and packaging materials, or over an extended period as in the case of appliances, vehicles, machines and structures. Recycling is essentially only applicable to paper, bottles, cans and metal scrap, which cumulatively amounts to a tiny fraction of the total materials flow.

A summary of the major mass flows in the US economy for the year 1993 is shown in Figure 3.2. (The date does not matter, for this purpose.) The units are million metric tons (MMT). We included overburden and erosion in this diagram, since estimates were available. The mass-balance principle was used in constructing Figure 3.2 to estimate a number of flows that could not be measured directly. For instance, we used the mass balance to calculate the amount of oxygen generated by photosynthesis in agriculture

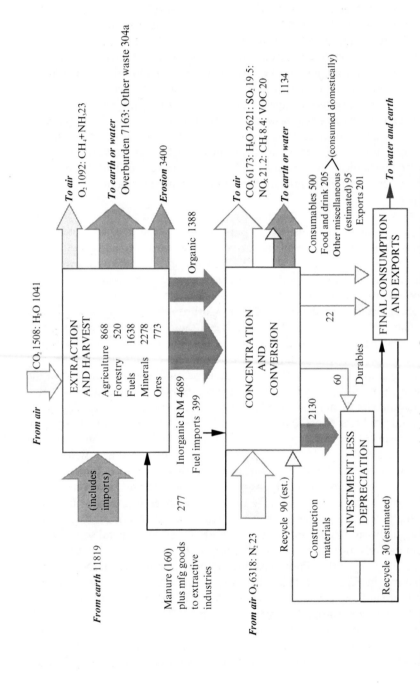

Figure 3.2   US economic system as a whole from a mass flow perspective (1993 in MMT)

and forestry, the amount of atmospheric oxygen required to burn all the fossil fuels and wood, and the amount of water vapor generated by the combustion process. We used official estimates of carbon dioxide production from fuel combustion, and calculated the others as ratios, based on chemical reaction formulae. (Erosion is a special case, constituting topsoil losses from plowed fields, resulting in silting and sediment in rivers. Hence erosion 'losses' in the figure are not balanced by inputs.)

As the life-cycle perspective makes clear, economic value is added at each stage by human labor, capital services and the application of energy (exergy) services, while material and exergy wastes are discarded. Value-added is sometimes equated with *embodied information* that increases the order embodied in useful products. In this view, usefulness is equated with order, or orderliness. Georgescu-Roegen, in particular, has argued that each stage of the process converts low entropy (ordered) materials into high entropy (disordered) wastes. In fact, he has insisted that, thanks to the second law of thermodynamics (the 'entropy law'), this process is irreversible (Georgescu-Roegen 1971). While his view on that score was much too apocalyptic, he was the first economist to characterize the economic system as a materials processor.

The word 'useful' is potentially ambiguous. In economic terms, useful products are those outputs with a well-defined market and market price. In general, many outputs are inputs for other 'downstream' products. Yet some of the physical outputs of the system are useful without having market prices. An industrial example of this is so-called 'blast furnace gas', a mixture of carbon monoxide, carbon dioxide and nitrogen (plus other pollutants), with some heating value that makes it usable in the near vicinity of the source, but not marketable outside the firm. An agricultural example would be forage and silage fed to animals on the farm. Manure generated and recycled by grazing animals on the farm is another example; it would clearly be inappropriate to regard it as a waste (in India this material is harvested, dried and used as domestic fuel).[5] A domestic example is heat for rooms, water and cooking. Finally, oxygen and water vapor – by-products of photosynthesis – are useful. All of these are *unpriced*, but not *unvalued* intermediates.

Raw agricultural products harvested in the US in 1993 amounted to 868 MMT, of which 457 MMT was crops and the rest was silage, hay and grass. Of this, 83 MMT (net) was exported, mostly for animal feeds. Animal products amounted to 119.5 MMT. The food-processing sector converted 374 MMT of harvested inputs (dry weight) to 286 MMT of salable products, of which 203 MMT was food consumed by Americans, 66 MMT was by-products (such as starch, fats and oils), animal feeds and food exports, and 14 MMT was a variety of non-food products including natural fibers, leather, tobacco and ethanol. Evidently 500 MMT, more or less, was 'lost' en route to the consumers, mostly as water vapor and CO_2, though other wastes were significant.

Consider forest products. Inputs (raw wood harvested) amounted to 520 MMT in 1993, not counting timber residues left in the forests (about 145 MMT). About 200 MMT of this weight was moisture. Finished dry wood products (lumber, plywood, particle board) weighed about 61 MMT. Finished paper products amounted to 83 MMT, which included some paper made from imported wood pulp from Canada and some recycled waste paper. The output weight also included 3.7 MMT of fillers (mainly kaolin), hydrated aluminum sulfate (alum) and other chemicals embodied in the paper. Again, the difference between inputs and output weights was very large. Quite a lot was lignin wastes from the paper mills, which are burned on-site for energy recovery, but some of the mass still ends up as pollution. About 168 MMT of harvested wood, including paper mill wastes, were burned as fuel, producing about 230 MMT of CO_2 as a waste by-product.

Conceptually, it seems reasonable to mark the boundary of the extractive sector by counting the weight of *finished materials*, that is, materials that are embodied in products, or otherwise used, without further chemical transformation. Steel is an example. There is relatively little difference between the weight of raw steel produced (89 MMT in the US in 1993) and the weight of 'finished' steel products. The small losses of steel in the rolling, casting and machining stages of production are almost entirely captured and recycled within the steel industry.[6] The same can be said of other 'finished materials', from paper and plastics to glass and Portland cement: very little or none of the finished material is lost after the last stage of production, except as consumption or demolition wastes.

What of fuels and intermediate goods like ammonia, caustic soda, chlorine and sulfuric acid? Raw fuels are refined, of course, with some losses (such as ash and sulfur dioxide) and some fuel consumption (around 10 percent in the case of petroleum) to drive the refineries. But refined fuels are converted, in the course of use, mainly to heat, mechanical power and combustion wastes. Fuels cannot be recycled. The mass of raw hydrocarbon fuel inputs was a little over 1600 MMT in 1993. It was mostly combined with atmospheric oxygen. The combustion of hydrocarbon fuels in the US, in 1993, generated around 5200 MMT of CO_2, the most important 'greenhouse gas' (Organisation for Economic Co-operation and Development 1995, p. 39). This may be a slight underestimate, since some of the hydrocarbons produced by refineries do not oxidize immediately (asphalt and plastics, for instance) but, except for what is buried in landfills, all hydrocarbons oxidize eventually.

Minerals such as salt, soda ash and phosphate rock, as well as petrochemical feed-stocks, are converted to other chemicals. Some of these – mainly polymers – end in finished goods (like tires, carpets, packaging materials and pipes). Others are converted to wastes in the course of use. Examples include fuels, lubricants, acids and alkalis, cleaning agents, detergents and solvents, pesticides and fertilizers. A model scheme (and accounting system) appropriate for environmental analysis should distinguish between *dissipative* intermediates, such as these, and *non-dissipative* materials embodied in finished durable goods that might (in principle) be repaired, re-used or re-manufactured and thus kept in service for a longer period.

'Final' goods are goods sold to 'final' consumers in markets. This class of goods is reasonably well-defined. But so-called 'final goods' (except for food, beverages and medicinals) are not physically consumed. They are, in a sense, producers of services. By this test, all final outputs (not excepting food and beverages) are immaterial services and therefore weightless, the mass being discarded.[7] However, it is natural to consider finished products as a category, which do have mass, as well as monetary value (counted in the GNP). In fact, this category marks the downstream boundary of the manufacturing sector.

To summarize, raw outputs of the US extractive sector, not including overburden, topsoil, air and water, amounted to 1388 MMT organic (biomass) and 4689 MMT inorganic, in 1993. All of this, plus 400 MMT of imported fuel and 90 MMT of recycled metals, paper and glass, were inputs to the concentration and conversion sectors. Manufactured 'final' outputs amounted to a little over 2700 MMT, of which 2130 MMT were for buildings and infrastructure, 82 MMT were durables (mostly producer durables) and 500 MMT were consumables, of which two-fifths were exported.

The weight of all metals produced, and consumed, in the US in 1993 was less than 100 MMT. By far the greater part, especially of steel, was used for construction purposes and motor vehicles. Except for some packaging materials (cans and foil), the metals were mainly embodied in durable goods such as infrastructure, buildings, transportation equipment and other machines and appliances. Motor vehicles accounted for about 28 MMT of mass. The weight of other consumer products is modest. For example, the weight of all textiles produced, including cotton, wool and all synthetics, amounts to around 5 MMT. Products of textiles, partly clothing and partly furnishings (including carpets) must be of the same order of magnitude.

As regards wastes, an important distinction might be made, namely between 'potentially reactive' and 'inherently inert' materials. Most metals,

paper, plastics and so on are in the 'reactive' category, insofar as they
can oxidize or react with other environmental components. (Most of
these, especially paper and plastics, can be burned for energy recovery.)
However, as a practical matter, these potentially reactive materials are
vastly outweighed by the inert materials utilized in structures, such as
glass, brick and tile, concrete, plaster, gravel and stone. All of the latter
group of materials are chemically inert, even though some of the manufacturing processes involve heating.[8] The total mass of 'finished' chemicals
processed in the US economy in 1993 was about 0.5 metric tons per capita
or 140 MMT, including fertilizer chemicals. Of this total, no more than 30
MMT were embodied in long-lived materials, such as plastics and synthetic
rubber. The remainder was dissipated into the environment. The total
mass of thermally processed building materials (cement, plaster, bricks,
ceramic tiles and glass) consumed in the US in 1993 was 125 MMT. On
the other hand, chemically inert structural materials (sand, gravel, stone,
etc.) consumed in the US in 1993 without thermal processing amounted to
about 1870 MMT.

Total consumption of extractive materials (fossil fuels, harvested biomass,
construction materials, minerals and metals in the US – disregarding mine
wastes) increased from about 1100 MMT in 1900 to nearly 2000 MMT in
1929, followed by a drop of over 40 percent in the Depression years. But
since then there has been a steady increase to over 8100 MMT in 2004
(Figure 3.3a). Figure 3.3b shows the same consumption in terms of exergy.
The exergy consumption is completely dominated by fossil fuels.

Of course population nearly tripled during that time, so the per-capita
figures are more revealing. The next five figures show per capita consumption in both mass and exergy terms for fossil fuels, harvested biomass,
construction materials, metals and chemicals, respectively, plus their total
(Figures 3.4a–f). It is interesting to note that fossil fuels in raw form consumed per capita have almost tripled since 1900, but most of the increase
was in the first three decades of the century, when consumption per capita
doubled, and there has actually been a small decrease since the peak years
of the early 1970s. Biomass harvested per capita has actually decreased, but
most of the decrease was also in the first three decades, with a slight increase
since the Depression years and a slight decrease since 1980. For construction materials, the overall per capita increase has been by a factor of five,
but with major ups and downs, including a big boom in the 1920s, a very
sharp drop in the early 1930s and a huge postwar boom from 1950 until
the 1970s, which included the materials-intensive US national highway
program. The pattern for metals consumption is similar to that for fossil
fuels. Chemicals, of course, show a dramatic increase (over ten-fold since
the 1930s), but that is mostly due to exploding demand for petrochemicals

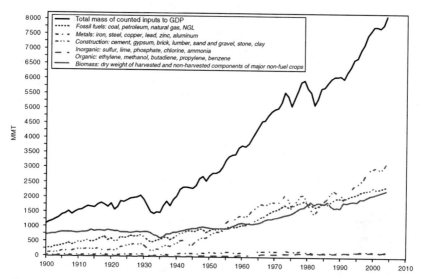

Figure 3.3a   Total major inputs to GDP (fuels, metals, construction, chemicals and biomass): in terms of mass (USA, 1900–2004)

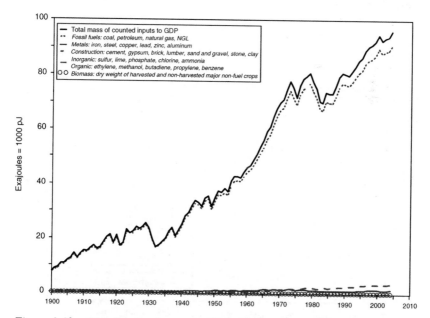

Figure 3.3b   Total major inputs to GDP (fuels, metals, construction, chemicals and biomass): in terms of exergy (USA, 1900–2004)

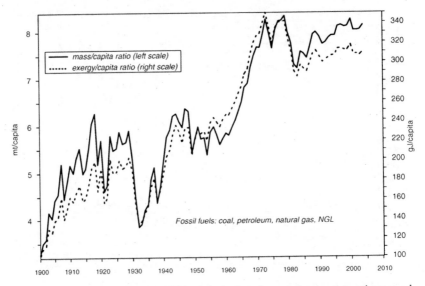

Figure 3.4a   Major inputs of fossil fuels (coal, petroleum, natural gas and
NGL): mass/capita and exergy/capita (USA, 1900–2004)

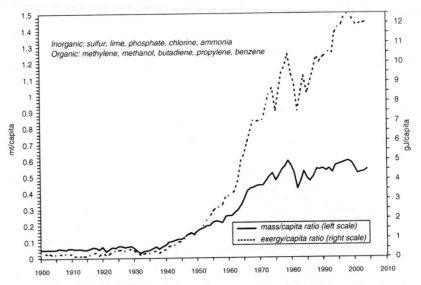

Figure 3.4b   Major inputs of chemicals to GDP: mass/capita and exergy/
capita (USA, 1900–2004)

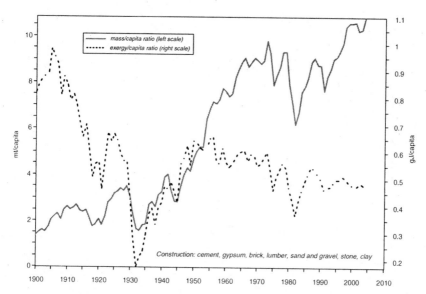

Figure 3.4c Major inputs of construction to GDP: mass/capita and exergy/capita (USA, 1900–2004)

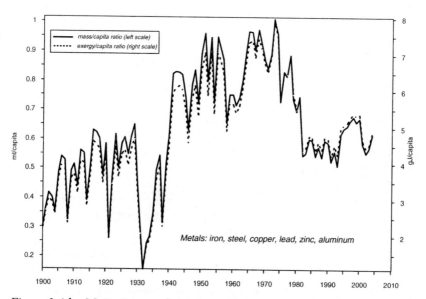

Figure 3.4d Major inputs of metals to GDP: mass/capita and exergy/capita (USA, 1900–2004)

*Figure 3.4e   Major inputs of biomass to GDP: mass/capita and exergy/
capita (USA, 1900–2004)*

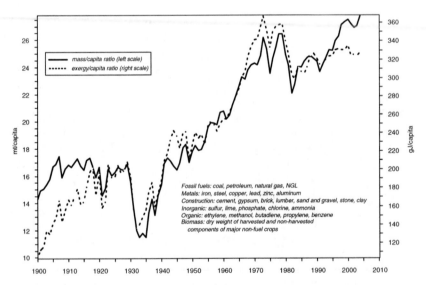

*Figure 3.4f   Total major inputs to GDP (fuels, metals, construction,
chemicals and biomass): mass/capita and exergy/capita
(USA, 1900–2004)*

(which are double-counted, being derived from fossil fuels). Demand growth has slowed sharply since the 1990s.

3.4 EXERGY AS A MEASURE OF MATERIAL QUANTITY AND QUALITY

Almost everybody uses mass as the measure of quantity applicable to material substances. On the surface of the earth, the mass of an object is proportional to its weight, which can be measured quite easily. To be precise, weight is equal to mass times the force of gravity.[9] However, mass is not particularly interesting in resource accounting, except for comparisons of changing requirements for specific materials or groups over time (as illustrated in Section 3.2), or similar comparisons between countries. Aggregate mass is also probably proportional to the energy (exergy) requirements for mining and transportation. Yet many authors have attempted to establish the importance of 'dematerialization' as a strategy for achieving long-run sustainability (for example, Herman, Ardekani, and Ausubel 1989, 1990) (Wernick 1994; von Weizsaecker, Lovins, and Lovins 1998). Other authors have attempted to justify the total mass of materials consumed by an economy as a measure of their potential harmfulness (Factor Ten Club 1994 and 1997; Hinterberger and Schmidt-Bleek 1999; Schmidt-Bleek 1993).

However, in either context, total mass as such is almost irrelevant. Most of the mass of extractive resources consists of fossil fuels, biomass or abundant and relatively inert materials such as sand and gravel, limestone and iron ore. On the other hand, apart from fossil fuels, and iron, aluminum and silicon, it is scarcer metallic elements such as copper, molybdenum, cobalt, chromium, nickel, silver and platinum, plus reactive halogens (chlorine, bromine, fluorine) that are most essential to industrial activity. And, along with combustion products and pesticides, it is comparatively tiny amounts of highly toxic by-product metals such as arsenic, cadmium, lead and mercury that dominate the environmental health literature (for example, Nriagu and Davidson 1986; Nriagu and Pacyna 1988).

Yet, for reasons of familiarity, mass is the usual – virtually universal – measure of physical quantity for all material substances used in the economic system. Clearly it is inconvenient to keep separate accounts for all the different categories of materials. This has prompted efforts to aggregate material flows, using total mass as a measure in a macroeconomic context (Adriaanse et al. 1997; World Resources Institute 2000). But the value of such aggregates is questionable, to say the least, due to the very important differences between materials as disparate as hydrocarbons, crops, inert construction minerals, toxic metals and reactive chemicals.

Table 3.1   Typical chemical exergy content of some fuels

Fuel	Exergy coefficient	Net heat. value (KJ /kg)	Chemical exergy (KJ /kg)
Coal	1.088	21 680	23 588
Coke	1.06	28 300	29 998
Fuel oil	1.073	39 500	42 383.5
Natural gas	1.04	44 000	45 760
Diesel fuel	1.07	39 500	42 265
Fuelwood	1.15	15 320	17 641

Source: Expanded from Szargut et al. (1988).

However it is not necessary to aggregate mass flows. As pointed out by several authors, another measure, called *exergy*, is available and more suitable for the purpose (Wall 1977; Ayres and Ayres 1998). Unfortunately, exergy is still an unfamiliar term, except to engineers, chemists or physicists. Exergy is a measure of *potential work*: specifically it is the maximum amount of work that can theoretically be recovered from a system as it approaches equilibrium with its surroundings reversibly (that is, infinitely slowly). In effect, exergy is also a measure of distance from equilibrium, which makes it a measure of distinguishability of a subsystem from the surroundings. But it is really what non-technical people usually mean when they speak of energy?

When people speak of energy consumption or energy production, it is usually exergy that they mean. The exergy embodied in a fuel can be equated approximately to the heat of combustion (or *enthalpy*) of that fuel. But an important difference is that exergy cannot be recycled; it is used up, or 'destroyed', to use the language of some thermodynamicists. On the other hand, energy is always conserved; it cannot be destroyed. There are several kinds of exergy, including physical exergy (kinetic energy) and thermal exergy (heat). However for our macroeconomic purposes – as in this book – only *chemical exergy* need be considered. The exergy content of various fuels is given in Table 3.1.

Combustion is a process whereby a substance reacts with oxygen rapidly and generates combustion products – such as carbon dioxide and water vapor – that subsequently diffuse and thus equilibrate with the atmosphere. Combustion generates heat, which can do useful work by means of a Carnot-cycle heat engine. Of course, oxidation need not be rapid. Rusting of iron is an example of slow oxidation. Heat is generated, but so slowly that it is not noticeable. But iron (like most other metals) in finely divided form, with a lot of surface area, will burn and liberate heat rapidly at a high enough temperature. Similarly, the respiration process in animals is another form of oxidation. This is why the energy – actually exergy – content of food is expressed in units of heat energy, namely *calories.*

There are some economically important processes that are essentially the reverse of combustion, in the sense that chemical exergy is concentrated (but not created) and embodied in a target substance. Photosynthesis is an example where exergy from solar radiation is captured and embodied in carbohydrates, which are combustible chemical substances. Carbo-thermic reduction of metal ores and ammonia synthesis are other examples. In the metals case, a metal oxide in contact with red-hot carbon is converted to a pure metal plus carbon dioxide. The exergy of the smelted metal is less than the exergy of the fuel used (for example, coke) because the combination of oxygen from the metal oxide with carbon from the coke is disguised combustion. In the ammonia case, natural gas plus air is converted to ammonia plus carbon dioxide by a series of catalytic processes at high temperatures and pressures, which also amount to disguised combustion.

There are other non-combustion processes that can do work, in principle. So when salt is dissolved in water, some heat is generated and work could be done if the heat were not rapidly diffused away. Desalination is the reverse of this diffusion process, and quite a lot of heat is required for the purpose of separating salt from water. It follows that any useful material that is present in concentrations above the average in the air (if it is a gas) or the ocean (if it is soluble) or the earth's crust (if it is neither a gas or soluble) also embodies some exergy. Thus, pure rainwater contains some exergy as compared to seawater, which has zero exergy by definition. Pure salt also contains some exergy for the same reason. Similarly pure oxygen or pure nitrogen contains some exergy, whereas the mixture that is air has zero exergy content, by definition. Finally, mine overburden has little or no exergy if it is chemically indistinguishable from the surrounding earth or rock.

Fuels, hydro-power, nuclear heat and products of photosynthesis (biomass) – crops and wood – are the major sources of exergy input to the economy. Most other materials have very little exergy in their original form, but gain exergy from fuels, as in metal reduction or ammonia synthesis. Nevertheless, the exergy content of materials is an interesting comparative measure, especially in contrast to the traditional measure (mass).

We emphasize that the exergy content of fuels and other raw materials can be equated to the theoretical maximum amount of physical work that can be extracted from those materials as they approach equilibrium reversibly. We will point out later that the actual amount of useful work done by the economic system is considerably less than the theoretical maximum. Moreover, the ratio of actual to theoretical maximum can be regarded as the *technical efficiency* (as opposed to *economic efficiency*, a very different concept) with which the economy converts raw materials into finished materials. This, in turn, as we will demonstrate later, can be regarded as rather a good measure of the state of technology. Over time, technical efficiency is a useful measure of technological progress or total factor productivity (TFP).

3.5   TRENDS IN EXERGY/MASS AND EXERGY/ GDP, FOR THE US

The next group of charts, Figures 3.5a–f, shows materials consumption in the US during the 20th century as measured in terms of mass and exergy in relation to economic activity (GDP). Though the exergy embodied in any given material is proportional to its mass, the mass/exergy ratio is not necessarily constant for groups of materials (for example, construction materials or fuels) due to shifts in the mix or composition of the group. Thus, Figures 3.4a and 3.5a for fossil fuels exhibit not-quite parallel curves for mass/GDP and exergy/GDP. Both curves peak in the early 1920s, and decline more or less monotonically thereafter.

The ratio E/GDP is sometimes called the Kuznets curve, although it is properly attributable to others (Schurr and Netschert 1960). It is often observed that, for many industrialized countries, the E/GDP (or E/Y) ratio appears to have a characteristic inverted-U shape, at least if E is restricted to commercial fuels. However, when the exergy embodied in firewood is included, the supposedly characteristic inverted-U shape is much less pronounced. When non-fuel and mineral resources, especially agricultural phytomass, are included, the inverted-U form is no longer evident. Figure 3.6 shows the two versions plotted from 1900 to 2004.

Similar peaks have been observed in the energy/GDP curves for a number of other countries, but at different times. The earliest peak (for the UK) was higher, while later ones for Germany, Japan, China etc. are progressively lower. This peak, followed by a declining trend, has been interpreted as a measure of relative industrialization. However, when biomass (including wood as a fuel) and other materials are included, as in Figure 3.6, the US curve did not peak after 1900. In fact, it apparently reflects a long-term substitution of commercial fuels for non-commercial biomass (fuelwood).

Similarly, comparing exergy/GDP and mass/GDP for fossil fuels (Figures 3.3a, 3.4a), it is evident that the mass/exergy ratio keeps decreasing.[10] This is due to a long-term shift from coal, at the beginning of the

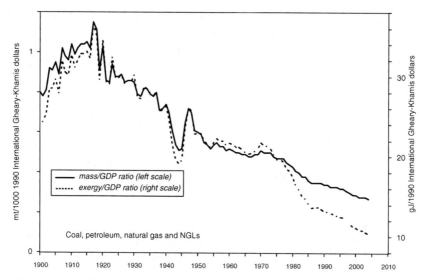

Figure 3.5a   Major inputs to GDP of fossil fuel: mass/GDP and exergy/GDP (USA, 1900–2004)

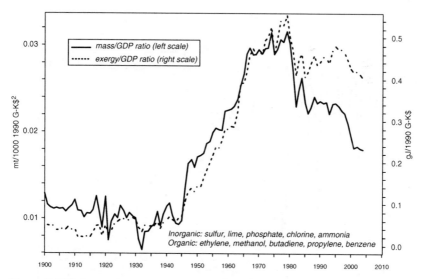

Note: G-K$ is International Geary-Khamis dollars.

Figure 3.5b   Major inputs to GDP of chemicals, major organic and inorganic: mass/GDP and exergy/GDP (USA, 1900–2004)

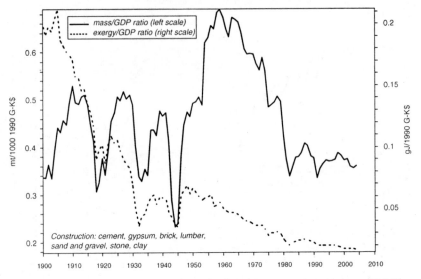

Figure 3.5c   Major inputs to GDP of construction materials: mass/GDP
and exergy/GDP (USA, 1900–2004)

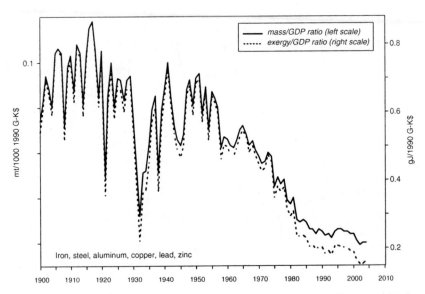

Figure 3.5d   Major inputs to GDP of metals: mass/GDP and exergy/GDP
(USA, 1900–2004)

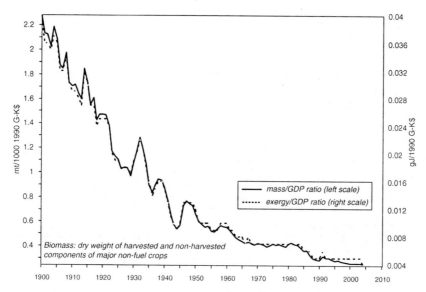

Figure 3.5e   *Major inputs to GDP of biomass: mass/GDP and exergy/
GDP (USA, 1900–2004)*

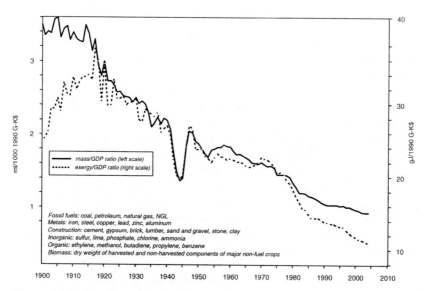

Figure 3.5f   *Total major inputs to GDP (fuels, metals, construction,
chemicals and biomass): mass/GDP and exergy/GDP (USA,
1900–2004)*

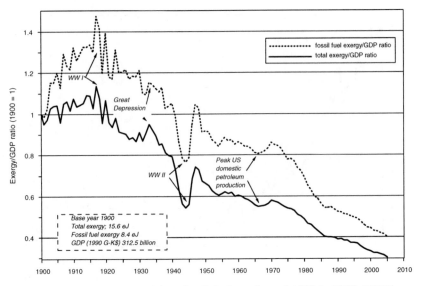

Figure 3.6   Exergy intensities: fossil fuels and total (USA, 1900–2005)

century, to petroleum and increasingly to natural gas. This shift reflects the increasing hydrogen fraction of fuels being used, and it is interpreted by some as the ongoing 'hydrogenation' of the economy. A similar shift in construction materials (Figures 3.4b and 3.5b) reflects the substitution of inert (non-flammable) materials for wood. And a comparable shift towards lighter and more flammable materials (i.e. organics) can be observed in the case of chemicals (Figures 3.4c, 3.5c). On the other hand, from the charts for metals (Figures 3.4a, 3.5a), it can be seen that the shift toward lighter metals, notably aluminum, is much less pronounced.

The other noteworthy long-term trend in the data is the decline, in every group including chemicals, in consumption per unit of GDP, although the turning point occurred earlier for fuels and metals, later for construction materials and still later for chemicals. Total mass/GDP (Figure 3.4f) also tends to exhibit declines (albeit with some exceptions for specific materials during certain periods). The overall decline from 1905 to 1995 is almost exactly by a factor of three. Since 1950 the decline has been a little faster (a factor of two). This is interpretable, in part, from efficiency gains in extraction and primary processing and in part from the overall shift from products to services in the economy. Another way of saying the same thing is that GDP has increased faster than either population growth or mass or exergy consumption. This decline has sometimes been interpreted as evidence of dematerialization (for example Greenspan, cited in Cairncross

1997). However, the most important conclusion from the evidence is that the consumption of mass per capita (except for inert construction materials) is not declining significantly.

3.6 EXERGY SUPPLY TRENDS FOR THE US AND JAPAN

In the remainder of this book we compare the US and Japan in considerable detail. The choice of Japan for this purpose is partly due to the availability of excellent historical data for the full hundred-year period. However, Japan also offers a fascinating contrast with the US. While the two countries are at comparable levels of development today, the history of development has been very different. Moreover, the two countries differ radically in terms of raw material base. The patterns of exergy supply and use differ substantially between the two countries, so if our theory of growth works well for both countries, it will increase our confidence in the new theory.

Inputs of exergy by source for the two countries are shown side by side in Figure 3.7a and Figure 3.7b. Note that exergy inputs from minerals and biomass are included explicitly. Breakdowns of the supply data in

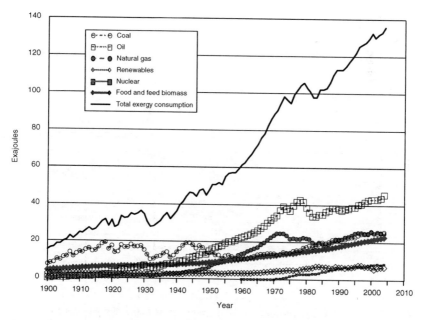

Figure 3.7a   Inputs of exergy by source (USA, 1900–2004)

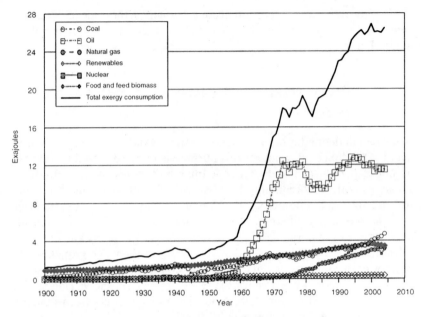

Figure 3.7b   Inputs of exergy by source (Japan, 1900–2004)

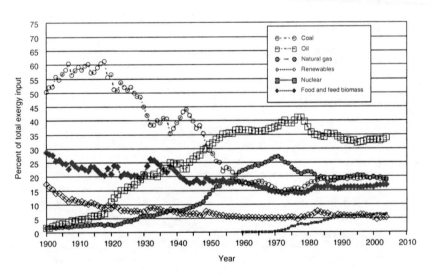

Figure 3.8a   Exergy input sources as percent of total exergy input (USA, 1900–2004)

Percent of total exergy input

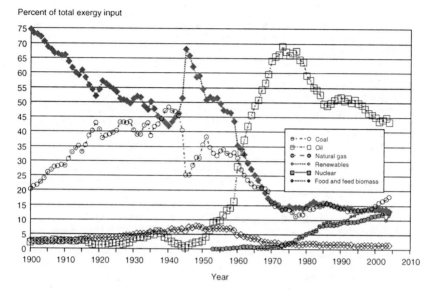

Figure 3.8b   *Exergy input sources as percent of total exergy input (Japan, 1900–2004)*

percentage terms are shown in Figure 3.8a and Figure 3.8b. Allocations of exergy inputs among the major categories of use are displayed and discussed in Chapter 4.

NOTES

1. The role of money is disputed. Most economists would agree that money is simply a convenient medium of exchange, and that it must be backed by an underlying stock of physical goods. As long as money was explicitly backed by gold, this point seemed self-evident. But now that money is backed only by the 'faith and credit' of the government in power, it is unclear whether money itself is also a component of wealth.
2. Actually it is mass-energy that is conserved. But apart from nuclear fission (or fusion), matter and energy are not interconvertible on the surface of the earth. Hence, as a practical matter, each is conserved separately.
3. The case of batch processes or continuous processes with time variability requires more careful consideration. In general, however, the accounting rule holds: stock changes equal inputs minus outputs. When stock changes are zero, or can be neglected, inputs equal outputs.
4. These conditions can be very helpful in filling in missing data. For instance, chemical engineering textbooks (for example, Faith et al. 1950) tend to provide 'recipes' for standard chemical processes that specify inputs (per unit output) in some detail, but neglect to specify waste products. While a detailed chemical characterization of the wastes requires very complex model calculations or direct measurements, one can derive some useful information about the elementary composition of the wastes.

5. On the other hand, animal manure generated in large industrialized feedlots *is* a waste.
6. Actually 51 MMT of the 89 MMT of steel produced in the US in 1993 was recycled scrap. Domestic pig iron inputs were only 48 MMT. The two input streams add up to 99 MMT; the weight difference consists mostly of slag and CO_2.
7. It can be argued that food and beverages are also service-carriers, inasmuch as they pass through the body and become wastes almost immediately, except for the tiny fraction that is retained in body mass. Even that is returned to the environment at the end of life, except for the annual incremental increase in the mass of the human population.
8. Glass is manufactured by a thermal process from a mixture of silica (sand), magnesia, kaolin and soda ash (sodium carbonate) plus traces of other metal oxides. Carbon dioxide is released. Portland cement is made by heating (calcining) a mixture of crushed limestone, clay, gypsum and other silicate minerals. Carbon dioxide is released. Concrete is made from cement, sand and other fillers, with added water. Brick and ceramic tiles are made from clay by heating to drive off water. Plaster is produced from natural gypsum by heating to drive off water, but the material is rehydrated (as in the case of Portland cement) to solidify.
9. However, in a more general physics context mass is a quantity only known from its influence. Originally the notion of mass was inferred from the observed fact of inertia. Some objects were more difficult to accelerate, or decelerate, than others. The 'something' that explained this difference was called mass (Newton's law was 'force equals mass times acceleration'). Isaac Newton applied this law to explain planetary orbits by equating the centrifugal force, proportional to mass, with the attractive gravitational force exerted by the sun, also proportional to mass. Later still Einstein proved that mass and energy are interconvertible through his famous formula: energy (E) is equal to mass (m) times the velocity of light (c) squared, probably the second most famous formula in physics. The reality of this interconvertibility was demonstrated over Hiroshima and Nagasaki in August 1945.
10. In effect, there has been a modest dematerialization of energy carriers since 1900. That is to say, the mass/exergy ratio for primary fuels consumed in the US has declined from 0.042 metric tons per tJ (teraJoule) in 1900 to 0.03 metric tons per tJ in 1995. This is an overall decline of 28 percent, due primarily to the increased use of natural gas and reduced use of coal. But, curiously, the minimum point was reached in the decade 1965–75 (0.028 metric tons per tJ). The trend has been rising since that time as coal has increased its share of the electric power generation market since the 'energy crisis' of 1973–4.

4. Exergy conversion to useful work

4.1 INTRODUCTION

In Chapter 3 we introduced the concept of exergy as a measure of quantity applicable to all materials (including fuels) as well as non-material energy fluxes. In the present chapter we continue the discussion in terms of resource (exergy) conversion efficiency. This leads up to the formulation, in the chapters which follow, of a new – and quantifiable – analytic model to explain past and future economic growth.

4.2 USEFUL WORK

Before embarking on a more technical discussion of 'work' in the thermodynamic sense, to be distinguished clearly from the ordinary everyday use of the term, it may be helpful to recall some words of one of the pioneers of energy accounting, Nathaniel Guyol. In a paper prepared for a conference in 1984 (but never published as far as we know), he wrote:

> The convenient correlation of energy (exergy) and national product exists mainly by virtue of the fact that both are related to population and the state of the national economy . . . *A proper model of energy consumption must take into account the reasons why energy is used* . . . Energy is used to do the *work* that must be done to supply the goods and services we need or want and can afford. (Guyol 1984; emphasis added)

Our use of the term 'useful work' in this book is somewhat more technical, and hopefully more precise, than his, but it is consistent with Guyol's argument. A brief explanation is needed, even though a precise definition is surprisingly elusive. In physics texts, work is usually defined as 'a force operating over a distance'. However, this definition is not helpful if force is also undefined. The best explanation may be historical. Useful work was originally conceptualized in the 18th century in terms of a horse pulling a plow or a pump raising water against the force of gravity.[1] During the past two centuries, several other types of work have been identified, including thermal work, chemical work and electrical work. For our purposes, we have also considered 'useful heat' (as delivered to a user) as another form of work. Space heating, water heating and cooking are the primary examples.

In physics, *power* is defined as work performed per unit of time. Before the Industrial Revolution there were only four sources of mechanical power of any economic significance. They were human labor, animal labor, water power (near flowing streams) and wind power. (The advent of steam power in the early 18th century led to the first quantification of power in terms of equivalent 'horsepower' by James Watt.) Nowadays mechanical power is mainly provided by *prime movers*, which are either hydraulic or steam turbines (used to generate electrical power) or internal combustion engines. The three major types of internal combustion engines are *spark ignition* (gasoline) engines, *compression ignition* (diesel) engines and *gas turbines*.

More generally, one can say that whatever increases the kinetic or potential energy of a subsystem can be called 'work', it being understood that the subsystem is contained within a larger system in which energy is always conserved, by definition. Electricity can be regarded as 'pure' useful work, because it can perform either mechanical or chemical work with very high efficiency, that is, with very small frictional losses. Of course, electricity is also a commodity, produced by a well-defined sector and sold at a well-defined price in a well-defined market. Since electricity is not a material good, it is commonly regarded as a 'utility' service.

Unfortunately, this is not true of other kinds of physical work done in (and by) the economic system. Motive power, for instance is produced by human muscles, animals (horses and mules) or machines and also consumed within the productive sectors of the economy as well as within households (for example, motor cars). Similarly, heat is both produced and consumed within virtual sectors, as well as in households. It follows that non-electrical useful work and useful heat can be regarded as *exergy service*, even though this service is often consumed where it is produced and therefore it is not conventionally measured or priced.

If this concept seems strange at first, it may be easier to think in terms of the electrical equivalent of motive power (from an engine), or the electrical equivalent of chemical work or heat. The electrical equivalent of motive power is already a reality, for instance, in electrified railroads, where electric motors drive the wheels. The electrical equivalent of chemical work is also exhibited by storage batteries, for instance, which convert electricity into chemical potential, and vice versa, albeit with some losses in each direction. Similarly, high temperature industrial heat provided by fuel combustion and heat exchangers could be equated to the amount of electricity required to produce that heat, at the point of use, by an electric stove or toaster, or an electric arc furnace.

The above examples are slightly misleading to the extent that the conversion from electrical work (power) to other kinds of work is always subject to some loss, thanks to the second law of thermodynamics. But electric power can be converted into mechanical motion (via a motor) and *vice versa* (via a generator) with an actual efficiency over 90 percent. Fuel cells are not quite as efficient at converting chemical energy into electricity, although they are improving and the theoretical potential of fuel cells, at very high temperatures, is in the 80 percent range.

This interconvertibility does not apply to heat, however. As Count Rumford showed in a classic experiment, carried out while he was boring cannons for the Bavarian government, kinetic energy can be converted into heat with no loss. Similarly, it is true that electricity can be converted into heat (by a resistor) with 100 percent efficiency. But heat cannot be reconverted into kinetic energy or electricity with the same high efficiency. This is because of the entropy law or second law of thermodynamics, which was first explained in the context of heat engines by the French engineer, Sadi Carnot (Carnot 1826). Even the most efficient possible heat engine can only achieve a maximum efficiency based on the temperature difference between two reservoirs. For this reason, we use the term 'second-law efficiency' to characterize the efficiency of low temperature heating systems in relation to the theoretical limits (American Physical Society et al. 1975).

It is helpful for some discussions later in this book to define *primary* and *secondary* work. Primary work is done by the first stage of energy conversion for example, electric power generation by means of a heat engine or hydraulic turbine. Secondary work is work done by electrical devices or machines. We also introduce the notion of 'quasi-work' done by driving an endothermic chemical process or moving heat energy from one place to another across some thermal barrier (metal smelting is an example of the first; home heating is an example of the second). In all cases the physical units of work are the same as the units of energy or exergy.

The notion of *energy conversion* efficiency is commonplace in engineering and physics. It is easily generalized to exergy. As noted already, exergy is the maximum work theoretically obtainable from a subsystem as it approaches equilibrium with its environment. Exergy conversion efficiency is therefore the ratio of *actual* work (output) to *maximum* work (exergy) input, for any given process. For instance, a heat engine converts the heat of combustion of a fuel into useful mechanical work.[2] In recent decades, a number of authors have applied exergy analysis at the industry level.[3] We now generalize this concept to the economy as a whole. In order to do so we must identify the different types of useful work done in the economy as a whole and allocate the exergy resource inputs to each type of work.

Useful work can be divided into several categories. These include *muscle work* (by humans or farm animals), *mechanical work* by stationary or mobile prime movers (for example, heat engines), and heat delivered to a point of use (for example, industrial process heat, space heat, cooking). Electricity can be regarded as a pure form of useful work, since it can be converted into mechanical work, chemical work (as in electrolysis) or heat with little or no loss.

Figures 4.1a and 4.1b show the percentage allocation of coal exergy to various types of useful work in the two countries. Figures 4.2a, 4.2b, 4.3a and 4.3b show the same for petroleum and natural gas. Figures 4.4a and 4.4b show how useful work from fossil fuels as a whole is allocated among uses, in percentages. Food and feed are utilized exclusively for muscle work, while fuelwood is used for space heating. Hydro-power and nuclear heat also contribute to electricity. Using the exergy flow and conversion efficiency data, the aggregate useful work (exergy services) performed by the US and Japanese economies since 1900 can be calculated. However, such a calculation presupposes that historical energy conversion efficiency data are available. In practice, this is only true for electric power generation. For other sources of work it is necessary to collect historical data on the conversion efficiency of transportation, chemical processes, metallurgical processes and space heating. We discuss this problem later in the present chapter.

4.3   ANIMAL (AND HUMAN) MUSCLE WORK

There are no reliable estimates of aggregate animal or human muscle work as such, although the horsepower unit (of work per hour) was originally defined by James Watt to measure the output of steam engines, based on a comparison with the work done by a horse pumping water via a treadmill. It is possible, however, to estimate human and animal outputs of mechanical work crudely on the basis of food or feed intake, multiplied by a biological conversion efficiency. Human muscle work was already negligible by comparison at the beginning of the 20th century. The US population in 1900 was 76 million, of which perhaps 50 million were of 'working age'. Of these, only 25 million were men. Women worked too, perhaps even longer hours than men, but, except for some shopkeepers, teachers and nurses, their labor was not monetized and hence did not contribute to GDP at the time. Despite the impression created by 'working class' songs of the time, such as 'John Henry' and 'Sixteen Tons', at least half of the employed workers were probably doing less physical things like operating telegraphs, entering figures in accounts, driving carriages or trams, caring for animals, cooking or making furniture. In short, they were doing jobs

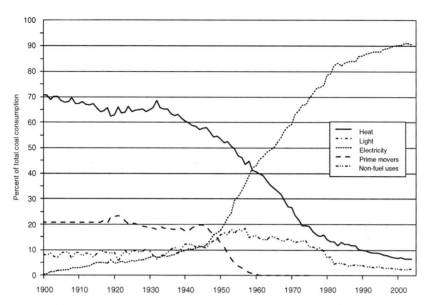

Figure 4.1a   Percent of coal exergy consumed by type of end-use (USA, 1900–2004)

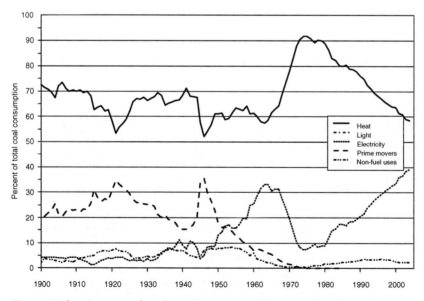

Figure 4.1b   Percent of coal exergy consumed by type of end-use (Japan, 1900–2004)

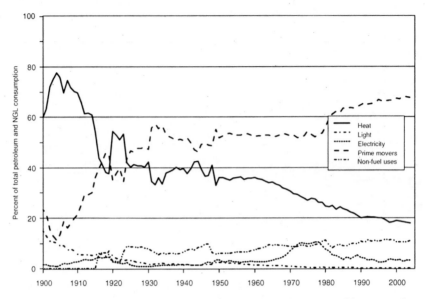

Figure 4.2a   Percent of petroleum and NGL exergy consumed by type of end-use (USA, 1900–2004)

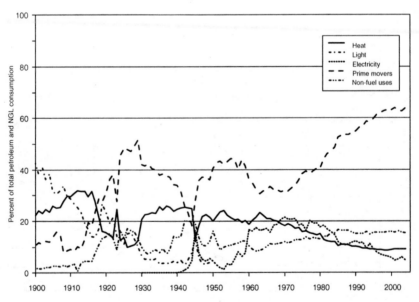

Figure 4.2b   Percent of petroleum and NGL exergy consumed by type of end-use (Japan, 1900–2004)

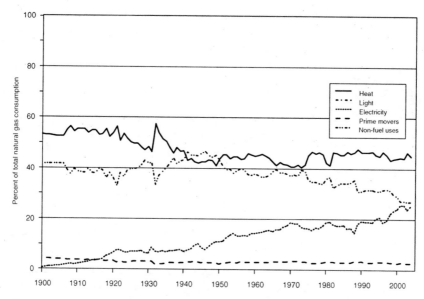

Figure 4.3a   Percent of natural gas exergy consumed by type of end-use
             (USA, 1900–2004)

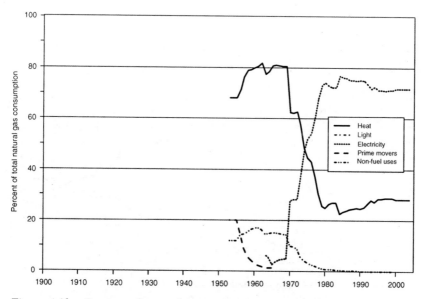

Figure 4.3b   Percent of natural gas exergy consumed by type of end-use
             (Japan, 1900–2004) (no usage prior to 1945)

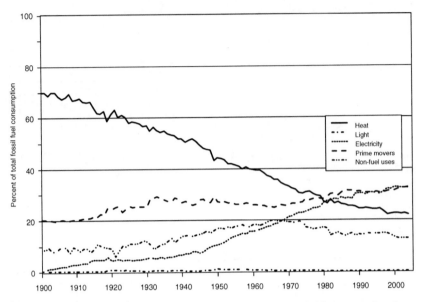

Figure 4.4a   Percent of total fossil fuel exergy consumed by type of end-use (USA, 1900–2004)

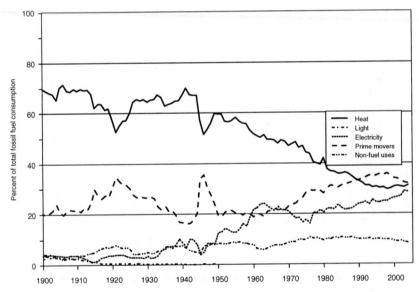

Figure 4.4b   Percent of total fossil fuel exergy consumed by type of end-use (Japan, 1900–2004)

that depended more on eye-hand coordination or intelligence than on sheer muscular effort.[4]

The minimum metabolic requirement for an adult man is of the order of 1500 calories per day, whereas the average food consumption for a working man was (and is) about 3000 calories per day. Thus, no more than 1500 calories per day were available for doing physical (muscle) work above and beyond metabolic needs, for example, to chew and digest food, breath air and circulate the blood. This comes to 18 billion calories per day or about 0.16 EJ per year of food exergy inputs for non-metabolic human muscular effort, as compared to aggregate fossil fuel consumption of 8.9 EJ in 1900. Assuming muscles convert energy into work at about 15 percent efficiency, the overall food-to-useful-work conversion efficiency for the US population as a whole would have been roughly 2.4 percent at that time. In recent years, of course, more and more women have joined the labor force. Given the changing (less physical) nature of modern work, and the much greater life expectancy and longer retirement time, the average conversion efficiency has probably declined significantly. We note, however, that in some developing countries, such as India, the human contribution to physical (mechanical) work, especially in agriculture, may not yet be negligible as compared to the contribution from machines.

Since human *labor* is treated independently in economic analysis – and since human muscle power is no longer an important component of human labor in the industrial world, as compared to eye-hand coordination and brainwork – we can safely neglect it hereafter. However, work done by animals, especially on farms, was still important in the US at the beginning of the 20th century and remained significant until trucks and tractors finally displaced most of the horses and mules by mid-century.[5]

According to Dewhurst, 18.5 units of animal feed are needed to generate one unit of useful (physical) work by a horse or mule (Dewhurst 1955, pp. 1113–16, cited in Schurr and Netschert 1960, footnote 19, p. 55). This implies an effective energy conversion efficiency of 5.4 percent for work animals. However, more recent estimates by several authors converge on 4 percent efficiency or 25 units of feed per unit of work done (for example, Gruebler 1998, box 7.1, p. 321 and references cited therein; also Kander 2002). We choose the latter figure, right or wrong. Evidently the work done by animals can be estimated from the feed consumption, which can be estimated with reasonable accuracy.

Luckily, higher precision is probably unnecessary for the quantitative estimates in the US case because even at the beginning of the 20th century the magnitude of animal work was relatively small compared to inanimate power sources. Inanimate sources of mechanical work (hydraulic turbines, steam engines and windmills) exceeded animal work in the US by 1870. However, again, in some developing countries animal work is still quantitatively important.

4.4   PRIME MOVERS AND HEAT

For purposes of empirical estimation of other types of work, it is helpful to distinguish between two categories of fuel use. The first category is fuel used to do mechanical work, via so-called 'prime movers'. These include all kinds of internal and external combustion engines, from steam turbines to jet engines, as well as nuclear steam power plants. (Electric motors are not prime movers because a prime mover – such as a steam turbine – is needed to generate the electricity in the first place.) The second category is fuel used to generate heat *as such*, either at high temperatures for industry (process heat and chemical energy) and domestic or commercial cooking, or at low temperatures for space heat and hot water for washing for residential and/or commercial users.

The percentage consumption by prime movers for the three major fossil fuels (coal, petroleum and natural gas) was plotted in Figures 4.1a, 4.1b, 4.2a, 4.2b and 4.3a, 4.3b for the US and Japan. Fuelwood has never been used to a significant extent for driving prime movers, at least in the US, except in early 19th-century railroads or Mississippi River steamboats. In Japan, charcoal from biomass was used for buses and trucks briefly towards the end of World War II, but otherwise not (there are no published statistics).

Figures 4.1a and 4.1b show the fraction of coal consumption allocated to mechanical work since 1900. During the first half of the century steam locomotives for railroads were the major users, with stationary steam engines in mines and factories also significant contributors. These uses are not distinguished in published US statistics prior to 1917. Industrial uses for heat and work were estimated by assuming that fuel consumption for each category is proportional to total horsepower in that category of prime movers, for which data have been estimated separately.[6]

Figures 4.2a and 4.2b, for petroleum, are based on published data for liquid fuels, by type.[7] At the beginning of the 20th century, the dominant product of the industry was 'illuminating oil' (kerosine) used for lamps in rural areas. Much of this was exported (in fact, the US was the major exporter of petroleum products until after World War II). Only 'natural' gasoline – a moderately volatile light fraction of the petroleum (15–18 percent) consisting of hydrocarbons with six to 12 or so carbon atoms – was used for early motor vehicles. The more volatile lighter fraction was mostly flared until after World War II. The fractions heavier than kerosine had little value except for fuel oil, lubricants, wax and asphalt.

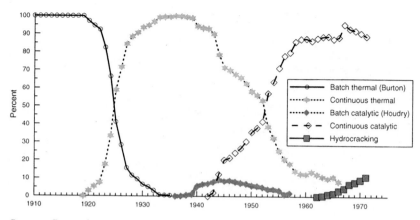

Source: Data prior to 1958 from Ayres; data from 1958 on from Lakhani (p. 54).

Figure 4.5 *Developments in petroleum 'cracking' fractions (USA, 1910–72)*

The rapid increase in motor vehicle production and use after 1900 created a correspondingly rapid growth in demand for gasoline, which exceeded consumption of kerosine for the first time in 1911. This led to a series of technological developments in 'cracking' heavier petroleum fractions. Burton's batch-type thermal cracking (1913) was succeeded by continuous thermal cracking, followed by batch (Houdry) catalytic cracking and finally continuous catalytic cracking (Enos 1962) (Figure 4.5). Evidently the fraction of crude oil used to drive prime movers, rather than for heating, has been increasing for a long time. This is a crude measure of the increasing efficiency of petroleum use (Figure 4.6). In the US, roughly half of the mass of crude petroleum is converted into gasoline, with other liquid fuels (diesel oil, jet fuel, residual oil) accounting for much of the rest (Figure 4.7). In Japan, the split between gasoline and diesel or heating oils is somewhat tilted toward the heavier fractions.

Figures 4.3a and 4.3b, for natural gas, show the uses of gas. In the US, gas is mostly used for heating and chemical processes (such as ammonia synthesis). A small fraction is used to drive compressors in the gas pipelines and another small fraction is used by electric utilities to generate electric power. In Europe and Japan, a much larger fraction is used for electric power generation.

Figures 4.4a and 4.4b, combining Figures 4.1a, 4.1b, 4.2a, 4.2b, 4.3a and 4.3b, show the fraction of all fossil fuel exergy used to drive prime movers and perform mechanical work – for purposes of generating either electric power or mobile power. This share has been increasing more or less

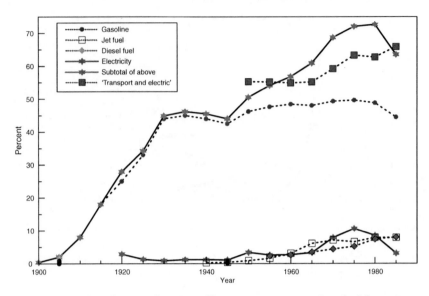

*Figure 4.6   Petroleum utilization efficiency: percent used as fuel for prime
              movers (USA, 1900–82)*

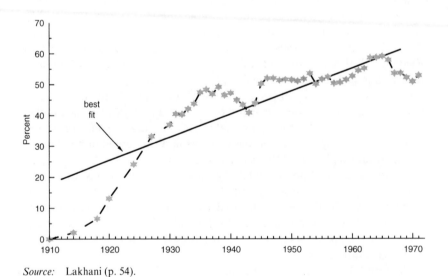

Source: Lakhani (p. 54).

*Figure 4.7   Percent of crude oil cracked to produce gasoline (USA,
              1910–72)*

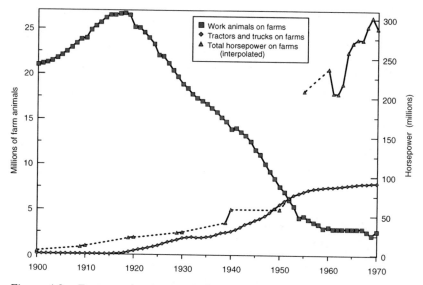

Figure 4.8   Farm mechanization: substitution of machinery for animals

continuously since the beginning of the 20th century, mostly because of the increasing fraction of the other fossil fuels, coal and gas that has been devoted to electric power generation. Transportation uses have remained roughly constant as a fraction of the total. The other major uses of fuel exergy are to do chemical or thermal work: they include industrial heating (direct or via steam), space heating, water heating and cooking. We classify the direct heat as 'quasi-work'.

Figures 4.4a and 4.4b, discussed above, reflect two different phenomena. One is structural change. For instance, the substitution of machines, especially tractors, for animals in agriculture (US) is shown in Figure 4.8. The other phenomenon is technical improvement in specific conversion processes, which we discuss next. Needless to say, efficiency gains, reflected in prices for exergy or power, drove some of the structural changes noted above.

4.5   EXERGY-TO-WORK EFFICIENCY IMPROVEMENTS SINCE 1900[8]

4.5.1   Prime Movers

In a very important sense the industrial revolution was powered by steam. The fuel required to perform a unit of mechanical work (for example, a

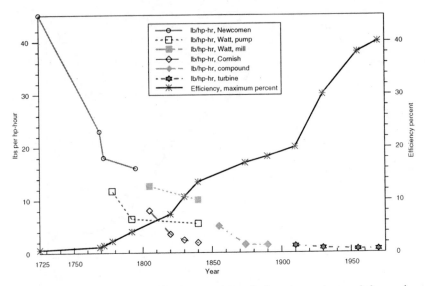

Figure 4.9   Performance of steam engines: fuel consumption and thermal efficiency

horsepower hour or kilowatt hour) from steam has decreased dramatically since 1800, and even since 1900, although the decline has been very slow since the 1960s. Steam engines have become more efficient (in both countries) since Watt's time, as shown in Figure 4.9. The largest stationary steam piston engines – cross-compound 'triple expansion' engines – generated up to 5 MW at efficiencies above 20 percent (Smil 1999, p. 145). In the case of large stationary or marine steam engines operating under optimal conditions (at constant loads), the thermal efficiency exceeded 15 percent in the best cases. However, single expansion (non-compound) coal-burning steam locomotives – the product of engine efficiency and boiler efficiency – were not nearly so efficient: about 6 percent on average, depending on boiler pressure, temperature, fuel and power output. Results from three sets of experiments, as of the late 19th century, for locomotives with indicated horsepower ranging from 130 to 692, ranged from 4.7 to 7.7 percent (Dalby 1911, table XXI, p. 847). The more powerful engines were not necessarily the most efficient. The lack of improvement in railway steam engine efficiency opened the door for diesel-electric locomotives, starting around 1930.

Factory engines were typically larger than railway engines, but not more efficient. Moreover, transmission losses in factories, where a central engine was connected to a number of machines by a series of leather belts, were enormous. For instance, if a stationary steam engine for a factory with

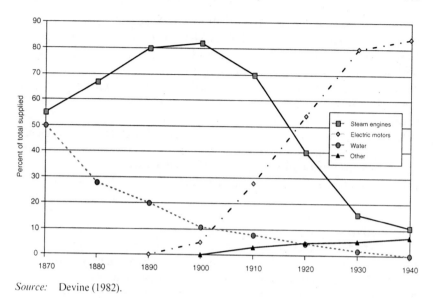

Source: Devine (1982).

Figure 4.10 *Sources of mechanical drive in manufacturing establishments (USA, 1869–1939)*

machines operating off belt drives circa 1900 had a thermal efficiency of 6 percent, with 50 percent frictional losses, the net exergy efficiency was 3 percent (Dewhurst 1955, appendices 25-3, 25-4, cited in Schurr and Netschert 1960, footnote 19, p. 55). The Dewhurst estimate, which took into account these transmission losses, set the average efficiency of conversion of coal energy into mechanical work at the point of use at 3 percent in 1900 (when most factories still used steam power), increasing to 4.4 percent in 1910 and 7 percent in 1920, when the substitution of electric motors for steam power in US factories was approaching completion (Figure 4.10) (Devine 1982). The use of steam power in railroads was peaking during the same period.

A steam-electric central generating plant together with its (local) transmission and distribution system achieved around 3 percent efficiency by 1900, and probably double (6 percent net) by 1910. Thermal power plants operated at nearly 10 percent (on average) by 1920 and reached 33 percent in the mid-1960s. Electric motors in factories were already capable of 80 percent or so efficiency in reconverting electric power to rotary motion, rising to 90 percent plus in recent times.[9] So, the combined efficiency of the generator-motor combination was at least 8 percent by 1920; it reached 20 percent by mid-century and nearly 30 percent by 1960. Hence the overall efficiency gain in this case (from 1920 to 1960) was of the order of five-fold – more than enough to explain the shift to electric power in factories. Motor drive for pumps, compressors and machine tools of various types, but excluding air-conditioning and refrigeration, accounted for nearly 45 percent of total electricity use in the peak year (1927), but the industrial share of motor use has declined quite steadily since then to around 23 percent in the year 2000 (Ayres et al. 2003).

In the case of railroad steam locomotives, average thermal efficiency circa 1920 according to another estimate was about 10 percent, whereas a diesel-electric locomotive half a century later, circa 1970, achieved 35 percent (Summers 1971). Internal friction and transmission losses and variable load penalty are apparently not reflected in either figure, but they would have been similar in percentage terms in the two cases. If these losses amounted to 30 percent, the two estimates (Dewhurst's and Summers') are consistent for 1920. Old coal-burning steam locomotives circa 1950 still only achieved 7.5 percent thermal efficiency; however, newer oil-burning steam engines at that time obtained 10 percent efficiency and a few coal-fired gas turbines got 17 percent (Ayres and Scarlott 1952, tables 6, 7). But the corresponding efficiency of diesel-electric locomotives circa 1950 was 28 percent, taking internal losses into account (ibid., tables 7, 8). The substitution of diesel-electric for steam locomotives in the US began in the 1930s and accelerated in the 1950s (see Figure 4.11).

The most attractive source of power for electricity generation has always been falling water and hydraulic turbines. Hydraulic turbines were already achieving 80 percent efficiency by 1900. The first 'large-scale' hydro-electric power plant in the US was built in 1894–5 at Niagara Falls. Alternating current was introduced at that time by Westinghouse, using Tesla's technology, for transmission beyond a few miles. The facility served local industry as well as nearby Buffalo. But most of the electricity consumers at that time were not located close to hydro-electric sites, so coal-fired steam-electric generation soon dominated the US industry.

On the other hand, Norway, Sweden, Switzerland, Austria, France, Canada and Japan relied entirely or mainly on hydro-electric power until the 1930s, and all but Japan, France and Sweden still do. Meanwhile Egypt, Brazil and Russia have also invested heavily in hydro-electric power, and China is doing so now. Unfortunately, most of the rest of the world does not have significant hydraulic resources today. Needless to say, those countries with hydro-electric power produce useful work more efficiently, on average, than the rest of the world.

In the case of steam-electric power, the so-called 'heat rate' in the US has fallen from 90,000 Btu/kWh in 1900 to just about 11,000 Btu/kWh by 1970 and 10,000 Btu/kWh today.[10] The heat rate is the inverse of conversion

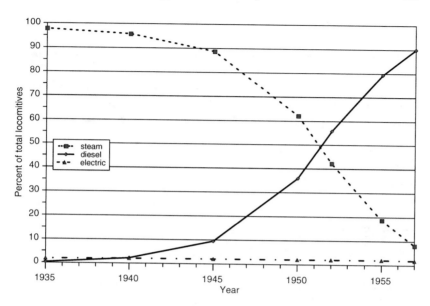

Figure 4.11   Substitution of diesel for steam locomotives in the USA, 1935–57

efficiency, which has increased by nearly a factor of ten, from 3.6 percent in 1900 or so to nearly 33 percent on average (including distribution losses). The declining price and increasing demand for electric power is shown in Figure 4.12.

Steam-turbine design improvements and scaling up to larger sizes accounted for most of the early improvements. The use of pulverized coal, beginning in 1920, accounted for major gains in the 1920s and 1930s. Better designs and metallurgical advances permitting higher temperatures and pressures accounted for further improvements in the 1950s. Since 1960, however, efficiency improvements have been very slow, largely because existing turbine steel alloys are close to their maximum temperature limits, and almost all power plants are 'central', meaning that they are very large, located far from central cities and therefore unable to utilize waste heat productively.

The retail price of electricity (in constant dollars) to residential and commercial users decreased dramatically prior to 1950 and by a factor of two since then. On the other hand, the consumption of electricity in the US has increased over the same period by a factor of 1200, and continued to increase rapidly even after 1960. This is a prime example of the so-called 'rebound effect'.[11] The probable explanation is that a great many new electrical devices and consumer products – from washing machines and

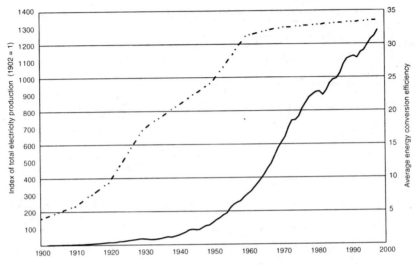

*Figure 4.12   Index of total electricity production by electric utilities
              (1902 = 1) and average energy conversion efficiency (USA,
              1902–98)*

refrigerators to electric ranges, water heaters, air-conditioners, TVs and
most recently, PCs and DVD players – were introduced after 1930 or so
and penetrated markets gradually (Figures 4.13a and 4.13b).

The work done by internal combustion engines in automobiles, trucks
and buses (road transport) must be estimated in a different way. In the case
of heavy diesel-powered trucks with a compression ratio in the range of
15:1 to 18:1, operating over long distances at highway speeds, the analysis
is comparable to that for railways. The engine power can be optimized for
this mode of operation and the parasitic losses for a heavy truck (lights,
heating, engine cooling, air-conditioning, power-assisted steering, etc.) are
minor. Internal friction and drive-train losses and losses due to variable
load operation can conceivably be as low as 20 percent, though 25 percent
is probably more realistic.

For vehicles operating in urban traffic under variable load (stop-start)
conditions, the analysis is quite different.[12] Gasoline-powered ICE engines
nowadays (2001) have an average compression ratio between 8 and 8.5.
This has been true since the early 1970s, although average US compression
ratios had been higher in the 1960s, in the heyday of the use of tetraethyl
lead as an anti-knock additive, as shown in Figure 4.14 (Ayres and Ezekoye
1991). The thermal efficiency of a 'real' fuel-air four-cycle auto (or truck)
engine operating at constant speed (2000 rpm) is around 30 percent. By

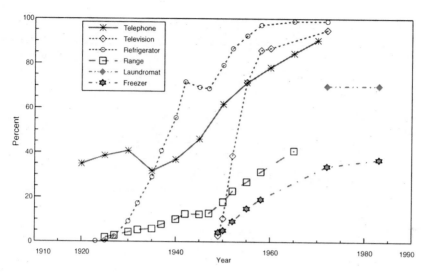

Figure 4.13a   Household electrification (I) (percent of households)

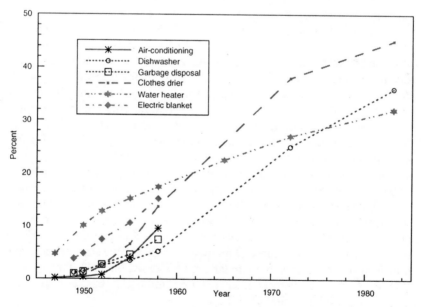

Figure 4.13b   Household electrification (II) (percent of households)

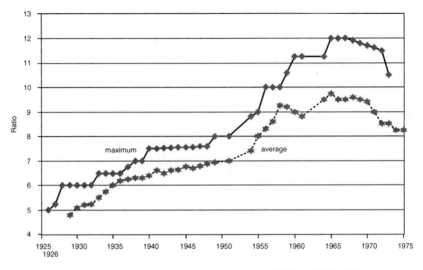

Figure 4.14   Compression ratio in auto engines (USA, 1926–75)

contrast, with a compression ratio of 4:1 (typical of engines in 1920) the *maximum* theoretical thermal efficiency would have been about 22 percent (Figure 4.15). Internal engine friction would reduce these by a factor of about 0.8, while the penalty for variable loads in stop-start urban driving introduces another factor of 0.75. With a manual transmission (European average), there is a multiplier of 0.95 to account for transmission losses, but for American cars with automatic transmissions, the transmission loss is more like 10 percent for small cars, less for larger ones.[13] Other parasitic losses (lights, heating, air-conditioning, etc.) must also be subtracted. These items can account for 4.5 bhp on average, and up to 10 bhp for the air-conditioning compressor alone, when it is operating.

The net result of this analysis suggests that for a typical 'mid-size' American car with automatic transmission, the overall exergy efficiency with which the engine converts fuel energy into so-called brake horsepower at the rear wheels – where the tire meets the road – was as low as 8 percent in 1972 (American Physical Society et al. 1975), and perhaps 10 percent for a comparable European or Japanese car of the same size with manual transmission. An earlier but similar analysis based on 1947 data arrived at an estimate of 6.2 percent efficiency for automobiles, based on gasoline input (Ayres and Scarlott 1952).[14]

Contrary to widespread assumptions, there has been little or no improve-ment in thermodynamic engine efficiency since the 1970s. Four and five-speed transmissions, overhead cams, four valves per cylinder, electronic

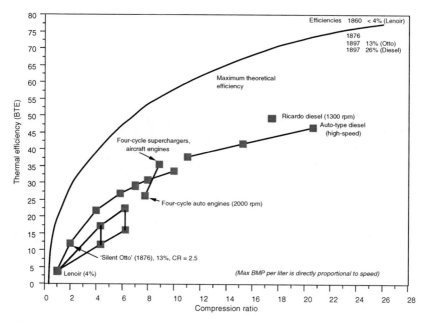

Figure 4.15 Internal combustion engine efficiency

control and fuel injection have been collectively responsible for perhaps 15 percent cumulative reduction in engine losses since 1972. Heavier vehicles (light trucks, vans and sports utility vehicles) exhibit lower fuel economy (10.3 mpg for 1972; 17 mpg in 1990). Heavy trucks exhibit still lower fuel economy, around 6 mpg. From 1970 to 1990, overall average motor vehicle fuel economy in the US increased from 12.0 mpg to 16.4 mpg; from 1990 to 1998 there has been a very slight further increase to 17.0 mpg (United States Department of Energy annual).[15]

Thanks to regulations known as the Corporate Average Fuel Economy (CAFÉ) standards, imposed in the aftermath of the 1973–4 Arab oil boycott, the US passenger vehicle fleet of 1990 achieved about 50 percent more vehicle miles per gallon of fuel than in 1972. This was only partly due to drive train efficiency gains but mainly to weight reductions, smaller engines, improved aerodynamics and better tires. However, these improvements must be classified as secondary, rather than primary, efficiency gains.

A more detailed analysis of energy losses in automobile transportation (circa 1990) that reflects the impact of CAFÉ standards and distinguishes between urban driving (12.6 percent) and highway driving (20.2 percent) is summarized in Figure 4.16. In that year, passenger cars in the US averaged 20.2 mpg. Unfortunately, the distinction between urban (stop-start)

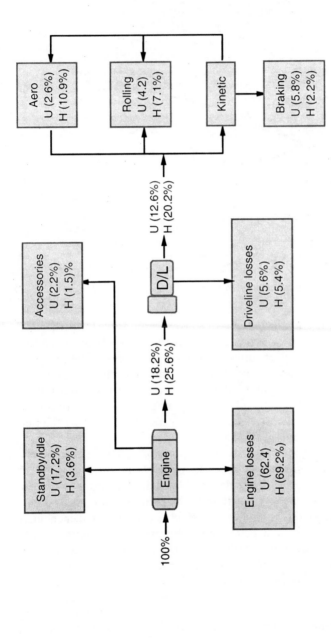

Note: U = Urban; H = Highway.

Source: Adapted from Green (1994).

Figure 4.16 Breakdown of energy requirements for a typical mid-size automobile (shown for US federal urban and highway driving cycles as a percent of the energy content of the fuel)

and highway driving is not clear in the highway statistics. Assuming urban vehicle miles traveled (VMT) accounted for something like 40 percent of the total, the average thermodynamic efficiency would have been between 15 and 16 percent.[16]

In the case of heavy diesel-powered trucks with a compression ratio in the range of 15–18, operating over long distances at highway speeds, the analysis is comparable to that for railways. The engine power can be optimized for this mode of operation and the parasitic losses for a heavy truck (lights, heating, engine cooling, air-conditioning, power-assisted steering, etc.) are minor. Overall thermodynamic efficiency for such trucks could be as high as 20 percent, even allowing for friction and parasitic loads.

For aircraft up to 1945, most engines were piston-type spark ignition ICEs and fuel was high (100 plus) octane gasoline. Engine efficiencies were comparable to those achieved by a high-compression engines (12:1) under constant load. This would be about 33 percent before corrections for internal losses (a factor of 0.8) and variable load penalty (a factor of 0.75), or roughly 20 percent overall. Aircraft are even more efficient in cruising, but there are heavy losses in takeoff and some in landing.

Gas turbines began replacing piston engines during World War II, and more rapidly thereafter. The turbo takeover in the commercial aviation market began around 1955 and accelerated in the 1960s. The fuel consumption index fell from an arbitrary value of 100 for the early turbo-jets of 1955 to 55 for the advanced turbo-fans of the year 2000. These improvements can be categorized as thermodynamic. Of course it takes a number of years before a new engine type penetrates the fleet, so fleet averages lag significantly (a decade or so) behind state-of-the-art.

In 1989, the US Environmental Protection Agency calculated that the average thermodynamic efficiency of *all* motor transportation (including trucks, buses, railroads and aircraft) was 8.33 percent.[17] Because of the increasing size of motor vehicles – pickup trucks and so-called sports utility vehicles (SUVs) – sold, it is unlikely that the average efficiency of the transport sector in the US has improved since then. On the other hand, thanks to a combination of factors, such as smaller vehicles and much more intensive use of electrified railways and subways, the corresponding efficiency in Japan reached nearly 15 percent by 1990, although there has been a slight decline subsequently. The efficiency of exergy use in Japan is reviewed in Chapter 6.

4.5.2 Direct Heat and Quasi-work

A declining, but still considerable, fraction of the fuel inputs to the economy is still used for heat (Figure 4.4a and b). Process heat and space heat do not 'perform work' in the usual sense, except in heat engines. However, process improvements that exploit improvements in heat transfer and utilization may be classed as thermodynamic efficiency gains, no less than the use of turbo-chargers or recuperators in modern auto, truck or aircraft engines. It is possible in some cases to calculate the minimum theoretical exergy requirements for the process or end-use in question and compare with the actual consumption in current practice. The ratio of theoretical minimum to actual exergy consumption – for an endothermic process – is known as the 'second-law efficiency' (American Physical Society et al. 1975). The product of second-law efficiency times exergy input can be regarded as 'useful' heat delivered to the point of use, or 'quasi-work'.

There are three different cases. First high temperature (say greater than 600° C). High temperature heat drives endothermic processes such as carbo-thermic metal smelting, casting and forging, cement manufacturing, lime calcination, brick manufacturing and glass-making, plus some use in endothermic chemical processes like ammonia synthesis and petroleum refining (for example, cracking). The second case is intermediate temperature heat, namely 100° C to 600° C, but mostly less than 200° C and mostly delivered to the point of use by steam. The third case is low temperature heat at temperatures below 100° C, primarily for hot water or space heat.

We know of very little published data allocating industrial heat requirements by temperature among these cases. Based on a detailed 1972 survey covering 67 four-digit SIC groups and 170 processes, it appears that roughly half of all US industrial process heat was required at temperatures greater than 600° C and most of the rest was in the intermediate category (Lovins 1977, figure 4.1). We assume hereafter that this allocation has been constant over time, although it may well have changed.

Intermediate and low temperature heat is required for many industrial purposes, usually delivered to the point of use via steam. Examples include increasing the solubility of solids in liquids, accelerating dehydration and evaporation (for example, in distillation units), liquefaction of solids or viscous liquids for easier transportation or mixing and acceleration of desired chemical reactions, many of which are temperature dependent. For purposes of back-casting to 1900, we have assumed that all coke and coke oven gas, as well as half of the natural gas allocated to industry, as opposed to residential and commercial usage, were used for high temperature processes. Most of the rest of the fuels used for industrial purposes are assumed to be for steam generation.

We consider high temperature industrial heat first. The iron and steel industry is the obvious exemplar. In this case, the carbon efficiency of reduction from ore might appear to be a reasonable surrogate, since the reducing agent for iron ore is carbon monoxide. Thus the C/Fe (carbon to iron) ratio is a true measure of efficiency, as regards the use of this resource. There was a reduction from about 1.5 tons C per ton Fe in 1900 to a little less than 1 ton per ton in 1950, or about 0.1 tons of carbon per ton of steel saved per decade. Total energy consumption for iron smelting has declined at almost the same rate, however. In 1900 the average was about 55 MJ/kg.

From 1953 to 1974 total exergy consumption per ton of steel declined by 35 percent (adjusted for the 1973 ratio of pig iron to crude steel) while the carbon rate (coke to iron) declined even more, by 45 percent. During that period fuel oil replaced some of the coke, while electric power consumption, for electric arc furnaces (EAFs) increased significantly (National Research Council National Academy of Sciences 1989). In 1973 the average exergy consumption was 20.5 GJ per tonne of steel in the US (with 36 percent EAF in that year), as compared to 18.5 GJ/t in Japan (30 percent EAF) and 24.5 GJ/t in Canada (Elliott 1991). The rate of improvement has certainly slowed since then, but final closure of the last open hearth furnaces and replacement of ingot casting by continuous casting has continued, as has the penetration of EAF scrap-melting furnaces as a share of the whole.

A recent study of the steel sector provides a useful update (de Beer 1998). A 'reference' integrated steel plant described in that study consumes a total of 22.6 GJ/t exergy inputs, of which 20.2 is coal and 1.87 is the exergy content of scrap.[18] Rolled steel output embodies 6.62 GJ/t, with other useful by-products from gas to tar and slag accounting for a further 4.28 GJ/t. The remaining 11.62 GJ/t is lost exergy. The second-law efficiency of such a plant would be very nearly 50 percent, counting salable by-products. Significant improvements are still possible, at least in terms of the primary product. The author expects future plants to achieve 12 GJ/t (with smaller by-product output, of course.) Of course EAF melting of scrap is much more exergy-efficient, current state-of-the art being around 7 GJ/t with near-term improvement potential to half of this, or 3.0 GJ/t.

Fairly detailed static (single-year) exergy analyses have been carried out for a number of major energy-consuming industries, including iron and steel, aluminum, copper, chlor-alkali, pulp and paper and petroleum refining. In second-law terms, the calculated second-law efficiencies based on 1970–72 data were as follows: iron and steel 22.6 percent, primary aluminum 13.3 percent,[19] cement production 10.1 percent and petroleum refining 9.1 percent (for example, Gyftopoulos et al. 1974; Hall et al. 1975; Ayres 1989c). The real question is how much improvement took place from 1900 to 1972.

If the 1974 performance was equivalent to a second-law efficiency of 22.6 percent – as noted above – the 1953 efficiency must have been about 14.5 percent and the efficiency in 1900 was probably between 9 and 10 percent, based on coke rates. If the best available technologies circa 1973 had been used, the second-law efficiencies would have been 35 percent for iron and steel, 12 percent for petroleum refining, 16.8 percent for aluminum and 17 percent for cement (Gyftopoulos et al. 1974). A 25 percent average efficiency for all high temperature industrial processes is probably a fair guess. Given a 20-year half-life for industrial plants (Landsberg et al. 1963; Salter 1960), it is probably safe to assume that the best-practice figures for 1975 became 'average' by 1995, due to incremental improvements and replacement of the last efficient facilities. If the overall second-law efficiency of the industrial sector's use of high temperature process heat was 25 percent in 1975, it is unlikely to be much better than that – perhaps 30 percent – in 2000. In countries industrializing from scratch (for example, South Korea), process efficiencies in recent years are likely to be a little higher, due to newer equipment.

Though exothermic in principle, pulp and paper manufacturing is a major energy consumer (2600 PJ in 1985 and 2790 PJ in 1994 – about 3 percent of the US national total). About half of the total energy (exergy) consumed was purchased electricity or fuel. The best short-term measure of progress in the pulp and paper industry is tons of paper output per unit of fuel (exergy) input. A similar measure would be applicable to the copper mining and smelting sector, which is also exothermic in principle (for sulfide ores). Unfortunately, we do not have reliable historical data for either of these industries. The major opportunity for future improvement is to make fuller use of the exergy content of the pulpwood feedstock, of which less than half (in mass terms) is incorporated in most grades of paper. (The exception is newsprint, which is made by a different process, known as mechanical pulping, that does not separate the cellulose from the hemi-cellulose and lignin fractions.)

For kraft (that is, 'strong') paper, the consumption of purchased energy per unit of output in the US has fallen more or less continuously, from 41.1 GJ per metric ton (air dried) in 1972 to 35.6 GJ/t in 1988 (Herzog and Tester 1991). Those improvements were largely triggered by the so-called 'oil crisis' of 1973–4, as well as environmental regulations on the disposal of so-called 'black liquor'. However, it is noteworthy that the state-of-the-art (best-practice) plant in 1988 consumed only 25 GJ/t or 70 percent as much energy as the average. Adoption of advanced technologies now being developed could bring this down to 18 GJ/t by 2010. At present, wet lignin waste is burned in a furnace for both heat and chemical recovery, but the first-law efficiency of that process is low (about 65 percent compared to 90 percent for a gas-fired furnace) (Herzog and Tester 1991). Gasification of the lignin waste followed by gas-turbine co-generation offers the potential of becoming self-sufficient in both heat and electricity (ibid).[20]

Significant process improvements have been recorded in the chemical industry. An example where a time series is available is high density polyethylene (HDPE). This plastic was first synthesized in the 1930s and is now one of the most important industrial materials. In the 1940s energy requirements were 18 MJ/kg, (= GJ/t) down to 11.5 MJ/kg in the 1950s. Improvements in compressors reduced this to 9.4 MJ/kg on average in the 1970s. But Union Carbide's UNIPOL process introduced in 1968 achieved 8.15 MJ/kg, which dropped to 4.75 MJ/kg in 1977 and 1.58 MJ/kg as of 1988 (Joyce 1991). The ten-fold reduction in energy requirements is one of the reasons why prices have fallen and demand has risen accordingly.

Nitrogen fixation is another example for which data are available. The electric arc process (circa 1905) required 250 GJ/t; the cyanamide process introduced a few years later (circa 1910) reduced this to something like 180 GJ/t. The Haber-Bosch ammonia synthesis process – the original version of the process now employed everywhere – achieved 100 GJ/t by 1920 (using coal as a feedstock) (Smil 2001, appendix K). Incremental improvements and increasing scale of production brought the exergy consumption down steadily: to 95 GJ/t in 1930, 88 GJ/t in 1940 and 85 GJ/t in 1950 (ibid.). Natural gas replaced coal as a feedstock subsequently, and the reciprocating compressors of the older plants were replaced by centrifugal turbo-compressors which enabled much higher compression ratios. By 1955 exergy requirements of the best plants had dropped to 55 GJ/t, and by 1966 it was down to 40 GJ/t. Global production soared, from 5 MMT in 1950 to around 100 MMT today. Since 1950 the decline in exergy cost has been more gradual, to 27 GJ/t in 1996 and 26 GJ/t in 2000 (ibid.). According to one author, the theoretical minimum for this process is 24.1 GJ/t (de Beer 1998, chapter 6). Smil states that the stoichiometric exergy requirement for the process is 20.9 GJ/t (Smil 2001). The latter implies that the second-law efficiency of ammonia synthesis rose from 8.3 percent in 1905 to over 77 percent in 2000. Clearly there is not much more room for improvement in this case.

Synthetic soda ash produced via the Solvay process is another documented case. The first plant (circa 1880) achieved 54.6 GJ/t. By 1900 this had fallen by 50 percent to 27 GJ/t and by 1912 is was down to 25 GJ/t. Then progress accelerated briefly during World War I and early postwar years. However, from 1925 to 1967, improvement was very slow (from 15 GJ/t to 12.9 GJ/t). Historical efficiency improvements for pulp and paper, ammonia, HDPE and soda ash are plotted in Figure 4.17, along with steel.

Extrapolating back to 1900 is always problematic. Except for the above examples, it is difficult to estimate an efficiency figure for 1920 or 1900, since for many industries there are virtually no time series data, at least

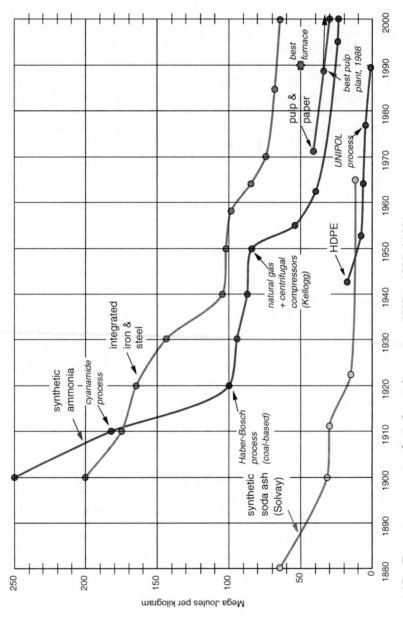

Figure 4.17 Exergy consumption by industrial processes (USA, 1880–2000)

in a convenient form. If one takes the efficiency improvement in the steel industry (roughly three-fold) as a model for the efficiency gains for high temperature heat elsewhere in manufacturing, it would follow that the average exergy efficiency of high temperature heat use in the industrial sector as a whole was around 9.5 percent in 1900. We make this assumption in Table 4.1 in Section 4.7.

As mentioned above, the second-law approach is also applicable to the use of direct heat for steam generation in the industrial sector and for space heating, water heating and cooking in the residential and commercial (R&C) sectors. The most optimistic assumption is 25 percent (American Physical Society et al. 1975; United States Congress Office of Technology Assessment 1983). A British study obtained a lower estimate of 14 percent (Olivier et al. 1983). The technology of boilers has not changed significantly over the years. The differences mainly depend on the temperature of the steam and the efficiency of delivery to the point of use. We think the lower estimate is more realistic. An important difference between this and most earlier (pre-1975) studies is that different measures of efficiency are used. The older studies used what is now termed first-law efficiency, namely the fraction of the chemical energy (enthalpy) of the fuel that is delivered to the furnace walls or the space to be heated.

Based on first-law analysis, in 1950 an open fireplace was about 9 percent efficient, an electric resistance heater was 16.3 percent efficient (allowing for 80 percent losses in the generating plant), synthetic 'town gas' was 31 percent efficient, a hand-fired coal furnace was 46 percent, a coal furnace with a stoker yielded 60 percent and a domestic oil or gas furnace gave 61 percent (Ayres and Scarlott 1952, table 12). Incidently, the authors calculated that a heat pump with a coefficient-of-performance of four would be 65 percent efficient. However, as noted earlier, if alternative ways of delivering the same amount of comfort to the final user are considered, the above efficiencies are too high. In 1950, space heating accounted for 42 percent of all exergy consumption in the residential and commercial sector, with cooking and hot water adding 2.5 and 3.2 percent respectively.

The APS summer study previously cited (American Physical Society et al. 1975) concluded that heat delivered by a conventional central oil or gas furnace to heat the rooms of a typical house to 70° F by means of hot water or hot air would correspond to a second-law efficiency of 6 percent, while the second-law efficiency for water heating was perhaps 3 percent. It made no estimate for cooking on a gas range, but similar arguments suggest that a 3 percent figure might be appropriate in this case too for 1970.

It is difficult to make a meaningful estimate for 1900, since the basic furnace technology from 1900 to 1970 changed very little, except that coal or coke were the fuels of choice in the early part of the century, whereas oil and gas had replaced coal by 1970. The oil burner or gas burner lost considerably less heat up the stack than its clumsy predecessor, and far less than a wood stove or open fireplace. We guess that the heating systems of 1970 were at least twice as efficient as those of 1900, in second-law terms. According to this logic, space heating systems in 1900 were probably 3 percent efficient in second-law terms.

A 'typical' wood-frame house in North America is poorly insulated and uses around eight times as much heat as a well-insulated one (Ayres 1989b). Assuming houses in 1900 were essentially uninsulated, while houses in 1970 were moderately (but not well) insulated, it appears that the overall efficiency of space heating in 1970 was something like 2 percent, whereas houses in 1900 achieved only 0.25 percent at best. It is interesting to note that the overall efficiency of space heating in the US by 1960 had already improved by a factor of seven-plus since 1850, due mainly to the shift from open fireplaces to central heating (Schurr and Netschert 1960, p. 49 footnote). However, we have to point out that most of the gains were due to systems optimization, rather than increased efficiency at the equipment level.

Recent investments in heating system modernization, insulation, upgrading of windows and so forth may conceivably have doubled the 1970 figure by now. Progress since 1970 has been slightly accelerated (thanks to the price increases of the 1970s), but space heating systems are rarely replaced in existing buildings, which have an average life expectancy of more than 50 years, based on average economic depreciation rates of 1.3 percent per annum (Jorgenson 1996). The penetration of new technologies, such as solar heating and electric heat pumps, has been very slow so far.

4.6   SECONDARY WORK

Secondary work refers to further conversion steps by means of which electric power produces either mechanical work (via motor drives) or high temperature heat, including electrolytic reduction processes, electric furnaces, air-conditioning and heat pumps, refrigeration or microwave cooking. The last four are thermodynamic insofar as they involve heat removal and heat delivery, respectively. These are types of work comparable to primary work or quasi-work and measurable in the same units, whence efficiency measures (output over input) are dimensionless numbers, as before. The efficiency of secondary work is, of course, the ratio of final work to primary work (for example, electric power) input.

Service output per unit of work refers to gains in the quantity of a specific product or service per unit of exergy or work input. The output should be a measurable intermediate or final service, such as transport (for example, tonne-km or passenger-km per unit of fuel), refrigeration (heat removal per kWh) or lighting (lumens per watt). These gains can be measured by index numbers with reference to a given year, but they are not thermodynamic efficiency measures.

Indeed, published data often refer to secondary work measures rather than primary work performed. In some cases, as will be seen, the secondary or tertiary service outputs from a unit of work have increased much more than the primary exergy efficiency *per se*. In this section we discuss secondary (downstream) services performed by electric power and mechanical power for transportation purposes.

Electrolytic reduction of aluminum, magnesium, chlorine and a few other materials are good examples of secondary work. Aluminum production from aluminum oxide (alumina) is a well-documented example. The Hall-Heroult electrolytic process for reducing aluminum oxide to metallic aluminum, discovered simultaneously in the early 1880s by Hall in the US and Heroult in France, was industrially established by the turn of the century. The electrolytic smelting step required 50 kWh/kg of aluminum when first introduced in 1888 and 30 kWh/kg in 1900. Average power consumption fell more or less gradually thereafter from 26 kWh/kg in 1935 to 20 kWh/kg in 1956, according to US government statistics (which included magnesium) (Schurr and Netschert 1960, table A-28). Exergy requirements of new cells had dropped to 25 kWh/kg already by 1905, however, and continued downward to 18 kWh/kg in 1940, with virtually no further improvement until 1960, then a further drop to 14 kWh/kg in 1970 and 13 kWh/kg by 1990 (Spreng 1988).

The 'practical limit' for electrolytic reduction is said to be 5 kWh/kg and the thermodynamic limit is 2.89 kWh/kg (Atkins et al. 1991). To this, of course, must be added the consumption of carbon anodes. The anode carbon is petroleum coke, which is a by-product of petroleum refining, or a synthetic version made from powdered coal and coal tar, amounting to 48 MJ/kg. About 0.44 kg of carbon is used per kg of aluminum, down slightly from earlier decades. It is clear that the potential for future efficiency gains is now rather limited. The above does not take into account the energy consumed in the prior bauxite calcination stage (currently 3 MJ/kg), where improvements in recent years have been modest. The practical limit for this process is said to be 1.75 GJ/t and the thermodynamic limit 0.75 GJ/t (ibid.). Despite historical improvements, considering all steps in the process, aluminum is still far more energy intensive (150 MJ/kg) than either steel (20–25 MJ/kg) or even copper (40–50 MJ/kg).

Comparing 1984 with 1972, US electric power utilities had to pay 240 percent more for oil and 385 percent more for gas (Blair 1986). Electricity prices rose with fuel costs, and a general recession in the mid-1970s pushed electricity demand growth down sharply, from 7 percent a year throughout the 1950s and 1960s, to only 2.5 percent per annum at the end of the 1970s (Blair 1986). In response, the use of electricity generally in the chemical industry became much more efficient in the immediate post-1973 period. For example, the electrical intensity of the US chemical industry, measured in terms of electricity consumption per unit of production, as measured by the Federal Reserve Board (FRB) Index, dropped from 570 in 1977 to 506 in 1981, a decline of 11 percent in just four years (Burwell and Reister 1985, table D-1). Even more dramatic changes were recorded in other countries. For instance, the chemical industry of East Germany (DDR) reduced its electric power consumption by 17 percent per unit output (in constant monetary terms) during those same years (1977–81) and by 35 percent from 1973 through 1983 (Schirmer 1986). Comparable reductions were achieved in Japan. Unfortunately, we know of no study covering the whole 20th century, or the whole postwar period.

Metal cutting, drilling and grinding, an important subclass of electric machine drive, is another example of secondary work. For instance, data from Sweden's Sandvik steel company record the number of minutes required to machine a steel axle of standard dimensions. From 660 minutes in 1860 it dropped to 100 minutes in 1895, mainly due to the introduction of Taylor-Mushet 'high speed' tungsten-steel cutting tools. Tungsten carbide-cutting tools cut the time to 40 minutes by 1916. By 1980 the time required was down to five minutes or less (Ayres et al. 1991). Higher rotational speeds of cutting tools were made possible by harder materials – starting with silicon carbide (carborundum) in the 1880s and synthetic abrasives like corundum, to tungsten carbide to synthetic diamond coatings – have accounted for most of this progress. In the early years of the 20th century, rotational speeds were limited to a few hundred rpm. Today state-of-the-art machines operate at much higher speeds, up to a few thousand rpm.[21] Higher rotational speeds mean faster cutting with less heat loss and lower energy requirements. Unfortunately, we have no absolute baseline efficiency data for metal cutting.

Non-industrial motors driving pumps, compressors, washing machines, vacuum cleaners and power tools also account for quite a lot of electricity consumption in the residential and commercial sector. (It has been suggested that motors use as much as half of all electric power.) Air-conditioning and refrigeration in the residential and commercial sectors accounted for just under 23 percent of all electric power consumed in 1979, while cryogenic oxygen-separation plants for the steel industry and freezers in the fish and frozen food sectors must have added significantly to this total (Ayres et al. 2005).

The APS study cited earlier estimated second-law efficiencies of 4 percent for refrigerators and 5 percent for air-conditioners in 1970 (American Physical Society et al. 1975). Prior to 1970 electricity prices in constant dollars had declined continuously. But after 1972 energy prices (in current dollars) increased sharply, if only temporarily, and this triggered a considerable effort by industry, encouraged by government and consumer groups, to improve the performance of appliances. According to one source, refrigerators improved by 95 percent, freezers by 80 percent and air-conditioners by 30 percent, between 1972 and 1987 – due largely to regulatory and public concern with energy efficiency provoked by the 1973–4 'energy crisis' (McMahon 1991). Another source records even greater progress in residential refrigerator efficiency, from 1726 kWh per year in 1972 to 690 kWh per year in 1993 (EPRI 1993). Even larger gains are possible (and have been achieved in Scandinavia and Japan).[22] These gains are mainly attributable to the use of more efficient compressors and better insulation. Note that, even if the efficiencies of earlier models have increased by 50 percent since 1970, this would only bring average efficiency up to 7 percent or so, which suggests quite a large potential for further gains.

As regards air-conditioning, it must be pointed out that the amount of cooling required (for a given climate) is a function of the design of the building. A very well insulated building can get by with very little supplementary cooling, even in a hot climate, by a variety of means, including very thick walls, reflective exterior surfaces and thermal barriers in windows. Unfortunately, we have no data on the absolute minimum cooling requirements of a structure, so no estimate of absolute end-use efficiency can be made. Nor is there any evidence that residential or commercial buildings have significantly improved in terms of thermal design since 1970.

Electric light can be regarded as another sort of secondary work. Electric light accounted for between 20 and 25 percent of US electric power output from 1900 to 1972, but dropped to 17 percent by 1980 and 16 percent as of the year 2000 (Ayres et al. 2005). Incandescent lights with tungsten filaments improved from about 1.5 percent in 1900 to 5 percent while fluorescent lamps introduced in the 1930s and halogen lamps used for street lighting provided further gains (up to 31 percent for the best compact fluorescent lamps) (Nordhaus 1994). Evidently the rate of progress from 1920 through 1990 – while electricity prices were steadily declining – was very slow. However, the events of the 1970s triggered changes, especially the diffusion of compact fluorescent lighting. This will sharply increase the apparent rate of improvement over the next decade or two. Unfortunately, we have no data on the average performance of installed lighting systems at the national level.[23]

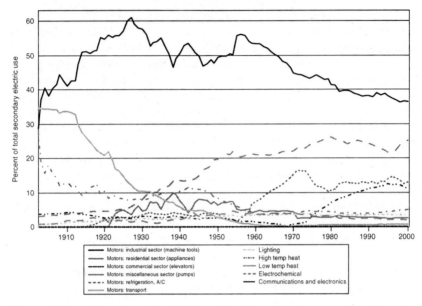

Figure 4.18   Secondary electrical work by function as percentage of total secondary electrical work (USA, 1902–2000)

   To calculate the overall efficiency of electric power usage, we need to weight the individual efficiency numbers by the corresponding shares of total electricity use, shown in Figure 4.18 (Ayres et al. 2005). The individual efficiencies of different electric power uses since 1900, as best we can estimate them, are plotted in Figure 4.19, taken from the same study. Evidently the sharp gains in some applications, such as lighting and electronics, have been vitiated or compensated by significant increases in low efficiency uses, such as low temperature heating, and air-conditioning. Overall efficiency remained roughly constant, around 55 percent since 1900, although there has been some improvement since 1975, partly attributable to higher prices in the period just after the oil embargo of 1973–4. It is not easy to make precise calculations, since the available data reflect best-available technology rather than averages. Also, we do not know the efficiency with which electric motors and other intermediate devices are utilized in some applications. Metal cutting, for instance, appears to be very inefficient in absolute terms. For pumping and other such uses, there is also reason to believe that system optimization offers major potential gains (von Weizsaecker et al. 1998). In short, we lack a baseline figure for the end-use efficiency with which electricity is used in the US economy.

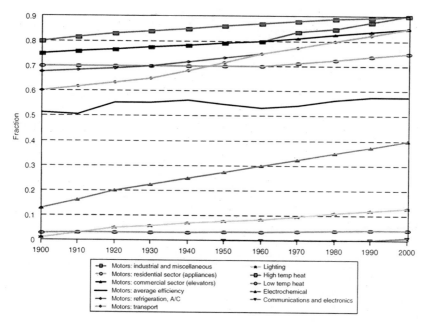

Figure 4.19   *Efficiencies in performance: secondary work from electricity by function (USA, 1900–2000)*

The service performed by transportation systems, such as motor vehicles and railroads, is to move people and goods from one place to another. A typical passenger car today weighs around 1000 kg, whereas passengers (plus baggage, if any) typically weigh only 100–200 kg, depending on occupancy. The measure commonly used is vehicle-km traveled, rather than passenger (or payload) km traveled. The latter would make more sense and would correspond better to measures used in bus, rail and air transport modes.

We can roughly equate vehicle-km traveled with work performed by motor vehicles, which implies (for the purpose of this discussion) that overall exergy conversion efficiency for all motor vehicles is roughly proportional to average mpg (or inversely proportional to the European measure, liters per 100 km). The proportionality constant is uncertain, but normalizing to 1989 (15.9 mpg, 8.33 percent efficiency) we estimate efficiency to be mpg times 0.52, as shown in Figure 4.20. It is important to emphasize that, in using mpg as a surrogate efficiency measure, we effectively assume that the objective is to move the vehicle itself, as well as the passengers and baggage it carries. The difference between exergy conversion efficiency and payload efficiency is not discussed here.

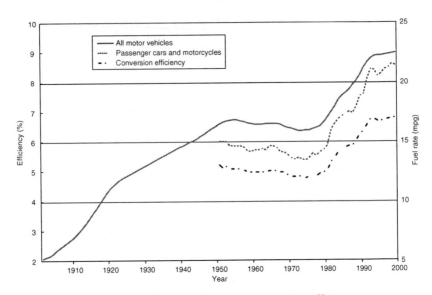

Figure 4.20   Vehicle fuel rates and energy conversion efficiency

The average fuel economy of the US vehicle fleet increased significantly from the early 1970s until about 1988, entirely thanks to government regulation, as already mentioned. The CAFÉ standard fuel economy standards were met primarily by reducing average vehicle size and weight (by using thinner steel sheet and more plastic). The average weight of new cars dropped by 1000 lb (450 kg) from 1970 to 1979, and by 600 lb (275 kg) from 1976 to 1979. The net effect was to increase system and payload efficiency, rather than thermodynamic efficiency. However, if the overall (primary and tertiary) efficiency of producing VMT from fuel is 15 percent (probably high) and if passengers plus luggage weigh (on average) 200 kg in a 1000 kg car – which is also optimistic – the real *payload efficiency* is only $0.2 \times 0.15 = 3$ percent or so. We have no quantitative information on how payload efficiency may have changed, if it has, although it is clear that there is still plenty of room left for future improvements.

On the other hand, for trucks which carry cargo, the mpg is lower (5.6 mpg in 1972; 6.0 mpg in 1990), but payload efficiency is significantly higher than for cars, probably as much as 75 percent for a fully loaded heavy truck. However, conventional wisdom has it that trucks typically operate at half capacity, mainly due to empty return trips. Unfortunately, we have no basis to estimate either absolute efficiency or improvements in recent decades, if any.

In the case of railroads the traditional performance measure is ton-mile or metric ton-km. From 1920 to 1950 the improvement by this measure was three-fold, most of which was due to the replacement of coal-fired steam locomotives by diesel-electric or electric locomotives. This substitution began in the 1930s but accelerated after World War II because diesel engines were far more fuel-efficient – probably by a factor of five[24] – and also required significantly less maintenance. But from 1950 to 1960 the service output (measured in vehicle-km traveled) per unit exergy input quadrupled and from 1960 to 1987 there was a further gain of over 50 percent (United States Department of Highway Statistics Bureau of Transportation Statistics 1994). The overall performance increase from 1920 to 1987 by this measure (tonne-km per unit of fuel input) was around 20-fold. In 1920 US railways consumed 122 million tonnes of coal, which was 16 percent of the nation's energy supply. By 1967 the railways' share of national energy consumption had fallen to 1 percent and continued to decline thereafter (United States Department of Highway Statistics Bureau of Transportation Statistics 1994; Summers 1971).

It is obvious that much of the improvement since 1950 has occurred at the system level. One of the major factors was that trucks took over most of the short-haul freight carriage while cars and buses took most of the passengers, leaving the railroads to carry bulk cargos over long distances at (comparatively) high and constant speeds and with much less switching – which is very exergy-intensive. Under these conditions, the work required to move a freight train is reduced because rolling friction and air resistance are minimized, while work required for repeated accelerations and decelerations was sharply reduced or eliminated.

Another factor behind the gains was that the work required to overcome air and rolling resistance had been reduced significantly by straightening some of the rights of way, improving couplings and suspensions, and introducing aerodynamic shapes. A third source of gain was increasing power-to-weight ratios for locomotives; locomotives in 1900 averaged 133 kg/kW. By 1950 this had fallen to about 33 kg/kW and by 1980 to around 24 kg/kW (Larson et al. 1986). The lighter the engine, the less power is needed to move it (this is an instance of true dematerialization contributing to reduced exergy consumption). If the railways in 1987 were achieving 30 percent thermal efficiency (almost certainly an overestimate), and if the coal-fired steam locomotives of 1920 were averaging 7 percent (for an overall factor of four and a fraction), then an additional factor of five or so was achieved by increasing system efficiency in other ways. In effect, the work required to haul rail cargos has declined dramatically since 1960, but the exergy input required per unit of mechanical work done has hardly changed since then.

In the transportation domain, fuel consumption per unit of service output by new passenger cars (measured in vehicle-km traveled) nearly halved between 1970 and 1989, thanks mainly to the CAFÉ standards. But for the motor vehicle fleet as a whole (including trucks) the end-use efficiency improvement since 1970 has probably been about 30 percent.

4.7   PUTTING IT TOGETHER: TOTAL PRIMARY AND SECONDARY WORK

Considering both primary and secondary work, we have arrived at something like Table 4.1. This table incorporates numerous assumptions, of course. The most surprising conclusion is that the exergy efficiency of transportation probably peaked around 1960, when gasoline engines (in the US automobile fleet) operated at higher compression ratios, and wasted much less power on accessories than is true today. Increased fleet average fuel economy since 1970 (discussed later) is not attributable to thermodynamic efficiency improvements at the conversion/transfer level, but to systems optimization. Much the same can be said of improvements in the utilization of heat. Improved performance in domestic and commercial space heating has been due mainly to better insulation and better design. However, since insulation is a normal method of improving heat economy in thermodynamic systems of all kinds, we take it into account here.

The end-use allocation by type of work by fossil fuels for the US and Japan were shown above in Figures 4.4a and 4.4b. We can calculate the total work done in each economy by multiplying the exergy consumed by each major category of end-use (work) by the average efficiency with which each type of work, both primary and secondary (electrical), is produced (for example, Table 4.1). Source data are too extensive to reproduce in this book, but they can be found in an earlier publication (Ayres et al. 2003). The estimated efficiencies by type of work are depicted in Figures 4.21a and 4.21b for the US and Japan, respectively. Major differences between the two countries are (1) that biomass plays a greater role in the US than Japan and (2) that hydro-electricity – which is very efficient – dominated Japanese electric-power generation during the first half of the 20th century, whereas it was never the dominant source of electric power in the US.

The total useful work done by the two countries is shown in Figure 4.22. Comparing total work output with total exergy input (including phytomass), we obtain the aggregate technical efficiency of exergy (resource) conversion to work in the US and Japanese economies, since 1900 as shown in Figure 4.23. In both countries, the curves are almost monotonically increasing, as one would expect. The overall thermodynamic efficiency of the Japanese economy, as estimated by the same method, is higher than the US case.

Table 4.1 Average exergy efficiency of primary work (percent)

Year	Electric power generation and distribution	Other mechanical work, e.g. auto transport	High temperature industrial heat (steel)	Medium temperature industrial heat (steam)	Low temperature space heat	Total secondary electrical efficiency
1900	3.8	3	7	5	0.25	0.52
1910	5.7	4.4				0.505
1920	9.2	7				0.55
1930	17.3	8				0.55
1940	20.8	9				0.56
1950	24.3	9				0.54
1960	31.3	9				0.53
1970	32.5	8	20	14	2	0.54
1980	32.9	10.5				0.56
1990	33.3	13.9	25	20	3	0.575

Source: Ayres et al. (2003).

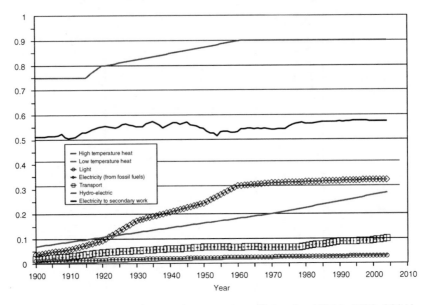

Figure 4.21a   Energy (exergy) conversion efficiencies (USA, 1900–2004)

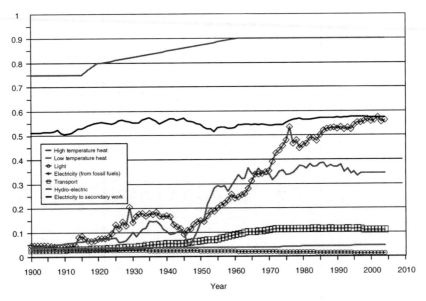

Figure 4.21b   Energy (exergy) conversion efficiencies (Japan, 1900–2004)

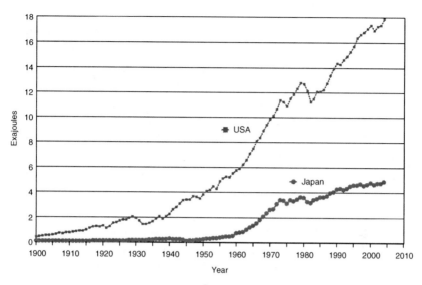

Figure 4.22   Useful work (U) for the USA and Japan, 1900–2004

Figure 4.23   Aggregate efficiencies for the USA and Japan, 1900–2004

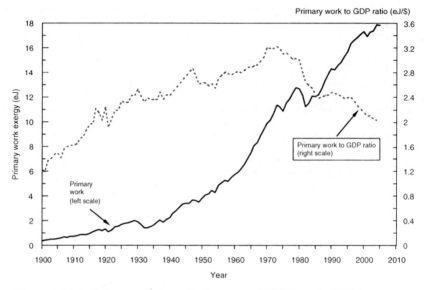

Figure 4.24a   Primary work and primary work/GDP ratio (USA,
                1900–2005)

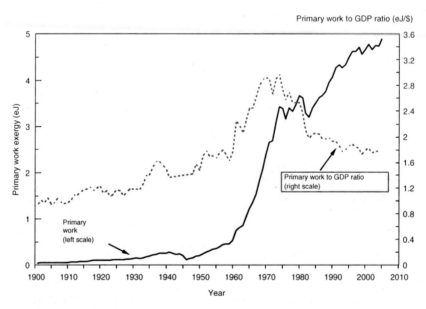

Figure 4.24b   Primary work and primary work/GDP ratio (Japan,
                1900–2005)

The work/GDP ratio for the US and Japan are also shown in Figures 4.24a and 4.24b, for the case in which biomass exergy is included. We note with interest that, whereas the exergy/GDP ratio does not exhibit a pronounced 'inverted-U' shape, when biomass is taken into account (as noted in Chapter 3), the work/GDP ratio does exhibit such a pattern, a sharp change of slope, with a peak in the years 1973–4. It is tempting to seek an economic interpretation of this peak, although it would lead us astray from the subject of this book.

NOTES

1. The first steam engines were used for pumping water from mines, an application where horses had previously been used. This enabled a direct comparison to be made. Ever since then power has been measured in terms of horsepower or a metric equivalent.
2. This particular conversion process was first analysed in detail by the French engineer, Sadi Carnot. The maximum efficiency of an idealized heat engine operating between two infinite reservoirs is a function only of the temperature difference between the two reservoirs. Real (non-ideal) engines are necessarily less efficient than the Carnot limit. Carnot's work was the real basis of modern thermodynamics.
3. Perhaps the best example comes from the Ford Foundation Energy Policy Study in the early 1970s, namely Gyftopoulos et al. (1974).
4. Obviously a lot of jobs, such as plowing and caring for animals, involved plenty of muscular effort as well as some brainpower. Our division is admittedly arbitrary. However, it is fairly clear that a modest revision of our argument would not make much difference overall.
5. The number of horses and mules, by year, in the US is given in United States Bureau of the Census (1975, tables K-201, 203).
6. United States Bureau of the Census (1975, table S 1-14, p. 818). Electric-power generation gradually became by far the dominant use of coal, as it is today (United States Bureau of the Census 1975, tables M-113, 114, p. 591 and S-100, p. 826; and United States Department of Energy annual).
7. The basic sources of data are United States Bureau of the Census (1975, M-162-177, p. 596), and United States Department of Energy (annual).
8. Much of the material from this section has been taken from Ayres et al. (2003).
9. That motors can be 80 or 90 percent efficient does not mean that they are in practice. Studies of individual plants have discovered that efficiencies tend to be much lower – more like 60 percent (and as low as 30 percent in extreme cases) (Lovins 1977).
10. Btu refers to British thermal units, a measure still widely used in industry and government. For instance, the most common measure of energy in US statistics is the 'quad', which is defined as 1015 Btus. The more usual metric unit of energy is kiloJoules (kJ) and 1 Btu = 1.055 kJ. One kilowatt hour (kWh) of electric energy is equivalent to 3600 kJ or 3412 Btu. The conversion efficiency is the ratio of output to input, in consistent units. Thus 3412 Btu divided by 90 000 Btu corresponds to an efficiency of about 3.6 percent.
11. The 'rebound effect' has recently preoccupied energy conservation advocates. The point is that efficiency gains do not yield reductions in energy use if cost/price reductions result in demand increases that overcompensate for the efficiency gains. This phenomenon can undermine attempts to achieve conservation through higher efficiency (Saunders 1992; Brookes 1979, 1990, 1992, 1993; Khazzoom 1980, 1987; Herring 1996, 1999; Lovins 1977).

12. The following analysis is taken largely from a report from Ford Motor Co. (Kummer 1974) and an American Physical Society (APS) summer study held in 1975 (American Physical Society et al. 1975).

13. Turbo-chargers were not considered by the APS study because they were rare at the time. Their principal advantage is to increase passing power at high rpms, rather than to improve fuel economy *per se*. However since a turbo-charged 100 hp engine may have the same performance at high rpm as a non-turbo-charged 150 hp engine, the net result could be a reduction in the size of engine needed to achieve a given performance level. This would improve low-speed fleet average fuel economy somewhat. Again, hp is the standard unit for automotive power in America, and (surprisingly) it is also used in Europe.

14. In 1972 US passenger vehicles averaged 13.5 mpg (United States Department of Energy annual), which – based on 8 percent thermodynamic efficiency – suggests that an idealized vehicle of the same size and weight capable of converting fuel exergy into work at 100 percent efficiency would have achieved a fuel rate of 165 mpg. (The European measure of fuel economy, liters per 100 km, is unfamiliar to Americans, and *vice versa*. However, the American unit is proportional to efficiency, whereas the European version is inversely proportional.)

15. In terms of vehicle-miles per gallon, the average in 1920 was 13.5, declining slightly to 13.2 in 1930 (as cars became heavier) and increasing to a peak of 13.8 in 1940, probably due to a Depression-era preference for smaller cars. From 1940 to 1970 the mpg declined steadily to 12.2 (Summers 1971).

16. This implies that 100 percent conversion efficiency would correspond to only 125–35 mpg. This seems rather low, considering the fact that the most fuel-efficient cars on the market today (2002) achieve 60 mpg and proposals for radically new vehicles capable of up to 100 mpg or more are not at all fanciful (for example, Goldemberg et al. 1987a, 1987b; Bleviss 1988a, 1988b; Lovins 1996; Lovins et al. 1996).

17. The Pollution Prevention Division of the USEPA prepared a graphical diskette document in 1990 entitled 'United States Energy System' using 1989 data. It defined 'useful work' as energy (exergy) dissipated in the brakes of the vehicles (1.6 Q). Fuel input to highway transportation was 19 Q. This corresponds to just 8.3 percent efficiency. The rest of the input energy went to idling in traffic jams (3Q), waste heat out of the tailpipe (9.5 Q), engine friction and parasitic accessories (2.4 Q), driveline friction (0.5 Q), and overcoming aerodynamic drag (1.6 Q).

18. A recent study for IISI (International Iron and Steel Institute) by Ecobilan (1998, p. 46) gives the average primary energy consumption as 24.98 GJ/kg for hot-rolled coil. The range was from 20.7 to 30.4.

19. As noted above, aluminum smelting is an electrolytic process (as are copper refining and chlor-alkali production).

20. Much the same argument can be made about the agricultural and food-processing sectors, which currently generate large amounts of combustible organic wastes, such as bagasse from sugar cane production, while consuming equally large amounts of fossil fuels (in other locations) for direct heat. There is considerable interest now in gasifying these wastes and using them as fuel for small gas turbines to generate electric power (Williams et al. 1992).

21. The increased drill speeds are very evident in dentists' offices.

22. The Swedish Electrolux company produced models back in 1958 consuming 3.8 kWh/24 hrs to cool a volume of 100 liters. In 1962 this had been reduced to 1 kWh/24 hrs. By 1993 the company was making refrigerators that consumed barely 0.1 kWh/24 hrs per 100 liters cooled (data from the Electrolux company).

23. The efficiency of light production is not the whole story, of course. Much more can also be done to increase end-use efficiency by distributing light where it is needed. A 15 W light focused directly on the page of a book is as effective as a 100 W light several feet away without a reflector. We have no data on the absolute efficiency with which electric light is currently being utilized. However, it is clear that further gains can be achieved

by optimum placement of lighting, better use of reflective surfaces and, incidentally, by automatic controls that turn off lights when people leave the room.

24.   According to a study published in 1952, diesel engines can perform ten times as much work as steam engines in switching operations, five times as much in freight service and three times as much in passenger service (Ayres and Scarlott 1952, p. 311). The overall gain might have been about a factor of five.

5.   Economic growth theories

5.1   INTRODUCTION

Although GDP is widely used by economists, its value as an indicator of development or wealth creation has been widely criticized. Two points of criticism are of particular relevance. First, GDP doesn't measure sustainable growth, as a country may achieve a temporary high GDP by over-exploiting renewable natural resources. Second, extraction and consumption of non-renewable resources is counted as national income and not (as it should be) as depreciation of capital assets (Repetto et al. 1989; Repetto 1992; Solorzano et al. 1991).

A third criticism of the GDP concept is that it does not subtract activity that produces no net welfare gain, but merely compensates for negative externalities. For example, if a factory pollutes a river, the cost of cleanup adds to the GDP but adds nothing to social welfare. Crime increases the demand for police, which adds to GDP. War destroys people and property, but the military expenditure adds to GDP, as does the postwar reconstruction. This concept is summarized by the self-explanatory titled 'parable of the broken window', created by Frederic Bastiat (Bastiat 2006 [1850]) in his 1850 essay *That Which is Seen and That Which is Not Seen*[1] to illuminate the notion of 'opportunity costs'. It is important to note that in our examples cleaning up the river, catching criminals or winning the war may provide no net (new) benefits, but can constitute important opportunity costs, diverting funds from other more 'productive' (wealth-creating) investments.

Additional concerns are that GDP, as a measure of economic activity, fails to measure well-being and standard of living accurately and doesn't take into account the 'black' (cash) economy, bartering, volunteer work, organized crime, or un-monetized work, such as unpaid childcare, household work by women, do-it-yourself construction or repair work, or subsistence agriculture. There are many more omissions in 'developing' countries, whence international GDP comparisons are potentially misleading. Finally, GDP does not provide information about the disparity of wealth distribution within a country. Certain groups of people within a country might not be benefiting from its economic activity. A high GDP could be the result of a case of a few very wealthy people contributing to the economy, while most of its citizens live at or below the subsistence level. Clearly then, well-being does not necessarily increase as the GDP increases, and we cannot assume that the quality of life is improving just because more money is earned and spent.[2]

Notwithstanding these criticisms, justified though they are, we continue to utilize GDP as a measure of economic activity – if not a measure of welfare – on the simple ground that 'everybody does it'. Actually there is a better reason: resource consumption, and waste, are intimately related to economic activity of any sort, irrespective of whether it is 'productive' in the sense of creating net new wealth, or simply digging holes and filling them in. Our focus in this book is on the growth of GDP (as activity), not welfare. Limited time and mental resources incline us to let others worry about the vexing problem of how to correct the deficiencies of GDP as a measure of well-being.

In this chapter we expand on the idea that the primary missing ingredient in growth theory (and for that matter in much of macroeconomic theory) is the role of natural resources, materials, energy (exergy) and a thermodynamic quantity known as *useful work*. It is also curious, in our view, that most neoclassical growth models assume a uni-directional causality, namely that natural resource consumption and use are strictly determined by the level of economic activity, while simultaneously assuming that increasing resource consumption – and its consequences, including declining costs of extraction and processing – do not affect economic growth in return. The origins of physical production in the neoclassical paradigm remain unexplained. The only endogenous driving variables in the original Solow model and its variants were accumulations of abstract labor and abstract capital, plus an exogenous driver variously called 'technological progress' or 'total factor productivity'. In more recent models, the exogenous driver has been endogenized as 'knowledge' or 'human capital', otherwise undefined or quantified. The possibility of a 'virtuous circle' or positive feedback cycle involving the exploitation and conversion of natural resources has, up to now, been neglected.

It must be acknowledged that we see no useful role in this book for optimal – consumption-maximizing – growth theories, for several reasons noted in Chapter 1. Quite apart from criticisms of the usual intertemporal discounting assumption, we distrust the assumption that the economy is always in or very near equilibrium. Nor, notwithstanding 'rational expectations', is the real economy necessarily always in or near a long-term optimal trajectory. In fact, thanks to path-dependence and 'lock-in', there is every reason to believe that the current US economy, and that of the industrialized countries, built as it is on intensive use of fossil hydrocarbon, is nowhere near a sustainable long-term trajectory. Surely the optimal long-term trajectory in these circumstances, must be one that minimizes waste (entropy) generation. That would seem to imply approaching a steady-state similar in concept to the ideas of Herman Daly (1973). However, the implications of such a steady-state would take us too far from the subject of this book, which is economic growth.

Meanwhile, Pigou's observation about the inherent myopia of humans with regard to planning for the future (Pigou 1920) is thoroughly exemplified by the behavior of governments, especially with respect to climate warming. Optimality depends in a fundamental way on the choice of objective function and discount rate. What is optimal for a given nation with a given technology at a given moment in time may not be optimal the next moment, due to unexpected technological or socio-political change. We prefer a semi-empirical approach, with some theoretical support, as will be seen.

5.2   PHYSICAL CONSTRAINTS: THE SECOND LAW OF THERMODYNAMICS

The second law of thermodynamics is commonly known as the 'entropy law'. It states, in effect, that spontaneous processes in isolated systems always tend toward long-run thermodynamic equilibrium. In simple terms, it means that no energy transformation process that goes spontaneously in one direction can be reversed without some expenditure of available energy, or *exergy*. This applies, incidentally, to materials-recycling processes, a point emphasized (though somewhat misunderstood) by the late Nicholas Georgescu-Roegen (Georgescu-Roegen 1971).

The essence of the law is that every non-reversible process tends to increase the degree of disorder in the universe. Another way of saying it is that all processes tend to decrease gradients; for example, between high and low temperature regions, or between high and low concentrations of substances, densities, pressures, electric charges and so on. In other words, the universe is a great homogenizer. Many industrial processes, however, separate different substances or create greater temperature, density or pressure differences. The second law allows this to happen, locally, but subject to the rule that local order can only be increased at the cost of increasing global disorder. (Commonly this occurs by burning fossil fuels and dissipating the combustion products.)

In more precise technical language, the second law implies that there exists a non-decreasing function of thermodynamic state variables, known as *entropy*. This function is defined for every thermodynamic system and subsystem. The entropy for any subsystem reaches a maximum when that subsystem reaches thermodynamic equilibrium with its surroundings (the system).[3] Similarly, there exists a measure of potentially available work (exergy) that is also defined and computable for all systems that are in local (internal) equilibrium. Energy is a conserved quantity. Exergy is not conserved; exergy is destroyed (lost) whenever a system performs physical work.

On the earth, where we live, thermodynamic equilibrium is a far distant static state of nature. Nevertheless, entropy is still a definable variable for every subsystem – such as a mass stream – although exergy is not defined for non-equilibrium situations. Changes in entropy can be calculated quantitatively for every 'event' in the physical world. In fact, it has been argued that the 'potential entropy' of products and waste residuals is a general – albeit imperfect – measure of potential environmental disturbance resulting from human economic activities (Ayres et al. 1993; Martinás and Ayres 1993).

However, in addition to the possibility of developing a general measure of potential harm to the environment, thermodynamic variables such as entropy and exergy also must satisfy explicit balance conditions. In particular, the exergy content of process inputs must be equal to the exergy lost in a process plus the exergy content of process outputs. Exergy lost in the process is converted into entropy. There is a balance equation for entropy, as well: the entropy of process inputs must also be equal to the entropy of process outputs *minus* the entropy generated within the process.

The above statements are probably not meaningful for most economists. They are included here only for the sake of completeness. In any case, computational details need not concern us here. All that really matters is that *entropy and exergy balance conditions constitute effective constraints on possible process outcomes*. If these conditions are violated – as in the case of the once sought-after 'perpetual motion machine' – the process or change cannot occur.

We note in passing that the simplest textbook version of the economic system, illustrated in Figure 5.1a, consists of two agents, namely a producer and a consumer, exchanging abstract goods and services for money and labor. More complex models can be constructed; for instance by adding agents such as producers of capital goods or central banks to create money (Figure 5.1c). But the system thus envisaged remains a sort of perpetual motion machine. The missing element, of course, is the fact that goods (unlike money or services) have a material basis; and real physical materials are not self-produced nor are they consumed, in the literal sense. Material goods are derived from raw materials, and converted first into useful goods and ultimately into waste residuals (Ayres and Kneese 1969). Entropy is created during this process.

A. Closed static production consumption system

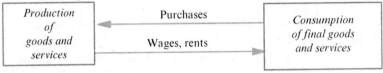

B. Closed dynamic production consumption system

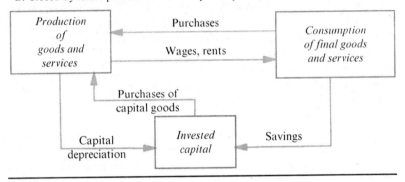

C. Open static production consumption system

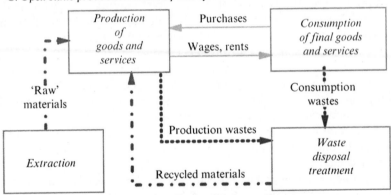

Figure 5.1   Production-consumption systems

As a practical matter, all *real, existing* materials-transformation processes must satisfy the second-law conditions, by definition. However, industrial systems can be modeled without explicit attention to second-law constraints. Moreover, in constructing hypothetical future industrial systems (based, for instance, on the substitution of biomass for fossil fuels), or modeling processes (such as the carbon cycle or the nitrogen cycle) in the natural world, under altered conditions, it is important to take second-law constraints into account.

The second law also has immediate importance for modelers in regard to energy analysis. Since energy is conserved in all transformation processes (the first law of thermodynamics), there is no way to compare two energy conversion processes without talking about thermodynamic (exergy) efficiency. Exergy efficiency is a simple way of expressing second-law constraints.

To recapitulate: the importance of the two laws of thermodynamics for economics is that they constrain possible physical processes. In particular, all material-transformation processes must satisfy both first-law (mass balance) and second-law (exergy and entropy balance) conditions. Hence economic models with physical implications should reflect these constraints.

5.3   THERMODYNAMIC CRITIQUE OF ECONOMICS

The first major economist to criticize neoclassical economics on thermodynamic grounds was Nicholas Georgescu-Roegen (hereafter G-R). He is best known for his 1971 book, *The Entropy Law and the Economic Process* (Georgescu-Roegen 1971). To summarize in the fewest possible words, his key point was that the economy is *not* a perpetual motion machine. In contrast to the standard neoclassical view, the economic system is a *materials-processing* system that converts high quality (low entropy) raw materials into goods and services, while disposing of, and dissipating, large and growing quantities of high entropy materials and energy waste (that is, waste heat). The economic systems of less developed countries are still driven by solar energy converted by photosynthetic plants into food and feed for human and animal workers. The economic systems of advanced industrial countries are driven mainly by exergy that was captured and accumulated hundreds of millions of years ago in the form of fossil hydrocarbons.

G-R understood, and emphasized many times, that economic goods are of material origin, while even immaterial services are almost all delivered by material goods or systems. It follows that processing raw materials into finished materials, machines, objects and structures (goods) requires a supply of available energy (that is, exergy). Moreover, the production of services, from transportation to communications to protection, also requires a flow of exergy. But for his unfortunate insistence on a so-called fourth law of thermodynamics (his phrase was 'matter matters'), he would probably have accepted the view of most physicists that exergy is the 'ultimate resource' (for example, Goeller and Weinberg 1976).

How then can exergy and the second law play a central role in economics? A few authors have invoked thermodynamic concepts as a way of conceptualizing the interface between the natural environment and the economic system, that is, the extraction, recycling and dissipation of resources (Berry 1972; Berry et al. 1978; Cleveland et al. 1984; Cleveland 1991; Costanza 1980, 1982; Costanza and Daly 1992; Daly 1986, 1992). This approach has become known as 'biophysical economics'. Others have probed the relationship between entropy, information and evolution (Prigogine et al. 1972; Prigogine and Stengers 1984; Faber 1985; Faber and Proops 1986, 1989; Faber et al. 1987, 1995; Ayres 1994a). Others have focused on the integration of natural capital into economic theory. Still others have tried to apply thermodynamic and economic ideas in ecosystem theory (Odum 1971, 1973; Hannon 1973; Kay and Schneider 1992; Brooks and Wiley 1986).

Possibly the most ambitious effort, so far, to integrate thermodynamics, economics and ecology has been by Matthias Ruth (1993). His perspective is summarized, in the introduction to his book, as follows:

> Economists' arguments – originating in the Walrasian tradition – suggest that under ideal conditions economic agents anticipate all relevant future costs associated with the use of matter and energy, and act rationally such that their choice of actions are reconciled on a complete set of current and future markets. At any given moment in time prices subsume all information on the availability of materials and energy, direct their optimal allocation, and induce the introduction of substitutes and the development of new technologies. Since substitution is assumed to be always possible, the scarcity of energy and materials is just a relative one. Thus the conclusions drawn from studies based on the Walrasian tradition are dominated by arguments of adjustment possibilities...
>   . . . Although during the past several decades economists have made tremendous advances in the relaxation of assumptions necessary to describe and analyze economy-environment interactions, physical interdependencies of the economic system and the environment receive attention only if they are associated with prices and costs.

We would have added the word 'explicitly' in front of the phrase 'associated with prices and costs'. It is precisely these physical interdependencies that Ruth seeks to clarify, as we do also. Here is another more recent view by Söllner (1997, p. 194):

> . . . environmental economics is faced with a profound dilemma: on the one hand, thermodynamics is highly relevant to environmental economics so that thermodynamic concepts seem to have to be integrated somehow to redress the deficiencies of neoclassical economics. On the other hand all approaches toward such an integration were found to be incomplete and unsatisfactory. On the basis of the neoclassical paradigm, thermodynamic constraints are able to take only the first law of thermodynamics into consideration, whereas the implications of the entropy law cannot be given due regard. But the radical alternative of an energy theory of value was even more of a failure . . .

The most perceptive, albeit tangential, critic of the treatment of energy in economics has been Philip Mirowski in his book, *More Heat than Light* (1989). Mirowski makes a case that some will find persuasive, namely that neoclassical economics suffers from 'physics envy'. The most obvious example of physics envy is the use in economics of the Lagrangian-Hamiltonian formalism for optimization, borrowed from 19th-century mechanics. Mirowski points out something that most economists are probably unaware of, namely that *the use of this optimization technique presupposes the existence of an underlying conservation law*. In 19th-century physics that law was the conservation of energy, as formulated in the 1870s. In neoclassical economics, the analog of energy is utility. Hence the implied conservation law in economics refers to utility, although the assumption is almost never made explicit. It is ironic that the actual laws of thermodynamics, which are highly relevant constraints upon the possible outcomes of real economic transactions, are neglected in neoclassical economics.

Looking more closely at how energy has been incorporated up to now into theories of production, and in particular production functions *per se*, we note an apparent inconsistency. Energy is not consumed. Yet, capital is consumed (via depreciation) and labor-hours are consumed. Why then include energy in the production function if it is a conserved quantity? The answer is, of course, that the terminology is misleading: the available part of energy (known as exergy) is *not* conserved at all.

In Chapter 3 we noted that exergy is defined as the maximum amount of useful work that can be extracted from a given amount of energy. It is sometimes regarded as a measure of energy quality. As energy is transformed into less useful forms according to the entropy law, exergy is destroyed. It is only the useful work from consumed exergy that is productive and that should therefore be included in the production function. Unused exergy, associated with material wastes released into the environment, including waste heat, is what we understand as pollution. At worst, pollution may be directly harmful to people's health; more commonly, the harm is indirect, as when fisheries are destroyed. To minimize harm requires countermeasures that cost money or inhibit economic growth. On a practical level, the problems of treating and disposing of waste exergy-containing materials, or waste heat, invariably require additional expenditures of exergy.

Perhaps the best example is that of atmospheric greenhouse gas (GHG) emissions – mainly carbon dioxide, but also methane, nitrous oxide and some other chemicals – from the combustion of fossil fuels and other industrial processes. There is no doubt that the useful work provided from 'energy carriers' such as fossil fuels has been central in providing the mechanical power to operate machines and drive processes that contribute to economic activity and growth. But GHGs also drive climate change.

Climate change has real costs, from droughts and floods to sea-level rise and, over time, the shifting of biomes from south to north, and loss of biodiversity.

But the carbon dioxide in the combustion products remains in the atmosphere for a century of more and when it is finally dissolved in the oceans, it remains in and acidifies the surface waters. Future costs to mankind are incalculable but potentially enormous. Current expenditures to limit carbon emissions are increasing, but represent only a small fraction of the eventual monetary (and exergy) requirements just to stabilize the climate and prevent further damage. The costs of reversal, that is, a return to the pre-industrial climate, are incalculable because the climate system is probably irreversible, at least by any means known, or at any tolerable cost.

For us, the answer to Söllner's discouraging assessment of the state of environmental economics (ibid.) is to incorporate exergy, and second-law efficiency, explicitly into an endogenous alternative to the neoclassical theory of economic growth. Indeed, the normative implication of Georgescu-Roegen's world-view, slightly re-stated, is that – thanks to second-law irreversibility – it is essential to utilize scarce exergy resources of all kinds (including metals and minerals) *more and more efficiently* in the future. In other words, increasing efficiency is the key to combining economic growth with long-term sustainability. Luckily, or perhaps unfortunately, depending on viewpoint, the efficiency with which raw material input (exergy) is currently converted into final services is still fairly low. Hence there is plenty of room for improvement, at least in the near and medium terms (Ayres 1989b). The long term must probably approach Herman Daly's elusive steady-state (Daly 1973).

It follows that, if the economy is a 'materials processor', as G-R evidently believed, and we concur, then useful work (exergy services) ought to be one of the factors of growth. We think that, after some grumbling, G-R would have agreed with the approach adopted hereafter.

5.4 THE TRANSITION FROM STATIC TO DYNAMIC THEORIES OF GROWTH

Most economic theory since Adam Smith has assumed the existence of a *static* equilibrium between supply and demand. It is this equilibrium that permits the beneficent functioning of Adam Smith's 'invisible hand'. The notion was successively refined by Ricardo, Say, Walras, Wicksell, Edgeworth, Pareto and others in the 19th and early 20th centuries.

In the 1870s Leon Walras formulated the postulate as a competitive (static) equilibrium in a multi-product system with stable prices where all product markets (and labor markets) 'clear', meaning no shortages and no surpluses (Walras 1874). He also postulated a sort of auction process, never really defined, known as *tatônnement*, by means of which prices are determined in a public manner, without individual pair-wise bargaining, such that all actors have perfect information. Walras' proposition that such an equilibrium is possible was widely accepted, though not proved until long after his death (Wald 1936; Arrow and Debreu 1954). Since then most economists have assumed that the real economy is always in, or very close to, a Walrasian equilibrium (for example, Solow 1970). We find this assumption troubling.

The Walrasian model applies only to exchange transactions, and does not attempt to explain either production or growth. Growth was and is, however, an obvious fact of economic life. It was attributed by theorists in the 19th century to labor force (that is, population) growth and capital accumulation. The latter was attributed to capitalist 'surplus' by Marx or savings by most of the marginalists. Apart from the work of Keynes (discussed below), the most influential models of the 1930s and 1940s were based on a formula attributed to Fel'dman (1928, 1964) equating the rate of growth of the economy to the savings rate divided by the capital-output ratio, or (equivalently) the ratio of annual savings to capital stock. The formula was 'rediscovered' by Roy Harrod and Evsey Domar (Harrod 1939; Domar 1946). These models, which emphasized the role of central planning, a relic of academic Marxism, dominated early postwar thinking about development economics.[4] For instance, a well-known 1950s-era text on the subject by an influential academic writer, Arthur Lewis, states without qualification that '. . . the central fact of development is rapid capital accumulation (including knowledge and skills with capital)' (Lewis 1955). *Development*, for most economists, is still just a euphemism for economic growth.

For a single-product, single sector model, modern growth theory actually began earlier with Frank Ramsey (1928). Ramsey assumed an economy producing a single all-purpose capital and consumption good produced by homogeneous labor and the all-purpose good itself. There is no role in the Ramsey model, or its successors, for physical laws such as conservation of mass, consumption of energy (exergy) or indeed for natural resources – or wastes and losses – of any kind. Note that the Ramsey model is a perpetual motion machine, as described at the beginning of this chapter.

In the closed multi-product, multi-sector static economic system described by Walras, it is only possible to generate a sort of growth process by mathematical sleight-of-hand. The trick is to assume – as in the Ramsey case – that every product is produced from other products made within the system, plus capital and labor services (Walras 1874; Cassel 1932 [1918]; von Neumann 1945 [1932]; Koopmans 1951). Von Neumann made the system 'grow' uniformly in all directions (sectors) – rather like a balloon – by the simple trick of increasing the output of all sectors equally. In his model, the rate of economic growth is determined by the allocation between investment and consumption. But all goods in his model are still abstract, immaterial and not subject to physical conservation laws. In fact, all goods in the model are derived from other goods in the model, which is not possible for material goods. There is no extraction of raw materials, consumption of energy (exergy) or disposal of wastes.

Abstract flows of money and services are presumably exempt from the physical law of conservation of mass-energy. But that law – the first law of thermodynamics – guarantees that waste residuals must be pervasive, just as the second (entropy) law guarantees that all economic processes are dissipative and irreversible and can only be maintained by a continuous flow of free energy (or exergy) from outside the system. Yet the neoclassical conceptualization implies that wastes and emissions – if they exist at all – are exceptional. The standard assumption is that they do not affect growth or decrease the wealth or welfare of society as a whole, and can be disposed of at no cost. We dissent sharply from that view.[5]

A brief digression on the influence of J.M. Keynes is appropriate here, although he is not regarded as a growth theorist today. However, he was probably the most influential economist of the first half of the 20th century and his influence has not entirely disappeared despite serious problems with his theories. His influence rests on his recommendation of deficit spending by governments to stimulate demand, during recessions, to be followed by a period of budgetary surplus to pay off the accumulated debt, during periods of high employment and inflationary pressure. The first half of his recommendation was adopted half-heartedly by the British government and whole-heartedly by Nazi Germany (though for other reasons), if not by the Roosevelt Administration's 'New Deal' in the US. We need not recapitulate the basis of Keynes' theory, except to note that he asserted (like Malthus) that under-consumption causes recession and unemployment. The debate still rages between so-called 'supply-siders' and 'demand-siders'. In the proverbial nutshell, the former group advocates tax cuts to stimulate investment while the latter group advocates deficit spending to create demand and thus increase employment.

We do not need to engage in this debate, nor to comment on the supply-side critique of Keynes, or his alleged misunderstanding of Say's law (Best 2007). However, there is no doubt that concern with unemployment was a primary feature of the Harrod-Domar models that dominated development economics during the two decades following Keynes' work (Domar 1946; Harrod 1948). Moreover, there is undoubtedly a business cycle that alternates between two 'regimes', namely periods of high employment and growth followed by periods of lower employment and recession (Schumpeter 1939; Kuznets 1940). In fact, we would seriously consider the possibility that the 'true' relationships between factors of production may have a tendency to flip-flop from one regime to the other, depending on stages in the business cycle or other factors (Hamilton 1996).

5.5 DIGRESSION: OPTIMAL CONTROL THEORY

In recent decades neoclassical growth theory has leaned heavily on a branch of mathematics known as optimal control theory. The idea that economic growth proceeds along an optimal path was first introduced by Frank Ramsey in 1928 to test Pigou's idea that people tend to save too little and under-invest due to myopia (short-sightedness) about the future (Ramsey 1928). Ramsey's model postulated a single homogeneous capital good, and assumed that future growth follows an optimal path determined by maximizing the time integral of 'utility' L. It assumed diminishing returns for both utility and capital productivity.

Utility in his model was a function of consumption C, defined as total output Y minus savings/investment. Evidently total output Y is equal to consumption C plus capital accumulation during the year. The latter is equal to new investment (equated with savings sY where s is the savings rate) minus depreciation.

$$Y = C + \Delta K = C + sY - \delta K \qquad (5.1)$$

Here δK is the annual depreciation of capital K. Rearranging terms we get,

$$C = Y - sY + \delta K \qquad (5.2)$$

Output Y is assumed to be a function of capital stock K, so output per capita y is a function of capital per capita k. We want to maximize the integral over utility L from the present to a distant future time t_x, where the integrand is a function of k:

$$W = \int L(k, \dot{y}, k) dt \qquad (5.3)$$

It is also usual (though Ramsey himself did not resort to this device) to introduce a discount function $\exp(-\gamma t)$ in the integral. This supposedly reflects the myopia or time preference mentioned above. For instance, one might choose a utility function L of the form:

$$L = C' \exp(-\gamma t) \tag{5.4}$$

where η and γ are parameters. Thus the utility L becomes a function of k, its time derivative $\dot{k}$ and time t. Several mathematical conditions also apply.

The condition for a minimum (actually any extreme value) of the integral is that the so-called Euler-Lagrange equation must be satisfied at all points within the range of integration, namely:

$$\frac{\partial L}{\partial k} - \frac{d}{dx}\frac{\partial L}{\partial k} = 0 \tag{5.5}$$

Lagrange also introduced a method of introducing constraints with undetermined multipliers. These multipliers later evolved into so-called *co-state variables*. The Euler-Lagrange differential equation determines k as a function of x. (This is the central result in the calculus of variations.) It is important to emphasize that the Euler-Lagrange equation is quite general: it determines the functional form of extremum of any line integral over a function L of some variable (such as k), the time derivative of that variable, and time itself. The next step, due to Hamilton, was to introduce a 'conjugate' variable, defined by

$$P = \frac{\partial L}{\partial v} \tag{5.6}$$

The Hamiltonian function *for a dynamical system* is now defined as

$$H = pv - L = T + V \tag{5.7}$$

and the canonical variable p is interpreted as the momentum of a particle. Note that if V is derived from a conservative force field, energy is conserved, so $T + V$ is a constant and the time derivative of H must vanish. Hamilton's equations can then be expressed in a neat canonical form:

$$\frac{\partial H}{\partial X} = \frac{\partial p}{\partial t}; \quad \frac{\partial H}{\partial p} = \frac{\partial x}{\partial t} \tag{5.8}$$

The assumption of a single homogeneous capital-cum-consumption good is obviously problematic. However, Samuelson and Solow showed how, in principle, to generalize the Ramsey model to the case of heterogeneous capital goods, and even 'more realistic utility functionals not having the independently additive utilities of a simple integral' (Samuelson and Solow 1956). They concluded, among other things, that

> Over extended periods of time an economic society can, in a perfectly straight-forward way, reconstruct the composition of its diverse capital goods so that there may remain great heuristic value in the simpler J. B. Clark-Ramsey models of abstract capital substance. (Ibid., pp. 537–8)

In short, the more complicated models are solvable, in principle, though hardly in practice.

The basic Ramsey scheme with homogeneous capital can also be generalized to several variables and their time derivatives. For instance, we could include a variable representing an exergy resource stock R and the rate of change (that is, extraction) of that resource, which would be the current exergy supply E, which also happens to be the negative time derivative of R, $\dot{R}$. (See for example Ayres 1988b). Integrals of this sort can be solved by well-known methods.

However, apart from mathematical tractability, there is really no reason to suppose that economic growth follows a consumption-maximizing path in equilibrium. Is maximizing aggregate consumption truly identical with maximizing utility? Are there no other growth drivers to be reckoned with? In fact, there are very strong reasons to suppose that the economy worships several gods, in different ways at different times. As pointed out earlier in this book, and emphasized by many economists, from Schumpeter to Kuznets, Schmookler, Abramovitz, Kaldor and Nelson, economic growth is not an equilibrium process.

But, as we have also noted, the standard model, in which energy plays no role or a minimal one, contradicts economic intuition, not to mention common sense. Indeed, economic history suggests that increasing natural resource (exergy) flows at ever-lower costs are a major fact of history. The declining costs of mechanical or electrical power (physical work per unit of time) in relation to the rising wages of labor have induced ever-increasing substitution of machines (mostly consuming fossil fuels) for human labor, as indicated in Figure 5.2. We think this long-term substitution has been the most important driver of economic growth since the industrial revolution.

5.6 GROWTH IN THE NEOCLASSICAL PARADIGM: THE STANDARD MODEL

Most economists are still using versions of a theory of growth developed for a single-sector model half a century ago by Robert Solow, who was awarded a Nobel Prize for his accomplishment (Solow 1956, 1957); a very similar model was set forth at about the same time by Trevor Swan (Swan 1956). The theory was developed further by Meade, another Nobel laureate (Meade 1961). The key feature of the Solow-Swan model was to

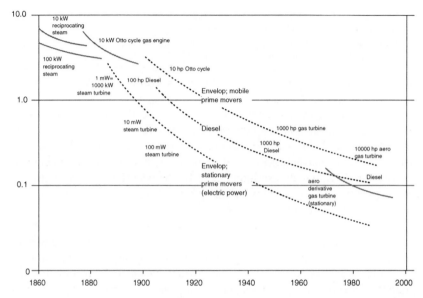

Figure 5.2   Cost of power per hour as multiple of hourly wage

express the logarithmic time derivative of output (growth rate) as the sum of output elasticities with respect to capital, labor and time multiplied by their corresponding growth rates.[6]

The growth rate for labor is normally taken to be equal to the population growth rate, although some models incorporate more detailed considerations (with regard to gender, retirement age, years in school, etc.), while the growth rate of capital is defined as the rate of savings (investment) less depreciation. The output Y is a function of capital stock K and labor employment L.[7] If the factor shares happen to be constants, they can be interpreted as output elasticities and the differential expression can be integrated to yield the familiar and convenient Cobb-Douglas form with an exogenous multiplier $A(t)$ depending only on time.

Solow did not specify a particular mathematical form for the production function in his 1956 paper, but in his 1957 paper he specified the Cobb-Douglas form (Solow 1956, 1957). Since then most economic models have utilized either the well-known Cobb-Douglas form, or the so-called 'constant elasticity of substitution' (CES) model (Arrow et al. 1961). One implication of the Solow-Swan model, or any production function model, is that capital and labor are perfectly substitutable for each other. Adding a third or fourth factor of production does not change this requirement for mutual substitutability.

In equilibrium, assuming many price-taking firms in equilibrium producing a single composite product, constant returns to scale, integrability, and factor substitutability, it can be proved that the elasticities of the factors are equal to factor cost shares. The formal proof of this theorem is given in Appendix A. The reasoning behind this argument is spelled out in many economic textbooks (for example, Mankiw 1997, pp. 50–55). It goes like this: imagine an economy consisting of a large number of firms making a single all-purpose product (call it bread!). They all use capital and labor as inputs. They all must hire labor and rent capital equipment – from an agency outside the economic system – to stay in business. In a competitive economy in equilibrium, the wages paid to labor must be equal to the marginal productivity of that labor, and similarly, the rents for capital equipment and infrastructure must be equal to the marginal productivity of the capital, which is proportional to the corresponding elasticity. In this idealized economy all workers are paid the same, so marginal productivity is less than average productivity, the difference being profit. The payments to labor and capital together exhaust the total of all payments which, in turn, equals the total output of the economy. Q.E.D. We discuss this issue further in the next section.

The origins of physical production in the neoclassical paradigm remain unexplained, since the only explanatory variables are abstract labor and abstract immaterial capital. The realism of the core assumption (that only labor force expansion and/or capital accumulation drives growth) was sharply challenged in the early 1950s. Research based on reconstructions of historical time series of the supposed factors of production (labor and capital) drastically reduced the apparent role of capital accumulation (Abramovitz 1952, 1956; Fabricant 1954). For example, Fabricant estimated that capital accumulation accounted for only 10 percent of US economic growth since the middle of the 19th century. The need for a time-dependent multiplier $A(t)$ arises from the observation that the GDP has grown faster than either capital K or labor L or any combination of the two that satisfies the requirement of constant returns to scale (Euler condition); namely that the production function must be homogeneous of the first order.

The neoclassical paradigm does not allow any role for 'real' material flows, except as consequences, but not causes, of economic activity. It considers the economy as a closed system in which production and consumption are linked only by flows of money (wages flowing to labor and expenditures flowing to production). The goods and services produced and consumed are supposedly measured in real terms, though in practice they are measured only in monetary terms. Of course, the simplest version of this model is too simple for serious analysis, since it presumes that a part of the composite product is diverted to producing more capital. The simple model is normally modified and extended to include an investment component that produces capital. A still more elaborate version of the basic model can incorporate extraction and waste flows, but it is still only an abstraction without physical properties.

Another implication of the Solow-Swan model is that technological progress is *not* created by capital or labor. Otherwise a 'sector' would have to exist, converting capital and labor into technological progress which, in turn, becomes an input to other sector(s). In other words, Solow's use of the single-sector assumption requires technological progress to be exogenous. Some economists have called it 'manna from heaven'. The analogy is apt.

The multiplier $A(t)$ is usually expressed, in practice, as an exponential function of time which increases at a constant average rate based on past history. The multiplier is now called 'total factor productivity' (TFP). Of course, naming a disease is not the same as explaining it. Nevertheless, thanks to the miracle of differential calculus, it is standard practice to speak of the productivity of labor, the productivity of capital and (in some circles) the productivity of resources. Productivity estimation and explanation has become a mini-industry (Kendrick 1956, 1961, 1973; Gollop and Jorgenson 1980; Kendrick and Grossman 1980; Hogan and Jorgenson 1991). Some economists, such as Denison, have made careers of decomposing observed productivity in terms of other variables (for example, Denison 1962, 1967, 1974, 1985). More recently the emphasis has been on international comparisons to explain differences in growth rates in terms of policy-related variables (for example, Barro 1991; Barro and Sala-I-Martin 1995; Sala-I-Martin 1996, 1997; Easterly and Levine 2001; OECD 2003). This activity is called 'growth accounting'. In some respects, our work, reported hereafter, can be regarded as a small contribution to this literature.

5.7 AGGREGATION, SUBSTITUTABILITY AND THE FACTOR PAYMENTS PROBLEM

In 1973–4 there was an oil crisis and an embargo. Oil prices in particular and energy prices in general rose rapidly. Economists wanted to assess the impact on economic growth. Dale Jorgenson and his colleagues introduced a four-factor version, known as KLEM (capital, labor, energy, materials). They also introduced a transcendental logarithmic production function of these four factors, expressed as prices rather than quantities (Jorgenson et al. Lau 1973; Jorgenson and Houthakker 1973; Jorgenson et al. 1982;

Jorgenson 1983, 1984). However, a simpler approach was to incorporate energy as a third factor E into a Cobb-Douglas production function (for example, Allen et al. 1976; Hannon and Joyce 1981). This approach retained the condition of constant returns to scale and the usual assumption that factor elasticities should correspond to factor payments' share in the national accounts.

What if a third factor (energy) is included? It is axiomatic that the sum of all money payments must exhaust the total output of the economy. The trouble is that payments to resource owners are not really payments 'to' energy. Indeed, energy is not a tangible commodity or substance. The term 'energy' is a conceptualization of physicists, which only evolved to the present level of understanding in the late 19th century (earlier names for this idea were 'phlogiston' and 'vis viva'.) Sunlight can be thought of as a pure form of energy but it cannot be owned or sold as such. Nor can the wind or the kinetic energy of tides or flowing water. What can be captured, whether by water or wind turbines, or in the products of photosynthesis (present or past), is value added to this non-substance by the investment of labor and man-made capital, plus some of the recovered energy (useful work) itself. There are no payments to or for energy *per se*, both because energy is a conserved quantity (that quantity which is consumed or used up is exergy) and because there is no entity with financial accounts to receive or disburse payments.

Economists have tried to get around this difficulty by assuming that energy (exergy) carriers (food, fuels) are equivalent to energy itself and that the owners of resources like land, coal and petroleum are the ones to be paid. Since Ricardo, these payments have been classified as 'rents'. But, from another perspective, land and mineral resources are really forms of capital (natural capital), whence useful energy ('useful work') is really a product of capital, both natural and man-made, plus labor. That seems reasonable, since both natural and man-made capital plus labor are obviously required for mining, drilling and agriculture. It is important to emphasize again, however, that capital and labor do not actually create the energy, which is either embodied in fossil fuels, flowing water, wind or sunlight, all of which are actually gifts of nature.

This seems reasonable at first sight. But then the energy (exergy) component of capital, which is *not* man-made, cannot be treated as a product of savings and investment. It is better to regard the extraction activities (agriculture, forestry, mining, drilling, etc.) as a distinct sector or sectors, whose inputs are man-made capital and labor and whose products are food, animal feed, wood, coal, petroleum, natural gas, etc. These products are derived directly from sunlight, movements of air or water or extracted from a stockpile of the above-mentioned gifts of nature. The costs of transforming them into marketed products are simply the payments to capital and labor used by the corresponding extraction and transformation sectors.

It is evident that, apart from rents to land or mineral resource owners, the extractive sectors *per se* account for a very small share of payments in the national accounts of an industrialized country. The more value is added to crude oil or coal in the chain of processes leading to a final service, the smaller the extractive component will be. Thus, as a number of influential economists have argued, if factor elasticities are equal to factor payments' share in the national accounts, factor price changes *cannot* make any significant difference in terms of explaining economic growth (for example, Denison 1979). But are output elasticities really equal to cost shares? Solow, Denison, Jorgenson et al. habitually thought in terms of a single-sector economy producing a single 'composite' all-purpose good. They also assumed equilibrium, perfect competition and homogeneous labor and capital. Finally, they assumed that all factors are mutually substitutable. Actually the formal proof of equivalence between output elasticity and cost share also depends upon the assumptions of constant returns to scale, that firms are profit maximizers (and cost minimizers) in equilibrium (Appendix A). Needless to say these assumptions are all open to serious question.

What if the economy is more complex than a single sector producing a composite good? Does the famous factor share theorem (Appendix A) still hold for a two, three or multi-sector economy? Setting aside the question of substitutability among the factors (capital, labor, useful work), the answer is provisionally 'yes'. Consider a two-sector economy such that sector 1 consists of all the extractive and primary energy conversion sectors, such as electricity generation, and sector 2 consists of all the rest. The inputs to sector 1 are capital and labor, and gifts of nature. The output of this sector is energy services, or what we call 'useful work', some of which is utilized within sector 1 itself. Subject to the usual assumptions, the factor share theorem still holds, meaning that the costs of useful work consist of the capital and labor costs used to produce it.

Sector 2 consists of all the activities that convert the net output of useful work, plus additional capital and labor, into final products and services. Once again, the theorem holds. The costs of the final output (GDP) consist of the costs of all the capital and labor inputs to the second sector plus the cost of the useful work inputs from sector 1. But the costs of the latter are simply the cost of capital and labor utilized by sector 1. The total of all capital and labor for both sectors are now accounted for.

Now suppose 'useful work' were to be treated as an independent factor of production (provided by an exogenous source; presumably the same agency that leases capital equipment and provides workers as needed). For purposes of argument we can now pretend that it is not actually a product of capital and labor applied to natural resources. In this case we can also dispense with the two-sector approximation and revert to the single-sector model similar to that of Solow, but with three factors. The factor share theorem still applies, subject to the usual assumptions, but with three factors, as proved in Appendix A.

However, one of those questionable assumptions is that both or all three factors are mutually substitutable. In the real world this is a very strong condition, because it implies that GDP could be produced by any one of the three factors alone, without either of the others. In reality, there is at most a narrow range of substitutability in the neighborhood of the actual combination of factors that exists at any one time. Substitution does occur, of course, but only over time, accompanied by capital investment. But there is also a considerable degree of complementarity. Machines require workers to operate them. (Only in a distant and hard-to-imagine future populated by intelligent robots might it be possible to produce all the goods and services we now enjoy without human labor.) Labor requires tools to be productive. Both humans and animals require food or feed. Heat engines require exergy (fuel) to do useful work, and other machines require useful work (for example, electricity or high temperature heat) to function. In short, both labor and capital equipment also require exergy inputs. *All three factors are essential and therefore not substitutable – except at the margin – in the economy as we know it.*

Of course the real economy is a multi-sector system, consisting of many products that are *not* substitutable for each other in the short term, of which 'useful work' is one of the most important examples. But quite apart from energy services, food cannot be replaced by paper, plastics cannot be replaced by cement, steel cannot be replaced (except in special cases) by aluminum, and copper has no effective substitute, at least for electrical wiring. The multi-sector character of the economy is determined by these limits on substitutability. Of course the multi-sector economy is characterized by important intersectoral flows and interdependencies. Crude extractive inputs are converted first into finished fuels and materials, subsequently into components, then subsystems, then complex products and structures, and finally into transport, information, entertainment and other services.

To deal adequately with the sectoral non-substitutability problem, an input-output approach would seem to be appropriate. Up to now, however, serious practical difficulties have prevented significant progress in that area. This issue is addressed briefly in the next section.

It is not clear to us whether the mathematical relationship that is proved in Appendix A is still applicable to a multi-factor, multi-sector economy where the factors are not totally substitutable and the output of one sector is an input to some other sector. True, quite a number of economists, including Jorgenson and Allen (cited above), have tried to include a third factor, namely commercial energy E, while retaining the single sector 'composite product' assumption. But this is conceptually dubious. There seems to be a fundamental contradiction in using a model that assumes perfect substitutability while assigning the cost of energy as the payments to primary resource extractive industries, thus identifying those industries as a separate sector.

Farm products are not made entirely by farmers, and coal, oil and gas are not created by the firms that extract them. Moreover, the energy carriers produced by these sectors are subsequently refined and converted into useful work or useful heat by other downstream sectors, from food-processing to petroleum-refining to electric-power generation, and further down the line by the engines in motor vehicles and the furnaces in industrial plants or the heating plants in commercial and residential buildings, not to mention the cooking stoves in kitchens. A moment's thought suggests that treating the fossil fuel extractive industries as the 'source' of energy is not only wrong in logic, but that doing so implicitly treats the economy as a two (if not multi)-sector system. From this perspective, it becomes clear that the real, but indirect (downstream) elasticity of useful work is far greater than the cost share of the extractive industries at the beginning of the chain.

The assumption that the elasticity of exergy service output should correspond to the payments to primary exergy extraction in the national accounts is still so widespread (despite being very dubious) that a few more paragraphs can justifiably be devoted to the subject. Here is a quotation from a 2005 Nobel Laureate, taken from the *Concise Encyclopedia of Economics*, available on the internet (Schelling 2002):

> Today, little of our gross domestic product is produced outdoors, and therefore, little is susceptible to climate. Agriculture and forestry are less than 3 percent of total output, and little else is much affected. Even if agricultural productivity declined by a third over the next half-century, the per capita GNP we might have achieved by 2050 we would still achieve in 2051.

This particular article is entitled 'Greenhouse Effect', which explains the context. But it is clear that Schelling assumes that a radical cut in agricultural production would affect only the agriculture sector. In other words, he ignores the chain of downstream impacts on food processing, agricultural chemicals, tractor sales, rail transport, wholesale and retail trade, hotels and restaurants, etc.[8] In effect, Schelling assumes that all the downstream sectors that consume agricultural products will easily find substitutes.

Yet it is perfectly clear that they will not. Suppose (with Schelling) that physical agricultural output (harvested crops) were cut in half, and suppose – for simplicity – that this cut applied to every crop. Based on existing intersectoral relationships, the immediate result would be that animal feed, other than grass, would be eliminated almost completely since humans would need all the grain, and the output of chickens, turkeys, pigs and grain-fed beef would fall to near zero. Only lamb and (some) veal would remain on the market, and the meat-packing industry would virtually disappear, as would most of the butchers. The dairy industry would also have to reduce its output substantially. Transport requirements for grain, potatoes and other bulky crops would be cut in half. Alcoholic beverages (which depend on grain) would also be cut sharply, as would leather goods, tobacco products and so on.

To be sure, these consequences would be modified by prices. Steak lovers and beer/whiskey drinkers would bid up the prices of beef and alcoholic beverages, thus reducing the amount of grain products available to millers and bakers to make bread and cereal products. The prices of those products would consequently increase dramatically, and the poor would have less to eat. Meanwhile many workers in agriculture, food processing and transportation, not to mention retail trade, would also lose their jobs, to the extent that they are related to the processing and movement of physical quantities. Clearly an input-output approach is needed to assess the real economic impact of a cut in agricultural production.

According to Schelling's argument, it would seem to follow that a sudden 50 percent cut in US energy supplies, which account for about 4 percent of GDP, would only result in a 2 percent reduction in US GDP. Virtually everybody in touch with reality knows this to be absurd. The transport sector, the construction sector, the chemical sector and even agriculture would be devastated by such a cut, precisely because there is no substitute for energy. The downstream and indirect impacts will have a multiplier effect several times greater than the primary cut. In short, the output elasticity of energy (exergy) services must be significantly greater than the cost share.

To take a more extreme, but equally pertinent, example, consider the sector that delivers water and sewer services to cities (SIC 680302). The total value added by this sector may be only in the tens or low hundreds of billions of dollars, which is insignificant in terms of the whole US GDP. But if these services were eliminated, the economy would collapse utterly. The multiplier effect in this case might be 100 or more. The point is that the real economy is not a homogeneous entity producing a single 'composite' good, as many simple models assume (and Schelling assumed in his ency-clopedia article). The reality is that we have a diverse multi-sector economy in which most sectors are dependent on inputs from others, and some intermediates – like water, food and electricity – are essential and non-substitutable.

In a multi-sector world the cost-minimizing strategy for the firm is *not* determined only by the elasticities of labor or of capital goods *per se*, but by a combination of labor, capital goods and other intermediates pur-chased from other sectors. Mankiw's textbook example was of bakers producing bread, *but only from capital and labor* (Mankiw 1997). Real products like bread cannot be produced from abstractions. In the real multi-sector world, the bakers must also purchase flour and yeast from a food-processing sector that buys grain from farmers. They must also purchase ovens from a manufacturer and fuel for their ovens from a gas distributor. Each of those sectors purchases from others.

Therefore, the idealized single-sector model of firms utilizing only labor and durable capital goods cannot be generalized to the economy as a whole. The cost-minimizing process at the firm level leaves its imprint on the overall picture, like the grin of the Cheshire cat.

5.8   DIGRESSION: INPUT-OUTPUT APPROACHES

As mentioned in the previous section, the fact that substitution between inputs, or sectors, is limited in reality suggests that an input-output model with fixed coefficients might be an appropriate tool for analysis, at least in the short run. Input-output models were first introduced into economics by Wassily Leontief (1936, 1941). Fundamental to these models is the existence of an effective sectorization[9] of the economy, normally represented as a square matrix with intersectoral transactions. The transactions table has rows that show fractional inputs to each sector from other sectors and columns that show fractional outputs from each sector to other sectors. This table is obviously dynamic; it changes from hour to hour, and certainly from year to year. But Leontief argued that the coefficients (matrix elements) represent technological relation-ships that do not change rapidly. By assuming fixed coefficients, the relationship in question becomes a model of the economy. The Leontief model assumes an exogenous final demand (including exports) vector Y which determines the vector of sectoral outputs X through a matrix relationship

$$X = Y + AX \qquad (5.9)$$

where A is a matrix of coefficients, representing fractional inputs to each sector from other sectors. Hence it follows that

$$X = (I - A)^{-1} Y = B^{-1} Y \qquad (5.10)$$

This famous relationship makes it possible to ascertain the sectoral impacts of an increase (or decrease) in some component of final demand. For instance, an increase in military spending will have implications for other sectors such as steel, aluminum and electronics. We note that the matrix inverse can be expressed as a power series

$$B^{-1} = B + B^2 + B^3 + \ldots \qquad (5.11)$$

where each term in the series after the first consists of a sum over all possible products of pairs, triples and n-tuples of coefficients. These n-tuples represent flows of products (or payments for products) from sector to sector through the economy. Of course, most sectors sell to only a few other sectors, so most of the possible products in the sums actually vanish, which is why the series converges. The non-vanishing combinations reflect actual flows of products (apart from some aggregation errors) or, in the case of interest to us, energy services, from any starting point – such as coal mining or petroleum and gas drilling to refineries, electric power generation and subsequently to other sectors.

For instance, one primary user of electric power (e-power) is the steel industry. A fraction of the output of the steel industry is produced in electric arc furnaces (including both recycled scrap and stainless steel). The recycled scrap is consumed mainly by the construction industry (for example, for concrete reinforcement), while stainless steel is consumed by a range of industries from kitchenware to plumbing products. These flows are represented by product terms of the form $A_{e\text{-power,steel}} A_{steel,construction}$ and $A_{e\text{-power,steel}} A_{steel,plumbing}$ and so on. The extension to products of three or more terms is obvious.

It is tempting to assume that the sum of all such product terms from electric-power generation to others will be a measure of the economic importance of electric power in the economy, and hence of the impact of a price increase, or a supply scarcity. This is partly true. However, one of the other implicit assumptions underlying the Leontief model is that, in the event of a change in some element of final demand Y, all input requirements – including the factors of production (capital, labor and energy) – will be met automatically and instantaneously, or at least within the statistical year. This implies the existence of unused capacity and elastic factor supply curves (Giarratani 1976). That assumption is rarely justified in practice.

An alternative scheme is known as the supply-side I-O model (for example, Ghosh 1958). In this version, the final demand vector is regarded as endogenous, whereas the value-added (expenditure) vector, including expenditure for imports, is given exogenously. In this model, an increase (or decrease) in some element of the expenditure (supply) vector has implications for the outputs of all the other intermediate sectors, as well as final consumption. But again, this model assumes perfect substitutability of inputs at the sectoral level, and at the final demand level. Indeed, cost minimization implies that each sector will consume only the cheapest input, or that a single combination applies to every sector equally, which is clearly not realistic (Oosterhaven 1988; Gruver 1989). In any case, the supply-side I-O model is not satisfactory for assessing the impact of scarcity of an essential – non-substitutable – input such as petroleum or electric power.

It has been suggested by R.A. Stone that the problem can be addressed by a hybrid I-O model with some supply-constrained sectors and some unconstrained sectors (Stone 1961 p. 98). The idea is to fix the value-added in some sectors and the intermediate or final demand of others, exogenously. The procedure has been explained in detail by Miller and Blair (Miller and Blair 1985, p. 330 ff.), and it has been applied to several cases, primarily in the context of agriculture and limited land availability (for example, Hubacek and Sun 2001). On reflection, it is clear that a reduction in petroleum output by, say, 10 percent will necessarily cut automotive and air transportation activity by almost the same fraction, at least in the short run. Labor or capital cannot replace liquid fuel, so people will have to fly less. The cut in electricity production will have a similar impact on virtually every manufacturing sector, as well as final consumption, because there is virtually no substitute for electric power, at least in the short run, although the allocation of cuts among users might reduce the impact somewhat. Again, labor and capital cannot replace electricity in the near term. The point is that a cut in the availability of a primary fuel will have a downstream impact much larger than the impact on the primary production sector itself.

It is intuitively clear that, because of non-substitutability, the 'weight' of energy (and energy services or useful work) in the economy is much larger than its cost share. The magnitude of the multiplier can be calculated, in principle, from an I-O model. However, the multiplier is *not* the simple sum of value-added fractions attributable to the primary input, because some downstream substitution between sectors – for example, communication substituting for transportation – does occur. The question is: how much? Unfortunately, the supply-constrained model has not yet been applied, as far as we know, to the problem of constrained petroleum or exergy supplies. Such an application would obviously be desirable, but it is beyond the scope of this book.

5.9 OTHER CRITICISMS OF THE CURRENT NEOCLASSICAL THEORY

Apart from its questionable simplifications, above, the standard Solow-Swan theory suffers from a crucial – and recognized – deficiency: it cannot explain the main – but exogenous – driver of economic growth, often identified as 'technical progress'. Unfortunately, there has never been any real theory to explain technical progress. Notwithstanding fancy packaging and the use of enormously sophisticated 'computable general equilibrium' algorithms, virtually all economic projection models nowadays are still driven by single-sector Solow-type models using either Cobb-Douglas or CES production functions of capital and labor.[10]

These models always assume some underlying long-term rate of productivity increase, while simultaneously remaining in Walrasian (static) equilibrium. As pointed out above, US economic growth is not explainable by an accumulation of the two standard factors of production, namely reproducible capital stock, and human capital stock. The unexplained residual is usually attributed to a homogeneous stock of technological 'knowledge' that grows (by assumption) smoothly and automatically, due to factors outside the economy.

There are serious problems with neoclassical growth-in-equilibrium. It assumes that technical change is exogenous, uniform and smooth. In fact, it assumes that labor (and capital) become steadily and continuously more productive, while the economy remains, at all times, in equilibrium. However, as we argued in Chapter 1 and, especially, Chapter 2 smooth, gradual change, uniform across all sectors – whether attributable to learning, experience or scale effects – *cannot* explain either technological or economic history. It is especially inconsistent with observed patterns of structural change that characterize the real world and would therefore have to be reflected in multi-sector models.

Walrasian static equilibrium is clearly inconsistent with inventive activity or innovation at the micro-scale or structural change at the macro-scale. Thus growth-in-equilibrium is essentially an oxymoron. Detailed critiques of the equilibrium assumption are hardly original with us (for example, see Kaldor 1971; Kornai 1973).[11]

The standard neoclassical growth model has other drawbacks. For instance, the Solow-Swan theory had a built-in tendency for declining productivity due to declining returns to capital investment. When this point of 'capital saturation' is reached, further growth per capita can only result from 'technical progress' or TFP, which (as noted) is itself unexplained.

This feature of the Solow model implies that countries with a small capital stock will grow faster than countries with a large capital stock. Thus the model also predicts gradual 'convergence' between poor and rich countries. In the late 1980s and early 1990s there was considerable interest in the theory of convergence, supported by a wide variety of examples. In fact, for a time, it appeared that a new regularity in empirical economics had been discovered, namely the existence of an underlying convergence within 'convergence clubs' at the rate of 2 percent per annum (Baumol 1986; Baumol et al. 1989; Ben-David 1994; Barro and Sala-I-Martin 1992; Sala-I-Martin 1996).

However, subsequently it has been discovered that the apparent statistical uniformity might be misleading and that, while convergence clubs apparently exist at both ends of the economic spectrum, the rich clubs and the poor clubs are polarized and diverging. Moreover, it appears that this divergence of the rich and poor dominates the apparent 2 percent convergence that had briefly been accepted as conventional wisdom (Quah 1996).

However, subsequently it has been discovered that the apparent statistical uniformity might be misleading and that, while convergence clubs apparently exist at both ends of the economic spectrum, the rich clubs and the poor clubs are polarized and diverging. Moreover, it appears that this divergence of the rich and poor dominates the apparent 2 percent convergence that had briefly been accepted as conventional wisdom (Quah 1996).

A consequence of the saturation effect predicted by the Solow model was that richer countries should grow more slowly, and developing countries should grow faster and gradually catch up to the more industrialized countries. In fact, economic growth in the industrialized countries has not slowed down to the degree suggested by the theory, while a major subset of the so-called 'developing countries' have not been catching up (Barro and Sala-I-Martin 1995). There is some evidence for convergence between rich clubs and poor ones in East Asia, but not in Africa or Latin America. Recent work suggests that there is convergence from above, but not from below (Okada 2006).

In response to this perceived difficulty, some theorists have suggested that capital and labor augmentation – in the sense of quality improvements – might enable the Solow-Swan model to account for the observed facts. For instance, education and training should (and does) make the labor force more productive. Moreover, knowledge and skills presumably do not depreciate. Similarly, capital goods have become more productive as more advanced technology is embodied in more recent machines, thus compensating for depreciation. Augmentation of labor and capital are, in some degree, observable and quantifiable facts. Allowing for it, a number of cross-sectional econometric studies were carried out in the 1990s to test this idea. Indeed, some of them seemed, at first, to provide empirical support for the idea that exogenous technological progress (TFP) can be eliminated from the theory and that factor accumulation alone could, after all, explain the observed facts of economic development (Mankiw et al. 1992; Mankiw 1995; Young 1995; Barro and Sala-I-Martin 1995).

However more recent research has contradicted that conclusion, based as it was on statistical analysis of imperfect data. Later results have essentially reinstated the original Solow view, namely that factor accumulation is *not* the central feature of economic growth after all (Easterly and Levine 2001). Easterly and his colleagues, having extensively reviewed the published literature of economic development studies, argue – as Solow did – that 'something else' accounts for most of the observable differences between growth experiences in different countries. Easterly et al. adopt the standard convention of referring to this 'something else' as TFP. In this and the next few chapters we hope to cast some new light on the origins of this unexplained driver of growth.

As we have said, the theory as articulated by Solow and others does not allow for 'real' material flows in the production function. Production and consumption are abstractions, linked only by money flows, payments for labor, payments for products and services, savings and investment. These abstract flows are governed only by equilibrium-seeking market forces (the 'invisible hand'). There is no room for path dependence and no deep fundamental connection in the neoclassical theory between the physical world and the economy. The equilibrium assumption is needed mainly to justify the assumption that output is a function of capital and labor inputs and that the output elasticities of the factors of production (that is, marginal productivities) should correspond to factor payment shares in the National Accounts.[12] This 'requirement' is a consequence of the equality of output elasticities with factor shares in equilibrium, proved for a single-sector, single-product economy in Appendix A.

The production function approach is generally coupled with an assumption of 'constant returns to scale' which essentially means that N copies of an economic system would produce exactly N times the output of one system. Putting it another way, a big country like the US will not necessarily be richer per capita, by virtue of its size, than a small one like Switzerland or Sweden. This assumption is in reasonable accord with observed facts. It is also mathematically very convenient, since it sharply limits the mathematical forms of allowable production functions to homogeneous functions of the first order, also known as the 'Euler condition'. On the other hand, even if the strict constant returns to scale postulate is violated in the real world (that is, if big economies grow slightly faster than small ones due to economies of scale, *ceteris paribus*), the violation cannot be very great. In other words, while the factor productivities of a Cobb-Douglas (C-D) production function might conceivably add up to slightly more than unity, *the deviation cannot realistically be large.*

Apparently there is (or has been) a widespread assumption among economists, that the constant returns to scale condition (the sum of the two exponents in the C-D function equals unity), is empirically based. This has been confirmed by many econometric tests. Paul Romer was puzzled to note that 'the exponent relating to labor can be substantially inferior to its share in (national) income' (Romer 1987b). Sylos Labini points out emphatically that many (most) econometric tests do not support the notion that the sum of the exponents is close to unity (Sylos Labini 1995, table 1, pp. 490–91).[13] He also offers an explanation. The three tests that did support the Douglas hypothesis over a period of about 20 or 25 years were all cross-sectional. The explanation of the sum of the exponents being close to unity in these cases was probably due to the fact, previously pointed out by Mendershausen and Phelps Brown, that, between one industry and another, the relationships between labor, capital and output tend to change in the same proportion (Mendershausen 1938; Phelps Brown 1957). This explanation has nothing to do with the marginalist theory of income allocation that is usually cited.

5.10 SO-CALLED 'ENDOGENOUS' THEORIES OF GROWTH

Solow's 1956–7 model (cited above) implies that capital should exhibit diminishing returns, that is, that either savings and investment as a fraction of output must increase or the growth-rate must slow down as capital stock increases. For the same reason it also implies that less developed economies will grow faster than more mature economies. As mentioned above, neither slowdown nor convergence has been observed as a general characteristic of the real world (Barro and Sala-I-Martin 1995). This fact, among others, stimulated interest in the late 1980s in new models capable of explaining continuous steady-state growth. They attempt to overcome the limitations of Solow's production function approach by modifying the traditional feature of diminishing returns to capital.

In response to this problem, neoclassical development economists began thinking about other possible ways to endogenize the standard theory without making drastic changes. Although not emphasized in neoclassical growth theory, there is an endogenous mechanism that can explain a part of this residual, that is, beyond that which is accounted for by labor and capital accumulation. The part that can be explained *without* radical (structure-changing) technological innovations is due to learning, economies of scale and the accumulation of general knowledge (for example, computer literacy) that leads to cost savings and product improvements.

As explained in Chapter 2, the mechanism in question is a simple positive feedback between increasing consumption, investment, increasing scale and 'learning by doing' or 'learning by using' at the societal level (Figure 1.1). This feedback cycle, first suggested by Arrow, results in declining costs leading to declining prices, stimulating increases in demand, increased production and new investment to increase capacity (Arrow et al. 1961; Kaldor 1966, 1971; McCombie 1982).[14] Increasing production generates learning by doing and increasing capacity gives rise to further economies of scale, both of which drive costs down. Lower costs result in lower prices (in a competitive equilibrium), greater demand, more production and so forth.

However, the dominant neoclassical endogenous growth theories now in the literature do not explicitly depend upon feedback. On the contrary, they are all 'linear' in the sense that they assume a simple uni-directional causal mechanism. The endogenous theory literature can be subdivided into three branches. The first is the so-called AK approach, harking back to the older Harrod-Domar 'AK' formalism mentioned above. In the newer version, capital K is taken to include human capital (hence population and labor force). The growth of human capital is not subject to declining returns – as in the Solow model – because of the supposed (exactly) compensating influence of factor augmentation and technology spillovers. Spillovers are, of course, externalities, which – surprisingly – enables increasing returns to remain compatible with general equilibrium and thus with computable general equilibrium (CGE) models.

Neo-AK models began with Paul Romer (1986, 1987b, 1990). Romer postulated a tradeoff between current consumption and investment in undifferentiated 'knowledge'. He assumed that knowledge can be monopolized long enough to be profitable to the discoverer, but yet that it almost immediately becomes available as a free good (spillover) accessible to others.[15] The original Romer theory also postulated positive returns to scale – because knowledge begets knowledge – as an explanation for economic growth. A closely related approach by Lucas, based on some ideas of Uzawa, focused instead on 'social learning' and the tradeoff between consumption and the development of 'human capital' (Lucas 1988; Uzawa 1962). In the Lucas version the spillover is indirect: the more human capital the society possesses, the more productive its individual members will be.

This externality is embedded in the production function itself, rather than in the knowledge variable.

Other contributors to this literature divide capital explicitly into two components, 'real' and human (King and Rebelo 1990). An alternative version assumes one kind of capital but two sectors, one of which produces only capital from itself. Another approach was to allow increasing returns by preserving the distinction between cumulable and non-cumulable factors (for example, labor, land) and modifying the production function to prevent capital productivity from vanishing even with an infinite capital/labor ratio (for example, Jones and Manuelli 1990).

The second approach to endogenous growth theory emphasizes active and deliberate knowledge creation. This is presumed to occur as a result of maximizing behavior (for example, R&D). Knowledge is assumed to be inherently subject to spillovers and dependent on the extent to which benefits of innovation can be appropriated by rent-seeking Schumpeterian innovators. Most models assume that inventors and innovators have negligible success at appropriating the benefits of their efforts. A recent empirical study suggests that this assumption is quite realistic (Nordhaus 2001).

The development of endogenous growth theory along neoclassical lines seems to have culminated, for the present, with the work of Aghion and Howitt (1992, 1998) and Barro and Sala-I-Martin (1995). The former have pioneered a 'neo-Schumpeterian approach' emphasizing the research-driven displacement of older sectors by newer ones. This is essentially equivalent to the process of *creative destruction* originally described by Schumpeter (1912, 1934). These authors (like Romer) focus on investment in knowledge itself (education, R&D) as a core concept. In fact, the idea that the investment in education might be the key to long-term economic growth has political resonance and has been taken up rather enthusiastically by, for example, the British 'New Labor' party.

The neoclassical endogenous theory has interesting features, some of which are shared by our semi-empirical approach, discussed hereafter. However, all of the so-called endogenous growth models based on 'human capital' or 'knowledge' share a fundamental drawback: they are and are likely to remain essentially qualitative and theoretical because none of the proposed choices of core variables (knowledge, human capital, etc.) is readily quantified. At best, the obvious proxies (like education expenditure, years of schooling, and R&D spending) exhibit significant multinational cross-sectional correlation with economic growth. In other words, countries with good school systems are likely to grow faster than countries with poor schools, *ceteris paribus*.

Before leaving the topic, it is worth pointing out where we differ substantively from Romer's theory. His article on economic growth in the on-line

Concise Encyclopedia of Economics contains the following explanation of the growth process, as he sees it:

> Economic growth occurs whenever people take resources and rearrange them in ways that are more valuable. A useful metaphor for production in an economy comes from the kitchen. To create valuable final products, we mix inexpensive ingredients together according to a recipe . . . Human history teaches us . . . that economic growth springs from better recipes, not just from more cooking. New recipes generally produce fewer unpleasant side effects and generate more economic value per unit of raw material.
>
> Every generation has perceived the limits to growth that finite resources and undesirable side effects would pose if no new recipes or ideas were discovered. And every generation has underestimated the potential for finding new recipes and ideas. We consistently fail to grasp how many ideas remain to be discovered. The difficulty is the same one we have with compounding. Possibilities do not add up. They multiply . . . The periodic table contains about a hundred different types of atoms, so the number of combinations made up of four different elements is about $100 \times 99 \times 98 \times 97 = 94,000,000$. A list of numbers like 1, 2, 3, 7 can represent the proportions for using the four elements in a recipe. To keep things simple, assume that the numbers in the list must lie between 1 and 10, that no fractions are allowed, and that the smallest number must always be 1. Then there are about 3,500 different sets of proportions for each choice of four elements, and 3,500 94,000,000 (or 330 billion) different recipes in total . . . (Romer 2006)

We don't suppose that Romer really thinks that growth is simply a matter of finding new 'recipes' for combining the elements. However his illustrations make it very clear that he thinks that the magnitude of knowledge capital (and the rate of growth) depends on the number of new recipes – in the broader sense – discovered, and not on their quality or (more important) sector of application.

For us, as we have pointed out already in Chapter 2, knowledge capital is emphatically *not* a homogeneous entity, consisting of a collection of recipes, to use Romer's analogy. Nor is knowledge in every field equally productive. On the contrary, some ideas are far more productive than others.[16] An innovation that cuts the cost of electricity by a fraction of a cent is far more productive than an idea for a golf ball that flies further, an improved corkscrew, a better mosquito repellant, a longer-lived razor blade, a stronger stiletto heel, or a new computer game. Hundreds or thousands of such innovations may not have the impact of a more efficient power transformer design or an improved tertiary recovery process for oil. We differ with the theorists cited above, and Romer in particular, on this issue. In the Romer theory, all ideas are equally productive and it's just the number of ideas that counts. In our theory it is mainly innovations that increase the quantity and reduce the cost of 'useful work' that have caused the economy to grow in the past. Future economic growth may depend on innovations in another area, of course: probably information technology and/or biotechnology.

5.11   EVOLUTIONARY THEORY

The evolutionary approach emerged as a distinct branch of economic theory in the 1980s, although it was inspired by Schumpeter's early work (1912, 1934). In standard neoclassical economics, competition in an exchange market near equilibrium is mainly driven by some inherent comparative advantage, attributable to climate, soil, mineral deposits or a harbor; for instance, capital invested or knowledge and skills due to past experience. In Schumpeter's world, by contrast, competition is driven by competitive advantage resulting from innovation by 'first movers', taking advantage of returns to adoption, imperfect information transfer to competitors, and (in some cases) legal monopolies during the life of a patent. The neoclassical picture is consistent with equilibrium; the evolutionary picture is not.

Neoclassical economists like Alchian and Friedman argued that Schumpeterian competition is consistent with profit maximization, because only maximizers will be 'selected' (in the Darwinian sense) by the market (Alchian 1950; Friedman 1953). This might be true in a static environment. But even in the case of biological evolution, where the environment changes relatively slowly, the work of Moto Kimura has shown that some mutations can spread through a population by random drift, without possessing any selective advantage (Kimura 1979). His theory of so-called *selective neutrality* is now conventional wisdom in population genetics. The evolutionary view in economics is more consistent with 'satisficing' or 'bounded rationality' in the sense introduced by Herbert Simon (1955, 1959).

In other words, if the selection mechanism is fairly slow and not very efficient, it is not necessary to optimize in order to survive, at least for a great many generations or in an isolated niche. Meanwhile, the environment and the conditions for *competitive* advantage can change enough to modify the conditions for *comparative* advantage. If this is so in population genetics, why not in economics? We all know of inefficient firms that survive in isolated locations or specialized niches, simply because there is no nearby competition. In any case, Sydney Winter argued as long ago as 1964 that variation and selection need not bring about either optimality or equilibrium, whence predictions made on the basis of these postulates need no hold in the real world (Winter 1964). In later work Winter, working with Richard Nelson, pointed out that the Darwinian 'selection' analogy is imperfectly relevant to economics because of the lack of an inheritance mechanism to assure perpetuation of whatever strategic behavior is successful at a point in time. However, Nelson and Winter introduced the notion of inheritable 'routines' as a crude analog of genes (Winter 1984; Nelson 1982; Nelson and Winter 1982a, 1982b).

The main difference between evolutionary economics, as it has developed so far, and the neoclassical mainstream has been characterized as follows: that neoclassical theory postulates 'representative' firms operating on the boundary of a well-defined region in factor space, whereas evolutionary biology – and evolutionary economics – lays primary stress on the existence of diversity (Boulding 1981; Nelson and Winter 1982a and b; Hanusch 1988; Silverberg and Verspagen 1994; Van den Bergh 2003). In fact, the mechanism that drives the economic system, in the evolutionary view, is a kind of conflict between diversity and selection. In biology, diversity of populations and species is assured by mutation combined with diversity of environments. In economics, diversity among firms is the result of a wide range of talents and ideas among entrepreneurs operating in a heterogeneous environment of competitors, institutional constraints, cultures and other external circumstances.

The selection mechanism in biology has been called 'survival of the fittest', although the details of what constitutes 'fitness' are still very unclear, even a century and a half after the publication of *Origin of Species*. In economics *competitiveness* seems to be the common term for whatever quality or strategy is effective in assuring survival and growth. It is generally assumed that one of the explicit strategies for survival is product or process innovation. Innovation is modeled as a search and selection process. Selection, in evolutionary economics, is essentially equated to survival into the next period as a viable competitor in the market (Nelson and Winter 1982 a and b). Nelson and Winter have shown that a plausible growth process can be simulated by postulating a population of firms (not in equilibrium), displaying bounded rationality, and interacting with each other on the basis of probabilistic rules.

However, most evolutionary theorists share with mainstream economists a simplistic view that the specific features of technological change are essentially unpredictable, except in the statistical sense that investment in R&D can be expected to generate useful new ideas. The contemporary orthodox view is reasonably well summarized by Heertje among others:

> Technical knowledge, being the product of a production process in which scarce resources are allocated, can be produced. We do not know exactly what will be produced, but we are certain that we will know more after an unknown period. (Heertje 1983)

The Nelson-Winter model of technological progress is consistent with the view quoted above. In brief, it assumes (for convenience) that the probability of a successful innovation is a function of R&D investment and is more or less independent of past history or other factors. If discovery, invention and innovation were really so random, technological progress would be much smoother than it actually is. Our contrasting view of the process of technological change has been summarized in Chapters 1 and 2. In brief, we insist that some innovations, especially those contributing to energy (exergy) efficiency, are much more pervasive and economically potent than the vast majority of innovations which affect only a single firm or a small market segment. (Innovations in information technology may have a comparable potential for universal application.)

Evolutionary theory has yielded a family of models that simulate many of the important features of structural change and economic dynamics. However, they have not, up to now, produced an explicit quantifiable model to explain past macroeconomic growth or forecast the future.

5.12   THE ECONOMY AS A MATERIALS PROCESSOR

The economy has been interpreted as a self-organized system, far from thermodynamic equilibrium (Jantsch 1975, 1980; Prigogine 1976; Ayres 1994a). It converts low entropy-low information materials into high entropy wastes and high information products and services. Another way of putting it is to say that the economy creates useful order from natural disorder, and embodies this useful order (mostly) in material form, using large quantities of exergy from biomass (that is, the sun) or from fossil fuels.

Energy (exergy) flux, is transformed into an intermediate service ('useful work'), driving machines and substituting for human and animal labor. By driving down the cost of other products, and thus increasing demand and production, this long-term substitution has been the dominant driver of economic growth in the past two centuries. In this context, exergy or exergy services (useful work) can be regarded as a factor of production, playing a role complementary to capital services and labor services.

This interpretation explains the close observed correlation between exergy input and economic output (Cleveland et al. 1984) without any necessary implication that energy (exergy) content of physical products is proportional to value. It also allows us to interpret technological progress on a macro-level in terms of the efficiency of conversion of exergy inputs-to-service (= work) outputs (Ayres and Warr 2003).

From an evolutionary perspective, the economic system can be viewed as an open system that extracts and converts raw materials into products and useful services. The economy consists of a sequence of processing stages, starting with extraction, conversion, production of finished goods and services, final consumption, and disposal of wastes. Most of the non-structural materials are discarded in degraded form. These conversion processes correspond to exergy flows, subject to constraints, including the laws of thermodynamics. The objective of economic activity can be interpreted as a constrained value-maximization problem or its dual, a cost-minimization problem. Value is conventionally defined in terms of preferences for consumption goods, or services.

The simplest 'model' representation of the economy consists of a single sector producing a single all-purpose product that is both a capital good and a consumption good. This simplification is widely accepted in undergraduate textbooks, despite its unrealism, because two or three sector models are far more difficult to analyse mathematically, yet not much more realistic. For example, one might consider a model of two sectors with a single intermediate product. The first sector would include extraction and primary processing, for example, to finished materials. The second sector would include manufacturing and service activities. Three or more sectors would obviously add a little more to the realism of the scheme, but the mathematics for a three-sector model is almost impenetrable. Of course, the more stages in the sequence, the more it is necessary to take into account feedbacks, for example, from finished goods to extraction of primary processing sectors. The N-sector version would be an input-output model of the Leontief type in which the sequential structure tends to be obscured.

An adequate description of a materials-processing system, must include materials and energy flows as well as money flows. These flows and conversion processes are governed by the laws of thermodynamics, as well as accounting balances. At each stage, until the last, mass flows are split by technological means into 'useful' and 'waste' categories. Value (and information) are added to the useful flows, reducing their entropy content and increasing their exergy content per unit mass (thanks to exogenous inputs of exergy), while the high entropy wastes are returned to the environment.

The conceptualization of the economy as a materials processor is further developed in Chapter 6.

5.13 FURTHER IMPLICATIONS OF THE FIRST LAW OF THERMODYNAMICS

As mentioned earlier (Chapter 3), the first law of thermodynamics (conservation of mass) implies that mass outputs from any process equal mass inputs. However, useful outputs are almost invariably a fraction of total inputs, sometimes a small fraction (as in the case of refining low grade ores).

In some cases, the output mass is entirely wasted, as with combustion processes. Thus wastes are an unavoidable by-product of physical production.

The law of mass conservation, on the other hand, is far from trivial. The so-called 'mass-balance principle' states that mass inputs must equal mass outputs for every chemical process (or process step), and that this must be true separately for each chemical element.[17] All resources extracted from the environment must eventually become unwanted wastes and pollutants. Waste emissions are not exceptional phenomena that can be neglected or treated as exceptions. The standard multi-sector economic model of commodities produced from other commodities is misleading (Walras 1874; Sraffa 1960; von Neumann 1945 [1932]).

It follows, too, that virtually all products are really joint products, except that wastes have no positive market value. On the contrary, they have, in most cases, a negative value. A producer of wastes will need a 'sink' for disposal. Options for free disposal are becoming rarer. Producers must, increasingly, pay to have waste residuals removed and treated, safely disposed of, or recycled. The implication that there exists a price-determined equilibrium between supply and demand (of commodities) must therefore be modified fundamentally (Ayres and Kneese 1969).

This means, among other things, that 'externalities' (market failures) associated with production and consumption of materials are actually pervasive and that they tend to grow in importance as the economy itself grows. Materials recycling can help (indeed, it must), but recycling is energy (exergy) intensive and (thanks to the second law) imperfect, so it cannot fully compensate for a declining natural resource base. Long-term sustainability must depend to a large extent upon dematerialization and 'decoupling' of economic welfare from the natural resource base (Ayres and Kneese 1989).

The mass-balance condition provides powerful tools for estimating process wastes and losses for industrial processes, or even whole industries, where these cannot be determined directly. Even where other data are available, the mass-balance condition offers a means of verification and interpolation, to fill in gaps (Ayres and Cummings-Saxton 1975; Ayres 1978; Ayres and Simonis 1999; Ayres 1995).

5.14   FURTHER IMPLICATIONS OF THE SECOND LAW OF THERMODYNAMICS

Many economists, and most physical scientists, assume that the relationship between economics and the second (entropy) law of thermodynamics concerns resource depletion and scarcity. In this belief they are, in a sense, disciples of the late Nicholas Georgescu-Roegen, who famously said: 'The entropy law is the taproot of economic scarcity' and many other words to that effect (Georgescu-Roegen 1971, 1977). As noted at the beginning of this chapter, the economy is a system that extracts low entropy resources from the environment and rejects high entropy wastes back into the environment. While solar energy was the original source of fossil fuels that accumulated in the earth's crust during the Carboniferous era, several hundred million years ago, we humans are dissipating those resources at a rate thousands or even millions of times faster than they were created.

An aspect of the depletion argument concerns recycling. One consequence of the second law is that recycling can never be 100 percent efficient. At first sight, this would imply that scarce materials like platinum must actually disappear from the surface of the earth, which is not the case. What is true is that as the quality of the resource base declines towards the average in the earth's crust, the amount of exergy required to extract and re-concentrate it increases to a maximum. In a finite planetary environment, the concentration of a scarce metal can never fall below the average. This means that recycling will become more difficult over time, but it will never become impossible (Mayumi 1993; Ayres 1998a, 1999).

The popular notion of perfect recycling in a 'circular economy' (by industrial analogs of decay organisms) with 'zero emissions' is off base in a real economy. Contrary to Georgescu-Roegen's assertions, perfect recycling is theoretically possible given a flow of exergy from outside the system (for example, from the sun).[18] But zero emissions can be ruled out as a practical matter, if only because there is always a point at which the benefits of more complete waste treatment (or recycling) are less than the costs. This is the fundamental basis for benefit-cost analysis (for example, Herfindahl and Kneese 1973; Boadway 1974.) In fact, even the notion that natural ecosystems are perfect recyclers is quite false. The biosphere recycles carbon, oxygen and nitrogen with fairly high efficiency. Yet lignite, coal, petroleum and natural gas are actually transformed biological wastes.[19] Other elements needed by living systems are not recycled biologically to any significant degree, including phosphorus, sulfur, potassium calcium and iron. Chalk, limestone, iron ores and phosphate rock are all accumulations of biological wastes. The fact that they are sufficiently concentrated to be extracted economically as 'ores' is very fortunate for us, but somewhat irrelevant to the question of recycling. The ways in which materials are extracted, transformed and used in the real industrial economy, and the environmental implications, are the substance of the new field of Industrial Ecology.

The idea that economic growth must be limited by physical resource scarcity actually has quite a long history. It goes back, at least, to Thomas

Malthus, who saw arable land as the limiting factor (Malthus 1946 [1798]). Jevons in the 19th century worried about future availability of energy from coal (Jevons 1974 [1865]). Since 1919, there has been a series of predictions that petroleum reserves are about to run out, each 'crisis' followed by new discoveries and another glut (Yergin 1991). Scarcity worries were behind the neo-Malthusian 'limits to growth' thesis, propounded in the 1970s by the Club of Rome (Meadows et al. 1972). However, an authoritative study published by Resources for the Future Inc. had strongly indicated that scarcity – as indicated by price, production and reserve trends – was not yet a problem for any exhaustible mineral resource (Barnett and Morse 1963). A follow-up in 1979 seemed to confirm that result (Barnett 1979). This optimism might now have to be modified, at least with respect to oil and natural gas (Campbell and Laherrère 1998; Campbell 2004; Deffeyes 2005; Rutledge 2007).

The long-running debate between neo-Malthusians, who worry about scarcity, and 'cornucopians', who do not, remains unresolved to the present day. It is, in any case, beyond the scope of this book.

NOTES

1. Bastiat uses this story to introduce a concept he calls the *broken window fallacy*, which is related to the law of unintended consequences, in that both involve an incomplete accounting for the consequences of an action.
2. The problem was first recognized and discussed by economists in the 1970s (Tobin and Nordhaus 1972). It has been revisited more recently by Daly, Jackson and Marks and others (Daly 1989; Jackson and Marks 1994). There exist several examples of alternative welfare measures, including the Fordham Index of Social Health (FISH), the Genuine Progress Indicator (GPI) and the United Nations Human Development Index (UNHDI), to mention just a few.
3. The absolute minimum of entropy would correspond to absolute zero temperature. It is an unreachable state.
4. The idea that economic progress is explained mostly by capital investment, while long since abandoned as regards the industrialized countries, was still taken very seriously by many development specialists until very recently. The Harrod-Domar model predicts that the rate of growth of an economy in a year is proportional to the capital investment during the previous year. Harrod intended this as a way of explaining short-run fluctuations in output of industrial countries and disavowed its use for developing countries. Yet it was widely adopted by international institutions in the early 1950s for purposes of growth accounting and to estimate the so-called 'financing gap' for developing countries. This capital investment-centered approach was supported by the 'stages of growth' model of W.W. Rostow, who asserted that 'take-off' into sustained growth occurs only when the proportion of investment to national income rises from 5 to 10 percent (Rostow 1960). Several econometric studies have failed to find any evidence for this theory, however (for example, Kuznets 1963; United Nations Industrial Development Organization 2003).
5. The unrealistic neglect of materials (and energy) as factors of production in the economic system was pointed out long ago by Boulding (1966), Ayres and Kneese (1969) and Georgescu-Roegen (1971). Unfortunately, the mainstream view has not adapted.

This is extremely significant for policy, in the new century, because if resource consumption is only a consequence – and not a cause – of growth, then 'decoupling' growth from resource consumption is conceptually easy: they were never 'coupled' in the standard theory. On the other hand, if increasing resource consumption is inseparable from the 'growth engine' (as we argue), decoupling is impossible and dematerialization will be extremely difficult.

6. Virtually all models consider only man-made capital as a factor of production, although some attempts have been made to incorporate education and skills into something called 'human capital'. However, no role is generally assigned to natural capital as a factor of production, although many countries count the sale of raw materials as income, thus a contribution to GDP and hence a source of capital investment in the traditional sense. This issue is discussed briefly in Chapter 10.

7. Problems of defining and measuring capital gave rise to a well-known debate between Robert Solow et al. at MIT (Cambridge, Massachusetts) versus Joan Robinson and others at Cambridge University in the UK. The theory of capital (and the debate) was later reviewed by Harcourt (1972). A key part of the dispute was whether (or how) capital could have a value independent of its rate of return. This issue has been forgotten in recent years. Capital stock, in current models, is an accumulation based on monetary investment and depreciation, along the lines of the 'perpetual inventory' approach, which starts from a base year and adds new investments in various categories (for example, residential housing, non-residential buildings, machinery, roads and bridges, etc.) at current prices adjusted to a standard year, while simultaneously depreciating existing capital stocks based on assumed lifetimes.

8. In fairness it should be noted that Schelling is not the only important economist who has made this assumption in the context of discussions of the costs and benefits of greenhouse gas abatement policy. See Daly (2000).

9. In principle, the way a sector is defined in practice is that products within a sector are assumed to be similar enough to be mutually substitutable whereas products of different sectors are not substitutable. This is obviously a very strong assumption, since sectors are often defined in terms of a generic process (for example, agriculture or mining) or a generic use (for example, automobile parts). Yet the products of olive orchards and wheat farms are not substitutable; the products of iron mines, copper mines and gold mines are not substitutable; and the only link between engines, transmissions, headlights, brakes and axles is that they all get combined in a motor vehicle.

10. The major exceptions are the multi-sector models built by Dale Jorgenson and his colleagues (Christensen et al. 1983; Gollop and Jorgenson 1980, 1983), using the so-called 'trans-log' production function devised by Lauritz Christenson, Dale Jorgenson and Lawrence Lau (Christensen et al. 1973, 1971). Unfortunately these models are extremely data-intensive and lacking in transparency, making them hard to use and interpret.

11. Indeed, Kaldor tried to explain growth in terms of a positive feedback between demand, induced by increases in supply induced by increased demand (Kaldor 1966, 1972, 1979). He regarded the empirical 'Verdoorn Law' as evidence of this feedback (Verdoorn 1951). Our own theory can be regarded as an extension and elaboration of Kaldor's.

12. N.B. the national accounts reflect payments only to capital (as interest, dividends, rents and royalties) and to labor (as wages and salaries). The accounts therefore do not explicitly reflect payments to inputs (for example, energy, raw materials or environmental services from 'nature'). It is possible, of course, to distinguish payments to some tangible resource owners (royalties), and to natural resource extraction (labor), but these payments constitute only a very small percentage of the total.

13. Indeed, for 17 tests where the condition was *not* imposed as a constraint, values for alpha (the exponent for labor) ranged from 0.11 to 5.03, while values for beta (the exponent for capital) ranged from −0.74 to 1.35. Values for the sum of the two ranged from −0.09 to 4.29. Three of those tests were carried out in the original study by Paul Douglas himself, yielding values for the sum of the exponents of 1.04, 1.07 and 0.98 (Douglas 1948). In 14 other time series tests, where the sum of the two exponents was constrained to be unity,

the values for alpha ranged from −0.35 to 1.12, while the values for beta ranged from −0.12 to 1.35.

14. The positive feedback cycle is essentially identical to the 'rebound effect' cited by some economists to argue that increasing energy efficiency may not result in energy conservation (for example, Khazzoom 1980, 1987; Saunders 1992).

15. This assumption has been tested empirically by Nordhaus, who found that only a very small fraction (<10 percent) of the Schumpeterian profits of most innovations are captured by the innovators (Nordhaus 2004).

16. Paul David has emphasized this point (for example, David 1991, 2003).

17. Nuclear processes (fission or fusion) are apparent exceptions to the mass-balance rule, because they convert mass into energy. However, the conservation law, as applied to mass-energy, still holds.

18. We reject Georgescu-Roegen's so-called 'fourth law' (Mayumi 1993; Ayres 1999).

19. In the case of petroleum and natural gas, there is an alternative theory, attributing some hydrocarbons to geological processes, but it is thought that anaerobic decay accounts for most deposits.

6. The production function approach

6.1 INTRODUCTION

In this chapter we seek to explain economic activity and growth in terms of a 'production function'. A production function hereafter can be thought of as a model to explain output (GDP) consisting of a function of two or three independent variables. The traditional two-variable scheme involves only capital stock – or capital services – (K) and labor supply (L). For reasons explained at length in previous chapters, we do not consider the one-sector two-factor model hereafter, except as a point of departure. The three-factor scheme involves energy or natural resource use – call it X for the moment. In most studies, the factors of production (K, L, X) are regarded as independent variables. The assumption is that some combination of these variables can explain changes in a fourth dependent variable, namely the gross domestic product (Y) over a long period of time. We also assume (in common with most practitioners) that the production function exhibits constant returns to scale. Mathematically this implies that it is linear and homogeneous, of degree one (the Euler condition), which implies that the individual variables are subject to declining returns.

The usual formulation is deterministic, with output treated as a dependent variable. In our model, the four variables (including output) are regarded as mutually dependent (and cointegrated) in the long run. Each is determined (over time) by the others. Statistical evidence in support of this conjecture is provided in Chapter 7.

On the other hand, we do not suppose that all of the short-term fluctuations, whether attributable to business cycles or other causes, are fully accounted for by the above set of four variables. Any or all of them can be subject to external influences, whether natural disasters, conflicts, shortages or government fiscal or monetary policy changes. For instance, the labor supply may be decimated quite suddenly by epidemics, as happened during the various episodes of the 'black death' in Europe, or by wars. Wars, floods, storms or fires can destroy capital goods. Energy supplies (and prices) can be affected by political events, such as the oil embargo of 1973–4 or the Iranian revolution of 1979–80. We postulate, however, that most of these influences lead to short-term effects that are smoothed out over time. The exceptions might be major wars, like World War II, revolutionary changes of regime such as the downfall of the Soviet system, or major policy changes, such as the end of the gold standard.

6.2   ARGUMENTS AGAINST THE USE OF AGGREGATED PRODUCTION FUNCTIONS

However, there are a number of strong arguments against the use of production functions that we need to acknowledge and address if possible. The argument may be dated to the years immediately after World War II when economists were busy reconstructing historical statistics and national accounts, and the aggregate production function was in the process of being implemented as a practical tool.

The first question that arose was, not surprisingly, how the aggregate macroeconomic function should be related to the microeconomic production functions that characterize individual firms. There were two schools of thought with regard to this issue. Klein argued that the aggregate function should be strictly a technical relationship, comparable to firm-level production functions, and not reflecting behavioral assumptions such as profit maximizing (Klein 1946, p. 303, cited by Felipe and Fisher 2003):

> There are certain equations in micro-economics that are independent of the equilibrium conditions and we should expect that the corresponding equations in macro-economics will also be independent of the equilibrium conditions. The principal equations that have this independence property are the technological production functions. The aggregate production function should not depend on profit maximization but purely on technical factors.

Klein's view would be consistent with that of Leontief (1941). However the 'technological' view was immediately disputed (for example, May 1947; also quoted by Felipe and Fisher 2003):

> The aggregate production function is dependent on all the functions of the micro-model, including the behavior equations such as profit maximization, as well as all exogenous variables and parameters . . .

It will be clear in due course that the latter viewpoint has prevailed in the literature.

The next obvious problem was how to account for capital. Here again, two views emerged. One view, most strongly espoused by Joan Robinson at Cambridge (UK), was that capital stock should be measured in physical terms (Robinson 1953–4).This left open the question of how to measure heterogeneous physical capital stock in monetary terms. This question initiated the so-called 'Cambridge controversy' which has never really been resolved in the literature, notwithstanding Robinson's title-page assertion in 1971 (Robinson 1971). However, it has been resolved in the sense that the so-called 'perpetual inventory method' or PIM, developed especially by Angus Maddison, is now widely used in practice. This method measures capital stock as the accumulation of real (deflated) capital investment, less depreciation.[1] The standard objection to this approach is that the monetary value of capital depends upon prices, which can change for reasons unrelated to productivity. For example, the costs of capital equipment clearly reflect energy (exergy) prices at the time of manufacture.

In this book, we propose a partial reconciliation of the physical interpretation of capital and the economic interpretation. In short, we can adopt Kümmel's view that capital equipment is 'productive' only insofar as it contributes directly or indirectly to the function of extracting exergy resources, transporting them, converting energy (exergy) into useful work and work products including information, or utilizing such products for purposes of subsistence or enjoyment (for example, Kümmel et al. 1985). Obviously some types of capital – notably engines and related machines – convert energy directly into work, or perform work on work-pieces that eventually become components of products, including machines. Other types of capital protect the machines, or the associated infrastructure. The point is that virtually all types of capital (economically speaking) are involved in the exergy-work-production-service function and can therefore by measured in terms of exergy embodiment or exergy consumption.

A related problem is the implicit assumption that only two, or three, independent variables can really account for the output of the economy, as a dependent variable, over periods. Furthermore, it is a fact that any smooth twice-differentiable function of several variables – whether homogeneous of degree one or not – implies that the function exists for all possible combinations of the arguments. Since any combination is possible, the implication is that the variables can be substituted for each other throughout their ranges. In the two-factor case, this means that a specified output can be obtained with infinitesimal labor if there is enough capital, or conversely, with infinitesimal capital, with enough labor. The introduction of a third factor does not affect this conclusion: it implies that economic output is possible without any input of X (energy or useful work). In short, an attribute common to all production function models is the *built-in* assumption of complete substitutability between all of the factors.

Difficulties with the assumption of substitutability were discussed at some length in the previous chapter. Indeed, we know that there are limits to substitutability. In fact, all three inputs to the current economy are essential, which means non-substitutable except at the margin and over time. It is the *essentiality* of certain inputs (not only capital, labor and exergy) that imposes a multi-sectoral structure on the real economy. This, in turn, makes the output elasticity of an essential input – whether it be food, fresh water, copper or petroleum – much greater than its apparent cost share in the national accounts.

Evidently, substitutability is a variable concept, depending on the time element. It is arguable that instantaneous (for example, overnight) substitutability is essentially null. The economy has a great deal of inertia and there is really no possibility of substituting labor for capital, or capital for useful work – or conversely – in the very short term. A theoretical distinction was made between the movement of firms *along* a production frontier, versus movement *between* production frontiers (Solow 1957). Instantaneous substitution of this kind (if it were possible) would correspond to movements along the production frontier. This would correspond to increasing capital intensity (or 'capital deepening') without technological change.

However, the production frontier moves outward to a new frontier due to the combined effect where new capital (machines) also incorporates technological improvements. The importance of embedding technological change in new capital equipment and 'learning by doing' was emphasized by Arrow (1962). There is an important asymmetry between the degree of choice (of techniques) available before and after new machines have been installed. The flexible situation before installation of new machines has been characterized as 'putty', while after the machines are in place it becomes 'clay' (for example, Fuss 1977). For a broad survey, see Baily et al. (1981). Applications to the specific case of energy use have been reviewed by Atkeson and Kehoe (1999).

Within the standard theory of growth, there is a range of specifications with regard to the relative importance of these two modes: 'pure capital deepening' versus 'pure technological advance'. The standard Cobb-Douglas model allows for the former, and the notion of constant elasticity of substitution between capital and labor is embodied in the so-called CES production function introduced by Arrow et al. (1961). An alternative possibility is to rule out the possibility of capital deepening without accompanying technological change, that is, assuming that it is impossible to incorporate technological improvements without embedding them in new capital equipment (for example, Solow et al. 1966). However, while the two phenomena – capital deepening versus technological advance – can be distinguished in principle, there is apparently no satisfactory test to distinguish them in practice (Nelson 1973). Evidently, in the real world, virtually all opportunities for substitution require time and technological investment. The greater the degree of substitution, the more time and investment may be needed. We postulate that movements of the frontier are reflected and can be captured in time series data over a long enough period.

The need to distinguish between short-term and longer-term behavior seems to have been noticed in a different context by Levine (1960) and Massell (1962). It was rediscovered by Nelson (1973). The problem is that the sum of incremental short-term changes in the contributions of the factors of production (K, L) do not necessarily account for long-term changes. In Nelson's words (ibid., p. 465):

> Experienced growth is unlikely to be the simple sum of the contributions of separate factors. One could take the position that the degree of interaction among the factors is small, and that the separable contributions of the different factors are like the first terms of a Taylor expansion. This is an arguable position, but it rests on an assumption about the nature of the production function and about technical change. The approximation might be good and it might be poor. If the time period in question is considerable, Taylor series arguments are questionable.

Since the Cobb-Douglas and CES functions do not exhibit sharply changing gradients, it seems likely that interaction terms will have to be incorporated in the production function.

There is a further difficulty, namely that the three driving variables – and especially capital and useful work – are also to some extent *complements*. Machines need workers to operate and maintain them, and they need energy to function. In other words, they must be present in fixed (or nearly fixed) combinations. There is ample statistical, as well as anecdotal, evidence of complementarity between energy and capital (for example, Berndt and Wood 1975). This situation is inconsistent with the Cobb-Douglas production function or, indeed, any other smooth function of two or three variables. A production function with fixed ratios of inputs is called a Leontief function, because fixed ratios of inputs are characteristic of the Leontief model. Note that the plot of a Leontief production function in two (or three) dimensions is like a right angle or a corner. Except at the point of intersection (the corner), either some capital, or some labor (or some X) will be unutilized. It is not a smooth or differentiable function.

Assuming that aggregate production functions can be justified at all, the real situation at the national level is certainly somewhere in between the Cobb-Douglas and Leontief cases. That is to say, a realistic production function allowing for some degree of complementarity as well as some substitutability may not incorporate a sharp corner, but it should exhibit a sharply changing gradient, in the range where substitution is possible, as well as with a maximum second derivative near the optimum combination of the three variables. The three cases are shown graphically in Figure 6.1.

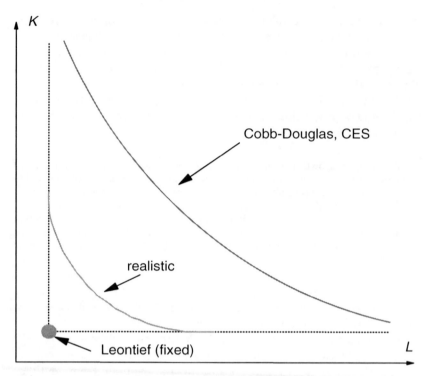

Figure 6.1   Substitutability in aggregate production functions

Another major problem is estimating capital stock *per se*. As we noted in the previous chapter, the so-called Cambridge controversies in the 1960s highlighted many of the problems, notably the difficulty of aggregating heterogeneous capital-comprising machines, structures, inventories, infrastructures, money and even natural resource stocks (Harcourt 1972). In practice, we adopt Maddison's 'perpetual inventory' method (PIM) to measure capital in monetary terms, accumulating capital from new investment less depreciation (Maddison 1982). But this method has certain drawbacks. As a subtraction from potential consumption, it makes reasonable sense, but it makes no allowance for changes in monetary values arising from price fluctuations, or for the non-equivalence and non-substitutability of different kinds of capital within the category. Machines are not equivalent to or interchangeable with structures or inventories, and a truck is not equivalent to 100 wheelbarrows. Indeed, some other implicit assumptions of neoclassical production theory can be violated. Unfortunately, no one knows how seriously these distortions bias the results.

The next class of difficulties concerns estimation of the parameters of the production function by regressing time-series data for a few highly correlated variables (for example, Mendershausen 1938; Griliches and Mairesse 1998). It was discovered long ago that almost any set of collinear capital and labor time series can be fitted to a Solow-type Cobb-Douglas function with a residual $A(t)$ subject to the Euler condition (constant returns) and constant savings rate. This is partly due to the fact that the residual $A(t)$ absorbs deviations from the actual data (for example, Hogan 1958). For other critiques along these lines see Shaikh (1974), Simon (1979) and Shaikh (1980).

More recently the problem with production functions has been restated more broadly by Felipe and Fisher as follows:

> The *ex post* income accounting identity that relates the value of output (VA) to the sum of the wage bill (wL where w is the average wage rate and L is employment) plus total profits (rK where r is the average *ex post* profit rate and K is the stock of capital) can be easily rewritten through a simple algebraic transformation as $VA = A(t)F(K, L)$ . . . The implication of this argument is that the precise form . . . corresponding to the particular data set $VA = wL + rK$ has to yield a perfect fit if estimated econometrically (because all that is being estimated is an identity); the putative elasticities have to coincide with the factor shares and the marginal products have to coincide with the factor prices . . . it says nothing about the nature of production, returns to scale and distribution. (Felipe and Fisher 2003, pp. 252–3)

Felipe and Fisher also note that the accounting identity does not follow from Euler's theorem if the aggregate production function does not exist. Finally, the *ex post* profit rate r in this identity is not the same as the cost of capital to users; it is merely the number that makes the accounting identity hold (ibid).

A consequence of this is that a production function derived from empirical data cannot be used to determine output elasticities with high reliability. Apart from the implicit accounting identity, estimated parameters tend to pick up biases from mis-specification or omitted variables. For us, a further question is whether the third variable in our formulation (exergy or useful work) really captures enough of the impact of other aspects of technological advancement, structural change and human capital. We will attempt to address this question again later.

In some ways, the case against using aggregate production functions of a very few variables seems overwhelming; certainly stronger than the case for using them.[2] The major reason for taking this approach, despite problems, is that it is familiar and both relatively transparent and relatively convenient. The conclusions, if any, must, necessarily, be considered carefully in the light of the criticisms.

6.3   SOME BACKGROUND CONCEPTS

Because of the *essentiality* (non-substitutability) condition noted several paragraphs above, we conceptualize the economic system as a multi-sector chain of linked processing stages, starting with resource extraction, reduction, refining, conversion, production of finished goods and services, including capital goods, final consumption (and disposal of wastes). Each stage has physical inputs and physical outputs that pass to the next stage. At each stage of processing, value is added and useful information is embodied in the products, while low value, high entropy, low information wastes are separated and disposed of.[3] Global entropy increases at every step, of course, but the value-added process tends to reduce the entropy of useful products, while increasing the entropy of the wastes. An adequate description of the economic system, viewed in this way, must include all materials and energy flows, and information flows, as well as money flows. These flows and conversion processes between them are governed by the first and second laws of thermodynamics, as well as by monetary accounting balances.

It is evident that there are also feedbacks – reverse flows – along the process chain. For instance, capital goods are manufactured products that are important inputs to all stages, including the extraction and processing stages. Electric power and liquid motor fuels are intermediate products that are utilized in all sectors, including the extraction sectors. Information services, including financial services, produced near the end of the chain are also utilized by all sectors. This feedback is the fundamental idea behind Leontief's input-output model (Leontief 1936). When monetary flows are considered, the feedbacks are significant. Certainly they cannot be ignored. However, for the present, we are less concerned with monetary flows than with flows of mass/exergy (or useful work). From this perspective, the reverse flows are quantitatively small compared to the main mass/exergy flows in the forward (downstream) direction.

The next step must be to justify the use of a so-called aggregate production function in a situation where an input-output (I-O) model with fixed proportions might seem to be more appropriate, at least for short-run analysis. However, in the longer term, substitution between factors does occur – in conjunction with investment – whence the Leontief model with fixed coefficients is inappropriate.[4] We expect to show that the relative importance of capital and energy (as useful work) have increased significantly over time *vis-à-vis* labor. This change reflects the long-term substitution of machines (in the most general sense) driven by exogenous energy sources mainly fossil fuels, for human and animal muscles, and human brains.

In the standard theory of productivity growth, beginning with Solow, firms produce goods and services – actually, a single composite product

– while households produce labor. Firms are assumed to be very small profit-maximizing price-takers, subject to constant returns to scale, producing a single composite good, and using capital and labor to the extent justified by marginal productivity of these factors. Consumers (households) sell labor and own capital, while firms may also own capital. In this idealized case, the cost shares for capital and labor in the national accounts would be equal to the corresponding output elasticities. We could, of course, generalize the Solow model by adding energy flows or useful work flows, provided by an exogenous utility. Each firm would purchase the amount of useful work justified by its marginal productivity. The question remains: what is the marginal productivity of useful work and what is its cost share? The latter question is particularly vexing. It can best be approached by means of an input-output model, as noted in the last chapter (and again later).

However, (in the spirit of evolutionary models) we do *not* assume that firms must operate on or move along the 'frontier' of a region in factor-space, as they would have to do if they were profit-maximizers with perfect information in a perfectly competitive market. On the contrary, we postulate (in the spirit of Milton Friedman (1953)) that if an assumed relationship explains (that is, reproduces) the empirical observations, one need not worry too much about the realism of every one of the underlying assumptions.[5] We also concede, in common with most neoclassical theorists, that the notion of a 'frontier', where all firms exist at all times, is quite a stretch from reality.[6] In reality, the collection of firms in factor-space constitutes a sort of turbulent cloud (Figure 6.2). The 'frontier' idea is useful only to the extent that it describes the average of an ensemble.

We also recognize that the economy is really multi-sectoral. Firms operate in sectors where they compete with others within the sector, but not with firms in other sectors. This assumption reflects intersectoral non-substitutability, as mentioned above, but does not exclude the possibility that generic inputs (capital, labor and energy services as useful work) may substitute for each other even in the short run, within some small range.

In short, we argue that a postulated functional relationship among aggregates (capital, labor and mass/exergy – or useful work) flows is an adequate representation of the real world, at least for the purposes of explaining economic growth. Almost all firms are operating at some distance from this fictitious frontier, either inside it and outside it. The only further assumption needed to account for this picture is that firms do not have perfect knowledge or foresight, and that competition is not perfectly efficient. A firm too far inside the cloudy frontier is likely to be unprofitable and risks being selected out, in time, if it does not change its strategic behavior. On the other hand, a firm on the outside is likely to be above average in profitability, and may grow at the expense of its competitors.

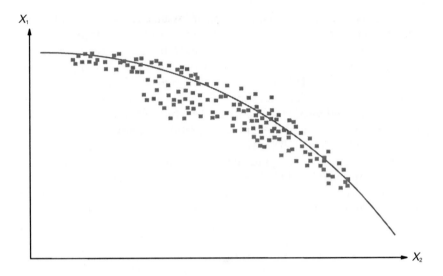

Figure 6.2   The production frontier as a turbulent cloud

If the condition of constant returns to scale is retained, it can be shown without difficulty (below) that adding a third term for materials and energy (exergy) resource inputs in a conventional Cobb-Douglas function for a single sector, while retaining the interpretation of output elasticity as share of payments in the national accounts, does not explain past economic growth any better than the original Solow model without a multiplier $A(t)$. It is also inconsistent with the usual assumption that the economy is a single sector with a single composite output, as noted in Chapter 5. In other words, an exogenous time-dependent multiplier to reflect technical progress or total factor productivity is still required in this case.

However, if only for historical purposes, we start with the old Cobb-Douglas function.

6.4   EXERGY IN THE COBB-DOUGLAS MODEL OF GROWTH

The simplest mathematical form that satisfies the constant returns to scale (Euler) condition and integrability conditions (Appendix A) is the single-sector, two-factor Cobb-Douglas production function:

$$Y = A(t)K^\alpha L^\beta \tag{6.1}$$

where the constant returns condition implies that

$$\alpha + \beta = 1 \tag{6.2}$$

It is traditional (as noted in Chapter 5) to interpret the marginal productivities α and β (elasticities of output) as factor payments shares for capital and labor in the national accounts. This is convenient because the national accounts are actually constructed in terms of payments to labor (wages, salaries) and payments to capital (interest, dividends, royalties). This makes such an interpretation seem natural.

It seems natural in this spirit to add a third factor such as exergy E, as follows:

$$Y = A(t)K^\alpha L^\beta E^\gamma \tag{6.3}$$

where $A(t)$ is the 'Solow residual', that is, the growth component that is not explained by either capital accumulation or increased labor supply. The constant returns condition implies that

$$\alpha + \beta + \gamma = 1 \tag{6.4}$$

The factor payments shares interpretation is not valid, however, when a third factor is introduced. As already explained, this is because segregating 'payments to exergy' amounts to considering exergy production as a separate sector, or sectors. Payments to 'exergy' are really payments to farmers, lumber companies, coal mines or oil and gas producers, mostly for labor and capital. These firms taken as a group constitute a sector or sectors. As a fraction of all payments (GDP), payments to this sector are comparatively small, that is, only 4 percent to 5 percent for most OECD countries. This implies – according to the standard neoclassical (single sector) interpretation noted in the last chapter – that the marginal productivity of resource inputs must be correspondingly small, too small to account for consumer price changes or GDP growth changes (for example, Denison 1979). The income allocation theorem (Appendix A), which is based on a single sector, single 'composite' product model, does not hold for a multi-sector, multi-product model.

The growth equation is the total time derivative of the production function,

$$\frac{dY}{dt} = Y\left(\frac{\alpha}{K}\frac{\partial K}{\partial t} + \frac{\beta}{L}\frac{\partial L}{\partial t} + \frac{\gamma}{E}\frac{\partial E}{\partial t} + \frac{1}{A}\frac{\partial A}{\partial t}\right) \tag{6.5}$$

The last term reflects the possibility that some part of the growth cannot be explained in terms of K, L, E and is therefore a function of time alone.

We can now define the four output elasticities α, β, γ and δ, where δ can be thought of as the marginal productivity δ of 'technical progress' as follows, assuming constant returns to scale:

$$\alpha = \frac{\partial \ln Y}{\partial \ln K} = \frac{K}{Y}\frac{\partial Y}{\partial K} \tag{6.6}$$

$$\beta = \frac{\partial \ln Y}{\partial \ln L} = \frac{L}{Y}\frac{\partial Y}{\partial L} \tag{6.7}$$

$$\gamma = \frac{\partial \ln Y}{\partial \ln E} = 1 - \alpha - \beta \ \text{(constant returns)} \tag{6.8}$$

$$\delta(t) = \frac{A}{Y}\frac{\partial Y}{\partial t} = \frac{\partial A}{\partial t} \tag{6.9}$$

where α, β and γ are all functions of K, L and E. The integrability conditions are not trivial. Mathematically, they require that the second-order mixed derivatives of the production function Y with respect to all factors K, L, E must be equal. In words, these conditions imply that the integrals along any two paths between two points in factor space are equal. It is quite conceivable that this condition might not hold. If it does not hold, integrals along different paths between the same two points would depend on the path. The economic interpretation of such a situation might be a regime change, such as the breakdown of the centrally planned Soviet economy in 1989 and its replacement by free-market capitalism.

The integrability condition requires that

$$K\frac{\partial \alpha}{\partial K} + L\frac{\partial \alpha}{\partial L} + E\frac{\partial \alpha}{\partial E} = 0 \tag{6.10}$$

$$K\frac{\partial \beta}{\partial K} + L\frac{\partial \beta}{\partial L} + E\frac{\partial \beta}{\partial E} = 0 \tag{6.11}$$

$$L\frac{\partial \alpha}{\partial L} + K\frac{\partial \beta}{\partial K} \tag{6.12}$$

The most general solutions to these three equations are:

$$\alpha = a\left(\frac{L}{K},\frac{E}{K}\right) \tag{6.13}$$

$$\beta = \int \frac{L}{K}\frac{\partial \alpha}{\partial L}dK + J\left(\frac{L}{E}\right) \tag{6.14}$$

The simplest (trivial) solutions are constants, namely: $\alpha = \alpha_0$, $\beta = \beta_0$ and $\gamma = 1 - \alpha - \beta$. We consider other solutions of the above equations later. For the single-sector two-factor case, we then obtain the original Cobb-Douglas function where $\alpha_0 + \beta_0 = 1$ ($\gamma = 0$) and the usual choices for α_0 and β_0 are 0.3 and 0.7, corresponding to the time-averaged cost shares for capital and labor, respectively, in the national accounts.

Figures 6.3a and 6.3b graph the key factors of production, for the US and Japan, over the period 1900–2004. Figure 6.4 (for the US) shows clearly that the C-D function with resource inputs E as a third independent variable, but retaining the constant returns condition and with an exponent (corresponding to marginal productivity) proportional to the share of payments to resource inputs in the national accounts, does not explain historical US growth over the long run. Similar results could easily be shown for Japan and other industrialized countries.[7]

Reverting to the standard Solow model, and its accompanying assumptions, $A(t)$ can be fitted independently to the unexplained residual that was once called 'technological progress' or, more recently, total factor productivity (TFP). We have done this, as shown in Figure 6.5. The 'best fit' for the technical progress function over the whole period 1900–98 (shown in the graph) is $A(t) = \exp[0.0388(t - 1900)]$ where t is the year. In other words, throughout the 20th century, growth attributable to exogenous technical progress or TFP in the US has averaged 3.9 percent per annum. However, there have been significant deviations from the average growth rate in certain periods, for example, below trend in the 1930s and above trend in the early postwar decades.

It is important to recognize that the third factor E is not truly independent of the other two. This means that not all combinations of the three factors are actually possible. In particular, capital and resource flows are strongly – and obviously – synergistic, hence correlated. Indeed, capital – except for residential housing and money – can be defined for our purposes as the collection of all energy-conversion machines and information-processing equipment plus structures to contain and move them. Thus capital goods are activated by energy (exergy) flows, while exergy has no economic function in the absence of capital goods.

The Cobb-Douglas function assumes constant marginal productivities over the entire century from 1900–98. This is also unrealistic. The essential result that holds true in general is the following: including resource (exergy) inputs in the model as a third factor of production cannot explain long-term growth, but the imputed marginal productivity of resource inputs is much greater than the factor-payments share (for example, Kümmel et al. 1985, 2000; McKibben and Wilcoxen 1994, 1995; Bagnoli et al. 1996). We will arrive at a similar conclusion subsequently by a different route, in Chapter 7.

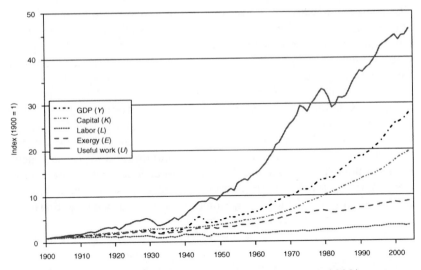

Figure 6.3a   GDP and factors of production (USA, 1900–2005)

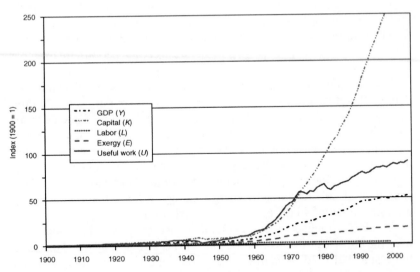

Figure 6.3b   GDP and factors of production (Japan, 1900–2005)

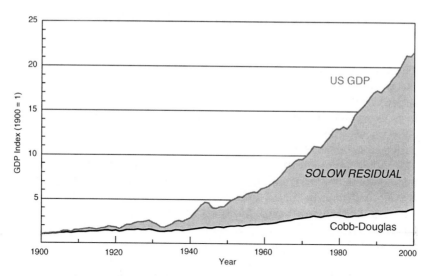

Figure 6.4 US GDP, 1900–2000 (actual versus three-factor Cobb-
Douglas function, L (0.70), K (0.26), E (0.04))

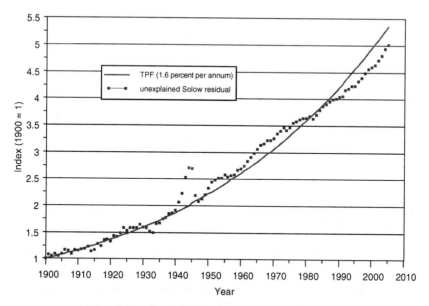

Figure 6.5 Technological progress function and Solow residual (USA,
1900–2005)

6.5 EXERGY IN THE LINEX PRODUCTION FUNCTION

The Cobb-Douglas function discussed above is the simplest solution of the growth and integrability conditions. However, the C-D function has serious weaknesses. The major weakness from our perspective is the built-in assumption that marginal productivities and elasticities of all factors are constant over the whole century. That assumption would be inconsistent with technological change.

Another approach (first demonstrated by Kümmel) is to choose the next-simplest *non-trivial* solutions of the growth equation and integrability equations (Kümmel 1980; Kümmel et al. 1985). This was done by selecting plausible mathematical expressions for the output elasticities α, β and γ based on asymptotic boundary conditions. To satisfy the Euler condition, these must be homogeneous zeroth order functions of the independent variables. Since the elasticities are partial logarithmic derivatives of the output Y (by definition), one can perform the appropriate partial integrations to obtain the corresponding production function, except for a constant term.

The first of Kümmel's proposed solutions can be thought of as a form of the law of diminishing returns (to capital). It is an asymptotic boundary condition conveying the notion that even in a hypothetical capital-intensive future state, in which all products are produced by machines, some irreducible need for labor L and exergy E will remain, namely:

$$\alpha = a\frac{L + E}{K} \qquad (6.15)$$

Kümmel's second equation reflects the continuing substitution of labor by capital and exergy as capital intensity (automation) increases:

$$\beta = a\left(b\frac{L}{E} - \frac{L}{K}\right) \qquad (6.16)$$

The assumption of constant returns to scale implies that, at every moment in time,

$$\gamma = 1 - \alpha - \beta \qquad (6.17)$$

which is the constant returns condition. Partial integration of the growth equation yields the so-called LINEX (linear-exponential) function:

$$Y = AE\exp\left[a(t)\left(2 - \left(\frac{L + E}{K}\right)\right) + a(t)b(t)\left(\frac{L}{E} - 1\right)\right] \qquad (6.18)$$

The functions (of time) $a(t)$ and $b(t)$ have been characterized by Kümmel as 'capital efficiency' and 'energy demand' respectively. It turns out that the multiplier A can be set equal to unity.

Not surprisingly, with time-dependent parameters $a(t)$ and $b(t)$, the GDP fits can be extremely good. On the other hand, neither $a(t)$ nor $b(t)$ has a straightforward economic interpretation. Hence, such a model is not ideal for forecasting. What is interesting, however, is the resulting calculated time-dependent productivities, which show a significant increase in exergy productivity and a decline in labor productivity, over time.[8]

6.6 INTRODUCING USEFUL WORK U

We now propose a true two-sector model with a third factor consisting of 'useful work' (denoted U) performed by the economy, as a whole. By definition, the product of resource (exergy) inputs E times conversion efficiency f is equal to useful work performed U. There are two ways to measure E, one of which includes biomass (agricultural and forest products) plus non-fuel minerals, while the other version is limited to commercial fuels and other commercial energy sources.[9] Having adopted the convention of an aggregate production function of the variables K, L and E, and a multi-sector 'process chain' approximation, we can write:

$$Y = E \times \frac{I_1}{E} \times \frac{I_2}{I_1} \times \frac{I_3}{I_2} \times \ldots \times \frac{Y}{I_n}$$

$$= E \times f_1 \times f_2 \times \ldots g \qquad (6.19)$$

Evidently f_1 is the conversion efficiency of the resource (exergy) inflow E into the first level intermediate product I_1; this occurs in the first (extractive) sector. In the second sector, I_1 is converted with efficiency f_2 into the second intermediate product I_2, and so on. The term g is just the ratio of output Y to the last intermediate product. Equation 6.19 is still an identity. It becomes a model only when we specify the intermediate products and functional forms.

As a first approximation, it is now convenient to assume that the economy is a two-stage system with a single intermediate product, denoted U. (To those skeptics who correctly point out that a two-stage approximation is much too simple for realism, we note that most of economic growth theory to date postulates a single-stage, single-sector, composite product model.) Then we have, to a first approximation:

$$Y = Efg = Ug \qquad (6.20)$$

where f is the overall technical efficiency of conversion of 'raw' exergy inputs E into useful work output U. Note that E and U are measured in the same (energy) units, whence the ratio $f = U/E$ is a dimensionless number. It can be interpreted as the efficiency of conversion of raw materials taken from nature into useful work (including finished materials).

To summarize: while discarding most of the neoclassical equilibrium and optimality assumptions as unnecessary, we retain the assumption that a production function of three factors (variables) is definable and meaningful.[10] We also retain (notwithstanding some reservations) the assumption of constant returns to scale, meaning that the production function must be a homogeneous function of the first order (Euler condition). Hence, the term g on the right-hand side of Equation 6.21 can be interpreted as an aggregate production function provided it is homogeneous of order zero with arguments labor L, capital K, and useful work U.

The calculation of E and U and the calculation of the efficiency factor f are major computational undertakings in themselves, since much of the underlying data is not published, as such, in official government statistics. The time series for useful work U must be constructed from other time series and information about the history of technology. Details of these calculations, for the US, were presented in Chapter 4.

As already noted, the new variable U is an *intermediate product*, meaning that it is an output generated by one sector and utilized by another sector (or sectors) within the economy. A single-sector model is not adequate for the same reason already explained: at least two sectors are necessary. The first sector produces the intermediate product U from inputs of capital K^*, labor L^* and some fraction of the useful work U^* (the exergy inputs to useful work can be regarded as free gifts of nature). It follows that the capital K^*, labor L^* and U^* needed to produce the aggregate useful work output U should therefore be *subtracted* from the total inputs of K and L in the production function, to avoid double counting. In principle, as inputs to the first sector, one should calculate K^*, L^* and U^* and subtract them from the totals K, L and U, respectively. Let

$$U = Y_1 (K^*, L^*, U^*) \qquad (6.21)$$

On the other hand, the second sector Y_2 produces all 'downstream' goods and services (that is, GDP) from inputs of capital $K - K^*$, labor $L - L^*$ and useful work $U - U^*$.

$$Y = Y_2 (K - K^*, L - L^*, U - U^*) \qquad (6.22)$$

However, it seems reasonable to postulate, as a first approximation, that capital, labor and useful work are used in the same proportions in the production of useful work U as they are in the economy as a whole. In fact, we assume that the mathematical form of the production functions Y_1, Y_2 and Y are identical in form, except for a constant multiplier. This being so, it follows that

$$\frac{K - K^*}{K} = \frac{L - L^*}{L} = \frac{U - U^*}{U} = \lambda \qquad (6.23)$$

whence we can write

$$K - K^* = \lambda K \qquad (6.24)$$

$$L - L^* = \lambda L \qquad (6.25)$$

$$U - U^* = \lambda U \qquad (6.26)$$

It follows that

$$Y_1(K^*, L^*, U^*) = (1 - \lambda) Y(K, L, U) \qquad (6.27)$$

$$Y_2(K - K^*, L - L^*, U - U^*) = \lambda Y(K, L, U) \qquad (6.28)$$

and therefore

$$Y_1 + Y_2 = Y \qquad (6.29)$$

Actually the above logic is not only applicable to the simple Cobb-Douglas case. It also applies to any production function that is homogeneous and of order unity, including the so-called LINEX function discussed next. To be sure, it is possible that the 'mix' of labor, capital and useful work inputs to the primary sector is slightly different than the mix of inputs applicable to the secondary (or other) sectors. For instance, the primary extraction and conversion sector may be slightly more capital-intensive and less labor-intensive than the downstream sector(s). However, adjusting for such small differences is a second-order correction.

Conceptually, the cost of producing useful work can be equated with the monetary value of the capital and labor consumed in the extractive and primary processing sector, plus the amount of useful work consumed within that sector. However, there are no quantitative data for any of these factors. Among the components of useful work, only electric power has a market price. This is undoubtedly a limitation on our model, although hopefully not a critical flaw.

6.7 THE LINEX MODEL WITH USEFUL WORK AS A THIRD FACTOR

It is clear that the argument for introducing exergy E as a third factor in Equation 6.3 applies equally well to useful work U. We have therefore modified the scheme of Kümmel et al. by substituting useful work U for commercial energy (exergy) inputs E in their LINEX production function, bearing in mind that our underlying model economy must have at least two sectors because U is explicitly an intermediate product.[11] The major justification for this formulation is the hope that all of the time dependence of 'technical progress' can be explained in terms of K, L and U. We also postulate that $\delta = 0$ and that a and b may be taken to be constants, independent of time, although we also consider the time-dependent case.

The assumed marginal productivities are given by Equations 6.15 and 6.16. The constant returns to scale (Euler) condition, Equation 6.4 (also Equation 6.17), also holds. Partial integration and exponentiation yields the time-independent linear-exponential (LINEX) function analogous to Equation 6.18, except that U replaces E and $A = 1$:

We note that the above LINEX function satisfies the three so-called Inada conditions with respect to capital K, namely $Y(0) = 0$; $Y'(0) = \infty$; $Y'(\infty) = 0$ (Inada 1963). Comparing Equation 6.18 with Equation 6.21, it is clear that the function g can be written

$$g = \exp\left[a\left(2 - \left(\frac{L + U}{K}\right)\right) + ab\left(\frac{L}{U} - 1\right)\right] \qquad (6.30)$$

which is a zeroth order homogeneous function of the variables, as required for constant returns to scale. In principle, a and b could still be functions of time.

It is interesting to note that by equating the two models for GDP, namely the C-D function (Equation 6.1) and the LINEX function (Equation 6.18), one can obtain an expression for the $A(t)$ multiplier in Equation 6.1, in terms of K, L and U, namely

$$A(t) = K^{-\alpha}L^{-\beta}U^{\alpha+\beta}\exp\left[ab - 2a + a\frac{L + U}{K} - ab\frac{L}{U}\right] \qquad (6.31)$$

It is evident that $A(t)$ in this formulation is strongly dependent on U, and more weakly (and inversely) dependent on K and L. These variables are functions of time, of course, and U is the product of resource exergy input E times exergy conversion efficiency f as in Equations 6.19 and 6.20. In short, if the model (Equation 6.31) can be parametrized to fit the actual

GDP data reasonably well, $A(t)$ can be explained approximately as a function of resource conversion efficiency. Numerical results and interpretations are discussed in Chapter 7.

NOTES

1. Maddison subdivides capital into several categories (machines, structures, etc.) with different average lifetimes. The method is obviously subject to criticism, but to date nobody seems to have come up with an improvement that is workable.
2. The most consistent and persistent skeptic over the years has probably been Franklin Fisher (Fisher 1965, 1968, 1969a, 1969b, 1987, 1993; Felipe and Fisher 2003).
3. The language here is suggestive of an energy (or information) theory of value. Unfortunately, perhaps, the term 'value-added' is so thoroughly established in economics that it cannot reasonably be avoided. In any case, we are not espousing the discredited energy theory of value. For a more thorough discussion of the economy as a self-organized system of concentrating 'useful information', see Ayres (1994a, chapter 8).
4. It is worthwhile pointing out that Robert Solow's (1956) criticism of the Harrod-Domar model was to note that the so-called 'razor's edge' property of that model (which called for a very precise and impracticable matching of capital investment to labor-force growth) was a consequence of the assumption of fixed coefficients. Solow (and Swan) subsequently offered a theory that characterized technological advance as a shift in the production function (Solow 1957; Swan 1956).
5. Friedman actually said 'truly important and significant hypotheses will be found to have "assumptions" that are widely inaccurate, descriptive representations of reality, and in general the more significant the theory, the more unrealistic the assumptions, in this sense'. He went on to say 'To be important, therefore, a hypothesis must be prescriptively false in its assumptions'. His remarks have been generally interpreted to mean that the validity (that is, non-falsification) of a theory depends only on its predictive ability, not on the realism of its assumptions (van den Bergh et al. 2000). It should be noted that Friedman's remarks were intended to defend the unrealistic assumptions of neoclassical microeconomics against critics.
6. The theory of 'distance functions' that has recently emerged explicitly recognizes this fact (Faere and Grosskopf 1994; Faere 1988; Faere and Grosskopf 1993; Faere et al. 1994).
7. Retaining the constant returns condition but relaxing the (one-sector) assumption that productivity equals payments share in the national accounts enables a crude statistical fit, using OLS regression, with E as a third variable, and no time-dependent multiplier. (As it happens, this procedure is spurious, because the underlying distribution of residuals is not Gaussian, as it should be for OLS regressions to be valid.) In this case, the regression yields a negative value (-0.76) for the exponent of labor (L), a positive value (0.56) for the exponent of capital (K) and a positive value ($+1.20$) for the exponent of exergy E. In the case of Japan, the OLS 'best fit' exponents, with exergy as a third variable, are all positive and in the range [0–1]. But the fit itself is rather poor after 1980. In both countries, the fit is considerably better with U as the third factor. (Again, the OLS regression is spurious.)
8. Kümmel and colleagues have obtained extremely close fits for three countries using the LINEX function with energy (exergy) as the third variable, and fitting the functions $a(t)$ and $b(t)$ by a logistic function or a Taylor expansion, resulting in a five-parameter model. Fits have been obtained for the US and the Federal Republic of Germany (total economy, 1960–98), and for Japan (industrial output) over the period 1965–95. In all three cases, the R^2 value is 0.999 and the Durbin-Watson coefficient is quite good

(DW= 1.46 for the US, 1.64 for Germany and 1.71 for Japan). The German results are remarkable, since they refer only to West Germany before 1990 and the merger with the so-called German Democratic Republic (GDR) in that year (Lindenberger et al. 2007).

9. Both versions of each variable, r and u have been tested statistically (see Ayres and Warr 2003). Both versions are defined and measured in terms of the thermodynamic measure already introduced. The more inclusive definition of resource inputs consistently provides a significantly better fit to the GDP data, regardless of choice of production function. We have done the OLS fits both with and without the constraint of constant returns. Without constant returns, the sum of the three calculated output elasticities turns out to be of the order of 1.3, which is implausibly high.

10. We do *not* assume that firms must operate on, or move along, the 'frontier' (by substitution among factors) as they would have to do if they were price-taking profit-maximizers operating at the least-cost point with perfect information in a perfectly competitive market. On the contrary, we regard the 'frontier' as the (fuzzy) locus of points in K-L-E space such that firms operating inside at a given time are uncompetitive and likely to decline, whereas firms outside the frontier are more likely to survive and grow. However, success or failure in an evolutionary model is not instantaneous, and a firm operating inside the frontier may be able to restructure or innovate to improve its competitive situation. This view is theoretically inconsistent with constant returns, atomistic competition, differentiability and various other assumptions underlying the notion of the production function (Sylos Labini 1995). For our purposes, we rely on the fact that there seems to be an empirical phenomenon that is consistent with the notion of aggregate capital.

11. The three-factor version of the Cobb-Douglas and LINEX models are already implicitly two-sector models since, in practice, the cost of exergy input E is *not* defined in terms of payments to 'nature' but rather to extractive industries that own natural resources, namely coal-mining, oil and gas drilling and hydro-electricity.

7. Numerical results for the US and Japan

7.1 INTRODUCTION

There are two types of time series data used in this chapter. Details of the data and sources are given in Appendix B. One type consists of standard economic data, originally compiled and published by governments or international agencies (such as the OECD). These data are based on a variety of sources that need not concern us particularly, since the published results are accepted and utilized by most economic modelers. This applies to labor supply (man-hours) and – in the US case – capital stock. Since our first test case is the US, we have used publications of the US government – notably the Bureau of Labor Statistics and the Bureau of Economic Analysis – since 1970. These data are available on the internet. For earlier periods, we use a compilation by the US Department of the Census (United States Bureau of the Census 1975).

In the case of Japan (and most other countries we are aware of), long time series for capital stock data are not published by governments, as such. The most convenient source for long-term comparative analysis is Maddison (1995a, chapter 5).

For purposes of extending the economic analysis beyond the US, consistency of definition is important. The most convenient international economic database is now maintained by the Groningen Growth and Development Centre, in the Netherlands (Groningen Growth and Development Centre 2006).

Exergy and useful work time series are derived for the US from 'energy' data published by the Energy Information Agency, which is part of the Department of Energy (United States Energy Information Agency 1991, 1994, 1995, 1997, 1998) and from historical statistics prior to 1975 (United States Bureau of the Census 1975). In this case, there have been some changes of category that require minor adjustments for earlier periods as far back as 1949, but the details of those adjustments do not concern us here. Detailed calculations of exergy and useful work for the US can be found in our original publications (Ayres et al. 2003, 2005), which are summarized in Chapter 4.

Energy data for Japan are taken from the International Energy Agency publications and from a publication co-authored by Dr Eric Williams (Williams and Warr 2008). Detailed Japanese data sources are given in that paper and in Appendix B.

7.2   EXERGY AND USEFUL WORK

The calculation of E and U for the US – or any country – and the calculation of the efficiency factor f are major computational undertakings in themselves, since much of the underlying data are not collected or published, as such, in official government statistics. The time series for useful work U must be constructed from other time series, for example, on energy consumption by category and information about the uses of energy and the history of technology. However, the results for exergy/GDP and work/GDP, in graphical form, are shown in Figures 7.1 and 7.2, for the US and Japan, respectively.

Note that the exergy required to produce a unit of GDP in Japan is just about half of the amount required by the US economy, and this

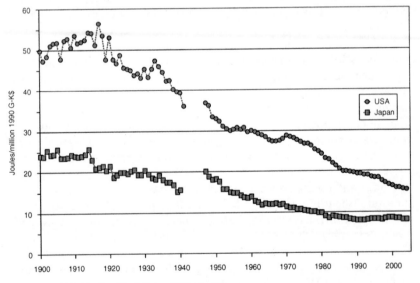

Note: G-K$ is International Geary-Khamis dollars.

Figure 7.1   Exergy to GDP ratio (USA and Japan, 1900–2005, excluding 1941–47)

Figure 7.2   Useful work (U) to GDP ratio (USA and Japan, 1900–2005, excluding 1941–47)

relationship has been consistent throughout the 20th century. There is no peak or 'inverted U' when biomass exergy is included along with fossil fuels, although the US data show a slight increase from 1900 to 1925 or so. However the work/GDP ratios for both countries exhibit a very well-marked peak, occurring in the early 1970s. That peak corresponds in time to the Arab oil embargo and the so-called 'energy crisis' that triggered a spike in petroleum prices and prices of other fuels.

From the data plotted in Figures 7.1 and 7.2 it is possible to calculate aggregate exergy-to-work *efficiencies* for the economies of the two countries. Results are shown in Figure 7.3. It is noteworthy – and surprising – that, according to our calculations, the efficiency of the Japanese economy actually peaked in the early 1970s and began to decline, albeit slowly, whereas the (lower) efficiency of the US economy has increased more or less monotonically up to now, while remaining significantly lower than that of Japan. The explanation is, probably, that as Japan has become more prosperous since the 1960s, inefficient uses of energy (exergy) have grown faster than aggregate efficiency gains. The fact that favorable hydro-electric sites were already exploited has necessitated increased use of less efficient steam-electric generation. Similarly, inefficient personal automobiles have shifted quite a bit of urban traffic away from more efficient public transportation. Finally, household uses of electricity such as hot water and air-conditioning

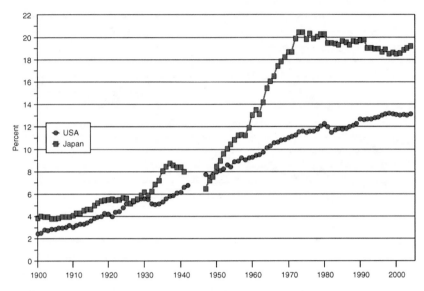

*Figure 7.3   Exergy to work efficiencies (f) (USA and Japan, 1900–2005,
           excluding 1941–47)*

have become widespread. Details of these calculations, and preliminary
results for the US, have been presented in previous publications (Ayres et
al. 2003; Ayres and Warr 2005; Warr and Ayres 2006). Details of the calculations for Japan have been submitted elsewhere for publication.

As will be seen below, we think that the increase in total factor productivity (TFP) for both countries is very closely related to – and largely
explained by – the exergy-to-work efficiency trend.

7.3   ESTIMATING THE PRODUCTION FUNCTION

For a theory of growth, if one does not want to wait 20 or 30 years for
confirmation, the best hope is to explain past economic growth reasonably
well for a very long period, such as a century. This is what we attempt here
in this chapter. The starting point is to specify the form of a production
function that fits historical data with as few independent parameters as
possible, subject to certain statistical requirements. This was the aim of
Chapter 6. The next step looks simple, at first glance: plug in the time series
data and turn the crank.

Alas, things are not so simple. Important questions about the time series
data themselves remain to be addressed. They have implications for the

method to be used for parameter estimation. The five economic variables in question are capital K, labor L, energy (actually exergy) E, useful work U and output (GDP) Y. Questions that might be asked include: are the variables well-behaved? Do the variables exhibit a systematic trend or do they vary randomly? Is there evidence of transitory shocks or structural breaks? Is there evidence of a stable long-run relationship among the variables, an essential precondition for a production function to be meaningful? Can we say anything about the direction of causality between the factors of production and GDP?

Before we can have great confidence in the outcome of calculations with a production function, especially if after introducing a new and unfamiliar factor of production (U), it is desirable to conduct a number of statistical tests on the variables. To do statistical analysis on time series variables, they must be converted to logarithmic form, to eliminate any exponential time trend. The next step is to determine whether the time series (of logarithms) is 'covariance stationary', meaning that the year-to-year differences are finite, random and not dependent on previous values of the variable. In statistical language, the mean and covariances are normally distributed and do not increase or decrease systematically over time. It happens that many macroeconomic variables, including the ones of interest to us, are not covariant stationary. When this condition is *not* met, there is said to be a 'unit root'. The first statistical test for this situation is known as Dickey-Fuller (DF) (Dickey and Fuller 1981).

The first question is whether the unit root is 'real' (that is, due to a missing variable) or whether it is due to an external shock or structural break (discontinuity) in the time series. We have carried out extensive tests, not only using the Dickey-Fuller statistic but also several more recent variants, to determine whether our time series do, in fact, exhibit structural breaks (Phillips and Perron 1988; Zivot and Andrews 1992). The results, as is often the case, are somewhat ambiguous: unit root tests of the time series show some evidence of 'mini-breaks' in individual time series. But rarely do these mini-breaks occur in the same years in all series. These mini-breaks may be due to various possible causes, from external events to major changes in government policy, especially in Japan. Some of the years correspond to identifiable events (such as the onset of the Great Depression in 1930), but others do not.

However the unit root tests we have carried out all point to the existence of one major structural break for both the US and Japan closely corresponding to the dates of World War II. Thus we have carried out our model-fitting procedures for two cases, namely for the entire 100-plus year period (1900–2005) and separately for the prewar (1900–41) and postwar (1946–2005) periods.

The next step is to test specific model formulations, such as the Cobb-Douglas or LINEX forms discussed in the last chapter. The most familiar statistical fitting procedure is known as 'ordinary least squares' (OLS). The question is whether OLS is legitimate for testing a model. The answer is easily stated: it can be shown that, when the model variables are not covariance stationary in the above sense, OLS model fits are likely to be spurious, except in one very special case which we return to below. Because of this special case, we cannot reject the use of OLS just yet.

The Durbin-Watson (DW) statistic is another test frequently applied to the residuals of econometric models. It checks for *serial auto-correlation*, meaning that the residuals (errors) of a model are (or are not) correlated (Durbin and Watson 1950, 1951). N.B. the DF test, as applied to a model, has the same purpose, but the DW test does not apply to an individual time series. The DW test statistic is defined as

$$DW = \frac{\sum_{t=2}^{T}(e_t - e_{t-1})^2}{\sum_{t=1}e_t^2} \qquad (7.1)$$

where e_t is the model residual error at time t. The statistic takes values ranging from 0 to 4, where a value of 2 means that there is no statistical evidence of auto-correlation, positive or negative, meaning that the errors are truly random. A DW value less than 2 implies positive auto-correlation between successive error. A DW value greater than 2 implies negative auto-correlation, which is extremely unlikely. A value close to (but less than) 2 is regarded as very good. A value less than 1.5 is regarded as 'cause for alarm'. A very small positive DW value means that successive error terms are consistently very close to one another. This implies that the errors are systematic, probably due to a missing variable, and hence not randomly distributed. Thus the smaller the DW statistic, the more likely it is that some important factor has been omitted.

However, like many statistical tests, the DW test is very specialized. It is quite possible for a model fitted over a short period to have a better (that is, larger) DW statistic than a model fitted over one long period. This could happen, for example, in the case of a model characterized by several segments, each displaying serial correlation, where the errors in different segments have opposite signs. The DW statistic is also perverse, in the sense that it bears no relationship to the magnitudes of the errors. The errors could be very small and yet give rise to a small DW statistic.

Having established that we are dealing with variables that are not covariance stationary, the second issue of importance is *multi-collinearity*. This means that the variables, and their logarithms, tend to be highly correlated with each other, although their year-to-year differences may not be. In such a case, high values of the correlation coefficient (R^2) are meaningless, and goodness of fit must be assessed in other ways. However, our variables are 'first-difference stationary'. This means that we could construct a model that explains past year-to-year differences very accurately but that has lost essential long-term information about the future. In fact, apart from the special case noted earlier, it has been shown that where the variables are first-difference stationary any OLS regression is likely to be spurious, meaning that no robust relationship can be detected between the variables (Granger and Newbold 1974).

The next step was to examine the residuals from OLS estimates, for both C-D and LINEX models both over the whole century and over the pre- and postwar periods taken separately. In the US case, the C-D model appeared to show breaks in 1927, 1942, 1957 and 1986. The implication is that the model should be re-calibrated for each period. This can be done by introducing dummy variables that modify the exponents and multipliers for each period, of which there are $(5 \times 3) - 1 = 14$ parameters in all. As it turns out, even with so many additional parameters, the fit is not particularly good (in fact, some of the fitted coefficients are negative). Hence, we decided to use the simpler two-period version of the model. To make a rather long story short (we have tested literally dozens of combinations), we found that the period of World War II (1942–5) is the only structural break that needs to be taken into account in both the US case and the Japanese case.[1]

To anticipate results shown in the following pages, it turns out that OLS regressions of the Cobb-Douglas model are indeed spurious, as expected, despite high values of R^2, because of both the existence of unit roots in the model residuals and extremely small values of the DW statistic (strong serial correlation).

The LINEX model is not estimated by OLS, however, but by a method of constrained non-linear optimization. The constraints we imposed on the optimization are that the output elasticities be non-negative and add up to unity (constant returns). It happens that there are multiple solutions that satisfy the constraints, because of multiple collinearity. Ideally, the independent variables would each be positively correlated with the dependent variable, but not correlated with the other independent variables. However, we think that in our case the variables do not divide neatly into 'independent' and 'dependent' categories. Rather, they are all mutually dependent. In simple terms, the problem with multiple collinearity is that the variables are measuring the same phenomenon (economic growth) and are consequently – to some extent – redundant. This situation can theoretically result in over-fitting.

We must also acknowledge at the outset that a good fit of the output (GDP) to the input variables (capital, labor, exergy or useful work) – even though not arrived at by OLS – does *not*, by itself, constitute proof of a postulated model relationship. It is theoretically possible that the causality runs the other way, that is, that the changes in the input variables (factors of production) in the model were consequences of changes in the state of the economy. However, recalling Figure 1.1 from Chapter 1, we actually expect causality to run both ways, although not necessarily at the same time. In fact, we suspect that the business cycle may consist of two alternating 'regimes' in the sense of Hamilton (1989, 1996).

The last step is to determine whether the variables (K, L, U, Y) cointegrate. In other words, we want to know if there is a stable long-term relationship among them. As pointed out earlier, the logarithms of most macroeconomic variables are not covariance stationary. However, in most cases, they are 'first-difference' stationary. Two such variables with non-stationary residuals (unit roots) are cointegrated if and only if there exists a linear combination of them, known as a vector auto-regressive (VAR) model, that has stationary residuals (that is, no unit root). A single integrating equation suffices in the bi-variate case. However, the general multivariate case is more complicated, because if there are N variables, there can be up to $N - 1$ cointegrating relationships. The challenge is not only to prove that such a linear combination exists – this is the special case, mentioned earlier in which the use of OLS is legitimate – but to find the best one. The form of the relationship is to express the rate of change of the target variable (say GDP) at time t in terms of a linear combination of the previous years' values of the variables (the cointegrating equation or error-correction term or ECT). Each variable in the ECT is weighted by a coefficient that describes the rate at which each variable adjusts to the long-term relationship. The cointegrating model also incorporates a number p of lagged values of the differences (rates of change) of each of the variables at prior times $t - 1$ through $t - p$. The system (with p specified) can be expressed most conveniently as a matrix equation, called a vector error-correction model or VECM (for example, Engle and Granger 1987; Johansen 1988, Johansen 1995). The absence of constant returns and non-negativity constraints on elasticities means that the VECM cannot usually be interpreted as a conventional production function.[2]

Cointegration analysis is a prerequisite of testing for causality when the variables are not covariance stationary (that is, they exhibit unit roots). The first application of cointegration analysis to the specific case of GDP and energy consumption was by Yu and Jin, using a bi-variate model (Yu and Jin 1992). These authors concluded that there is no long-run cointegration between energy consumption, industrial production or employment.

However, Stern (1993) used a multivariate VECM and reached the opposite conclusion, that is, that cointegration does occur among the variables and that energy consumption, adjusted for quality, does Granger-cause GDP growth (Stern 1993). He explains this contradiction of Yu and Jin's results as the consequence of the inclusion of two more variables, which allow for indirect substitution effects that are not possible when only two variables are considered. Stern's results were reconfirmed by a later study by himself (Stern 2000). A more recent application of the multivariate method, as applied to Canada, concluded that Granger-causation runs both ways (Ghali and El-Sakka 2004).[3]

7.4 NUMERICAL RESULTS

The ordinary least squares (OLS) fit can be done in two ways: either by using the log-variables and the ratios or, and alternatively, by using the year-to-year differences. As already noted, a simple two or three parameter production function, whether of the Cobb-Douglas or LINEX type, cannot be expected to explain short-run, year-to-year differences accurately. The fact that such a function has any short-run explanatory power at all is fairly remarkable. It is tempting, therefore, to do a fit with year-to-year differences instead of values *per se*. In the latter case, the model essentially forecasts the differences for the next period and uses them to adjust the current GDP for one period at a time. At each step, the actual GDP is used rather than the GDP calculated from the previous period. It turns out that the difference method can 'explain' the local variations in history extraordinarily well. As one might expect, the residual error is extremely small when the time series are differenced, except for the years of World War II. However, this method filters out the changes in the mean and hence *cannot* be used to forecast the future, or even to explain the major trends in the past, with any confidence. Hence we do not utilize the year-to-year difference approach hereafter.

Using the simpler two-period approximation with five independent parameters (two exponents for each period plus one for normalization at the beginning of the second period), the Cobb-Douglas model for the US yields results for GDP that are still not very good, especially after 1980, as shown in Figure 7.4a. There is quite a large and growing discrepancy between predicted and actual GDP after 1985. For Japan, the situation is slightly better. There is only one significant break in the C-D residual, again corresponding to World War II (1942–5). In this case, again, only five parameters are needed, two exponents for each period, plus a normalization for the second period. The resulting fit is also shown in Figure

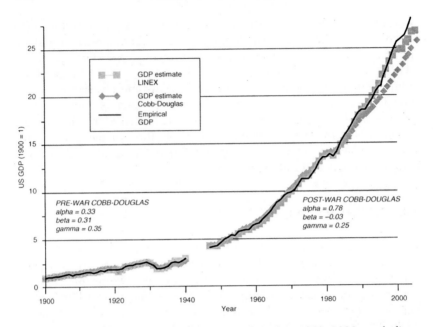

Figure 7.4a   Empirical and estimated GDP (USA, 1900–2005, excluding 1941–48)

7.4b. The parameter values needed to define the models are indicated on the graphs. The Cobb-Douglas residuals themselves are shown in Figure 7.5a for both countries.

The LINEX case for two periods is somewhat different, for both countries. In this case, again, there is only one significant break in the residuals, corresponding to World War II (1942–5). The LINEX residuals are shown in Figure 7.5b. The LINEX fits for the US and Japan were shown in Figures 7.4a and 7.4b. The fits are obviously very close. However, it will be recalled that Kümmel's generic LINEX model (Equation 6.18) included two time-dependent parameters, $a(t)$ and $b(t)$. The optimal choices for $a(t)$ and $b(t)$, corresponding to Figure 7.5, are graphed in Figures 7.6a and 7.6b. Time-averaging these functions in each of the two periods yields a simpler parametric form of the production function, with only four independent parameters, two in each period. The resulting fit (not shown) is only slightly less good than Figure 7.5.

In the US case, we note that the LINEX function provides a significantly better fit than Cobb-Douglas from the beginning of the century until the break in 1942, and again after 1945 to 1992 or so. But it underestimates economic growth significantly thereafter. We suspect that the

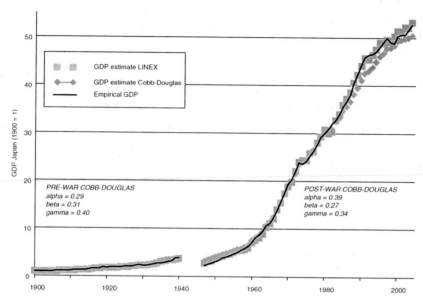

Figure 7.4b Empirical and estimated GDP (Japan, 1900–2005, excluding 1941–48)

underestimate may be due to either or both of two different factors. The first is the increasing importance of information and computer technology (ICT). The second is the increasing US trade deficit in recent years, which results in an underestimation of the role of domestic exergy services (useful work) in propelling growth in GDP. The point here is that the ratio of value-added to useful work-added to imports is significantly greater than the corresponding ratio for domestic production. This is because most of the useful work is done in extraction and primary processing, increasingly done abroad, rather than in later stages of the production chain carried out in the US. As a partial confirmation of our conjecture, it is noteworthy that in Japan the gap between model and GDP data for recent years is reversed in sign. In fact, Japan exports a significant amount of exergy (and useful work) embodied in the automobiles, machinery and other products that leave its shores. Clearly, these conjectures must be tested statistically at a later time.

In the case of Japan, the LINEX model is very slightly inferior to the C-D model in terms of residual error before 1926, again 1939–43 and again 1995–8. But the LINEX model provides a better fit for the rest of the time, and overall throughout the century. The statistics are summarized in Tables 7.1 and 7.2.

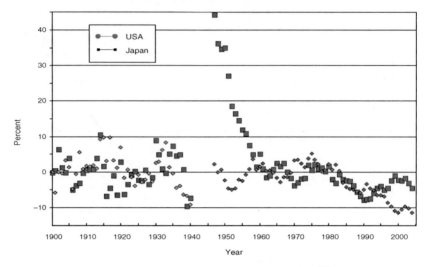

*Figure 7.5a   Cobb-Douglas residuals (USA and Japan, 1900–2005,
            excluding 1941–48)*

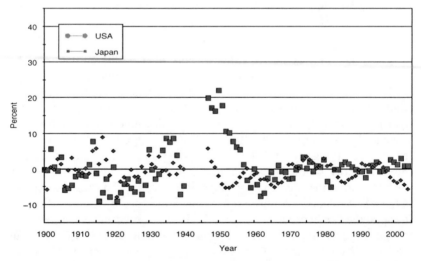

*Figure 7.5b   LINEX residuals (USA and Japan, 1900–2005, excluding
            1941–48)*

Elasticities of output are constant, by assumption, for C-D models,
although fitted values are not necessarily positive in all periods. In fact,
fitting the Cobb-Douglas model for the US seems to imply negative elasticities for both labor and useful work since 1984, probably due to the fact

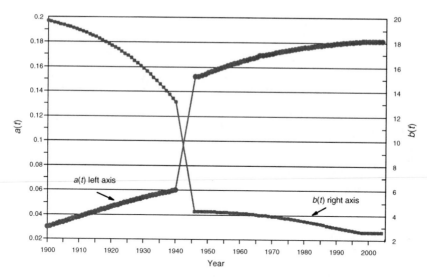

Figure 7.6a   Parameters of the LINEX function (USA, 1900–2005)

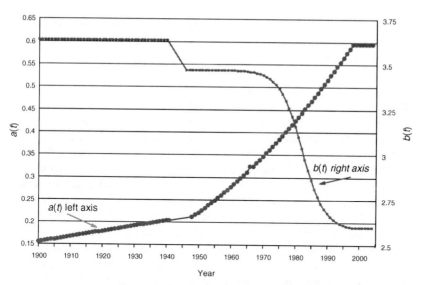

Figure 7.6b   Parameters of the LINEX function (Japan, 1900–2005)

noted earlier that the OLS regressions in this case are spurious. However, constant elasticities over long periods of time are unrealistic, in any case. Hence we prefer to concentrate on the LINEX production function hereafter. As a condition of the fitting procedure (mentioned earlier), the fitted

The economic growth engine

Table 7.1   Statistics of model fit

	1900–1940		1947–2005	
	Cobb-Douglas	LINEX	Cobb-Douglas	LINEX
USA				
Durbin-Watson	0.59	1.72	0.03	0.15
Dickey-Fuller	−1.816*	−5.427***	3.540	2.306
R^2	0.987	0.994	0.997	0.999
Japan				
Durbin-Watson	0.55	0.96	0.11	1.10
Dickey-Fuller	−1.317	−3.162***	−1.451	−4.355***
R^2	0.985	0.992	0.999	1

Notes: Critical test values for the Dickey-Fuller unit-root test: *90%−1.606, **95%−1.950, ***99%−2.366.

values of the elasticities of output remain positive throughout the century in the LINEX case, for both countries (Figures 7.7a and 7.7b). As expected, based on the Dickey-Fuller and other tests, also mentioned earlier, there are sharp breaks between 1942 and 1945 for both countries.

Since the national accounts do not distinguish payments for 'useful work' from other payments, it must be assumed that the payments for 'useful work' are accounted for indirectly as payments to capital and labor used in the production of useful work. However, even if all the payments to useful work are really attributable to labor, and none to capital, it can be seen from our results (Figures 7.7a and 7.7b) that the calculated labor share has fallen well below the traditional 70 percent of GDP and the capital share is much higher than the traditional 30 percent. This is disturbing. It suggests, at least, that our model overestimates the output elasticity for useful work and underestimates the output elasticity of labor.

Nevertheless, it is interesting to observe that for both countries the elasticity and hence the marginal productivity of labor falls throughout the century (except during World War II) and becomes very small at the terminal point (2004). Since labor still accounts for something like 70 percent of total costs (payments), the elasticity calculations suggest that marginal productivity of labor in both the US and Japan has been declining for a long time and is now quite low. In fact, the model results shown in Figures 7.7a and 7.7b suggest that adding a unit (man-hour) of labor, by itself, produces almost no added value in either country.

Table 7.2   Coefficients of production functions

Coefficients of Cobb-Douglas functions

USA	Capital (a)	Labor (b)	Useful work $(1-a-b)$
1900–1940	0.33 ±0.064	0.31 ±0.038	0.35
1947–2005	0.78 ±0.037	−0.03 ±0.018	0.25
Japan	Capital (a)	Labor (b)	Useful work $(1-a-b)$
1900–1940	0.37 ±0.094	0.44 ±0.033	0.19
1947–1998	0.51 ±0.038	0.34 ±0.009	0.15

Coefficients of logistic-type models for LINEX parameters $a(t)$ and $c(t)$

USA 1900–1940	k	p	q	r
$a(t)$	0.08	97.86	10.26	
$c(t)$	−4.12	80.85	63.04	2.6
USA 1947–2005	k	p	q	r
$a(t)$	0.19	107.6	11.50	
$c(t)$	−0.27	53.44	89.10	0.47
Japan 1900–1940	k	p	q	r
$a(t)$	0.15	74.24	6.38	
$c(t)$	9.5	9.5	9.5	9.5
Japan 1947–1998	k	p	q	r
$a(t)$	0.21	138.96	57.82	
$c(t)$	−0.35	19.03	83.99	1.26

Notes: Where

$$a(t) = k/1 + \exp\left[-\frac{\ln 81}{p}(\text{time} - 1900 - q) \right]$$

$$c(t) = k/1 + \exp\left[-\frac{\ln 81}{p}(\text{time} - 1900 - q) + r \right]$$

This is consistent with our observations (i) that output elasticity may not coincide with cost share in a real economy where the several conditions – equilibrium, profit maximization and constant returns – required for the proof (Appendix A) do not hold and (ii) that the elasticity calculations, based as they are on parameters determined by a non-linear fitting procedure, are not statistically robust.

Regarding the first possibility, there is evidence that the real economy is indeed quite far from equilibrium. The theoretical arguments against the equilibrium hypothesis have been discussed in the literature (Kaldor 1971, 1972, 1979; Kornai 1973; Day 1987). The mechanisms responsible (for example, 'lock-in' of sub-optimal technologies) have been analysed extensively by Arthur (1994). We certainly cannot rule out that possibility. As regards profit maximization, there is extensive empirical evidence that firms neglect profitable options (for example, Nelson 1989) and that the

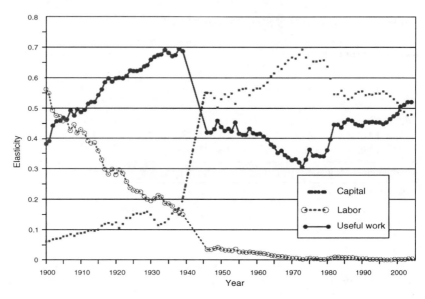

Figure 7.7a   Elasticities of factors of production – LINEX function (USA,
1900–2005, excluding 1941–47)

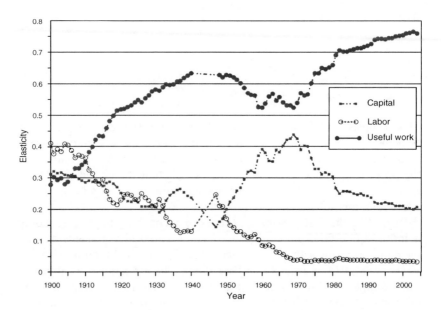

Figure 7.7b   Elasticities of factors of production – LINEX function
(Japan, 1900–2005, excluding 1941–47)

real economy uses considerably more energy than the least-cost solution, due to a variety of regulatory and oligopoly barriers (Sant and Carhart 1981; Morris et al. 1990; Casten and Collins 2003). Finally, several of the so-called endogenous growth models actually postulate positive returns to scale (Young 1928; Romer 1986, 1987b).

From another perspective on the equilibrium question, natural capital is clearly being underpaid today. The earth's stock of natural capital – from forests to topsoil to mineral resources – is now being depleted without being 'paid' (or replaced) at all. In an equilibrium economy, depleted capital stocks would have to be replaced. As existing stocks of cheap petroleum are exhausted, new and higher cost resources will have to be exploited. Natural capital in the form of oil or gas in easy-to-reach geological formations will have to be replaced by man-made capital in the form of nuclear fission or fusion reactors, wind farms or large-scale photovoltaic facilities.

7.5 WHAT CAN BE DEDUCED FROM THE GOODNESS OF THE FITS?

A professional statistician, seeing our results, is likely to respond with some skepticism, at least at first. We have acknowledged already that the fact that the OLS correlation coefficients are extremely high does *not* mean that the underlying model is 'correct'. In the first place, it is well-known that with enough free parameters one can model nearly anything, including the traditional elephant. However, our close fits over quite long periods are achieved with very few parameters. In fact, our most lavish use of parameters was to create the rather *ad hoc* 'bridge' between the two historical periods (pre- and post-World War II). Most economists will probably agree that the second World War constituted a major shock or 'break' that justifies re-calibration of the production function. The real question might be whether other significant breaks may have occurred, such as the Korean War, the Viet Nam War, the 'oil shock' in 1973–4 and so on.

Granted we have not utilized many free parameters, the skeptical statistician will note that a very close correlation between two (or more) variables need not mean that there is a causal connection between them. The close correlation between any two variables, such as exergy consumption and GDP, might be attributed, in principle, to some third independent variable driving them both. However, it is difficult to imagine what such a meta-driver might be (population? migration? education?). This difficulty becomes more acute when there are four variables to be explained simultaneously by a fifth variable that we cannot identify *a priori*. We think it is much more likely that the four variables linked in our production function drive (and explain) each other, in the sense of a positive feedback relationship. There is statistical evidence to support this hypothesis of mutual causation. What can be concluded from the cointegration analysis we have carried out thus far is that in both the US and Japanese cases the four variables (K, L, U, Y) do cointegrate, except during the 1942–5 break (and, for Japan, subject to a caveat below). This means that a stable long-term relationship really does exist among these variables for both countries. It is tempting to think of this hypothetical relationship as an expression of the rather elusive dynamic equilibrium that most growth theorists have always postulated.

In Japan, the situation is more complicated than for the US case, because of a long period between the 1950s and the 1980s during which our unit-root tests indicate a significant departure from equilibrium occurred for the capital stock variable, in particular. That departure from equilibrium is almost certainly attributable to the Japanese postwar 'economic miracle'. The unprecedented growth rate from 1952 on into the 1980s was brought about by a series of government–industry policies that strongly favored savings and investment over current consumption. Gross private investment increased from a solid 17.2 percent of GDP in 1952–4 to a high of 30.5 percent in 1970–71, when annual growth rates in excess of 10 percent were being achieved. Private savings followed a parallel path, rising from 16.5 percent in 1952–4 to 31.9 percent during 1970–71. By contrast, private savings in the US between 1961 and 1971 averaged only 15.8 percent of GDP (Henderson 2002).[4]

Having established that the variables are cointegrated, it is possible to carry out Granger-type causality tests regarding the question as to whether energy (exergy) and/or useful work drive growth or *vice versa*.[5] Because of the extreme complexity of the procedure, we have done this in detail only for the US. The results are summarized in Table 7.3.

We have tested Granger-causal relations for both exergy (Model A) and useful work (Model B), and considered short-run and long-run causality separately. For Model A we find evidence of both short-run and long-run causality from exergy to GDP, but no evidence for the reverse. However, in the case of Model B, where useful work replaces exergy as an input, we find no evidence of short-run causality from useful work to GDP, but strong evidence of long-run causality from useful work to GDP. We find this result very plausible, for the simple reason that aggregate exergy efficiency changes very slowly and therefore cannot explain short-term changes in GDP growth. On the other hand, we also found evidence that capital and labor Granger-cause useful work consumption in the short run. These results taken together are reasonably consistent with Stern's work (Stern 2000) and they refute the so-called neutrality hypothesis (that growth is independent of energy consumption/production).

Table 7.3   *Causality tests*

Independent variable (source of causation)	Dependent variable Model A				Independent variable (source of causation)	Dependent variable Model B			
	ΔGDP	ΔExergy	ΔCapital	ΔLabor		ΔGDP	ΔExergy	ΔCapital	ΔLabor
Short run					Short run				
ΔGDP		0.66	2.1	0.54	ΔGDP		0.51	2.07	0.82
ΔExergy	20.46***		6.17**	12.55	ΔWork	0.34		8.35**	1.51
ΔCapital	4.58	2.34		0.03	ΔCapital	1.06	4.65*		0.98
ΔLabor	0.68	0.53	4.63*		ΔLabor	1.67	5.06*	0.75	
Long run					Long run				
ECT/ΔGDP					ECT/ΔGDP				
ECT/ΔExergy		5.63	3.89	18.25***	ECT/ΔWork		1.99	2.19	6.18
ECT/Capital	56.78***		11.03***	25.96***	ECT/Capital	17.71***		12.89**	12.80***

In brief, we have found that there is reasonably good evidence of cointegration and mutual causality among the four variables, for both the US and Japan. Admittedly, while the evidence for causality is strong, it is not absolutely conclusive. This is because the residual errors for both models are not quite normally (Gaussian) distributed, as one would like. Hence, the statistical tests might still be spurious. We also find, as already noted, that there are significant structural breaks in the 100 plus year time series, for some variables, for both countries. This implies that the models being tested (Cobb-Douglas and LINEX) should be re-calibrated at the break points, or (better) that appropriate dummy variables should be introduced into the fitting equations. As previously noted, refitting after re-calibration might well result in better DW statistics for the segments.

Moving on, and regardless of the caveats above, the extraordinarily good fit to past GDP data exhibited by our LINEX model strongly suggests that it can be useful as a forecasting tool. The argument, in brief, is that if the model 'explains' the past with so few free parameters, there is no reason to suppose that the relationship will become invalid overnight, or in the course of a few years. In other words, other things remaining equal, the model should also provide strong clues as to what can be expected over the next few decades, even though some departures from historical trends can be expected. We develop this idea in Chapter 8.

As regards the past, our results clearly reflect the substitution, during the past century, of 'useful work', mostly by fossil-fuel-powered machines, for muscle work by humans and animals. In fact, the calculated output elasticity of energy, as useful work, is up to ten times higher than earlier estimates based on the factor cost-share theorem (Appendix A). Although the factor of ten may well turn out to be somewhat too high (because our model is still too simplistic), the fact that the difference is large is hard to ignore. While the calculated values of the elasticities are not absolutely trustworthy, having been obtained from non-linear fits, the results are still qualitatively consistent with the idea that 'pure' (unskilled) labor, in the absence of machines and sources of power, is now nearly unproductive *at the margin*. This result holds for both the US and Japan. In effect, our results suggest that labor is no longer a scarce resource. One more unskilled worker, without tools and mechanical or electrical power, adds almost nothing to economic output.

This result, tentative though it may be, has important implications for the future. Among them is that it contradicts the assertions by many politicians and pundits in Europe that a declining birth-rate needs to be reversed. On the contrary, it is getting harder to keep everybody who wants a job productively employed. The declining birth-rate in Europe and Japan may be more positive than negative.

Luckily there is some other evidence to support our qualitative results.

7.6 OTHER EVIDENCE OF THE ELASTICITY OF EXERGY AS USEFUL WORK

As noted several times in this book, standard neoclassical theory says that the elasticity of output with respect to energy (exergy) E should be equal to the dollar share of energy to total output. Recently, thanks to price rises, this share – just for oil – is about 4 percent of US GDP. Based on this presumed equality, a cut in petroleum output of 10 percent would result in a GDP reduction of 0.4 percent, from the 'normal' GDP increase of 3.4 percent per year. But the actual oil shock-related declines, relative to trend, were nearer 4.0 percent, on average, or ten times that predicted by the conventional factor share argument (Hamilton 2005).

The original debate about cost shares was prompted by efforts to explain the impact of oil price spikes in the 1970s on US consumer prices and economic growth (Perry 1977; Solow 1978; Denison 1979, 1985). There was a heated debate beginning in the 1980s about the relationship between oil consumption, prices and GDP, with a number of econometric studies on each side of the issue. One group of economists reported econometric results suggesting oil price rises have little or no effect on GDP (for example, Darby 1982; Bohi 1991; Darrat and Gilley 1996), while another group came to the opposite conclusion (for example, Tatom 1981; Hamilton 1983; and Burbridge and Harrison 1984, among others). The differences between these studies are difficult to summarize, except to say that they appear to be largely due to different testing hypotheses, choices of econometric techniques and different sample periods (mostly focusing on the 1970s).

Recent studies based on a longer history seem to be converging toward some agreement. One study that seems to have anticipated elements of ours deserves particular mention (Moroney 1992). Moroney investigated the effects of changes in capital and energy per unit of labor on labor productivity for 1950–84, leading to estimated output elasticities of similar magnitude (as compared to ours) for the two variables. Moroney estimated that increased energy consumption per unit of labor contributed 1.17 percentage points to growth during the period 1950–73, while declines in energy consumption cut 0.5 percentage points from growth during 1974–84.

Many econometric studies focused on price effects. The correlation between oil price rises and economic recessions is such that accidental coincidence can be ruled out (Hamilton 2005). In nine out of ten cases, a price increase was followed by a recession. Moreover, oil price rises, as compared to declines, tend to have non-linear (disproportionally negative) effects on GDP growth. To be sure, the fact that these price increases were mostly linked to military conflicts leaves open the possibility that other events associated with the conflicts, rather than the oil price increases *per se*, may have caused the recessions (Hamilton 2003). The negative effect of price volatility in oil markets on GDP has been confirmed by others, and provides support for Hamilton's non-linear measure (Guo and Kliesen 2005). Still, despite the enormous literature on the topic, the problem of explaining these non-linear effects remains open. In any case, no single explanation of recessions is necessary or sufficient (Barsky and Kilian 2004). But the non-linear negative impact of energy price increases, as opposed to decreases, on growth seems to be reasonably well established today.

Evidence of a completely different nature may eventually be provided by input-output models that take into account the non-substitutability of exergy and useful work.

Taking all the evidence into account, we argue that there is a strong case for asserting that either exergy or useful work can be regarded as factors of production. The virtue of useful work is that it also incorporates a large component of what we mean by technological progress. On the other hand, we would not seriously expect a simple production function model of four variables to explain all the vagaries of past economic behavior. While exergy and useful work are important, and should never have been neglected, there are many other macroeconomic phenomena (and policy interventions) that have had, and continue to have, an important role.

7.7   REPRISE: REALITY OR ARTIFACT OF THE MODEL?

A strong implication of our main results is that future economic growth depends either on continued declines in the cost of primary exergy or on an accelerated increase in the output of useful work from a decreasing exergy input, that is, increasing exergy-to-work conversion efficiency. Energy prices have increased significantly in the last few years and are almost certain to increase further, both because of increased demand and because of the need to cut greenhouse gas emissions. If the rate of technological progress in conversion efficiency slows down, we believe that economic growth will necessarily slow down as well. Hence it can no longer be assumed, without question or doubt, that growth along the 'trend' will continue indefinitely and that 'our children and grandchildren will be much richer than we are' as some economists have asserted. Though not discussed here, it is clear that policies that can deliver a 'double dividend' in the sense of decreasing carbon-based fuel consumption and greenhouse gas emissions, while simultaneously cutting costs, must be sought more intensively than ever before.

There is an obvious case for interpreting our model results as a reflection of the real situation. They are consistent with the observed effect of energy (oil) price spikes on economic growth. They are also consistent with the fact that big firms frequently find ways to cut large numbers of jobs to increase profits without cutting output. Typically, such a move is welcomed by the stock market. The implication is that the real economy has been distorted in a number of ways to create or preserve unnecessary and unproductive 'paper shuffling' jobs. The fact that redundant employees usually find other work, sooner or later, is a fortunate consequence of economic growth.

On the other hand, there is also a case for regarding our results as an artifact of the model. The use of a production function of capital, labor and useful work implies that these factors are perfectly substitutable, which is clearly not the case, except in the very long run, as we have noted repeatedly. It is true that consumers can be flexible about their use of auto transportation, heating, air-conditioning and so on. Similarly, workers using hand tools can replace power tools and machines in some applications, especially construction and local goods transportation. But invested capital in most industrial sectors is not flexible, either in regard to labor requirements or exergy requirements. While new investment (for example, in systems optimization) can reduce the need for both labor and useful work per unit of output, this happens only in the intermediate or long run.

Hence labor and capital are not truly substitutes, except at the margin. Workers in the existing economy require power tools, machines and places to work. The relationship between useful work and capital is ambiguous. The two factors are evidently complementary, at least in the short run. Machines require energy (useful work) inputs to perform their functions. This fact, together with the complementarity of labor and capital, also in the short run, casts doubt on the appropriateness of a production function that implies perfect substitutability, as does the Cobb-Douglas function.

The LINEX function also implies substitutability between factors, to be sure. But it implies substitutability between *ratios* of the factors (in the exponent) while it also allows for some degree of complementarity insofar as both numerator and denominator can increase or decrease together. In mathematical terms, factor substitutability should be near zero for large values of either variable but should be finite, and maximum, near the optimal combination, that is, as the function approaches the limiting case, which is the Leontief (zero substitution) production function (for example,

Diewart 1974). However, we confess that it is not yet clear whether the cost-share proof in Appendix A applies to a function of ratios.

If we had used a Cobb-Douglas model with no third factor, the calculated elasticity of labor would be automatically equal to the cost share, subject to all the other assumptions needed for the proof in Appendix A. Of course, in the Cobb-Douglas model, output elasticity is a constant. It is a generally accepted 'stylized fact' of economics that the capital-labor ratio remains constant, or nearly so, over time. Similarly, the ratio of the capital and labor shares of payments in the national accounts tends to remain rather constant over time. Our model results should be consistent with these stylized facts. We can only say that consistency is possible, but not guaranteed, by the results obtained up to now.

NOTES

1. We note in passing here that for both countries there are several 'mini-breaks' that suggest the possibility of re-calibration of the model parameters. This leads, in practice, to a series of 'mini-models' covering as few as 20 or 30 years. However, an obvious constraint that is impossible to incorporate explicitly in the mathematical optimization process is the need for each variable to be continuous across breaks. Ignoring that condition leads to extremely implausible results.

2. However, the very long-run relationship, as reflected by the error-correction term, might be interpreted in this way (Stern 2000).

3. The literature of Granger-causation includes studies for a number of other countries, such as Taiwan, Korea, Singapore and the Philippines. However, the developmental history of those countries is so different from the US and Japan that we hesitate to draw any conclusions from them.

4. One reason for the surge in private savings was the traditional 13th month end-of-year 'bonus', much of which went into the postal savings system, despite low interest rates. More important was the role of the Japan Development Bank, which provided cheap capital to industry – especially coal, electric power, steel and ship-building – from the Fiscal Investment and Loan Plan (FILP), which controlled the postal savings as well as other pools of capital. FILP controlled more than four times the capital of the world's largest private bank at one time. Perhaps the most important device was the policy, begun in 1954, of 'over-loaning', which enabled many firms to borrow more than their net worth from local banks, which in turn over-borrowed from the Bank of Japan (Wikipedia 2006). This gave the Bank of Japan total control over the entire financial system of the country. A further partial explanation of the phenomenon was the tremendous increase in Tokyo land prices, followed by the painful collapse in 1992. Land values were included as part of companies' capital assets, and of course many loans were secured by land values. The over-loaning policy was unsustainable, of course, and it led to a huge non-performing loan 'overhang' that was never accurately measured (because of leverage effects), but was still estimated to be in excess of $500 billion, as of 2005. Economic growth in Japan averaged only 1 percent per year from 1993 through 2005, largely because of the banks' reluctance to make new loans.

5. There is an extensive literature on this issue, covering a number of different countries and time periods. The older literature has been summarized by Stern (1993) and reviewed again by Stern in a more recent paper (2000). The earlier papers, mainly based on bi-variate models, were generally inconclusive or the results were not statistically significant. Stern's (1993) paper reached a more robust conclusion, based on a multivariate analysis

in which energy *quality* was taken into account (based on prior work by several authors: Jorgenson 1984; Hall et al. 1986; Kaufmann 1994). Energy quality, as defined by Hall et al., defines a hierarchy of qualities, with firewood and coal at the bottom, followed by crude oil, refined petroleum products, natural gas, and electricity, rated by relative price per unit of heat production. This scheme resembles our term 'useful work' insofar as it gives electricity a much higher quality rating than coal or crude oil. Using this scheme, Stern (1993) found that Granger-causality ran from energy consumption to GDP.

8.   Growth forecasting

8.1   ON FORECASTING THE FUTURE

There are several methods of forecasting the future. The oldest, no longer taken seriously in the West, is to rely on the positions of the stars, the entrails of a sheep, the flight of a bird, or some version of the Oracle at Delphi. One wonders how such ideas got started, but they were well established in various times and places. All of these methods had the advantage of ambiguity, so that a powerful 'client' could hear what he wanted to hear. In 546 BC King Croesus of Lydia, in Anatolia, asked for advice from the Oracle at Delphi in regard to a possible conflict with the Persians. The Oracle replied 'If King Croesus goes to war he will destroy a great empire.' Accordingly, Croesus attacked the Persians under King Cyrus, and was utterly defeated. The Lydian empire (such as it was) was duly destroyed. The most famous example of comparatively recent times was the French doctor Nostradamus, who wrote his predictions in a book. Nostradamus' trick was much like the Oracle's, namely to make his pronouncements so ambiguous that they could be interpreted at will. Yet Nostradamus still has believers.

The modern version of a seer is a 'futurologist' or simply an expert in some field of interest. Examples of bad predictions by experts abound. A fascinating collection of embarrassing pronouncements by experts can be found in a little book entitled *Profiles of the Future* by Arthur C. Clarke (Clarke 1958). Clarke unhesitatingly added several of his own. A more 'scientific' use of experts, known as 'Delphi Forecasting' was introduced by Olaf Helmer at RAND Corp. in the mid-1960s. The method amounts to voting. A panel of experts in the field of interest is asked to put a likely date on some future event of interest, along with measures of uncertainty. The idea is that some of the experts will be too optimistic, others will be too pessimistic and the errors will tend to cancel out. The problem is that the panel of experts often share the same assumptions, perhaps without knowing it. If they do, all of them can be equally wrong.

A Delphic forecast was carried out at RAND in 1966, in which all of the scientists were asked about the future of nuclear technology. Every single one of those polled predicted that thermonuclear fusion power would be in use by electric utilities before the year 2000 (Helmer 1967). A similar poll today would probably put the probable date of fusion power adoption by utilities around 2050 or so, and that could turn out to be equally optimistic.

Economists often use the Delphic approach, in effect, by assembling a panel of experts, for example, to forecast short-term growth rates, interest rates and so on. Panel forecasts are probably slightly more reliable than individual expert forecasts, but panels usually miss important changes of direction.

In any case we prefer a different approach.

8.2   EXTRAPOLATION

Extrapolation is the word which describes the continuation of a trend, usually quantitative. As applied to time series, the idea is that, barring unexpected events, the future will be like the past. If the sun has come up every morning for 10 000 years, it seems reasonable to assume it will come up again tomorrow. If the moon has waxed for 14 days and waned for 14 days for 10 000 years, it seems reasonable to assume that the pattern will be repeated next month. If spring, summer, fall and winter have followed each other regularly for 10 000 years, we feel comfortable in assuming that they will do so again in the coming year.

It has been said that man is a pattern-making animal. More accurately, some of us are good at pattern-recognition. The discovery of regularities in the observed motions of the stars and planets by the Babylonians was certainly the first step towards developing the science of astronomy. Copernicus was the first to provide a theory of sorts to explain the observable patterns, while retaining the notion that Earth was the center of the universe. His theory of cycles and hyper-cycles was soon overturned by Kepler and Galileo, who realized that the earth and planets revolve around the sun in elliptical orbits. Newton asked himself what sort of force law would account for an elliptical orbit, and concluded that such a force would have to be inversely proportional to the square of the distance from the point of attraction. From this kind of reasoning came Newton's laws of motion and the law of gravity. Newton's theory of gravitational attraction was accepted for 250 years. But some small but persistent deviations from the Newtonian scheme, notably the precession of the perihelion of the orbit of Mercury, inspired Einstein to formulate his more general theory. And so it goes. From patterns one can postulate and test cause-effect relationships. As competing hypotheses are winnowed, 'laws of nature' may emerge.

Evidently pattern recognition is a basic tool for forecasting. The simplest pattern of all is a geometrically straight line. Motion in a straight line is likely to continue along the same line unless it is deflected by some force. Newton's law of gravity is a more complex extrapolation, but no different in principle. Different 'laws of motion', such as exponential growth (compound interest), the logarithmic, sinusoidal and logistic functions, are commonplace in physics and economics. Quite elaborate statistical methods have been developed to identify superimposed sinusoidal patterns, such as business cycles, from apparently random fluctuations. But the underlying 'force laws' explaining such behaviors remain obscure. However, if a Delphic forecast panel of leading economists were created today and the question to them were 'what average real growth rate do you expect the US to enjoy during the 21st century?' we think the answer would fall between 1.5 percent and 2.5 percent per annum. But that is because virtually all economists assume that economic growth is automatic and costless, and that it is independent of energy price or availability.

Since the US economy has grown at a relatively steady rate for well over a century (nearer two centuries), it seems reasonable to suppose that it will continue to do so. In fact, it is usually reasonable to assume past trends will continue for some time to come, absent definite reasons for expecting a change of direction. A supertanker has enormous inertia. It cannot turn on a proverbial dime. The economy also has a lot of inertia.

We need to digress for a moment, here, to define the term 'trend'. The most common sort of trend in economics is exponential. Extrapolation of an exponential trend is tantamount to extrapolating the logarithms of the appropriate time series as a straight line. Of course there is an enormous gap between simple extrapolations of single variables and elaborate and complex models intended to capture a variety of interacting trends simultaneously. Nevertheless, it happens that most complex economic models depend on several extrapolations, as will be seen.

8.3   THE ROLE OF EXTRAPOLATION IN INTEGRATED ASSESSMENT MODELS

Integrated assessment (IA) models are at the heart of current efforts to assess policies and prospects for the future. The relationships between technological progress, economic activity and global environment are the focus of most of this area of research. Each model is designed to address different policy questions, for example, to quantify the potential costs of climate stabilization policies such as the Kyoto Protocol (Manne and Wene 1994; Weyant 1999), or to assess our ability to meet future energy demands (Nakicenovic 1993) and maintain future rates of economic growth (Gerlagh and van der Zwaan 2003).

Examples of 'top-down' (or macroeconomic) models, include GEMINI-E3, MERGE, CETA, DICE and RICE (Bernard and Vielle 2003; Manne and Wene 1994; Manne and Richels 2004; Nordhaus 1993, 2004). Examples of 'bottom-up' (energy system) models, include MESSAGE, DEMETER or FREE (Messner and Strubegger 1994; Fiddaman 1998; Gerlagh and van der Zwaan 2003).

Whether bottom-up or top-down, most share a common set of assumptions based on Robert Solow's neoclassical model of economic growth (Solow 1956, 1957). One of the simpler integrated assessment models, the top-down DICE model, was specifically focused on the economics of climate change (Nordhaus 1992, 1998). Nordhaus concluded that the costs of mitigating climate change today would cause a reduction in the rate of future economic growth. The logic underlying this conclusion is that (by assumption) the economy is currently on an optimal trajectory. It follows that any interference by government must inevitably force a departure from the optimal path. That would presumably cause a reduction in the growth rate. But is the current trajectory really optimal?

Gross output in DICE was given by a two-factor (capital and labor) Cobb-Douglas production function, together with an assumed rate of total factor productivity (TFP) and an assumed rate of decline in the energy intensity of the economy. The utility of future consumption was discounted at an assumed rate.[1] All of these parameters are essentially extrapolations. This is equally true of other large-scale models. For instance, the TFP assumption is a direct extrapolation based on an exponential fit of the ratio between the actual GDP (adjusted for inflation) and the 'naked' Cobb-Douglas model (assuming $A(t) = 1$) for the US economy from 1900 through 2004. The residual (TFP) grew at an average rate of 1.6 percent per annum while the 'naked' C-D function of capital and labor grew at an average annual rate of 1.67 percent. Adding the two rates together, the GDP increased at an average annual rate of about 3.3 percent per annum from 1900 through 2004. Most models, like DICE, simply assume that the TFP – a measure of technological progress – will continue to grow at the same rate, or slightly less, in the future. They also extrapolate standard labor force growth rates to estimate the labor component of the C-D function. Finally, they extrapolate an average historical savings rate and depreciation rate to estimate future capital stock growth.

Nordhaus also assumed that the energy/GDP ratio (known as 'energy intensity') would continue to decline at a fixed rate. This again is an extrapolation of past behavior, obtained from a similar exponential fit to an historical time series. The assumed social discount or time preference rate is somewhat open to debate, but the most common choice by economists would be to equate it with the 'prime' rate of interest or the average historical GDP growth rate (Hanke and Anwyll 1980; Markandya and Pearce 1988; Gerlagh 2000).

These are all extrapolations and, consequently, they all assume implicitly that the structure of the economy and the behavior of consumers will not change in the foreseeable future. Yet many of the underlying trends have actually changed significantly in the past several decades. Examples include family size, retirement ages, working hours per week, female participation in the labor force, household savings, investment, the decline of manufacturing in the US, the increasing US trade gap, and the increasing national debt, among others.

8.4   RISKS OF BLIND EXTRAPOLATION (I)

The macroeconomic changes between 1998 and 2005 alone are far from trivial. In the year 2000 the US Federal budget had a surplus of 1 percent of GDP. By 2006 the surplus had become a deficit close to 6 percent of GDP, a figure more usually associated with Latin America. From 2001 to 2003 President Bush lowered taxes for the richest Americans quite dramatically, sharply increasing the income disparity between rich and poor. To complicate the story, there are indications that the large investment in computers and software during the 1990s is finally beginning to pay off. In 1987 Robert Solow was quoted in an interview as saying 'you can see the computer age everywhere except in the productivity statistics' (Solow 1987). The phenomenon behind this remark became known as the 'Solow Paradox'.

But labor productivity, which grew at an annual rate of barely 1.4 percent per annum during 1975–95 jumped to 2.3 percent per annum in 1995–2000 and hit 6.8 percent in the second quarter of 2003. In 2003 the *Economist* asserted that the Solow paradox has been explained at last (Anonymous 2003). Most economists believe that rising labor productivity is unalloyed good news. But experience since the 1990s can be interpreted otherwise.

'Free trade' has been promoted as the secret to global growth for the past several decades, largely as a reaction to the very negative experience that resulted from the counter-productive US trade restrictions that followed the stock market crash in 1929. The Smoot-Hawley tariff of 1930, together with ill-timed credit tightening by the Federal Reserve Bank, triggered a worldwide protectionist chain-reaction that deepened and lengthened the recession into the Great Depression (Eichengreen 1989). Since World War II there have been a series of international conferences aimed at reducing tariffs and freeing up trade again. However, free trade for non-agricultural goods and for capital, *but not for labor*, has resulted in the movement of manufacturing, and more recently services, away from the so-called 'rich' countries into countries with cheap labor and minimal health, safety or environmental protection. Even jobs in the field of information technology (IT), which were supposed to replace jobs in manufacturing, started to move away from the US in the 1990s. As many as two million such jobs may have gone already, to such faraway places as Ireland and India. Despite the apparent dominance of US-based computer hardware producers such as Intel, Dell and HP, most of the production of components, and even the assembly, has moved to Asia and virtually all new investment in that field is now outside the US.

The result of the disappearance of US manufacturing jobs thanks to (partial) globalization has been a massive growth in the US trade deficit since the 1980s. The trade deficit has – in turn – been financed by foreign – mainly Asian – investment in US government securities. This reverse flow of capital amounts to borrowing not only to finance the government budget deficit, which has also grown by leaps and bounds, but also to finance a consumer spending binge. By the end of 2005 foreign creditors owned $13.6 trillion in dollar assets, a figure that is increasing at the rate of $600 billion per year.

In short, many extrapolations that would have seemed reasonable in 1990 have turned out to be radically erroneous. A closer look is warranted.

8.5   RISKS OF BLIND EXTRAPOLATION (II)

The 2003–05 'recovery' of the US economy is clearly attributable to excessive consumption paid for by deficit spending. This spending was encouraged by low taxes and low interest rates, the latter financed in turn by foreign investment in US government bonds.[2] That investment has been explicitly intended to keep US interest rates low and the US dollar overvalued in comparison with the Chinese and other Asian currencies. An overvalued US dollar is very good for Asian exporters and US consumers, especially of oil, but very bad for US workers and manufacturers. The US consumption boom is being financed by a large fraction – as much as three-quarters – of the net savings of the entire world. This obviously cannot continue for long. How it will end nobody can say with certainty, but clues are beginning to emerge.

The extraordinarily low interest rates of 2003–04, together with unwise deregulation of the banking sector, led to the proliferation of 'sub-prime' mortgages, with adjustable rates that come into effect after the first two or three years. This 'teaser' induced many under-qualified people to buy homes they cannot really afford, while simultaneously creating a housing boom and rising real-estate prices. Meanwhile many of the risky mortgages have been packaged into mortgage-backed securities and sold to investors around the world. The rather sudden discovery that these securities are nowhere near as safe as they were advertised to be, has already caused the virtual collapse of one savings bank in the UK. As of this writing (October 2007), other financial ripples are feared. And the US housing market, booming until spring 2007, has also suffered a dramatic setback.

Apart from immediate problems, there are a number of other drivers of past growth that are now showing signs of exhaustion. These include: (1) the benefits of free trade (globalization), (2) monetization of domestic and agricultural labor, (3) job specialization (division of labor), (4) borrowing from past accumulation of capital to consume in the present, (5) borrowing from the future to increase consumption in the present, (6) increasing technological efficiency of converting resource inputs to useful work and power and (7) borrowing – in the sense of using without payment – from the waste assimilation capacity of nature.

The efficiency benefits of free trade today are considerably exaggerated by many mainstream economists who like the theory of international division of labor and ignore the reality. The major benefits are enjoyed by dominant producers who can exploit the fact that larger markets permit greater economies of scale and experience, thus cutting costs and prices (in a competitive market). But opening product markets to cheap imports also weakens smaller local producers and domestic trade unions, in both the US and developing countries. The net result is to intensify competition, driving weaker firms out of business and enabling surviving producers to keep wages low and to export jobs to low wage countries. Globalization is certainly one of the factors driving the increasing gap between income levels enjoyed by the top executives and the ordinary workers. It is not surprising that big businessmen favor free trade. But it is very questionable whether the lower consumer prices offered by Wal-Mart and other large-scale importers ultimately justify the adverse consequences to most wage earners and smaller companies, especially in the long run.

GDP growth during the past two centuries has been partly due to the monetization of (formerly) un-monetized domestic labor (by women) and subsistence farm labor. This process of monetization is now largely complete in the industrial world, though barely beginning in many third world countries. Specialization of labor was very important at the beginning of the industrial revolution, as pointed out by Adam Smith. It probably peaked a century ago during the heyday of Taylorism. Today, workers are actually less specialized than in the past, as specialized skills are increasingly embodied in machines and human workers are increasingly valued for their flexibility and ability to respond to change. Future GDP growth in the US cannot be driven by further monetization or specialization of labor.

In principle, wage earners are able to do one of two things with their income: spend or save. As mentioned earlier, simple economic models tend to attribute growth to saving and investment, even though higher savings must necessarily cut spending. 'Optimal' growth, in the Ramsey tradition, is determined by the tradeoff between spending in the present and spending in the future, which boils down to 'time preference' (Ramsey 1928). In reality, there is a third option that allows spending in the present: namely, to borrow. In principle, people borrow to purchase cars or houses, and the loan is secured by the object of the loan. When people take second mortgages, they are borrowing from their own accumulated assets. But unsecured credit card loans and sub-prime mortgages are a different matter. In principle, unsecured credit enables people to exist with negative assets. This problem is just now becoming acute.

More importantly, the population in the US, Europe and Japan is aging. The ratio of workers to retirees is declining rapidly, even faster in Japan and Europe than the US (which has more young immigrants, mainly from Mexico). Result: fewer workers to support more non-workers in coming years. Early retirement, longer life and declining birth-rates have exacerbated this situation. An aging society, like an aging individual worker, depends increasingly on wealth accumulated from past investments by others to pay for current consumption. When a society, or an individual, is young – has few assets – it (or he/she) must save and invest out of current income in order to enjoy greater income in the future. For a society, long-term investments range from education and research to infrastructure to factories and enterprises.

An aging society, politically controlled by its older citizens, tends to introduce social welfare programs instead of investing. These amount to income redistribution from the young to the old. Taxpayers from the working age groups are asked to pay for social welfare services, health services and pensions for the elderly, from current income. Insofar as these transfer payments shift spendable income from the well-off to the less well-off, they tend to increase immediate demand for basic products and services. However, redistribution from the young for consumption by the old also cuts the pool of disposable income available for savings and investment, as the Ramsey model indicates. It is tantamount to living on capital.

Just as the monetization of (formerly) unpaid labor has contributed to past GDP growth, monetization of unearned future wages and profits

– via stock prices and bond issues or rising real estate values – enables individuals and firms to spend the money (in a rising market) *before it has been earned*. Business firms are able to monetize future earnings by issuing equity shares to the public. Stock market valuations often reflect 'technical' analysis, which amounts to bets on what other investors will buy or sell, rather than fundamentals. This phenomenon helps to explain what would otherwise be very difficult to understand, namely the fact, periodically emphasized by investment advisors, that stock market returns have far outpaced economic growth for many decades.

Another form of indirect monetization is the increase in value of real estate. As consumers' net worth, including borrowing capacity, has grown, demand for scarce goods, and especially urban land, has increased more or less in parallel. But rising demand leads to higher prices, which are reflected in increasing the equity – and net worth – of the existing land-owners and home owners. This enables them to borrow and spend still more, for example by remortgaging existing properties or 'trading up' to more expensive ones.

The monetization of expected future earnings for individuals also occurs partly through the growth of unsecured personal credit (credit cards). Clearly the underlying assumption on the part of creditors and investors is that the loans, or investments, can and will be repaid from future income, without reducing future consumption. This can happen – it has happened in the past – thanks to the magical 'growth dividend'. But future economic growth is not guaranteed by any law of nature.

Unsecured consumer credit card debt in the US more than quadrupled from 1990 to 2005. In 1990 the average balance outstanding by 88 million card-owners was $2550. By the end of 2003, 144 million people had cards (up 75 percent) and the average balance was up to $7520 (Walker 2002). More disturbing, credit cards have become so easy to get that debt has increased most rapidly, by far, among the lowest income families. Consumer debt, mostly secured by durable goods (automobiles) or real estate, has also risen steadily during the past two decades. It was slightly over 65 percent of household income in 1983. In 2003, consumer debt reached 110 percent of household income. In all of these cases, the net effect is to allow firms and individuals to increase current consumption by borrowing (in effect) from the future.

Most politicians, and even most economists, seem unaware of the severity of the combined entitlement and consumer debt problems. But the 'solution' they all hope for is faster growth, fueled by lower taxes and increased borrowing. If economic growth does not accelerate to levels *above* the historical average – well above 4 percent per annum, year in and year out – these structural imbalances can only get worse.

8.6 RISKS OF BLIND EXTRAPOLATION (III)

Another more urgent problem is the approaching end of 'the age of oil' when global output peaks and begins to decline. The received wisdom on this subject is that there is still plenty of oil, at least when rising prices 'unlock' resources that are currently too costly to exploit. The situation has been obscured up to now by cheerful forecasts by industry figures and government agencies (such as the IEA, the USGS and the US Department of Energy), suggesting that increasing global demand, for the next two or three decades at least, will be met at stable prices (Energy Information Administration (EIA) 2004; International Energy Agency 2004). These optimistic forecasts are strongly influenced by mainstream economists who still argue – as they did in their response to the *Limits to Growth* book – that there is plenty of oil in the ground and that rising prices will automatically trigger more discovery and more efficient methods of recovery (Meadows et al. 1972). The optimists note that oil prices declined dramatically in the 1980s and early 1990s because high prices in the 1970s stimulated both exploration and investment in energy conservation, the latter for the first time.

However, in the past few years many petroleum geologists have become convinced that global output of petroleum (and of natural gas soon after) is about to peak, or may have peaked already. US petroleum discovery peaked in 1930 and production has been declining since 1970. Globally, discovery peaked in 1960 and discoveries in a given year have exceeded consumption only twice since 1980 (1980 and 1992), and the ratio of discovery to depletion is continuously declining. It would not be surprising if global output had already peaked or will do so in the next year or so.

So-called 'proved resources' (90 percent certain) are still increasing (barely) because formerly 'proved and probable' resources (50 percent certain) are being converted to 'proved' as existing fields are fully explored. But the latter category is the one that best predicts future supplies – and the two curves are converging. Big publicly traded oil companies are showing increased reserves, but what they do not mention is that this appearance of growth is mostly from 'drilling on Wall Street' – that is, buying existing smaller companies – rather than drilling in the earth (companies that did not follow this path, like Shell, have faced strong pressures to meddle with their reserve statistics in order to reassure stockholders.) The fact is, new oil provinces are not being discovered; no super-giant field has been discovered since the Alaska North Coast.[3]

In any case, we think basic energy prices, especially for hydrocarbons, are more likely to increase than to fall in the next few years. The 'peak of oil' is only one of the reasons. Another reason for this is the perceived need to limit emissions of sulfur dioxide, nitrogen oxides, particulates and, especially, of greenhouse gases (GHGs) such as carbon dioxide. Emission controls are already a significant element of costs to electric-power producers, refiners and other industrial fuel users.

Oil (and natural gas) are not the only physical resources for which prices may rise in coming decades. Copper – essential for electrical wiring – is a serious candidate, along with platinum (the catalyst for petroleum cracking and automobile exhaust emissions control) and lithium (for rechargeable high-energy batteries). It must be acknowledged that none of these natural resources has exhibited a long-term increase in prices up to now, although it is hard to distinguish a major fluctuation from a long-term trend reversal (such as we might now be seeing in the case of copper). But, in general, extrapolation from past experience seems to suggest that declining trends in commodity prices will continue indefinitely.[4] We think such extrapolation is unjustified, at least for petroleum and gas and some of the metals.

What this means is that cheaper energy from new discoveries or more efficient extraction of petroleum (or natural gas) can no longer be expected to drive economic growth. This is because the fundamental mechanism for economic growth has always been that lower prices stimulate increasing demand. Clearly the reverse case must be considered: a trend toward higher prices will – other things being equal – result in reduced demand for energy and therefore for energy services, which we call 'useful work'. The only way to compensate for more costly primary energy (exergy) is to increase the efficiency with which primary energy is converted into useful work and mechanical power.

Electric power and mobile power (from internal combustion engines, mostly for transportation or construction) are the two most important types of useful work. The other two are muscle work, which is no longer important in industrialized countries, and heat delivered to the point of use (Ayres et al. 2003). But it is often forgotten that the cheapest source of electrical power – falling water – has already been largely exhausted in the industrial countries. Higher electricity prices won't create another Niagara Falls, although a large number of small streams may still be tapped for power. Coal-burning steam electric power plants are a much less efficient substitute for falling water and nuclear power is even less efficient. Declining prices for electric power, due to economies of scale, are also largely exhausted. Only fundamental improvements in technology – for example, combined cycle or combined heat and power (CHP) plants – offer near-term opportunities for future cost reduction for electric power.

8.7 EXTRAPOLATING TECHNOLOGICAL PROGRESS

The standard neoclassical growth model assumes growth in equilibrium, driven by an external force called 'technological progress' or total factor productivity (TFP). Goods and services are abstractions. Demand for energy (exergy) or other resources is a consequence, not a cause of economic growth. Silly as it sounds when stated explicitly, resources in such models are treated as if they were created by some combination of capital and labor. This is why growth, in this idealized model, does not depend in any way on the rate or quantity of consumption of natural resources, as such.

In contrast to the neoclassical model, the real economic system depends very much on material and energy (exergy) inputs, as well as on labor and capital. The real economic system can be viewed as a complex process that converts raw materials (and energy) into useful materials and final services. Evidently, materials and energy do play a central role in this alternative model of economic growth. The first stage is to convert raw materials into finished materials and raw fuels into finished fuels and electricity. These can be aggregated into a single category, namely 'useful work'. Later stages convert useful work into products and services. Over the past two centuries, as we saw in Chapters 6 and 7, successive improvements in the efficiency of these various exergy-to-work conversion stages have apparently accounted for most of the economic growth our Western civilization has enjoyed.

As we have noted earlier, the economic growth engine is a kind of *positive feedback* system. Demand growth for any product or service, and hence for raw materials and energy services, is stimulated by declining prices. Lower prices enable present consumers to buy more, and marginal consumers to enter the market. Higher prices have the opposite effect: they induce consumers to buy less or seek cheaper alternatives. Increased demand induces suppliers to add new capacity (such as new factories), which also tends to result in greater economies of scale, and savings from 'learning by doing', thus enabling further decreases in prices. Production experience also cuts costs by stimulating technological improvements in the production process itself. Finally, firms may invest in R&D to cut manufacturing costs or to increase product quality, which also helps sales. Evidently the system feeds on itself, which is why the 'engine' of growth can be described as a positive feedback cycle.

The feedback began operating in the 18th century when coal began replacing charcoal for a number of industrial applications, canals carried the coal and other goods, and steam engines began substituting for horses or watermills to operate machinery (Singer et al. 1958). One of the first significant applications of steam engines was to pump water out of coal mines, replacing horses. Coal-fired Newcomen 'atmospheric' engines, even very crude ones, could do this more cheaply than horses on a treadmill. The steam engines could use the coal from the mine to make steam, whereas the hardworking horses, unable to graze, had to be fed oats. The result of using coal to drive the pumps at the mine was cheaper coal. Coal (and later, coke) then began to replace charcoal in iron-smelting and brought about the widespread availability of cast iron, then wrought iron and finally steel (Landes 1969).

This is not the place to trace the operation of the feedback cycle in greater detail through the last two centuries. But throughout the 19th century, and the 20th, the basic mechanism has been the same: lower costs, lower prices, increased demand, increased investment, increased supply and, again, lower costs. Machines helped cut the costs of raw materials, especially fuels, which induced growth in demand for raw materials and energy, and induced continued substitution of fossil fuels for human (and animal) labor, and so on. This was – and still is – the basic recipe for economic growth (Ayres 2005). It has also been called the 'rebound effect' in another context (for example, Saunders 1992).

The technological efficiency of converting raw materials (and fuels) into useful work and power also increased enormously during the past two centuries, but the rate of increase has slowed down significantly since the 1960s. Unfortunately, the commonly cited 'renewable' alternatives to existing fossil fuel-burning steam electric power plants, notably wind power, biomass and photo-voltaics (PV) are not yet price-competitive with centralized electric-generating facilities. Moreover, costs are unlikely to fall rapidly unless there is a rapid increase in demand for such renewables, triggering dramatic economies of scale in manufacturing. Such an increase in demand can only be driven by subsidies to producers (as in Europe) or by regulation of some sort (such as the CAFÉ standards in the US). At the moment, subsidies are out of political favor in the US, and demand is not increasing fast enough to have a significant impact on costs.

As we have pointed out at some length, the costs of power and heat to users depends upon the thermodynamic efficiency with which primary fuels are 'converted' and delivered. The thermodynamic efficiency with which electric power is generated, on average, increased nearly ten-fold from 3 percent in 1900 to 30 percent in 1960, but it has remained almost constant at 33 percent since 1970 (Ayres et al. 2005). The reason for this slowdown is partly technical. A more efficient (up to 60 percent) technology does exist, notably the so-called 'combined cycle', consisting of a gas turbine whose hot exhaust drives a steam turbine. But this technology is only applicable where natural gas is plentifully available at low cost. Combined cycle with coal gasification is a future possibility but it is not yet enough of an improvement over existing older plants to justify their replacement.

Similarly, the efficiency of internal combustion (gasoline and diesel) engines increased by several times in the earlier period, but hardly at all since the 1960s, especially since refiners were forced to eliminate tetraethyl lead and auto manufacturers cut compression ratios to accommodate lower octane fuels. In automotive applications, the average efficiency of gasoline engine-powered vehicles, in typical stop-start applications, is not much over 12 percent, on average (American Physical Society et al. 1975; Ayres et al. 2003). The thermodynamic efficiency with which low temperature heat is produced (mostly by oil or gas-fired heaters) and used to heat air or water to comfortable temperatures in houses or office buildings is very low, in the range of 4 to 6 percent (ibid.).

Currently electric-power generation is much the most efficient of these three forms of useful work, so future increases are likely to be slow and expensive in coming. On the other hand, the least efficient form of 'work' is low temperature heat, such as space heat or hot water. But these forms of work are unlikely to get much cheaper in the near future, if only because raw forms of energy inputs, such as petroleum and gas, are unlikely to get much cheaper, and may well rise significantly in price when the present supply glut disappears. In the case of low temperature heating, the most promising source of improvement is more and better insulation and better windows (double or triple glazing). Mobile power systems and electric-generating systems have not improved significantly since the 1960s, and although efficiency gains are possible, they will require significantly higher capital investment. As regards mobile power, much better fuel economy is possible, especially with turbo-diesel direct injection, and later with electric-hybrid propulsion units.[5]

However, there is one other interesting possibility that has not yet been exploited to a significant extent in the US (unlike some other countries). This possibility, known as decentralized combined heat and power (DCHP), is to utilize the waste heat from a large number of small, decentralized electric power-generating units in factories and commercial buildings, thus reducing the need for fuel for space heating or water heating at the same time (Casten and Downes 2004; Casten and Ayres 2007; Ayres et al. 2007). This approach could simultaneously reduce overall fuel combustion and the accompanying unwanted emissions into the atmosphere.

The only technology that is still getting cheaper rapidly – thus driving economic growth in some sectors – is information and communications (ICT). But, while information processing is getting cheaper fast, information *products* are not (yet) capable of replacing, or significantly improving, the efficiency of older long-established materials-intensive technologies, notably agriculture, transportation and housing. Science fiction writers, notably William Gibson, have imagined a virtual world in which people live in tiny cubicles and work and travel mostly in a non-physical 'cyberspace'. Until that day comes, if ever it does, ICT will continue to have a marginal role.

Our point is that except for 'energy recycling' – or decentralized combined heat and power (DCHP) – there are no technologies on the immediate horizon that promise to cut the costs of electric power or mechanical power significantly below current levels. This means that, unless ways can be found to sharply increase the use of decentralized CHP, industrial society effectively faces an end to the positive feedback 'engine of growth' that has operated for two centuries. It remains to be seen whether the growth torch (as it were) can be passed to decentralized combined heat and power – or 'energy recycling' as it has been called – soon enough to keep the growth engine ticking over.

8.8   THE REXSF MODEL OF THE US ECONOMY

Since US economic growth for the past century, at least up to 2000, can be explained with considerable accuracy by three factors, K, L, U, it is not unreasonable to expect that future growth for some time to come – several decades, at least, will be explained quite well by simulated extrapolations of these variables, plus a growing contribution from information and communications technology (ICT). A powerful qualitative argument for this approach is that, no matter which direction the causality runs between useful work performed and growth (and we believe it runs both ways), it is hard to believe that a model that has high explanatory power for a century will suddenly spring a leak at the end of that time. But we are getting ahead of ourselves.

The simplest method of extrapolation of labor, capital and exergy consumption and conversion efficiency would be to do an econometric fit of each variable against a suitable mathematical function, such as an exponential. The simplest procedure would be to extrapolate output Y by fitting an exponential to past economic growth, and assuming future growth will continue at the same average rate r. This is, essentially, what most economists actually do in practice.[6] The next simplest procedure is to extrapolate aggregate labor supply L, capital stock K, exergy intensity (E/Y) or exergy/capital (E/K). We can then calculate the aggregate thermodynamic conversion efficiency (U/E), by a similar technique.

However, our basic mental model of the *feedback* process which drives growth suggests that, while GDP is indeed a function of capital, labor and useful work (which is a product of exergy inputs times conversion efficiency), all of these driving variables, except (arguably) labor supply, are also functions of past GDP. In short, the model must be recursive.

The solution we propose differs fundamentally from other forecasting models discussed in the literature. It is called the REXSF (Resource Exergy Services Forecasting) model. The model is based on the explanatory model (for growth in the US and Japan) developed in Chapters 6 and 7. But in contrast to the historical explanatory model (REXSH), the forecasting version REXSF treats the form and the parameters of the LINEX production function as given.[7] It focuses on forecasting capital and useful work output, not by simple extrapolation (as illustrated above), but by means of well-known techniques from the field of 'systems dynamics', originally pioneered by Forrester and his followers (Forrester 1961). Briefly, systems dynamic models differ structurally from most simple economic models in that the variables are not divided into dichotomous categories, *independent* or *dependent*. On the contrary, systems dynamic models assume *mutual dependence*: each of the variables may influence several of the others, while simultaneously being affected by the others, through feedback loops. Thence causality is always mutual, rather than uni-directional. To be more specific, it is no longer assumed that GDP is a dependent variable, causally determined by labor, capital and/or exergy services. On the contrary, each of those variables is also dependent on previous, or even current, values of GDP. Similarly, future values of the capital, exergy and useful work variables are partly dependent on future values of the GDP, with a time lag.

We extend the model into the future by introducing two explicit learning processes. In the first, production *experience* drives down the energy and materials intensity of output. (Recall that experience models were discussed in Chapters 1 and 2, especially Section 2.7). In the second, *experience* gained in supplying energy to the economy acts to increase the efficiency with which energy services (useful work) are supplied to the economy. The REXSF model formally consists of four distinct linked modules, namely (1) capital accumulation, (2) population growth, (3) resource consumption and (4) technological change dynamics, all of which are linked together by the production function derived previously for the explanatory model developed in Chapters 6 and 7.

The labor supply module of REXSF operates like a birth and death process, where births are considered equivalent to hires and deaths to retirements or layoffs. This simple formulation by-passes the need to model population growth, male and female labor force participation, length of active working life, and so forth, even though a more sophisticated model

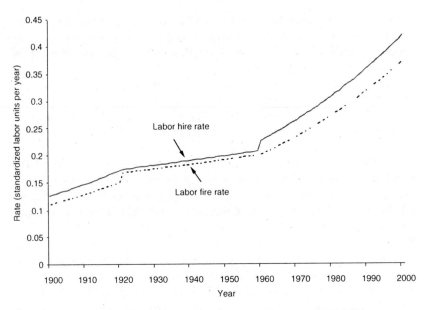

Figure 8.1   Simulated labor hire and fire rate (USA, 1900–2000)

would have to include these considerations. Nevertheless, our simple formulation is sufficient to create a simulated time series for labor supply. First order fractional entry and departure rate parameters were assumed to be constants, although they were not. To correctly reproduce the historical time series, it was necessary to allow each of these parameter values to change only once (discontinuously) over the entire 100-year period. Standard optimization methods were used to identify the years when the constant parameter values should change. In 1920, the fractional retirement rate shifted from 0.10 to 0.12. In 1959, the fractional entry rate increased from 0.124 to 0.135. These independent shifts generate three identifiable periods of relatively constant labor force dynamics, from 1900–20, 1920–59 and 1959 to the present day. The empirical and simulated results are presented in Figures 8.1 and 8.2.

In the case of capital stock at any moment, annual increments can be crudely equated with savings, which can be assumed roughly proportional to GDP, with some adjustments, such as a declining savings rate, as wealth grows, minus losses due to depreciation. The rate of depreciation is usually taken to be a constant, based on the useful life of the capital good, but adjustments may be needed to reflect a changing mix of capital goods (more computers with a life of four years, fewer bridges, etc.) There is at least a second-order relationship between depreciation and investment: the

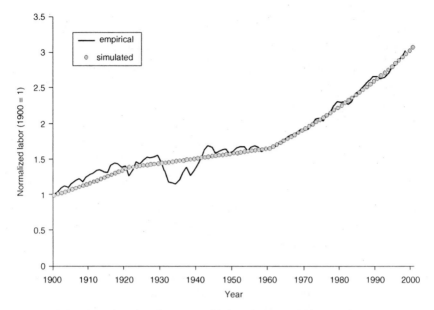

Figure 8.2   Simulated and empirical labor (USA, 1900–2000)

greater the latter, the faster the obsolescence rate, which accounts for part of the depreciation.

There is also a second-order relationship between investment and population cohort aging, because individuals save little or nothing during their first working years with young children, and they are likely to consume previous savings after retirement. Maximum savings are generated by age groups in their 40s and 50s. This phenomenon has been related to capital investment by Sanderson et al. (Sanderson 2006). Again, these relationships tend to change slowly, which means that the historical data can be used for parametric selection.

For REXSF model purposes, time series of total fixed capital were taken from standard published sources, as calculated by the so-called perpetual inventory method (Maddison 1995). We assume that future investment is a percentage of gross output, proportional to a savings rate, allocated among capital types (for example, infrastructure, equipment, structures, etc.). In principle, capital stock, by type, is depreciated based on appropriate estimates of useful lifetime. We assume that the mix of long-lived capital (infrastructure and structures) and short-lived capital (for example, vehicles and computers) has shifted significantly in favor of the latter, and that aggregate depreciation was about 3 percent per annum in 1900 compared to about 8 percent per annum today. This assumption fits the

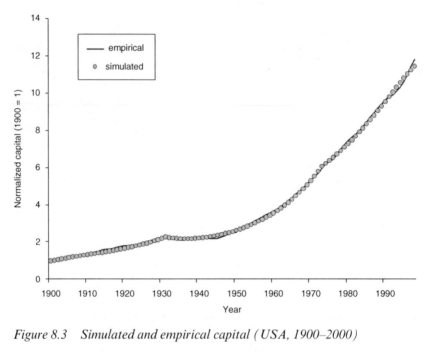

Figure 8.3   Simulated and empirical capital (USA, 1900–2000)

historical capital stock series with a savings (investment) rate of about 6 percent of GDP as shown in Figure 8.3. For forecasting purposes we extrapolated the fitted parameters for recent decades into the future. To construct more detailed scenarios it is possible to vary the future rates of investment and depreciation as well.

In the case of useful work (exergy services), there are two components. One is exergy consumption, which is almost proportional to GDP, except with a slight annual reduction in the *E*/*GDP* ratio. This decline arises from annual efficiency improvements and the structural shift away from exergy-intensive manufacturing and processing activities and towards services. In this case, a straightforward linear extrapolation of the *E*/*GDP* ratio may be appropriate, for a few decades, at least.

Existing models, as far as we know, consider only the commercial fuel exergy (energy) inputs, *E*. In several models, the energy intensity of *capital* (the *E*/*K* ratio) is also assumed to be a monotonically decreasing function of time. However, using either the usual definition of *E* (commercial fuels) or the broader definition that includes biomass, Figure 8.4 shows the actual exergy intensity of capital for the two definitions of exergy (*E*/*K*) for the US (1900–2000). Evidently, the actual curves are not smooth or monotonic at all.

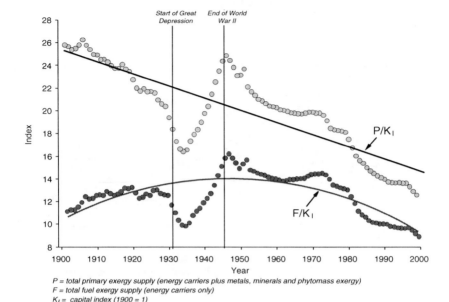

Figure 8.4   Energy intensity of capital (USA, 1900–2000)

The alternative is to use the energy intensity of GDP (E/Y) ratio. Then, for each year – starting with the present – knowing Y we can calculate the probable exergy input E for the next year from

$$\Delta\left(\frac{Y}{E}\right) = \frac{\Delta Y}{E} - \frac{\Delta E}{E}\left(\frac{Y}{E}\right) \tag{8.1}$$

whence, rearranging terms

$$\frac{\Delta E}{E} = \frac{\dfrac{\Delta Y}{E}}{\dfrac{Y}{E}} + \frac{\Delta Y}{Y} \tag{8.2}$$

where the energy intensity Y/E and its average rate of change $\Delta(Y/E)$ are both determined from the energy intensity graph Figure 8.5. Note the two definitions of energy (exergy) E. The narrower definition, correspond-ing to the lower curve, includes only commercial fuels, and the historical use pattern is an inverted U, with a peak in the mid-1920s (typical of the so-called environmental Kuznets curve). Breaks in the slope in the years 1930, 1940 and 1970 are clear evidence of the sensitivity of structural shifts

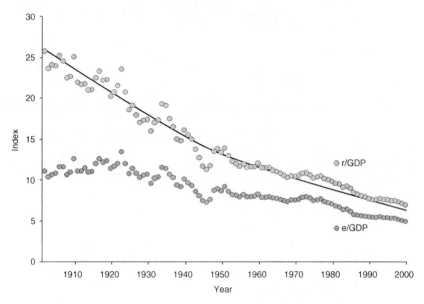

Figure 8.5   Energy intensity of GDP (USA, 1900–2000)

in the economy. The upper curve, which includes all forms of exergy from biomass, is also somewhat smoother and more nearly monotonic.

Of course, $\Delta Y/Y$ is the average historical economic growth rate r, also extrapolated. Then, knowing E and $f = U/E$ we can calculate U. This is sufficient to calculate Y for the next year from the LINEX production function (Equation 6.32). However, if any of the four input variables (K, L, E, U) or their ratios are departing from a smooth historical trajectory, the calculated Y for the next year will differ from the simple extrapolation assuming growth rate $\Delta Y/Y = r$ or a comparable rate of change for E/K.

In the REXSF model, we use the more general exergy/GDP (E/Y) ratio – including biomass – to define future exergy requirements. They are assumed to be proportional to GDP, but adjusted by a gradually decreasing exponential function of time. Based on data for the past century, the average rate of decline is 1.2 percent per annum. This assumption serves two purposes. First, it is simple. Second, it avoids the need to assume a constant capital-exergy relationship, for which there is little or no evidence. In the REXSF model, the rate of change of the E/Y decline is, as in other models, exogenously determined. Its value can be changed to reflect alternative 'dematerialization' policy efforts. In future versions of the model, we could envisage further developing the model to endogenize this aspect of technological progress, using a learning process controlled by production experience or R&D efforts.

The other component of useful work is the conversion efficiency itself, which reflects partly the mix of resource inputs and partly the state of the conversion technology *per se*. The former refers to structural shifts, for example, away from inefficient working animals to ICE-powered tractors on farms. The latter measures 'pure' technological improvements, for example, increasing thermal efficiency of electric power generation. Most of the primary exergy input to the economy is wasted due to an inefficient conversion process to physical work. Only the exergy services (useful work) delivered at the point of use can be considered productive. The lost fraction, at least its material component, is potentially harmful to the environment and can even hinder growth. As noted previously, the aggregate thermodynamic efficiency of exergy conversion f is a measure of the ratio of work (exergy service) delivered per unit of primary exergy consumed. This measure is a monotonically increasing function of time, as was shown in Figure 7.3.

Actually, we would expect the efficiency trend to have an elongated S-shape, rising slowly at first, then more rapidly as the mechanisms of technological advancement feed on themselves, but finally slowing down as the efficiency of conversion asymptotically approaches its theoretical maximum value (which is unity). As discussed in Chapter 1, the so-called logistic form of the elongated S-shaped progress or adoption-diffusion curve is observed in a wide variety of phenomena (for example, Fisher and Pry 1971; Marchetti and Nakicenovic 1979; Marchetti 1981). The logistic curve is the general solution of a simple differential equation, of the form

$$\frac{df}{dt} = kf(1 - f) \tag{8.3}$$

It happens to be symmetric around a point in time. Over the years, a wide variety of other non-symmetric functional forms have been suggested and analysed (for example, Martino 1983, chapter 4; Skiadas 1985). More recently, the notion of multiple logistic (or other) curves has been suggested (for example, Watanabe et al. 2001).

A variety of algorithms for extrapolating the thermodynamic efficiency curve can be envisioned. The simplest is to fit the historical data to a simple two-parameter logistic curve, plotting technical efficiency (f) against cumulative production, a surrogate for experience. However, the data provide some indication that a bi-logistic curve could fit better (Figure 8.6). Indeed the bi-logistic model gave a better fit (rms error = 0.001017), and successfully captures the trend of increasing efficiency. The bi-logistic model was

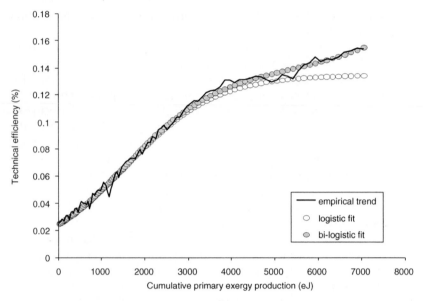

Figure 8.6   Logistic and bi-logistic S-curve fits to the trend of aggregate technical efficiency in the USA, 1900–2000

Table 8.1   Optimal logistic and bi-logistic model for technical efficiency f (USA 1900–98)

Parameters	1st logistic*	Parameters	2nd logistic
K_1	0.135	K_2	0.2
T_{m1}	1560	T_{m2}	12326
DT_1	4540	DT_2	10000
SSE	0.004**		0.001

Notes:

*nested within function for bi-logistic model.
**corresponding to the fit of the single logistic alone.

used to provide the forecasts that follow. Model parameters are shown in Table 8.1.

A ten-year moving average of the derivative of f versus cumulative GDP (Figure 8.7) reveals two peaks in 1962 and 1987, a valley in 1980 and another decline from 1987 to 1998. (We have not updated this particular graph.) The main conclusion is that technical progress is not as smooth as a first-order view, such as Figure 8.6, suggests. This irregularity results from

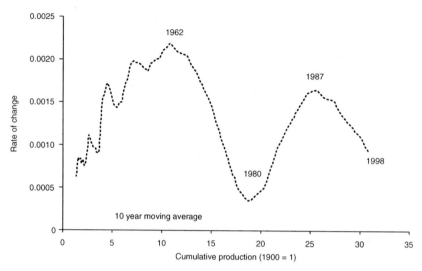

Figure 8.7   Rate of change of aggregate technical efficiency of primary exergy conversion (USA, 1900–98)

the combination of revolutionary and incremental engineering improvements, together with investment and behavioral changes. We do not propose any specific interpretation of the dates. However, this plot does provide some justification for the use of a bi-logistic S-curve to forecast technical efficiency growth into the future.[8]

8.9   EMPIRICAL RESULTS AND SENSITIVITY

Sensitivity tests have been performed by varying critical parameters of both the bi-logistic function and the rate of decline of the primary exergy intensity of output. Model parameters were assumed to vary according to a Gaussian distribution. Estimates of suitable minimum, maximum, mean and standard deviation were determined for each model parameter in isolation, while keeping all others at their empirically observed values, used in the REXSH (historical) model (Table 8.2). The parameters of the Gaussian probability distribution functions (pdfs) were chosen to provide plausible distributions about the forecast generated using the empirically observed parameter (Table 8.3). These pdfs were then used in a multivariate sensitivity analysis, which involved randomly drawing values for all parameters simultaneously, during 500 successive runs of the REXSF model.

Table 8.2   Forecast GDP growth rates for three alternative technology
             scenarios

| | Low | | Mid | | High | |
	f	GDP	f	GDP	f	GDP
Minimum	0.16%	−2.97%	0.43%	−1.89%	1.11%	1.94%
Average	0.40%	−1.29%	0.72%	0.38%	1.18%	2.20%
Maximum	0.62%	0.92%	0.89%	1.75%	1.23%	2.63%

Table 8.3   Sensitivity test Gaussian probability distribution parameters

	DT_2	T_{m2}	K_2	Dematerialization rate
Minimum	8 000	8 000	0.15	0.006
Maximum	12 000	16 000	0.4	0.016
Mean	10 000	12 326	0.2	0.012
St. Dev.	1 000	1 000	0.02	0.002

The results of this (multivariate) sensitivity analysis show how (simultaneous) perturbations of parameter values feed back to produce a range of plausible future trajectories of future output intensity, resource use efficiency and economic growth (Figures 8.8 and 8.9). In particular, Figure 8.10 shows how varying the exogenous assumption about the future rate of output intensity (E/Y) decline alters the accumulation of production experience and consequently the endogenous rate with which exergy conversion efficiency progresses. It is important to bear in mind, however, that one cannot conclude from the graph that accelerating the rate of decline *per se* will increase the rate of economic growth. On the contrary, what the graph really expresses is the fact that a higher rate of decline simply means that a given input of exergy generates more GDP. How to achieve that result is another question.

It may be of interest to note that the declining ratio E/Y can be interpreted as an indicator of *dematerialization*, bearing in mind that a major fraction of materials inputs to the economy actually consists of fuels and biomass. It follows that goals such as 'Factor Four' (von Weizsaecker et al. 1998) or 'Factor Ten' (Factor Ten Club 1994 and 1997) can be expressed roughly in terms of the intensity (E/Y) ratio.

Varying each of the parameters of the bi-logistic function produces a plausible spread of future trajectories for efficiency f and output Y, for a constant rate of decline (1.2 percent per annum) of the exergy intensity of

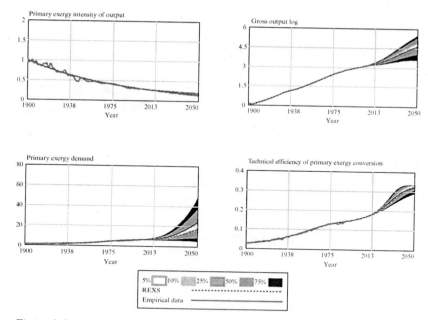

Figure 8.8 *Sensitivity test results varying the fractional decay rate of output exergy intensity*

output (Figure 8.11). When both E/Y and f are perturbed simultaneously, the range of possible outcomes is increased dramatically as the full impacts of feedbacks between resource consumption, production experience and end-use efficiency are manifest.

Combining these projections, and using the LINEX production function, corrected for ICT growth, we obtain the GDP projections shown in Figure 8.12. Although these forecasts are highly uncertain, it is very important to observe that the *most probable* forecast for US GDP is one in which growth ceases sometime between 2030 and 2040. Thus an important future implication of our model is that growth driven by the historical 'engine' is slowing and could possibly come to a halt a few decades hence. The reasons seem straightforward: (1) the efficiency gains in primary exergy conversion (to physical work) are getting harder to achieve (the S-curve has passed its point of inflection) and (2) the opportunities to substitute machines for labor are getting scarcer (because an increasing fraction of the GDP consists of services, where value is essentially equated to cost). In other words, there is a double saturation effect.

In order for economic growth to continue at historical rates without proportional increases in fossil fuel consumption and associated waste and pollution, it is vitally important to exploit new ways of generating value-added

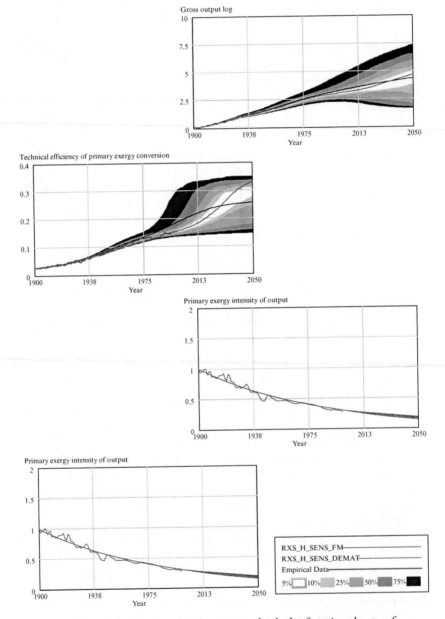

*Figure 8.9   Sensitivity test results varying both the fractional rate of
              output exergy intensity and selected parameters of the
              bi-logistic curve controlling the rate of efficiency growth*

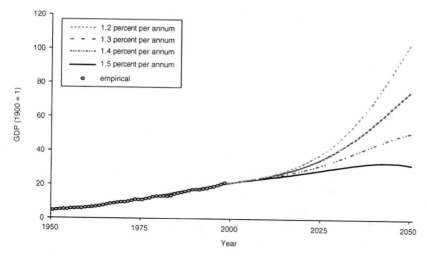

Figure 8.10   Historical (1950–2000) and forecast (2000–50) GDP for alternate rates of decline of the energy intensity of output, USA

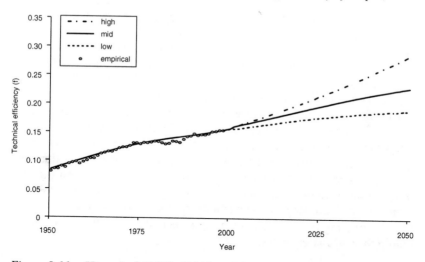

Figure 8.11   Historical (1950–2000) and forecast (2000–50) technical efficiency of energy conversion for alternate rates of technical efficiency growth, USA

without doing more physical work. Either basic resource costs must continue to decline relative to wages or it will be necessary to develop ways of reducing fossil fuel inputs per unit of physical work output. But major new cost-reducing resource discoveries seem quite unlikely. Moreover, economies

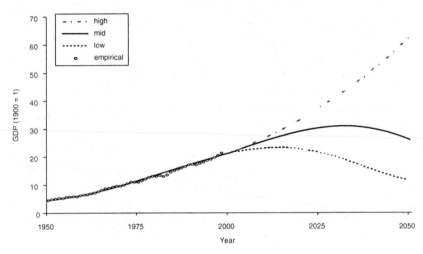

*Figure 8.12   Historical (1950–2000) and forecast (2000–50) GDP for
              alternate rates of technical efficiency growth, USA*

of scale and experience are unlikely to compensate for declining resource
discovery, and conventional energy conversion technologies are already so
high that future improvements are almost certain to be marginal.

The optimistic 'high' growth rate in Figure 8.12 implies a significant
increase in the efficiency with which useful work is generated from exergy
inputs. This is technically feasible, but it seems unlikely to occur without
drastic policy interventions to encourage the adoption of efficient technologies such as combined heat and power (CHP), rooftop photo-voltaics,
small mass-produced wind turbines, double and triple glazed windows,
domestic heat pumps, battery powered cars and so forth. In virtually all
cases, progress is still impeded by anti-competitive behavior on the part
of oligopolistic industries, reluctance by lenders to provide mortgages for
'non-standard' construction, reluctance on the part of insurers to insure
firms promoting innovative systems, and regulatory hurdles from zoning
requirements to safety rules.

NOTES

1. Some of the assumptions specific to the DICE model were challenged immediately, for
    instance the choice and sensitivity of the model to the assumed discount rate to which
    the model results are highly sensitive (Cline 1992), the uniform treatment of losses of
    tangible and intangible goods via the flexible production function, as opposed to a more
    rigid utility function (Tol 1994) and a lack of source and sink constraints on carbon and

the assumed linearity of the carbon uptake processes and instantaneous flexibility of emissions (Frankhauser 1995).

2. The peculiar phenomenon of sub-par mortgages for home buyers with poor credit is a direct consequence of Bush Administration policy. The sub-par mortgage lenders count on either raising their rates after a few years, or foreclosing and selling appreciated properties into a rising real-estate market. Declining house prices are disastrous both for the borrowers and the lenders, many of which went bankrupt in 2007–08.

3. The best source on all this is Strahan (2007). For the geological background see Campbell (1997), Campbell and Laherrère (1998), Campbell (2003) and Deffeyes (2001).

4. The outcome of the famous debate (and bet) between Julian Simon and Paul Ehrlich (and two colleagues) seems to confirm the optimists. However, this optimism about future costs and prices is really predicated on three other extrapolations, namely that the historical rate of technical progress in discovery and conversion will continue to outstrip the rate of decline in ore quality and the rate of increase of demand. The underlying economic theory has been set forth in detail in the book *Scarcity and Growth* by Barnett and Morse (1963), subsequently updated (Smith and Krutilla 1979).

5. Despite recent publicity, permeable membrane hydrogen fuel cells are unlikely to be used widely for private automobiles due to high costs and better uses for the natural gas or electric power used to produce the hydrogen (Romm 2004).

6. The actual procedure is to fit a straight line through the logarithms.

7. We used parameter values for REXSH, identified through empirical analysis of historical data (Ayres et al. 2003).

8. A more elaborate alternative could employ a punctuated-equilibrium model of technology adoption and diffusion, capable of modeling competing technologies (Loch and Huberman 1999). In the perspective of evolutionary economics, it might be appropriate to model efficiency as a birth and death process for Schumpeterian innovations. This formulation could also be considered a 'learning and forgetting' model (Benkard 1999). It is reasonable to consider the efficiency improvements as resulting from the birth of new technologies and the loss of memory of previous ones. Of course, this is a very simplistic interpretation, inasmuch as existing ideas are often incorporated into their successors.

9. Economic growth and development: towards a catch-up model (simplified REXSF model)*

9.1 BACKGROUND

The methodology described in the previous chapters is obviously too complicated to be applicable to developing countries with, in many cases, short histories and incomplete or unreliable historical data. Yet there is an increasingly urgent need to develop better forecasting and scenario-analysis tools that are simpler to implement and that do not depend from the outset on two critical but risky assumptions. The first assumption is that global economic growth is automatic and exponential, that is, that it depends on exogenous technological progress – or 'total factor productivity' (TFP) – which increases each year by something like 2.5 percent, on average, despite short-term fluctuations. The second critical but very risky assumption is that it (the growth trend) is independent of energy consumption and, therefore, independent of energy production and availability.

The dangers of making long-term policy decisions, and long-term capital investments, based on faulty assumptions, need not (indeed, cannot) be addressed here. However, it is worthwhile pointing out that a variety of organizations, including the World Bank, the International Monetary Fund (IMF), NATO, OPEC, the OECD, the Inter-governmental Panel on Climate Change (IPCC), the executive branches of the European Union (the EEC) and major national governments, routinely base policy decisions on long-term scenarios that incorporate such assumptions, albeit usually hidden.

Policies to respond to the challenge of global emissions of carbon dioxide and other greenhouse gas (GHG) emissions clearly depend upon forecasts of economic growth and energy consumption. Rapidly increasing demand for energy, especially by China and India, has introduced a significant new element into the equation. The likelihood of a peaking of global petroleum

---

* This chapter is based on a paper by Jie Li and Robert Ayres, entitled 'Economic Growth and Development: Towards a Catchup Model', in *Environmental & Resource Economics*, 2007 (Li and Ayres 2007).

output within the next decade or so magnifies the problem.[1] Finally, the fact that the bulk of known remaining petroleum resources is located in the Middle East, mostly in Islamic countries with unstable governments and rising Islamic fundamentalism, introduces a major uncertainty.

All the studies of strategies for minimizing the impact of climate change point to increasing costs of primary energy, whether by introducing carbon taxes, emissions regulation, carbon sequestration, or mandatory energy conservation technologies. Recent empirical and theoretical work suggests that the driver of growth is not energy (exergy) consumption as such, but exergy converted to 'useful work' in the economy (Ayres and Warr 2002; Ayres 2002; Ayres and Warr 2003; Ayres et al. 2003; Ayres and Warr 2005). This strongly suggests that higher energy prices could have a negative effect on economic growth, at least in the US.

The realism of the core assumption (that only capital accumulation per worker drives growth) was sharply challenged by empirical studies in the early 1950s. Research based on reconstructions of historical time series of the supposed factors of production (labor and capital) drastically reduced the apparent role of capital per unit of labor (Abramovitz 1952, 1956; Fabricant 1954). For example, Fabricant estimated that capital accumulation accounted for only 10 percent of US economic growth since the middle of the 19th century.

Most economists are still using versions of a theory of growth developed for a single-sector model exactly half a century ago (Solow 1956, 1957; also Swan 1956). The theory was developed further by Meade (1961). A key feature of the Solow-Swan model was the explicit introduction of a generic aggregate production function in which capital services are derived from an artifact called capital stock, discussed in previous chapters.

The Solow model, in its original form, depends on only two independent variables, or 'factors of production', namely, total labor supply and total capital stock (Solow 1956, 1957). Labor and capital services are assumed to be proportional to the corresponding stocks. However, as noted already, these two variables or factors of production could not explain the observed growth of the US economy from 1909 through 1949. The unexplained 'Solow residual' accounted for over 85 percent of the per capita growth in output. Solow termed this residual 'technological progress' and introduced it as an exogenous multiplier of the production function. The multiplier is usually expressed as an exponential function of time which increases at a constant average rate of about 2.5 percent per annum based on past history. The multiplier is now called total factor productivity, and it is commonly assumed to be exogenous to the economic system. The unexplained residual is usually attributed nowadays to a stock of technological knowledge that grows (by assumption) according to some unexplained principle.

9.2   ECONOMIC DEVELOPMENT THEORY

The theory of economic development is essentially growth theory as applied to the world as a whole, consisting of nearly 200 countries ranging in population from China to nearly unpopulated islands like Nauru or tiny city-states like Liechtenstein, Monaco, San Marino or Andorra. The range of political and economic circumstances is nearly as great. To explain the developmental behavior of such a diverse group is obviously a daunting task. However, the task has attracted, and continues to attract, considerable attention from economists. Attempts to explain economic development have a long history. Early theories were more theoretically than empirically based. By the middle of the 19th century, growth was an obvious fact of economic life. At that time, it was attributed to labor force (that is, population) growth and capital accumulation. The latter was attributed to 'surplus' (profits) or savings.

The most influential models of the 1930s and 1940s were based on a formula attributed to Fel'dman (1928, 1964), equating the rate of growth of the economy to the savings rate divided by the capital-output ratio, or (equivalently) the ratio of annual savings to capital stock. The formula was rediscovered (independently) by Harrod and Domar (Harrod 1939; Domar 1946). These models, which emphasized the role of central planning (a relic of academic Marxism), dominated early postwar thinking about development economics.[2] For instance, a well-known 1950s-era text on the subject by Arthur Lewis states, without qualification, that 'the central fact of development is rapid capital accumulation' (including knowledge and skills with capital) (Lewis 1955).

An influential theory of development known as the 'stage theory' was introduced in 1960 (Rostow 1960). Rostow's idea was, in brief, that economic growth 'takes off' only when a certain level of capital investment has been achieved, along with other conditions. In effect, the rate of growth depends upon the level of current income, using a relationship – based on a scatter chart – that is very difficult, if not impossible, to quantify sufficiently for forecasting purposes. As a consequence, the exact model specification is essentially arbitrary, since both the theoretical and empirical bases are weak. However, the characteristic growth trajectory in the Rostow theory would be a sort of elongated S-curve, characterized by rapid growth after 'takeoff', followed by progressively slower growth thereafter, that is, 'the poor get richer and the rich slow down'.

Actually the Solow-Swan theory has a built-in tendency for declining productivity due to declining returns to capital investment (Solow 1956, 1957; Swan 1956). This feature of the Solow model implies that countries with a small capital stock should grow faster than countries with a large capital stock. The same feature also predicts a gradual convergence between poor and rich countries. In the late 1980s and early 1990s there was considerable interest in the theory of convergence, supported by a wide variety of examples, mostly regional. In fact, for a time, it appeared that a new regularity in empirical economics had been discovered, namely the existence of a common underlying convergence rate within 'convergence clubs' at the rate of 2 percent per annum (Baumol 1986; Baumol et al. 1989; Ben-David 1994; Barro and Sala-i-Martin 1992, 1995).

However, as the voluminous econometric evidence was digested, it emerged that the apparent statistical uniformity might be misleading. There is some evidence for convergence in East Asia, but not in Africa or Latin America. However, while 'convergence clubs' apparently exist at both ends of the economic spectrum, the rich clubs and the poor clubs are polarized and diverging from each other. This large-scale divergence dominates the apparent 2 percent convergence that had been accepted as conventional wisdom (Quah 1996). Others have confirmed this conclusion. The results of our work, presented below, can be regarded as supportive of the 'diverging convergence clubs' notion, although we have arrived at our results (discussed later) by a completely different route.

In any case, economic growth in the industrialized countries has not slowed down to the degree suggested by the Solow theory, while most developing countries (with some notable exceptions, as noted hereafter) have not been catching up (Barro and Sala-i-Martin 1995). The failure of the rich countries to slow down as the model implied was one of the reasons for widespread interest in 'endogenous growth theory' that emerged in the late 1980s (Romer 1986, 1990; Lucas 1988).

In response to this perceived difficulty, some theorists have suggested that capital and labor augmentation in the sense of quality improvements might enable the Solow-Swan model to account for the observed facts. For instance, education and training make the labor force more productive. Moreover, knowledge and skills presumably do not depreciate. Similarly, capital goods have become more productive as more advanced technology is embodied in more recent machines, thus compensating for depreciation. Augmentation of labor and capital are, in some degree, an observable and quantifiable fact. Allowing for it, a number of cross-sectional econometric studies were carried out in the 1990s to test this idea. Indeed, some of them seemed, at first, to provide empirical support for the idea that exogenous technological progress (TFP) can be eliminated from the theory and that factor accumulation alone adjusted for augmentation could, after all, explain the observed facts of economic development (Mankiw et al. 1992; Mankiw 1995; Young 1995; Barro and Sala-i-Martin 1995).

However more recent research has also undermined that tentative conclusion, based as it was on statistical analysis of imperfect data. Later results have essentially reinstated the original Solow view that factor accumulation is *not* the central feature of economic growth after all (Easterly and Levine 2001). Easterly and his colleagues, having extensively reviewed the published literature of economic development studies, argue – as Solow did – that 'something else' accounts for most of the observable differences between growth experiences in different countries. Easterly et al. adopt the standard convention of referring to this 'something else' as TFP.

The standard theory up to now also shares a significant and even bizarre feature: it does *not* consider natural resource consumption and use to have any role in the growth process. Yet, though most economic historians date the beginning of the industrial revolution to the innovations in textile spinning, carding and weaving, it is evident that later developments depended on the works of James Watt and the 'age of steam'. Similarly, most non-economists immediately grasp the historical importance of the substitution of machines driven by the combustion of fossil fuels for human and animal labor. It seems to follow, of course, that the availability – or non-availability – of ever-cheaper fuels and sources of power will inevitably have a crucial impact on future economic growth.

Contemporary concerns about the price of petroleum are by no means irrelevant. It is simply not plausible that resource consumption is determined only by growth but not *vice versa*, or that GDP growth will continue indefinitely at a constant rate like manna from heaven. The rising price of petroleum will have very different effects on the growth trajectories of developing countries, depending on whether they are exporters or importers of oil, gas and coal. The failure of contemporary economic theory to recognize this 'disconnect' (as we see it) says more about the mind-set of contemporary economic theorists than it does about the real world.

Undoubtedly technological change, investment (and thus savings), capital accumulation, labor (workers and hours worked) and population growth are key driving forces of economic growth. These factors certainly differ widely across countries, and consistent long-term data series for some of the variables – especially technological change – are scarce or non-existent. We therefore seek a proxy for the latter variable.

9.3 'STYLIZED FACTS' ABOUT ECONOMIC GROWTH

Here is a list of 'stylized' facts from the economic growth literature:

1. Output per capita (Y/N) grows monotonically over time, during 'normal' periods.

2. Capital-labor ratio (K/L) grows also.
3. Rate-of-return on capital is nearly constant over time.
4. Capital-output ratio (K/Y) is nearly constant.
5. Share of labor and capital in national accounts is nearly constant.
6. Growth rate of output per worker differs substantially among countries.
7. Factor accumulation cannot explain increase in Y/N.
8. Fertility rate declines as output/capita grows, except at very low levels of Y/N.
9. (Hence) growth of population N is negatively correlated with Y and growth of Y.
10. Investment as a fraction of GDP (I/Y) and savings rate s tends to increase slightly with Y.
11. Workers tend to emigrate from poor countries to wealthy countries, as opportunity arises.
12. Cross-country convergence of Y/N is conditional on country characteristics.
13. Statistically robust determinants include initial level of GDP, life expectancy, investment, literacy, religious mix, and 'openness' (that is, to foreign investment and trade.

The first six items on the list were set forth originally by Kaldor (1961) while the others are extracted from the empirical growth literature of recent years, especially the work by Barro and Sala-I-Martin (Barro 1991; Barro and Sala-i-Martin 1992, 1995; Sala-I-Martin 1996, 1997; Mulder et al. 2001; OECD 2003; Baily 2003).

Much of the recent literature concerns the extent to which various modifications of the neoclassical model can explain why 'the poor get richer and the rich slow down' (or not), as the case may be. We suspect that neoclassical economics can never explain very much of the specific differences between countries, because institutional factors, especially political ideology, form of government and political stability, are so crucial. We do not doubt that sound macroeconomic policy, investment, education (investment in human capital), R&D spending, 'openness' (trade exposure), religion, natural resource endowments and others of the 60 factors that Barro and Sala-i-Martin and subsequently the OECD considered in their regressions are relevant, to various degrees in different countries. But that is the problem. There is no single overriding lexicographic hierarchy of importance among them that can be uncovered by elaborate multiple correlation analysis and used in a 'one size fits all' formula.

We add four more stylized facts that we think a theory of growth should explain, as follows:

14. Technological progress occurs in two varieties. Most progress (quantitatively) consists of incremental improvements to existing products or processes, but these improvements have no spillover effects and contribute little to growth. Radical innovations are much rarer but more important in the long run.

15. Technological progress is not homogeneous across sectors or continuous in time. The spillovers that drive long-term growth result from a few radical innovations that are discontinuous at the sectoral level. New sectors are created only by radical innovations.

16. Energy prices and growth are negatively correlated, while consumption of raw materials (exergy), exergy services (physical work, finished materials) are positively correlated with economic growth.

17. Economic growth is positively correlated with most kinds of waste generation, at least in the long term.

The first two items on our supplementary list (14, 15) are empirical observations that actually contradict most of the so-called 'endogenous growth' theories. In particular, they explain why 'human capital' as measured in the usual terms (years of school, educational expenditures, R&D, patents, etc.) *cannot* explain actual growth patterns as observed in the most technologically advanced societies, especially the US. During a 100-year time horizon this is a crucial point.

The last two items (16, 17) are directly linked to each other but also cannot be explained by neoclassical growth theory because the latter reserves no primary role for the production and consumption of materials, energy (exergy) or exergy services. In neoclassical theory these are assumed to be consequences of economic activity but not as causal factors. In fact, as we have emphasized several times previously in this book, the laws of thermodynamics are inconsistent with the standard theory of growth, which treats the economy, in effect, as a perpetual motion machine in which consumption of natural resources, and potential scarcity of resources, play no role. We think that resource consumption plays a central role in economic development.

9.4   WHAT THE STANDARD THEORIES EXPLAIN

Focusing on their list of 13 stylized facts, Mulder et al. present the core concepts of the standard Solow-Swan growth model followed by a mathematical elaboration of it, with an explanation of how the basic model deals with items 1–6, 9 and 12, as well as two of the determinants listed under 13, namely initial level of GDP and investment (Mulder et al. 2001;

Mulder 2004). They also propose an augmented version that incorporates human capital and thus satisfies some of the other criteria among the 13.

Mulder et al. present a series of five standard criticisms together with the responses offered by adherents of the standard theory. Two of the five major criticisms of the Solow model are concerned with demographic issues, notably the inhomogeneity of the workforce. These problems can be addressed by fairly straightforward modifications (augmentations) of the model. We quote only the most pertinent objection, number 2, namely that

> the Solow model essentially takes, as given, the behavior of the variables that are identified as the driving forces of growth, viz. population growth and technological change. In other words, it explains growth by simply postulating it. (Mulder 2004)

In response to this major criticism, Mulder et al. note the development of two classes of models in the past two decades, namely evolutionary growth models and neoclassical endogenous growth models (of which there are several sub-classes). They discuss the latter at much greater length than the former, which barely mention the seminal work of Nelson and Winter (Nelson and Winter 1982). As regards the neoclassical endogenous theorizing, three approaches are noted. The first is the so-called AK approach, pioneered by Romer and Rebelo, where capital K is taken to include human capital (hence population as well) (Romer 1986, 1987b; King and Rebelo 1990; Rebelo 1991). The growth of human capital in this approach is not subject to declining returns because of the compensating influence of spillovers, which are productivity-enhancing methods or technologies resulting from progress in another sector.

The second approach emphasizes knowledge creation as a result of maximizing behavior (for example, R&D), again subject to spillovers and dependent on the extent to which benefits of innovation can be appropriated by Schumpeterian innovators (Lucas 1988). More recent work has treated R&D as a separate sector, with capital flowing into it in proportion to the returns on R&D *vis-à-vis* other investments. Aghion and Howitt have pioneered a 'neo-Schumpeterian approach', emphasizing the research-driven displacement of older sectors by newer ones (namely the process of *creative destruction* postulated by Schumpeter) (Aghion and Howitt 1992, 1998).

It is worthwhile to note that none of our last four proposed stylized facts (14–17) are explained by any of the neoclassical theories. Indeed, facts 14 and 15 are explicitly inconsistent with the notion – common to so-called 'endogenous theories' – that technology is homogeneous, fungible and continuously improving. (We discussed this issue at some length in Chapter 2.)

9.5   WHAT THE STANDARD THEORIES DO NOT EXPLAIN

Much of the recent mainstream literature is concerned with the growing empirical evidence from growth-accounting studies, namely that factor accumulation – even with broad redefined factors, such as 'human capital' – matters less than TFP growth, which still remains essentially unexplained, except in qualitative terms. Models comparing growth over a large sample of countries are forced to make 'heroic' assumptions about the basic common growth rate, about the initial stocks of capital and technology and about the creation of and access to technology. As Mulder notes,

> The heroic assumption of an identical [growth rate] across countries goes back to the traditional neoclassical assumption that technology is a public good ('blueprints can be found in handbooks and now even on the internet, so everybody has free access to the latest innovations'). One needs not much empirical research to know that this can be far from the real life of technological change and technology diffusion, and technological progress can differ substantially across countries. (Mulder 2004)

In short, neoclassical growth theory does not reflect the patterns of technological progress in the real world, or our two 'stylized facts' 14 and 15.

Homo economicus is supposed to be a rational (utility-maximizing) decision-maker and *H. economicus* equates utility with money, at least in situations where a monetary calculation is possible. It follows that rational economic agents do not invest in projects that are known to have a negative rate of return or a negative expectation value (of utility). They do not buy lottery tickets or bet on horses, or prospect for gold to make money, though they might do so for the excitement. More important, some of the people who like risky adventures (including lottery tickets) are the crazy inventors who refuse to consider the very low odds of success and who nevertheless persevere. A very few, but a very important few, are the ones who come up with history-making 'radical innovations' in the Schumpeterian tradition (stylized fact 15). Standard theory cannot explain this fact.

Romer, in particular, argues that it is the number of innovations – or new 'recipes', in his words – rather than their quality, that contributes to economic growth (Romer 2002). But most inventions, and improvements, are so small and so narrowly focused on a particular product that they have essentially no spillover effect (see item, 14). This also means that formal R&D, in the aggregate, also has very little spillover effect. It is very hard to see how a razor with five blades, a new corkscrew, a new depilatory, a new lipstick color or hair-dye, a livelier golf ball, or a new fiberglass golf club can contribute even slightly to economic growth. Innovations such as these are very narrowly focused and in most cases merely replace an earlier product in the same market segment without increasing overall demand.

The radical innovations that yield major spillovers are comparatively rare and easily recognized. Practical applications of nuclear energy or superconductivity, or semiconductors, or space technology or lasers or gene splicing create fundamentally new products and services. They drive long-term economic growth by cutting costs and prices, keeping the economy far from equilibrium. They are not really accounted for in current neoclassical economic theory.

Most macro-models still assume (for convenience) that knowledge growth is exogenous, although microeconomists who work in the area of technology *per se* realize that the contrary must be true. However, there is another feature of technological evolution that has been given much less attention than it deserves, from the standpoint of macroeconomic theory. It is quite simply that 'knowledge', in recent economic models of the AK type, is regarded (for convenience) as *homogeneous and fungible* (that is, uniformly applicable across sectors).

On the contrary, we think technology is *inhomogeneous* and – with rare exceptions – *non-fungible*. Inhomogeneity means that some technologies have vastly more economic importance (that is, are more productive) than others. Indeed, it is fairly easy to identify some of those technologies, or families of technologies, that currently have the greatest impact. Candidates might include iron and steel, steam power, internal combustion engines, electric power and its many applications, telecommunications and information processing. Non-fungibility means that improvements in a specific technology may have no impact (that is, spillover) on others. That is true of all of the examples mentioned in a previous paragraph (five-bladed razors, depilatories, corkscrews, lipstick colors, golf balls, etc.).

Neoclassical growth theory also cannot explain the other two stylized facts, namely 16 and 17. It is important to note that the underlying accounting identities and physical conservation laws are applicable in any system, whether physical or economic, and whether or not the system is in, or near, equilibrium (in any sense). Granted that economics is not thermodynamics and economic equilibrium is somewhat different from thermodynamic equilibrium. But the basic characteristic of a system in any sort of equilibrium state is that 'nothing happens' spontaneously, that is, without exogenous intervention.

Nevertheless, the standard representation of the economic system is as an abstract box model, with production, investment and consumption linked by flows of money representing payments for labor services, capital services and consumption goods. In this model there is no special role for energy or raw materials, and there is no waste or dissipation.

We contend, on the contrary, that it makes more sense to view the economic system as a materials-extraction and processing system, in which raw materials are converted, through a series of stages, into physical work and finished materials, material products and finally, services. The materials that are extracted, whether or not they are embodied in products (or structures), and whether or not they are repaired, renovated, remanufactured or recycled, must eventually return to the environment in a degraded form (Ayres and Kneese 1969). While environmental and resource economists have for many decades recognized that these flows exist and that they have economic significance, they still play no role in the standard theory of economic growth.

9.6   ASSUMPTIONS

With the above as background, this chapter starts from the following assumptions (or stylized facts):

1. The United States is still the 'locomotive' of the world economy and will remain so for some time to come. There are two arguments to support this assumption. One is that the US is the main consumer of export goods from economies in East Asia that have kept their exchange rates artificially low precisely to maximize exports. The exporters, with large trade surpluses, have had to re-export capital to the US to prevent the financial markets from readjusting exchange rates and interest rates to compensate. This capital inflow is invested either in government bonds or other assets, such as existing firms. This, in turn, keeps US interest rates and inflation low. It also diverts much of the world savings away from the developing regions where it is most needed, to the US where it subsidizes excessive consumption. The second reason is that, since World War II, the US has been, and remains, the primary creator and generator of new advanced technologies. This is largely because of the existence of a number of autonomous elite universities that easily attract the world's top scientists and regularly spin off new business enterprises, subject to well-known and non-restrictive regulatory and labor market constraints and supported by plentiful venture capital, much of it created by previous successful spinoffs. The US model of university-generated high tech businesses exemplified by Silicon Valley is very difficult to imitate and has not, as yet, been imitated successfully elsewhere despite a number of attempts.

2. Economic growth and development in all countries is mainly driven by technological progress, reflected in increasing TFP. We assume

that the best quantifiable measure of technological progress (based on prior research on the US and Japanese economies) is the efficiency with which energy inputs (actually exergy)[3] are converted to 'useful work' (Ayres and Warr 2002; Ayres 2002; Ayres and Warr 2003; Ayres et al. 2003; Ayres and Warr 2005).

3. Technical progress in developing countries is almost entirely due to transfers from industrialized countries, either embodied in direct foreign investment (DFI) or in returning personnel who have studied or worked in an advanced country.

4. It is probably impossible to identify a set of necessary *and sufficient* conditions for economic growth. There are too many factors involved, many of which are interdependent. Certainly the extensive econometric work, mostly in the 1990s, seeking to identify the magic formula has utterly failed to do so. However, it is fairly easy to identify conditions that *prevent* or stunt growth, especially by inhibiting investment. Political instability, especially if accompanied by violence, is an absolute growth stopper. Monetary instability (as in Latin America for much of the past half century) is another. Rapid inflation essentially prevents planning and long-term investment. Central planning (as in the former Soviet Union) is a third. Excessive regulation and associated bureaucracy – also in Latin America – is a fourth. Excessive inequity between rich and poor is a fifth. Excessive corruption is a sixth. On the other hand, democracy or its lack seems to be largely irrelevant, or even negative for growth.[4] Growth-friendly factors previously identified include primary education (literacy and numeracy), religious mix, and advanced education (especially engineering). 'Openness' seems to help, given other conditions. The most important factor, after education, is probably 'rule of law', with active and honest enforcement of commercial agreements and necessary, but not onerous, government regulation.

9.7 HYPOTHESES

Based on the above, we test the following hypotheses:

I. That countries can be placed in three distinct groups, as follows: Group A consists of advanced countries (mainly OECD) that have largely caught up to the US, in terms of GDP per capita, but are no longer progressing in this area, for one reason or another. Group B consists of countries that are now growing faster than the US (that is, catching up) and have done so fairly consistently for the past 20 years

or so. Group C consists of countries, most of which are not growing
vis-à-vis the US, or have only started to do so very recently (such as
the transition economies of Eastern Europe and the former USSR).
Group C countries other than those in transition are overwhelmingly
characterized by one or more growth stoppers such as political-ethnic
or religious violence, monetary instability and/or lack of a legal
framework of laws that are enforced.

II.   That invested capital (K) and labor (L) are important factors of production, but that accumulation of capital and labor do not explain
economic growth. We conjecture that 'useful work' output – denoted
U hereafter – is a third factor of production and that U (or some
proxy thereof) has significant explanatory power both for Group A
countries and Group B countries, but not for Group C countries.

III. That electrification or electricity consumption per capita, plus some
fraction of petroleum consumption, is the most plausible proxy.[5]
The underlying reason is that electricity is, itself, essentially a form
of useful work, while the other major form of useful work in modern
economies (mechanical work by mobile internal combustion engines)
is based on the consumption of liquid petroleum products.

IV.   That some of the other factors affecting growth can be accounted for
by introducing dummy variables, equivalent to grouping countries
according to other criteria.

9.8   METHODOLOGY

The major objective of this simplified version of the REXSF model is to
estimate the gap (GDP fraction) between a target country and the leading
country (the USA for our purposes). The GDP fraction variable is the
country's GDP, in purchasing power parity (PPP) per capita, as a fraction
of the US GDP in the same year. The larger the fraction, the smaller the
gap with respect to the USA. The standard source of GDP data in PPP
since 1950 is the so-called Penn World tables (Heston et al. 2006). In principle, we would need international historical data on labor and capital as
well as useful work, to account for GDP. The World Bank Development
Indicators (WDI) is the standard source for employment data by economic activity (World Bank 2006). However, there is no readily accessible
standard source of international data on capital stock. The best available
source is the work of Angus Maddison, but his published work primarily
concerns a few individual OECD countries (Maddison 1995b). Hence we
focus in this work on the search for an alternative proxy, namely 'useful
work'.

It is well-known that the US GDP from 1900 to the present cannot be explained by the growth of capital stock or labor force alone, whence an exogenous multiplier, total factor productivity (TFP), is generally introduced. However Hypothesis II above is that a third factor, called 'useful work' (U), combined with the other two can explain economic growth in developing countries, at least those in Groups A and B. As noted above, useful work (U) is the product of the input energy (actually exergy) flow multiplied by the energy to work conversion efficiency for the economy as a whole (Ayres and Warr 2002; Ayres 2002; Ayres and Warr 2003; Ayres et al. 2003; Ayres and Warr 2005).

Electrification and urbanization are both fairly well documented variables that are also correlated with economic development. In fact, they are also closely correlated with each other, which means that they are not independent. (See Appendix C.1). Of the two, electrification is far better documented. Statistics on electric power production are widely available on a year by year – rather than decennial – basis. The efficiency of the energy conversion process is easily calculated and widely published. Electric power *per se* is also a form of useful work. It is by far the most flexible and adaptable, hence desirable, form of work, inasmuch as it can easily be reconverted to heat, light, motive power, or electromagnetic signals.

On the other hand, electricity is not the only, or even the most important, form of work in some countries. Human and animal muscles are still important in some of the less developed parts of the world where electricity is not yet widely available. Solar heat is still quite important for certain purposes – such as salt production, food and crop preservation and biomass desiccation prior to combustion – in some countries. Biomass combustion is a primary source of heat for cooking and space heating in many of the same countries. Finally, mobile mechanical power for transport, mining, agriculture and construction are not suitable for electrification except in a few exceptional cases.

The contribution of human and animal muscles to 'work' (in the thermodynamic sense) is largely a rural phenomenon. In cities, there is little need for human muscles and virtually none for animals. Hence the substitution of machine-work for muscle-work is closely correlated with urbanization. This is, essentially, the logic of suggesting urbanization as a proxy for work. As noted, urbanization is also closely correlated with electrification. As people move to cities they get electric light, TVs and other services. But space heat and hot water are mostly non-electric, while transportation and construction are almost entirely driven by mobile power sources based on internal combustion engines. Hence the simplest alternative (to using electricity consumption alone) is to add a fraction of petroleum (oil) consumption in order to reflect the non-electric types of work, especially transportation. Because of the low combined thermodynamic and mechanical efficiency of most internal combustion engines, we multiply total oil consumption by a fraction (typically around 0.1) before adding it to electricity consumption. The coefficient factor 0.1 might not be optimal. We test its sensitivity later. The symbol EP (energy proxy) is used to represent this new variable, also expressed as a fraction of the US value.

Of course, it is not to be expected that a single factor, such as EP, would explain all of the divergences among countries in regard to economic growth. There must be other factors affecting economic growth that are omitted from our simple hypothesis. Sources of divergence include: (1) the structure of the economy; (2) the form of government, (3) social and ethnic homogeneity, (4) bureaucracy, law and corruption, (5) the geographic location (and its influence on climate and energy consumption), (6) macroeconomic management, (7) openness to foreign investment, (8) educational level and capacity to absorb advanced technologies, (9) petroleum and gas exports in relation to consumption, and so on. Luckily, as emphasized later, some of these variables tend to occur in combination, which suggests the possibility of grouping.

All the other data are obtained from the IEA (OECD) database (2003) (Organization for Economic Cooperation and Development and International Energy Agency 2005). The periods that the IEA database covers are 1960–2001 for OECD countries and 1971–2001 for the others. There are 131 countries with reasonably good data records in the database.

9.9   SCATTER DIAGRAMS AND LINEAR REGRESSIONS

The first step is to plot the energy proxy variable EP against the GDP fraction. Figure 9.1 shows the plot for all (131) countries for which we have data. The time frame covers the period from 1960 to 2001 for OECD countries and from 1971 to 2001 for other countries. On the vertical axis is the GDP fraction, and on the horizontal axis is the EP fraction (proxy) as defined above. The US (by definition) is always at the point (1, 1). There is an obvious trend, on average, but with a significant number of outliers, especially countries with high GDP per capita and low EP. To reduce the scatter we can implicitly incorporate some of the other relevant variables discussed above by grouping the countries.

There are three obvious sub-groups based on the EP itself. The main sub-group includes most countries that are neither petroleum exporters nor major hydro-electric producers. The second sub-group consists of petroleum-exporting countries, including OPEC members and a few others

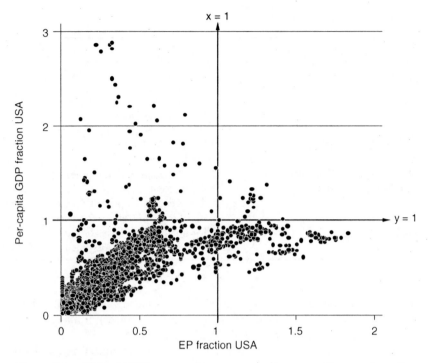

Figure 9.1   Plot of GDP gap against energy policy gap, all countries, all years

like Russia. In general, such countries significantly underprice motor fuel and heating oil, thus distorting the usual patterns of energy use. Moreover, petroleum exporters with very few exceptions, notably Norway, rely too much on export income, spend much of it on arms or consumer luxuries, and fail to develop other sources of revenue or employment. (This phenomenon has been called 'the curse of oil'.)

The third (small) sub-group consists of countries with significant hydro-electric power development, resulting in a very high level of electrification and encouraging inefficient uses such as electric heating. These countries are Norway, Sweden, Iceland, Canada, Austria and Switzerland. Norway is in both groups, and both Russia and China could be. Brazil and Paraguay potentially belong in the high hydro group also. Afghanistan, Nepal, Bhutan, Bolivia and Ecuador are high altitude countries with undeveloped hydro-electric potential.

By separating oil-exporters and countries with a high fraction of hydro-electricity, we obtain a much more concentrated scatter chart. However, without color the two scatter charts are difficult to distinguish, so we have

Table 9.1　　Dummy variables

Dummy variable	Value, Case
Petroleum export (Hi-Oilexp)	1 if exports > 1.5 × domestic supply; 0 otherwise
Hydro-electric potential (Hi-Hydro)	1 if hydroelectric power > 0.6 (60%) of total; 0 otherwise
Low GDP/cap (Lo-GDP)	1 if GDP fraction < 0.5; 0 otherwise
Medium GDP/cap (Mid-GDP)	1 if 0.5 < GDP fraction < 1; 0 otherwise
High GDP/cap (Hi-GDP)	1 if GDP fraction > 1; 0 otherwise
Low latitude (Lo-Lat)	1 for tropical countries roughly between the Tropic of Capricorn and the Tropic of Cancer; 0 otherwise
High latitude or altitude (Hi-Lat)	1 for northern countries or high altitude countries (identified in text)

omitted them. Since big countries could be subdivided – in principle – into a number of smaller units (for example, states, provinces), it makes sense to weight each country by its GDP. We have done this.

Clearly, variables such as hydro-electric fraction and fractional oil export are potentially important determinants of the relationship between economic growth and energy consumption. Also, a country's geographic location – whether in the tropics, with lower heating requirements or at high altitudes or high latitudes with high heating requirements but plentiful hydro-electric power, affects its per capita energy consumption. To reflect these, and other differences, we have incorporated several dummy variables in the regressions to indicate whether a country is low-latitude (tropical), temperate or northern/mountainous. To allow for this we introduce dummy variables in Table 9.1, shown above:

Four linear regressions are summarized in Table 9.2. They are all of the general form

$$Y = \alpha + \beta \times [EP + \textit{dummy variables}] \textit{ and cross-terms}$$

The first regression assumes that all the countries follow the same linear development relationship, which doesn't change over time. The coefficients α and β are the same for all countries. Even so, all the independent variables are very significant. The coefficient β of the energy proxy EP is 0.738. This means that, if the world average EP fraction increases by 1 percent the world average GDP fraction would increase by 0.738 percent *ceteris*

Table 9.2   Results of linear regressions

Regressions	Coefficients of Energy Proxy	R²	Significance of other factors
(1) Simple regression without considering fixed effects or time effects	0.738 (t = 39)	0.657	Very significant
(2) Regression (1) weighted with GDP	0.812 (t = 54)	0.875	Very significant
(3) Weighted fixed effect regression with each country as an intersection, considering time effects at the same time	0.346 (t = 7)	0.978	A lot of the *country dummies* and all of the *year dummies* are not significant
(4) Considering cross-terms so that each group of countries has not only a different intercept but also a different slope	Different slopes	0.99	Very significant

Table 9.3   Detailed results of regression 4

Independent variables	Coefficient	t
EP fraction	1.18	44.81
cross_GDP_high	−1.21	−3.8
cross_GDP_mid	−0.65	−24.33
cross_hydro_high	−0.13	−9.16
cross_large_oilex	−0.39	−8.22
GDP_high	1.25	5.81
GDP_mid	0.46	80.05
High_hydroele	0.06	9.56
Large_oil_expter	0.12	5.48
Low_lat	0.05	13.41
High_lat	−0.18	−13.53
Year	0.0001	* 0.32

Number of observations = 3906   cross_GDP_high = EP fraction GDP_high
$F(12, 3894) = 55,993.92$ cross_GDP_mid = EP fraction GDP_mid
Prob > F = 0.0000   cross_hydro_high= EP fraction High_hydroele
$R^2 = 0.9900$ cross_large_oilex= EP fraction Large_oil_expter
Root MSE = 0.06953

paribus. In this regression the R^2 is just 0.6566. In the second regression
GDP is used to weight the countries. The coefficient β for the energy proxy
is increased to 0.812, and the R^2 is much higher at 0.8746.

However, these two regressions are obviously very crude. They ignore
two categories of complications. The first is known to statisticians as 'fixed
effects'. In simple language, this allows for the fact that the regression
equations for different countries may have different values of the constant
α (that is, intercepts at the origin, where EP = 0), while having the same
slope β. The results are given in Table 9.2 as regression (3). It yields an
unreliable energy proxy coefficient β of 0.346. However, this assumption
is unrealistic. In reality, different countries or different groups of countries
have different slopes or even different growth relationships.

The second complication, known as 'time effects', allows for different
values of both the intercepts α and the slopes β. Regression (4) reflects
this. Several cross-terms are also included in regression (4). They are products of the energy proxy and some dummy variables which are used to
indicate countries' features. The details are given in Table 9.3. Figure 9.2
plots samples and fitted trends given by regression (4). There are several
different sets of data points with both different slopes and different intercepts. Evidently, the dummy variables included in our regression affect the

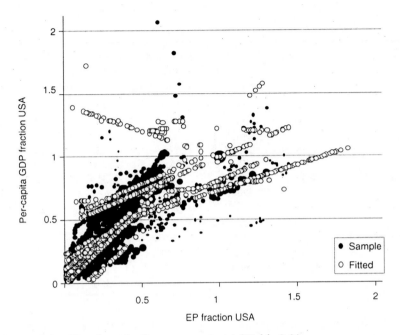

Figure 9.2   Fitted results from regression 4 (Table 9.3)

relationship between the GDP fraction and the energy proxy (EP). Among all the factors, GDP-high and GDP-mid are endogenous, appearing on both sides of the equation, as contrasted with the other dummies, which are exogenous. The fact that they are significant suggests that the underlying EP–GDP relationship is likely to be non-linear.

The exogenous dummy variables divide the set of all countries into several sub-groups. We then analyse the relationship for each group. Since we made no adjustments to the raw data, there might be some 'noise' among the samples. Therefore the next thing to do is to examine the development 'trajectory' of each country. By examining the development history for individual countries, we can eliminate the ones that failed to grow or catch up due to reasons that cannot be accounted for by our grouping scheme. Such reasons might include military conflicts, regional boundary changes, the breakup of the former USSR, failures in macroeconomic management and so on.

9.10   GROUPINGS AND NON-LINEAR REGRESSIONS

Three criteria (defined by three dummy variables) are used for grouping. They are (1) geographical (high, mid or low latitude), (2) a high or low

Table 9.4   The 12 groups

Group	Latitude	Hydro-electricity fraction	Oil-export important	No. of samples	Percent
1	Low	Big	Yes	124	4.12
2	Low	Big	No	341	11.34
3	Low	Small	Yes	465	15.46
4	Low	Small	No	728	24.21
5	Mid	Big	Yes	0	0
6	Mid	Big	No	219	7.28
7	Mid	Small	Yes	62	2.06
8	Mid	Small	No	816	27.14
9	High	Big	Yes	0	0
10	High	Big	No	168	5.59
11	High	Small	Yes	0	0
12	High	Small	No	84	2.79
Total				3 007	100

hydro-electricity fraction: and (3) high or low oil exporter. Based on the possible combinations of the three factors, we can divide all the countries into 12 groups, as shown in Table 9.4.

For all of the countries, hydro and oil export factors can and do change over time, mainly due to the building of new dams or the exhaustion of old oil or gas fields or the discovery and exploitation of new ones. To simplify the analysis, each country is assigned to the group where it appears for the longest period. Henceforth, we exclude countries that have experienced significant military conflicts and countries that have shifted from central planning to capitalism during the period for which we have data. After this adjustment, we obtain nine non-empty sub-groups of countries. Most countries belong to sub-groups 2, 3, 4 or 8. Figures 9.3a–d display the development tracks of countries in these four sub-groups respectively. Further analysis of the remaining five small sub-groups is not included here.

From Figures 9.3a and 9.3b it appears that low latitude countries (near the equator) with a lot of hydro-electric power or a lot of oil exports did not show any 'catch-up' progress with respect to the US during the last several decades. These countries exhibited development tracks with flat or even negative slopes. This suggests that there must have been exogenous political or institutional obstacles that have impeded economic growth. However in sub-groups 4 and 8, both of which are non-exporters of oil, most countries have been reducing their GDP gaps with respect to the US, as shown in Figures 9.3c and 9.3d.

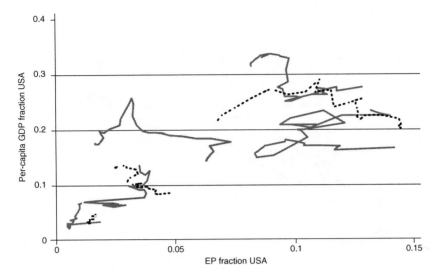

Figure 9.3a   Development tracks of countries in group 2

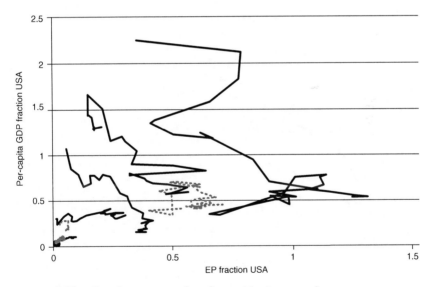

Figure 9.3b   Development tracks of countries in group 3

By grouping countries according to the criteria noted above, the non-linear relationship between GDP fraction and energy proxy (EP) becomes clearer. It seems that the non-linear growth path exhibited by 'catch-up' countries was disguised by the noisy information from sub-groups 2 and 3.

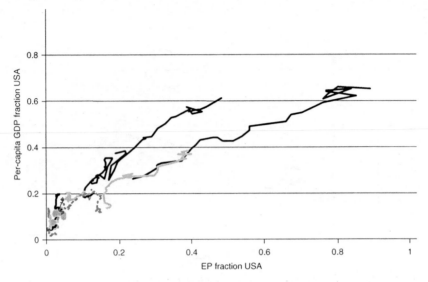

Figure 9.3c   Development tracks of countries in group 4

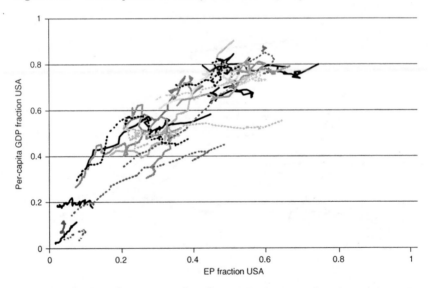

Figure 9.3d   Development tracks of countries in group 8

For sub-groups 4 and 8, the GDP fraction (with respect to the US) seems to evolve in time either as a natural logarithm or as a square root of the EP.

Assuming that, within each group, countries follow the same catch-up trajectory and that it doesn't change over time, we ran several regressions for each of the two non-linear functional relationships. The results are given in Tables 9.5a and 9.5b and Figures 9.4a and 9.4b and 9.5a and 9.5b. Since the fraction of oil combined with electricity in the energy proxy EP was given roughly in proportion to the efficiency of internal combustion engines, its sensitivity should be tested. The results are also set out in Tables 9.5a and 9.5b. Table 9.5a displays the results of unweighted regressions, and Table 9.5b displays the results of regressions weighted by GDP. Countries in sub-group 4 and sub-group 8 are listed in Appendix C, Table C.2. From the results in Table 9.5, it appears that the regressions are not very sensitive to the oil coefficient. The best values of the oil coefficient seem to be in the range 0.1 to 0.15, although the other choices are not significantly worse. For all the regressions, R^2 values are very good, and F-values are large. All the coefficients are very significant. The square root model is slightly better than the natural log model, but the differences between them are quite small and probably not significant.

9.11 CATCH-UP COUNTRIES ONLY

We have grouped the 131 countries according to several criteria and found that most countries in sub-groups 4 and 8 were catching up during the last few decades. However, not all countries in these groups were actually progressing. The regression results in Table 9.5 still reflect information from some countries that didn't progress *vis-à-vis* the US. If one assumes that all the information from countries that didn't make progress economically in the period we analyse is 'noise' and that only countries that really were catching up should be used to generate the parameters for our model, we should filter out the 'noise' and do regressions only for the remainder. All the catch-up countries in our samples, together with the US itself, are listed in Table 9.6. Most of them are in Group 8.

In 1971, the GDP in purchasing power parity (PPP) of the catch-up countries accounted for 66.34 percent of world GDP, including the US, and 43.1 percent of the non-US world GDP. It is fair to assume that all the countries that have been catching up during the past 30 plus years have had reasonably effective economic and political management during most of the period. We postulate that the energy–GDP relationship generated from these countries defines a theoretical trajectory that any country would follow, given reasonable economic management and in the absence of a 'growth stopper'.

Countries that did not catch up lagged behind or fell back for a variety of reasons. However, there are two groups of countries not on the list in Table 9.6, most of which were also not catching up with the US during

Table 9.5a Regression results with different oil coefficients for groups 4 and 8 (unweighted)

Oil coefficient	Group 4						Group 8					
	$Y = a + bx + c\ln(\times)$			$Y = a + bx + c(\times)^{1/2}$			$Y = a + bx + c\ln(\times)$			$Y = a + bx + c(\times)^{1/2}$		
	b	c	R^2	b	c	R^2	b	c	R^2	b	c	R^2
0	0.932	0.03	0.85	0.426	0.543	0.855	0.299	0.194	0.885	-0.57	1.783	0.893
0.1	0.624	0.03	0.867	0.257	0.483	0.875	0.343	0.19	0.901	-0.44	1.664	0.905
0.15	0.556	0.03	0.866	0.218	0.47	0.875	0.335	0.191	0.896	-0.43	1.651	0.899
0.2	0.51	0.03	0.865	0.191	0.46	0.875	0.319	0.193	0.889	-0.45	1.659	0.892
0.25	0.476	0.03	0.864	0.172	0.453	0.875	0.299	0.195	0.882	-0.48	1.678	0.885

Table 9.5b   Regression results with different oil coefficients for groups 4 and 8 (GDP weighted)

Oil coefficient	Group 4						Group 8					
	$Y = a + bx + c\ln(\times)$			$Y = a + bx + c(\times)^{1/2}$			$Y = a + bx + c\ln(\times)$			$Y = a + bx + c(\times)^{1/2}$		
	b	c	R^2	b	c	R^2	b	c	R^2	b	c	R^2
0	1.121	0	0.823	0.814	0.279	0.83	0.195	0.241	0.957	−0.63	1.934	0.959
0.1	0.662	0.02	0.862	0.324	0.419	0.878	0.245	0.224	0.965	−0.53	1.821	0.968
0.15	0.573	0.02	0.868	0.249	0.431	0.886	0.261	0.219	0.966	−0.5	1.779	0.969
0.2	0.515	0.03	0.871	0.205	0.435	0.89	0.272	0.214	0.966	−0.47	1.745	0.969
0.25	0.475	0.03	0.874	0.175	0.436	0.893	0.281	0.21	0.966	−0.45	1.716	0.968

Note: Countries that are far away from the main trend of each group were removed from the regressions. They are: in Group 4, Argentina, Jamaica, Netherlands, Antilles and Philippines; in Group 8, Luxembourg, South Africa and Turkey.
Y is the dependent variable, GDP fraction.
x is the independent variable, EP fraction.

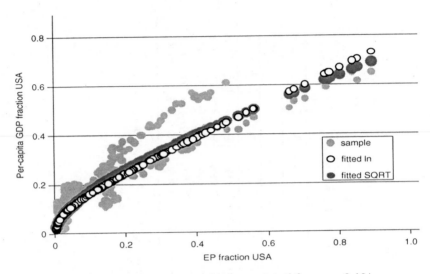

Figure 9.4a   Weighted regressions for group 4 (oil factor = 0.10)

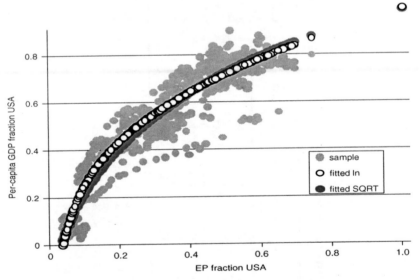

Figure 9.4b   Weighted regressions for group 8 (oil factor = 0.10)

the period. These are countries with high per capita GDP (Group A in the introduction) and countries with very low per capita GDP and development obstacles (Group C in the introduction). Figures 9.6a and 9.6b shows the trajectories of Group A and Group C countries, respectively. Instead

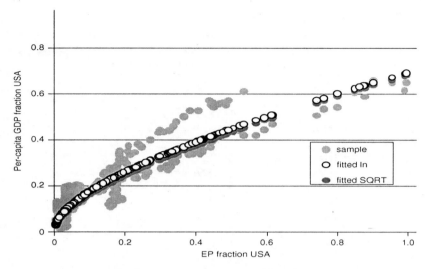

Figure 9.5a   Weighted regressions for group 4 (oil factor = 0.15)

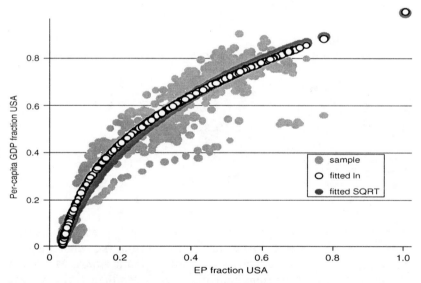

Figure 9.5b   Weighted regressions for group 8 (oil factor = 0.15)

of reducing their gaps with the US in per-capita GDP, most of them had been stagnant or even regressing.

In Figures 9.7a–e, the trajectories of catch-up countries are plotted for different values of the 'oil' coefficient in the EP, from 0.0 to 0.25. One can

Table 9.6   Catch-up countries

Country no.	Country	GDP of 2001 (PPP in billion 1995$)		Group no.
7	Austria	199.068		6
12	Belgium	256.049		8
21	Chile	130.826		6
28	Cyprus	14.629		4
32	Dominican Rep.	55.696		4
34	Egypt	213.128		3
40	France	1 394.529		8
43	Germany	1 922.029		8
46	Greece	165.226		8
52	India	2 707.164		4
53	Indonesia	560.887		3
55	Ireland	110.078		8
58	Italy	1 287.402		8
60	Japan	3 125.882		8
61	*Jordan*		*18.731*	*4*
64	*Korea (S.)*		*674.911*	*8*
73	Malaysia	181.962		4
74	*Malta*		*4.731*	*4*
91	P. R. China	4 707.822		8
95	Portugal	166.752		8
103	*Singapore*		*84.357*	*4*
107	Spain	739.499		8
108	Sri Lanka	56.746		6
114	Thailand	356.876		4
124	USA	8 977.8		8
Total GDP		2 733.05	782.73	28 112.8
World Total GDP		42 374.34		
% of World GDP		64.5%	2.85%	66.34%

see that, as the fraction of oil added to the energy proxy increases, several countries' imputed development tracks diverge from the major trend of the whole group. These countries are Jordan, South Korea, Malta and Singapore. Their oil consumption increases faster than their increase in electricity consumption and GDP. All four of these countries can be regarded as 'young': South Korea achieved formal independence in the mid-1950s after the very destructive Korean War. Singapore became independent of Malaysia in 1965. Malta became independent from Britain in 1964, while Jordan became independent of Palestine only after 1967, also after a war with Israel. It is possible that their abnormal behavior in regard

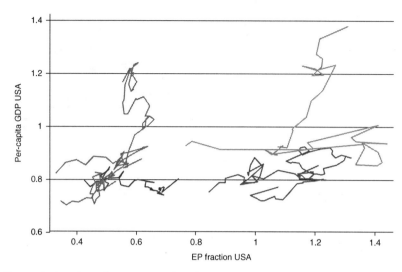

Figure 9.6a   Development tracks of group A countries

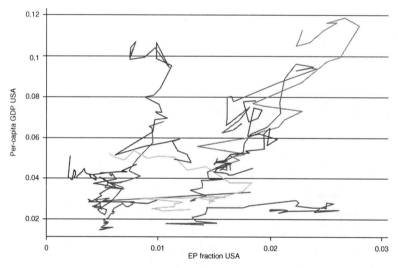

Figure 9.6b   Development tracks of group C countries

to oil consumption is due to having started from unusually low levels of motorization.

However, while the four outlier countries diverge, the others stay together. If we want to keep all the countries in our model, it is clear that electricity consumption alone is the best energy proxy. If we remove the

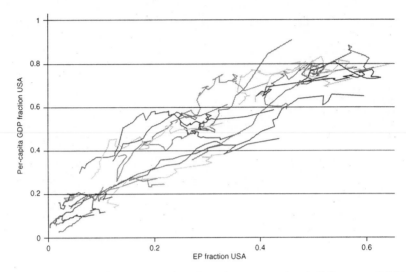

Figure 9.7a Development tracks of catch-up countries (oil factor = 0.00)

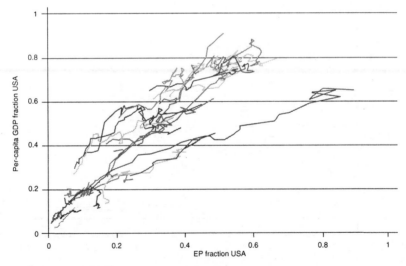

Figure 9.7b Development tracks of catch-up countries (oil factor = 0.10)

four countries from our simulation because of their too rapid increase in oil consumption, we still need to check whether including a fraction of oil consumption for the other countries in our proxy can improve the simulation. Regressions for the rest of the countries with different oil coefficients in the energy proxy were run and the results are given in Table 9.7. Table 9.7a

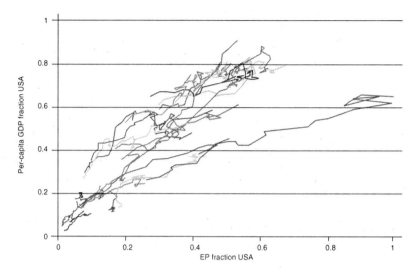

Figure 9.7c   Development tracks of catch-up countries (oil factor = 0.15)

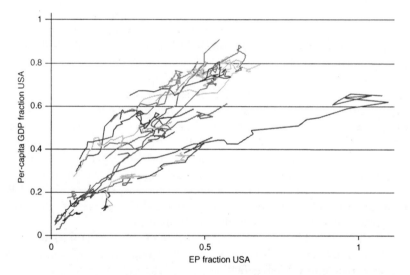

Figure 9.7d   Development tracks of catch-up countries (oil factor = 0.20)

shows the regression results with no weights, and Table 9.7b shows regression results weighted by GDP. Considering the values of R^2, the square root model is a little bit better than the natural log model. Even without weights, we get R^2 values higher than 0.94 with only one independent variable expressed in two terms. The linear terms in the square root model for

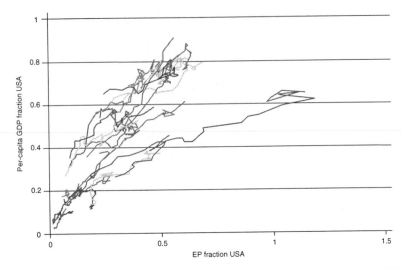

Figure 9.7e   Development tracks of catch-up countries (oil factor = 0.25)

some oil coefficients are not quite significant. However, in Table 9.7a all the other coefficients are significant. All the coefficients in Table 9.7b are also significant. The F-values are large.

By using GDP as weights, the R^2 values improve to above 0.98 for the square root model. Moreover, the regression results are not sensitive to the oil coefficient in the EP, especially for weighted results. The plot of the samples used in the regressions and the simulation results are given in Figures 9.8a–e. The simulation lines fit the samples very well. There is not much difference among different models (either natural log or square root, whether weighted with GDP or not) for different values of the oil coefficient.

There might be questions as to why only one independent variable (EP) is included in the regressions in Tables 9.5 and 9.7, given that there are obviously other factors that can affect economic growth. The explanation is that we are not seeking a complete theory to explain growth (or its absence) in developing countries. Instead, we are asking how much of that growth can be explained by a single factor: energy (exergy) consumption as converted to useful work. In effect, we are treating economic growth as a physical process, analogous to heating water. In our case, energy consumption is the input of the economic growth system and the output is GDP (of course both inputs and output are expressed relative to US values in our model).

In short, we believe that the evidence compiled in this chapter demonstrates that the EP, discussed above, is indeed an important factor of production, at least in situations where growth is not distorted or restricted

Table 9.7a   Regression results with different coefficients for catch-up countries only (unweighted)

Oil coefficients	$Y = a + b{\cdot}x + c{\cdot}\ln(x)$			$Y = a + b{\cdot}x + c{\cdot}(x)^{1/2}$		
	b	c	R^2	b	c	R^2
0	0.588 (t = 23)	0.108 (t = 20)	0.92	−0.211 (t = −6.8)	1.359 (t = 40)	0.94
0.1	0.600 (t = 25)	0.117 (t = 25)	0.93	−0.115 (t = −3.5)	1.298 (t = 37)	0.95
0.15	0.612 (t = 25)	0.116 (t = 24)	0.93	−0.081 (t = −2.4)**	1.266 (t = 35)	0.94
0.2	0.620 (t = 26)	0.114 (t = 23)	0.93	−0.057 (t = −1.6)*	1.241 (t = 33)	0.94
0.25	0.625 (t = 26)	0.113 (t = 23)	0.92	−0.039 (t = −1.1)*	1.221 (t = 32)	0.93

Table 9.7b   Regression results with different coefficients for catch-up countries only (GDP weighted)

Oil coefficients	$Y = a + b{\cdot}x + c{\cdot}\ln(x)$			$Y = a + b{\cdot}x + c{\cdot}(x)^{1/2}$		
	b	c	R^2	b	c	R^2
0	0.342 (t = 19)	0.169 (t = 31)	0.964	−0.465 (t = −15)	1.675 (t = 42)	0.976
0.1	0.345 (t = 23)	0.173 (t = 33)	0.973	−0.417 (t = −16)	1.632 (t = 45)	0.982
0.15	0.353 (t = 23)	0.172 (t = 33)	0.975	−0.397 (t = −15)	1.610 (t = 46)	0.983
0.2	0.360 (t = 24)	0.170 (t = 32)	0.975	−0.379 (t = −15)	1.590 (t = 47)	0.983
0.25	0.366 (t = 25)	0.168 (t = 32)	0.975	−0.365 (t = −15)	1.574 (t = 47)	0.983

Notes: 61 (Jordan), 64 (Korea), 74 (Malta) and 103 (Singapore) were dropped.
* Not significant at 5% level.
** Not significant at 1% level.
Y is the dependent variable, GDP fraction.
x is the independent variable, EP fraction.

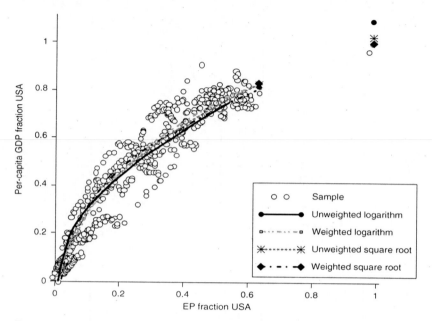

Figure 9.8a   Simulation results for catch-up countries (oil = 0.00)

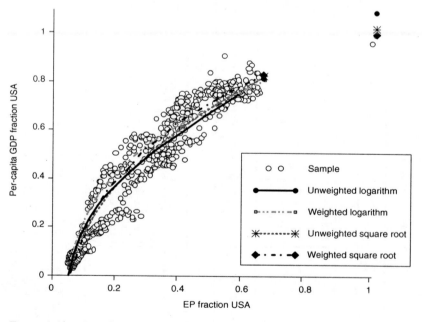

Figure 9.8b   Simulation results for catch-up countries (oil = 0.10)

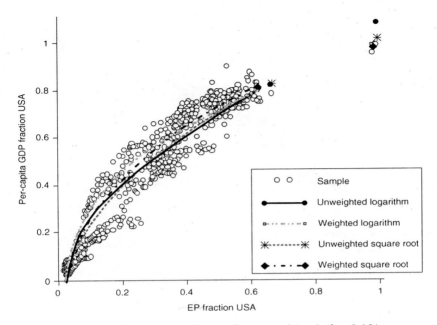

Figure 9.8c   Simulation results for catch-up countries (oil = 0.15)

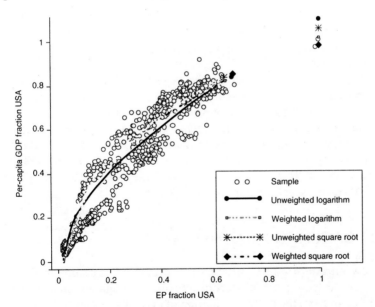

Figure 9.8d   Simulation results for catch-up countries (oil = 0.20)

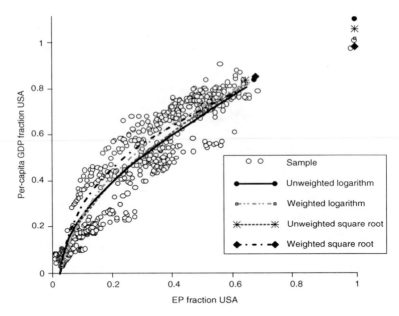

Figure 9.8e   Simulation results for catch-up countries (oil = 0.25)

by exogenous constraints. Factors such as political system, institutional situation and so on are beyond the consideration of our model. They constitute another dimension of the economic growth issue. However, there are factors, such as a country's location, its hydro-electricity fraction and so on, that can certainly affect the energy/work relationships.

Then what is the story these regression results can tell us? Mainly, the story is as follows: for countries whose per-capita GDP is very low (or which are at an early stage of development), energy consumption (as converted to useful work) can generate rapid (more than proportional) catch-up in terms of GDP. However, as countries' GDP approaches the US level, the catch-up rate slows down. Or, more accurately, the economic catch-up attributable to energy consumption decelerates.

9.12   CATCH-UP ELASTICITY

We now introduce a new variable, the 'economic catch-up elasticity of energy', or 'catch-up elasticity' from here on. Although we call it elasticity, it is different from the normal definition of elasticity in that the changes in percentage are with respect to the corresponding values of the US instead of the country itself.

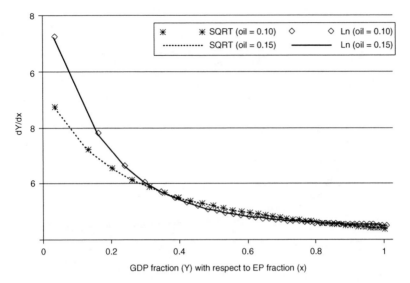

Figure 9.9a   Changes of catch-up elasticity of GDP with respect to EP for two models using weighted regression results

For the natural log (ln) model, we define

$$Y = a + bx + c \ln(x)$$

where Y is the dependent variable (GDP fraction), and x is the independent variable (EP), also expressed as a fraction. The catch-up elasticity is defined:

$$\frac{dY}{dX} = b + \frac{c}{x}$$

Similarly, for the square root model (SQRT), we have

$$Y = a + bx + cx^{\frac{1}{2}}$$

The catch-up elasticity in this case is:

$$\frac{dY}{dx} = b + \frac{1}{2}cX^{-\frac{1}{2}}$$

Using weighted regression results (from Table 9.7b) for oil coefficients of 0.10 and 0.15 as examples, Figures 9.9a and 9.9b show the calculated

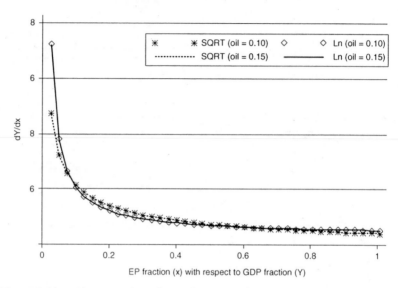

Figure 9.9b   *Changes of catch-up elasticity of EP with respect to GDP for two models using weighted regression results*

catch-up elasticity curves for the square root (SQRT) and natural log (ln) models. In both models, the catch-up elasticity diminishes both with the increase in *x* and with the increase in *Y*. There is no obvious difference between the two values of oil coefficients (0.10 or 0.15) for either model. In fact, the curves are essentially indistinguishable.

However, the difference in catch-up elasticity between the two models is relatively large for countries at early stages of development, for example, EP fraction $x < 0.1$, or GDP fraction $Y < 0.35$. Catch-up elasticity decreases faster with the increase in *x* than with the increase in *Y* at an early development stage and more slowly at a late development stage. A country's catch-up elasticity decreases to about 2 when its EP reaches about 10 percent of the US level, or when its per-capita GDP reaches about 30 percent of that of the US. A country's catch-up elasticity decreases sharply to about 1.0 and then decreases slowly after its EP reaches about 30 percent of that of the US, or after its per-capita GDP reaches about 50 percent of that of the US level. Catch-up elasticity seems to stabilize at around 0.5 as either *x* or *Y* approaches unity (we suppose that *x* and *Y* are always less than unity).

Until now, we have been looking at countries' development relative to the US. However, in order to have an idea of countries' absolute development we need to know the development trajectory of the US. Figure 9.10 shows the per-capita GDP expressed as a multiple of the 1960 value versus the EP for the US from 1960 to 2001. The overall trend lags below

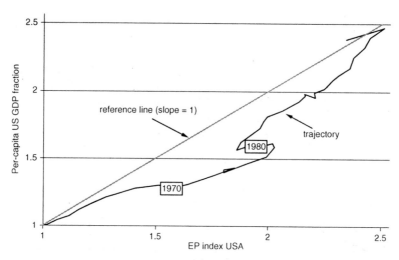

Figure 9.10 *Development trajectory (GDP versus EP) of the USA from 1960–2001*

the diagonal (the 45 degree slope line) until 1980 and then returns to the diagonal after that, except for a small reversal in 2001. The same information is presented in a different way in Figure 9.11, where US GDP and the EP are plotted versus time, from 1960 to 2001. The overall diagonal trajectory implies that the per-capita US GDP since 1960 has increased almost in proportion to the EP, except for a lag and a brief reversal in the 1970s (when there was a global oil crisis).

Evidently, the baseline we have been using for the catch-up model is growing more or less in proportion to its energy consumption proxy. This makes it easy to interpret the results of our model where relative values are used. For example, when a country's catch-up elasticity is bigger than unity, it is growing more energy-efficient than the US. Also, its absolute catch-up elasticity (percentage changes with respect to its own original values) is bigger than 1.

9.13 CONCLUSIONS

After the whole data analysis process, the following tentative conclusions can be stated:

1. Both electrification and urbanization are good indicators of economic growth, and they are highly correlated with each other during the

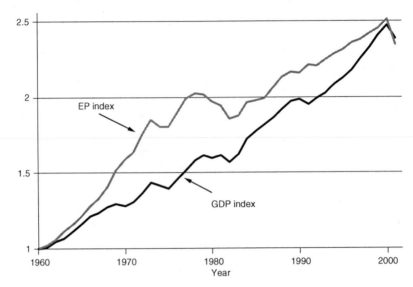

*Figure 9.11   Annual percentage change in US GDP and EP indices,
              1960–2001*

development trajectory, especially for countries that started industrialization late. We chose electrification instead of urbanization for
the first proxy mainly because electrification is more directly energy-
related and its data quality is better.

2. Per-capita electricity consumption plus some fraction of per-capita
    oil consumption can be used as a good proxy to simulate economic
    catch-up by using values relative to that of the US for both the proxy
    and per-capita GDP.

3. By dividing countries into groups based on criteria such as oil exports,
    hydro-electricity fraction and geographic latitude, we identified nine
    non-empty sub-groups, of which four sub-groups accounted for most
    of the countries (and the GDP). Only two of these sub-groups exhibit
    significant development *vis-à-vis* the US. Satisfactory regressions
    were obtained for these two groups (Table 9.5). Weighting by GDP
    significantly improves the quality of regressions. We have checked the
    residuals and found no problem of heteroskedacity.

4. Countries with high petroleum exports did not exhibit catch-up. (This
    phenomenon has been termed 'the curse of oil'.) Other 'growth stop-
    pers' include ethnic or religious conflict, transition from central plan-
    ning to market orientation, poor macroeconomic management and
    corruption.

5. For countries that are actually catching up, the relationship between the GDP gap and the energy proxy gap is not linear, but behaves like a logarithm or square root of the energy proxy. There is not much difference between the logarithm model and square-root model in terms of the fraction of oil added into the proxy, although 0.10 and 0.15 turned out to be a little bit better than higher values.

6. The catch-up countries exhibited very similar growth trajectories, relative to the US, except for four 'young' countries (South Korea, Singapore, Malta and Jordan) whose oil consumption increased relatively faster than electricity consumption and departed from the main trend. It is possible that these countries started from lower levels than others. After dropping these four countries, we obtained very good results for the relationship between the energy consumption gap and GDP gap.

7. The rate of increase in GDP with respect to the energy proxy ('catch-up elasticity') decreases as countries approach US levels (that is, the gaps decrease). The differences in 'catch-up elasticity' between the two non-linear models (square root versus natural logarithm) are surprisingly large for countries at early stages of development, suggesting that more research is needed on this question. Here we differ from the 2 percent per annum convergence 'law' that was suggested by a number of economists in the 1980s, and later (for good reason) discarded.

As a final concluding remark, we note that the empirical results obtained in this study tend to support the theoretical basis of prior work on the US economy by Ayres and Warr and discussed in the previous chapters of this book (Ayres and Warr 2002; Ayres et al. 2003; Ayres and Warr 2005; Warr and Ayres 2006). More important, in terms of the need for more credible forecasting and scenario-building tools, we think these results have an immediate application. While the underlying theory – regarding the role of energy and useful work as a driver of growth – is not yet fully tested even for the US, still less widely accepted, we think that the results demonstrated in this chapter are quite sufficient to justify extrapolation in a 'scenario' context, for several decades. In particular, we hope to use our model results to simulate future economic growth for important catch-up countries, such as India and China.

Also, to make the statistical results more statistically persuasive in the future, some additional statistical tests, such as auto-correlation and stationarity, should be run, since the data we use are panel data.

NOTES

1. There is increasing evidence that natural gas and coal reserves have been grossly over-estimated and that 'peak oil' will be followed by 'peak gas' and 'peak coal' within a few decades.
2. The idea that economic progress is explained mostly by capital investment, while long since abandoned as regards the industrialized countries, was still taken very seriously by many development specialists until very recently. The Harrod-Domar model predicts that the rate of growth of an economy in a year is proportional to the capital investment during the previous year. Harrod intended this as a way of explaining short-run fluctuations in output of industrial countries and disavowed its use for developing countries. Yet it was widely adopted by international institutions in the early 1950s for purposes of growth accounting and to estimate the so-called financing gap for developing countries. This capital investment-centered approach was supported by the stages of growth model of W.W. Rostow, who asserted that takeoff into sustained growth occurs only when the proportion of investment to national income rises from 5 to 10 percent (Rostow 1960). Several econometric studies have failed to find any evidence for this theory, however (for example, Kuznets 1963; United Nations Industrial Development Organization 2003).
3. Exergy is the technical term for available energy, or energy that can be converted into useful work. Energy is a conserved quantity, which means that it neither increases nor decreases in any process. By contrast, exergy is not conserved: it can be used up.
4. The most spectacular economic growth in East Asia, outside of Japan and Thailand, has been achieved by totalitarian or quasi-totalitarian regimes, including Indonesia, Malaysia, Singapore, Taiwan, South Korea and the People's Republic of China after the death of Mao Tse Tung. Indonesia, Malaysia, Taiwan and South Korea are now multi-party democracies, and Singapore is governed by an 'iron fist in a velvet glove'. Thailand has relapsed into authoritarian rule by a military junta.
5. Urbanization, another plausible choice, turns out to be very closely correlated with electricity consumption.

10. Conclusions, implications and caveats

10.1 REFLECTIONS AND CAVEATS

At the end of this book, we need to ask ourselves how far we have progressed towards several objectives. The first, which was clear at the outset, was a deeper understanding of the relationship between the laws of physics (thermodynamics) and economics. Another goal, also clear at the outset, was to develop a more realistic approach to explaining the relationship of 'technological progress', thermodynamic efficiency and economic growth. A third, which was only a glimmer at the beginning, might be characterized as a step toward integration of neoclassical and evolutionary perspectives on endogenous economic growth.

We think we can claim some progress on all three fronts, particularly the first two. As regard the third, the much criticized aggregate production function approach seems to be able to explain real-world behavior that cannot be explained by the restrictive assumptions of the formal neoclassical model. The formal model makes a series of unrealistic assumptions, including utility (profit) maximization, perfect information, perfect competition and optimal growth in equilibrium. The aggregate production functions seem to imply unlimited substitutability among the factors, which is clearly unrealistic. On the other hand, the fixed proportional input relationships required of Leontief's input-output framework are equally unrealistic because no substitution is allowed.

We suggest that the use of a three-factor LINEX aggregate production function constitutes a significant step toward reconciling these incompatibilities. It permits both substitution (in the long run) and complementarity between aggregate capital K and aggregate labor L (unlike the two-factor Cobb-Douglas function), while also allowing for substitution between ratios of pairs of the three factors. The third factor U plays a generic role, similar to that of capital services and labor, in the sense that it is an input to every sector of the economy. In fact, U is an essential input to the economy. Zero U would mean zero production and zero growth. Like capital, it is a product of the economy itself, but it is unlike capital and labor in that there is no stock and hence no accumulation. We treat U as a produced good that (with capital) can be substituted to a very large extent for labor. (The ratio K/U can substitute for the ratio K/L) However, the LINEX production function also allows for complementarity between pairs of the three factors insofar as the numerator and denominator of a ratio can increase or decrease in lock-step.

The third factor 'U' in our formulation is a thermodynamic quantity called 'useful work', which is the product of exergy inputs multiplied by aggregate conversion efficiency, f. The term 'work' is perhaps unfortunate, since common usage equates work with labor, whereas we make a clear distinction between the two. There is some etymological justification for the common usage, inasmuch as the two concepts – labor and work – were virtually indistinguishable in pre-industrial societies when almost all labor involved muscular strength, while intelligence or eye-hand coordination were of less importance.

Nowadays, it is understood in economics that 'labor' is what humans do mainly with brains and sensory feedback. However 'useful work' is mainly what machines driven by exogenous energy (exergy) flows do. Of course, the term 'work' is ubiquitous. People 'go to work'. They 'work for a living', in a 'workplace'. But physical work – requiring muscles – is no longer very important in the industrial countries, although human and animal muscles still play a part, especially in developing countries. All of this is admittedly quite confusing but unavoidable. We would happily introduce a less confusing term if possible; but to change the standard language of thermodynamics is beyond our scope.

Despite terminological confusion, we think that our original goal of integrating physical (thermodynamic) laws into economic theory is now much closer. The old neoclassical theory of growth-in-equilibrium along an optimal path driven by exogenous technological progress has already been discarded by both 'endogenous growth' theorists, as well as evolutionary theorists. The contribution of this book, we think, is to offer a fundamental explanation of endogenous growth that is both quantifiable and consistent with the laws of thermodynamics. Moreover, the new theory is consistent with the notion that the causal relationship between GDP and the so-called 'factors' (K, L, U) is not simply uni-directional and deterministic, as the standard (Solow) model implies. Rather, the relationship is a two-way street, analogous to Keynes' oft-quoted mis-statement of Say's law, namely that 'supply creates its own demand' (Keynes 1936).[1] In the case of useful work, the idea of growth as a positive feedback process was introduced in Chapter 1 and re-iterated in several places thereafter.

At this point, it is worthwhile to point out that a number of economists have discussed the so-called 'rebound effect' of energy efficiency improvements (for example, Brookes 1990, 1992, 1993; Saunders 1992). In brief, the 'rebound effect' has been introduced by skeptical economists to counter the claims of so-called 'efficiency advocates' in the context of discussions of energy conservation and greenhouse gas reduction policy.[2] The efficiency advocates' usually cited claim – on the basis of engineering studies – is that improved efficiency can sharply reduce the consumption of energy and hence of fossil fuels, which are the source of greenhouse gases and other pollutants.

The efficiency skeptics point out that improvements in energy efficiency generally result in less energy savings than the efficiency advocates claim, because lower operating costs make energy-using applications more attractive and thus increase demand for energy services over the baseline. In fact, it can be argued that the rebound effect is exactly the mechanism that drives economic growth, under another name.

In a mature economy, the increases in demand are not so great as to compensate for the savings. Econometric studies suggest that a 10 percent gain in efficiency in motor vehicles would only increase demand for vehicle use by 2 percent, not nearly enough to use up all the efficiency savings (Khazzoom 1987). Some other estimates suggest more dramatic rebounds, although the issue is highly contentious.[3] However, there is general agreement that greater efficiency and lower operating costs lead to greater consumption, thanks to a non-zero price elasticity of demand. By the same token, higher costs will certainly reduce consumption, just as the advocates of carbon taxes assume. However, the consequences of a permanent increase in energy costs and consequent increases in capital and other costs have not yet been taken into account in most long-range economic forecasts.

The most important implication of the new theory, up to now, is that future economic growth is not guaranteed because the efficiency gains that have driven growth in the past may not continue. Economic growth depends on producing continuously greater quantities of useful work. This depends, in turn, upon finding lower-cost sources of exergy inputs or more efficient ways of converting higher cost inputs into low-cost work outputs. In a world where the cheapest sources of exergy seem to be approaching exhaustion, the key to continued growth must be to accelerate the development of lower-cost alternative technologies, and policies, that increase conversion efficiency.

Meanwhile, if the rate of technological advance fails to compensate for the combination of approaching resource (notably cheap oil) exhaustion and policies needed to cut back on carbon dioxide emissions, we have to anticipate the possibility that economic growth will slow down or even turn negative. Global depression in the coming decades seems to us to be a serious risk.

10.2 ISSUES NOT ADDRESSED IN THIS BOOK

It would be foolish to claim too much. There are several issues that we have had to neglect. Taken together or individually, they offer sufficient reason for skepticism. A short list would have to include at least the following:

1. Data availability and quality, especially as regards capital stocks. Many time series are constructs, subject to assumptions that may be questioned. We have made the usual choices, with regard to labor (man-hours) and capital stock (perpetual inventory) without attempting independent scrutiny of the sources or the arguments. Our work does, however, depend on another unfamiliar constructed time series, namely the one for useful work. It was discussed in Chapter 4 and other publications cited. We have no doubt that the series could be improved by the application of some focused effort by historians of science and government statistical agencies.

2. The applicability of thermodynamic efficiency concepts to activities involving secondary (and tertiary) work. This issue seems straightforward at first glance, but we must acknowledge some room for argument. The primary difficulty concerns the definition of boundaries. In the case of an electric power plant, the boundary definitions are clear enough, but how should we define the efficiency of a heating system? Gas companies and furnace manufacturers define it in terms of the fraction of heat produced by the fuel that is radiated into the room (that is, not lost up the flue). This definition (known as 'first law') does not reflect the inefficiency resulting from the fact that the heat is produced by combustion at a very high temperature but only used at a much lower temperature. The high temperature heat is simply diluted in the air, which is wasteful. So why not use the high temperature heat to drive a steam engine producing electricity and heat the room with the waste heat from the condenser? Or, why not use electricity from a central power plant to drive a heat pump? All of these possibilities can be taken into account by adopting a different definition (known as 'second law'), which is the one we use. But there are further ambiguities, in the case of space heating, namely the role of insulation. Does more insulation increase the efficiency of the heating system? It doesn't affect the design of the heating system *per se*, but it obviously reduces the need for heat. This confusion is resolved by drawing the boundary around the room or the building rather than the heating plant. The concept of efficiency can be applied to other systems in a similar way. A well-designed road system with no traffic delays or congestion is obviously more efficient than a congested system, but to apply the

concept of efficiency, one must draw the boundary around the whole system.

3. The application of thermodynamic efficiency concepts to information processing. This is a topic that we have neglected for the present, but which will obviously be more and more important in the future. The thermodynamic efficiency of a computer is not easily calculated unless one can determine the power requirement of an idealized hypothetical quantum computer with equal performance. As far as we know, nobody has attempted this feat. The problem is quite analogous to the problem of calculating the efficiency of a communications channel, originally discussed by Claude Shannon (1948). We don't (yet) know how to do it.

4. The apparent neglect of economic efficiency in the sense of improved systems organization (for example, logistics, organization). This problem is partly addressed by item 2 above, that is; as a question of boundary definition. However, the other problem is that we don't have good ways to estimate the thermodynamic work equivalent of most services. At this point, it seems likely that the problem must be approached in terms of information theory (along the lines of item 3). Some work along these lines has been published by one of the authors (see Ayres 1994a).

5. The relevance of a two-sector approach to a multi-sector economy. We discussed this question briefly in Chapters 5 and 7 but we don't even know how to formulate a multi-sector model in full detail, allowing for both substitution and complementarity of factors. We have to leave it to others.

6. The relevance of classical notions like equilibrium and optimality to human behavior. Again, this topic is obviously important but outside our scope.

7. The adequacy of existing statistical methodologies and software for the purposes of extracting worthwhile results from extremely 'dirty' data, especially as regards developing countries. Again, this problem is outside our scope.

8. The complex and evolving relationships between GDP and underlying economic concepts such as welfare and wealth. See comments below.

9. The importance of 'natural capital' (apart from mineral resources) to economic activity and especially the impact of natural resource depletion and unpaid environmental costs on production. We do have some comments about the nature of the difficulties, also discussed below.

Most of the above questions are just that. We don't have the answers now, and perhaps nobody does. They are really topics for future research.

However, a few of the questions seem worthwhile exploring briefly in this chapter, beginning with the idea of wealth and its relationship with money.

Moreover, it must be said that the problems noted above also apply without exception to the current theories of economic growth. In some cases, at least, our approach is less problematic than the 'standard' neoclassical theory.

10.3   WHAT IS WEALTH, ANYHOW?

To a band of cave-dwelling proto-humans in the ice age, wealth must have consisted mainly of four or five survival necessities: (1) the cave itself (or other shelter), (2) a water supply, (3) a means of hunting or gathering edibles and (4) a fire and a fuel supply. These fundamental elements of wealth were not readily exchangeable, except by capture of territory. Other useful and portable objects, such as clothing (skins), smoked meats or other preserved foods, clay pots and crude tools or weapons would have been only slightly less valuable, but more easily obtainable by barter. Proto-money, consisting of scarce, difficult to make or fake, easily recognizable, intrinsically desirable and portable objects, from cowrie shells to blocks of salt, or gold nuggets, began to play a role in trade at some point in human history.

But modern economies did not evolve in a straight line from barter societies. By far the most important component of wealth in any society is power over the activities of other humans and domestic animals. The earliest source of power among proto-humans, as among social animals, was probably nothing more than physical prowess. The best fighter (alpha-male) became the tribal leader and remained so until he was killed in battle or by a stronger rival. It was natural for such a society to glorify victory in battle. It was also natural for a leader to try to control his own succession and – meanwhile – protect himself from rivals or enemies by relying on his male children or other relatives for protection. But human children themselves require a very long period of nurture and protection, which requires a long-lived family structure. The bodyguards of the leader had to be rewarded by privileges according to their rank. Of course, the leader's sons or brothers occasionally turned against him, but, on the whole, primogeniture was the most effective strategy for family survival.

As tribes became larger, leadership hierarchies evolved naturally. It became natural for the family of the tribal leader to develop into a dynastic succession, using daughters to 'trade' as marriage partners to other powerful families. Hierarchical status was confirmed by various symbolic actions to acknowledge submission of the lower orders to the higher ones. These symbolic actions have included saluting, kneeling or bowing, as well as titles and modes of verbal address ('sir', 'your excellency', 'your lordship', 'your majesty'), modes of clothing (uniforms), personal decoration (tattoos) and jewelry (finger-rings, ear-rings, nose-rings, diadems, crowns).

Of course, purely symbolic acknowledgment of hierarchical status was never enough. In the course of time, the higher orders persuaded themselves that they were inherently superior beings, cut from a finer cloth. They soon claimed legal and moral rights over the lower classes and demanded – as a matter of right – tribute (taxes) or physical service. Many, if not most, human societies formalized this hierarchical structure such that the lowest order were actual slaves, with no rights at all. Slaves were, of course, *property* – a form of wealth.

The road from feudalism to liberal democracy (using the words loosely) consists largely of an evolutionary shift in the hierarchy of 'rights' in law. The abolition of slavery in Europe and America during the 19th century was merely the final acknowledgment of a sea-change, which coincided roughly with the Protestant Reformation. The emergence of scientific modes of thought and humanist philosophy between the 16th and 18th centuries in Europe set 'human rights' – for example, 'life, liberty and the pursuit of happiness' – above property rights and hierarchical obligations to the King, or to one's feudal or caste superior. The remnants of the feudal hierarchical system have not totally disappeared. They remain, of course, in the military 'chain of command', the university and the Catholic Church. The 'values' debate between fundamentalist religions and secular society is about competing hierarchies of rights, especially as regards the roles of men and women in marriage and the conflict between 'right to life' and a woman's right to control her own body. The role of property rights *vis-à-vis* other rights such as the 'rights of animals' is also still evolving.

Thus, it is not surprising that wealth in a feudal society consisted partly in inherited rank with associated privileges, and partly in farmland with peasant labor attached, plus exchangeable wealth in the form of silver, gold or gemstones. The farmland may have produced most of the wealth, as the French physiocrats argued, but it was not equivalent to ready money. It is perhaps significant that dragons were reputed to sit on hoards of gold and precious gems. Certainly, the liquid wealth of traditional potentates took that form.[4] By contrast, wealth in modern society is mostly defined in terms of monetized property rights as expressed in markets. The theoretical insights of Adam Smith in *The Wealth of Nations* could not have preceded the actual evidence of economic benefits arising from markets ('the invisible hand'), joint stock companies, international trade and the 'division of labor'.

Property – for the majority of people – still consists of land or houses. A century ago animals were also a significant part of wealth. But for the wealthy it consists mostly of interest-bearing paper (bonds) or shares in profitable enterprises of some kind. In the 17th century, the enterprise could be a licensed trading ship, an insurance syndicate, a retail shop or a manufacturing establishment of some sort, such as a print shop. In recent years, the economic system has evolved in such a way that the source of profits itself may be a brokerage, an investment bank or a fund that makes its profits by trading in other financial instruments.

Today, wealth is usually defined as 'net worth'. For an individual or family, net worth as calculated (for example, for purposes of valuing an estate or a possible wealth tax) is the market value of exchangeable (salable) assets, including financial instruments (stocks and bonds), real estate, automobiles and 'collectibles', minus total indebtedness. It does not include personal clothing, most books and furnishings, or memorabilia. It does not include personal pension rights[5] or rights to public services such as health care, on the one hand, or potential financial liabilities such as the costs of illness, child support or alimony that would be payable in the event of divorce, on the other hand. Calculated net worth at the individual level does not include the value of formal education and training, or experience, even though these attributes – 'human capital' in current jargon – are very important assets in the job market. Finally, net worth does not take into account such assets as family or political connections, name recognition, friendships formed in school, special talents for sports or the arts, or personal appearance. Yet these assets may have greater financial value than all the others, as the case of George W. Bush illustrates.

While the imponderables noted in the last paragraph are not individually measurable, or exchangeable, they do have a financial value to a living person in terms of *earning and borrowing power*. In fact, some financial institutions are eager to offer unsecured credit backed only by the statistical probability of future earnings. Thus, borrowing power must be regarded as a significant element of individual wealth. Many individuals today – especially the young – have negative net worth, yet they are able to borrow significant sums based on the expectation of future earnings. Some of the borrowed money may be invested, for example, in higher education. But most of it, in practice, is consumed. This consumption expenditure evidently contributes to the GDP (next section), but only investment contributes to individual or national wealth.

10.4 GDP IS NOT A MEASURE OF EITHER WEALTH OR WELFARE

The quantity known as Gross Domestic Product (GDP) is regarded by most economists, financial journalists and politicians as a legitimate measure of national economic status, and – in the minds of many – of national welfare. GDP is actually defined as the total value of all final goods and services produced within a country, regardless of ownership. The value of the outputs must be equal to the sum of all labor costs (wages and salaries) and capital costs (interest, dividends and royalties). These costs are also equal to the total of money incomes or payments received by individuals. GDP is therefore a measure of economic activity, nothing more. Today the 'rich' countries are popularly supposed to be those with the greatest GDP per capita. But such an assumption may be quite misleading.

The fact that GDP is not an adequate measure of wealth is obvious from the definition. In the first place, it counts income obtained by depleting natural assets such as forests, fisheries or mineral deposits, but makes no allowance for the loss of wealth resulting from the depletion. Yet the bookkeeping accounts of any private enterprise would have to balance expenditure (or income) against changes in the stock of money in the bank. The most obvious examples are oil-exporting countries, but the argument applies equally to other natural resources such as forests and fisheries (for example, Repetto 1985, 1988; Repetto et al. 1989). To be sure, as the resource is gradually used up, its market price will rise, generating an apparent increase in the value of what remains. However, this process is clearly not sustainable in the long run. Rising prices to the consumers of the resource will reduce demand and induce substitution. As mentioned in the previous section, expenditures to repair damage from natural disasters are similarly included in GDP, whereas the property losses resulting from the damage itself are not included.

That GDP is also not a measure of welfare has been recognized for many years, at least since pioneering work by Tobin and Nordhaus, under the provocative title 'Is Growth Obsolete?' (Tobin and Nordhaus 1972). Their rhetorical question referred to the use of GDP growth as a *proxy* for welfare growth. They attempted to identify and quantify the – mostly defensive – components of GDP that clearly do not contribute to social welfare, even in the relatively narrow sense in which we understand it. Defense expenditures, police, health insurance and fire insurance are examples. For instance, as often pointed out, expenditures on recovery from a disaster such as a flood or fire can generate more economic activity without increasing welfare. Military activities are more likely to destroy wealth and welfare than to enhance it. Nevertheless, based on evidence from prior decades, Tobin and Nordhaus concluded that the use of GDP as a proxy was not unreasonable.

This issue has been revisited in recent decades by several groups, especially by Daly et al. (Daly and Cobb 1989; Cobb et al. 1995). In addition to eliminating additional activities that do not really contribute to human welfare (lawsuits are an example), the newer work tries to take into account missing components, such as non-monetized labor, leisure time and – especially – environmental benefits or damages. Alternative measures, such as the so-called Genuine Progress Indicator (GPI) and the Index of Sustainable Economic Welfare (ISEW), have been proposed which take into account other measures, such as energy conservation and environmental protection.

The concept of welfare can be much broader than the definition implied above, which essentially coincides with physical health and material comfort. The broader version encompasses non-physical (spiritual) aspects. A good illustration of the difference between the two is to be found in the long disagreement between Gandhi and Nehru on whether or not India should imitate the West, as exemplified by British industrialization, or return to traditional ways of life. Gandhi argued all his life that India should reject materialism and cultivate its ancient traditional values. Nehru won the argument (by default) when Gandhi was assassinated (Sachs 1992).

Unfortunately, there is no sign of convergence among present-day economists on several of these issues. Meanwhile, it is important to bear in mind that increasing GDP is *not* necessarily coincident with growing welfare or wealth accumulation.

10.5   CAPITAL, MAN-MADE AND NATURAL

Capital is a very tricky concept. Marx wrote an important and influential book about it (*Das Kapital*, volume I) without fully clarifying the topic.[6] He distinguished two important categories of productive capital, however, *circulating* (mobile) capital and *fixed* capital. The former is essentially financial; it consists of money and monetary instruments. Fixed capital, consisting of land, structures or machines, can be valued in monetary terms in several ways. One is to start from a base year and add new investments in various categories (for example, residential housing, non-residential buildings, machinery, roads and bridges, etc.) at current prices adjusted to a standard year, while simultaneously depreciating existing capital stocks based on assumed lifetimes. This is known as the 'perpetual inventory method' (PIM) (Maddison 1987). We have used Maddison's historical reconstructions of capital stock in our analysis.

Another approach, which is applicable only where the quantity of some form of physical capital is known, is to assess the replacement value at current costs. This might work for bridges or roads, but it is not practical for heterogeneous capital at the sectoral or national level. A third method, which is applicable at the sectoral level, would be to work backward from aggregated profits and some estimate of the rate of return to capital. In a totally monetized economy, it is tempting to argue that current income is equivalent to returns on capital. But that makes sense only for a business where all capital is invested in some sort of profit-making activity. It is clearly not true for individuals or nations. Another problem with that approach is that profits can and do vary significantly from year to year, whereas the capital stock is (presumably) much less variable and seldom decreases. The so-called 'Cambridge controversy' in the 1950s and 1960s was basically a debate about whether the term has any meaning independent of rate of return (Harcourt 1972). In recent decades, the issue seems to have been resolved in favor of the perpetual inventory method.

However, other kinds of capital need to be considered, notably human capital or knowledge, and natural capital. There are at least two fundamental difficulties, quantity measurement and valuation. As regards knowledge, including skills, 'know-how' and social organization, possible quantity measures include years of education, books, publications in scientific journals, and patents. Unfortunately, none of these measures correlates well with innovative performance by firms or nations. Other factors are obviously important, and probably crucial. Economists have also attempted valuation in terms of aggregate costs, for example, of higher education or R&D expenditures. Again, there is very weak evidence of a direct relationship between educational or R&D expenditure and contributions to useful knowledge. Most education is elementary: literacy and numeracy enable people to function in society and the economic system, but not to contribute anything new. Most non-military R&D in large firms is defensive, designed to cut costs of existing products, not to create anything new. Military R&D is focused on ways and means to destroy people and property, not to make the world better. It is no wonder that military 'spinoffs' are rare.

The fundamental problem of valuation is that the conditions for valuation of exchangeable goods in a competitive market do not apply to knowledge or natural capital. Exchange markets require exclusive ownership and control, and the ability to transfer that exclusivity. Knowledge can be sold, in principle, but it is also retained by the seller, so the exclusivity condition is violated. In the case of 'human capital', there is a market for certain kinds of expertise, embodied in people, such as lawyers, doctors, managers or entertainers. But the expertise in question is only slightly related to knowledge. Moreover, it is so distorted by institutional and other factors that the 'prices' (salaries) paid to such people are not even remotely related to the market value of specific contributions to the economy.

Inventions are no longer exclusive as soon as they are published, and they must be published to be patented. Very few inventions nowadays can stand alone. For the most part, they must be combined with many other inventions, constituting the technological assets of a firm. The firm has market value, to be sure, but there is no way to assess the value of its technology as such *vis-à-vis* the value of its commercial activities.

The statistical treatment of quantifiable natural resources, notably minerals and forests, is grossly inconsistent at present. Extraction of mineral or forest resources is treated as a form of national income, even though it is really a form of living off capital. Most resource-exporting countries and importing countries today are equally guilty of this form of deceptive accounting and many are actually (if unwittingly) impoverishing themselves (Repetto 1985; Repetto et al. 1989; Solorzano et al. 1991; Repetto 1992; Serageldin and Steer 1994).

In the case of unquantifiable natural capital – other than minerals, forests and fisheries – there is no market where they can be exchanged and hence no market price. This is because there is no possibility of exclusive ownership or possession. Nobody can own the sun, or the rain, or wind, or wild birds or biodiversity. Only by indirect hedonic analysis or survey techniques (for example, of 'willingness to pay') can quantitative values for the losses be assessed. The literature on these topics is large but ultimately inconclusive. However, a preliminary body of research carried out in the early 1990s by the World Bank, but never followed up, is important enough to be worth summarizing briefly below.

10.6   THE WORLD BANK APPROACH[7]

In the early 1990s a major effort was undertaken by the Environmentally Sustainable Development (ESD) unit of the World Bank to assess quantitatively the wealth of nations, taking into account monetary valuations of natural and human capital as well as man-made capital, for 192 countries for the year 1990. Man-made capital per capita was estimated by a perpetual inventory method (accumulated net investment in real terms less depreciation). A summary of this work is given in ESD (1995).

Natural capital per capita was estimated indirectly in terms of four types of assets: land, water, forest and subsoil assets. Land was subdivided into cropland, forest, pasture and other. Each was valued as a multiple of per-capita GDP, with some adjustment for 'protection', and quality. The appropriate multiple (of per capita income) was determined roughly by a statistical analysis and assumed to be the same for all countries, namely 3.0 for fertile irrigated cropland, 2.0 for other cropland, 1.75 for forest land, 0.75 for pasture and 0 for 'other' (for example, deserts, mountains). The value of standing timber was added to the value of forest land, at 50 percent of the international price for cut timber. Subsoil assets (coal, oil, minerals) were also based on then-current estimates of known or probable reserves and valued at 50 percent of the international price for the same minerals after extraction. Fresh water was valued at 1 (US) cent per gallon, for all countries – a (rough) geometric mean between the value for human use and the value for irrigation. (Industrial value, for example for cooling, was not considered.)

The value of human resources was calculated as a *residual*, after accounting for GDP (actually net national product, or NNP) in terms of contributions by man-made capital and labor, using a standard production function. Exchange rates were adjusted for purchasing power parity (PPP). Quantitative results for the year 1990 were presented for all 192 countries, and 'genuine savings' (adjusted for depreciation, sale of assets, depletion of natural resources and environmental degradation) were calculated for the period 1962–91 for 90 countries. Apparently, the results exhibited high correlation with educational attainment, but with enough variability to suggest that other factors are also involved.

Serageldin and Steer (1994) emphasized the preliminary nature of the results and repeatedly made the point that detailed results for any individual country could not be 'defended' without further work, although interesting patterns might be observed. The most 'stunning' result noted was that human capital for most countries exceeds the sum of both natural capital and man-made capital. In fact, produced (man-made) capital typically amounts to only 16–20 percent of the total, yet dominates economic policy.

The second important overall result was that savings calculated as a fraction of GDP can mask dis-saving by resource depletion and environmental degradation. In fact, it appears that Latin America as a whole experienced net dis-saving in 1980–84 and again after 1988 to the end of the period of analysis.

Serageldin and Steer were careful to note that the approximations made in the study were somewhat arbitrary, and might be modified significantly with further research. For instance, the value of land clearly depends on accessibility to markets, hence cities, whence population density or urbanization are likely to be important factors. The valuation of fresh water in the study was quite arbitrary and should be reconsidered, again in relation to population density, urbanization and industrialization, as well as possibly other factors. The valuation of subsoil resources in terms of known and probable reserves and current international prices is obviously very dubious, given the volatility of resource prices and the considerable uncertainty of reserve estimates. Undoubtedly, if the same calculations were carried out again today, the value of natural capital would appear to be much higher than it was in 1990, despite depletion since then.

Apart from these points, we would argue that the estimation of human capital, as a residual, should be reconsidered and revised to reflect the influence of energy (exergy) consumption and technological efficiency as drivers of GDP. If GDP can be explained largely in terms of labor, produced capital, exergy inputs and exergy conversion efficiency, it would follow that other components of human capital (including social institutions) must be of correspondingly less importance than the reported calculations suggest. In short, it does seem clear that much might be learned by revisiting and revising the research reported in *Monitoring Environmental Progress* (ESD 1995).

10.7   DEBT

At the national level, it is traditional for economists to distinguish investment income (profits, interest, dividends and royalties) from salaries and wages. These income items are equated to personal expenditures. Borrowing is implicitly equated to repayments. To the extent that the two flows are in balance, there is no effect on GDP. However, one source of 'economic growth' is the increased expenditure resulting from increased borrowing, whether secured (for example, by rising asset prices) or unsecured.

Government borrowing is a special case. It is secured only by financial markets' faith in the future ability to repay, based on the expectation of increasing tax revenues resulting from future GDP growth. There is no doubt that one significant source of US GDP growth in recent years is increasing private and public debt. Again, if future GDP growth is based on a valid expectation of increased productivity, there is no problem. However, to the extent that it is based on increased debt, we have a circular system where debt spawns more debt that can never be repaid. In effect, GDP growth in this case is achieved by consuming capital and decreasing real national wealth.

To the extent that the substitutes are also improvements, the original resource can eventually become worthless, just as whale oil is no longer needed and most natural drugs and dyes have been replaced. On the other hand, if the resource is finite and not readily substitutable, like petroleum or copper, the impact of increasing scarcity will cause depression at the macroeconomic level.

Evidently, there is no necessary correlation between national income (GDP) and national wealth. In a pioneer 'Robinson Crusoe' society such as the 19th-century US, they may grow together, but in a mature society the opposite can and does occur. For this reason (among others), GDP growth should not be regarded as necessarily 'good', however much we are apparently addicted to it.

10.8 SOME UNSUSTAINABLE CONVENTIONAL WISDOM

The conventional view of mainstream economists is that the US and world economies will enjoy perpetual growth, per capita, of around 3 percent per annum, driven by capital accumulation and exogenous increases in something called total factor productivity (TFP). The latter is presumed to be due to increases in knowledge or 'human capital'. Perpetual economic growth is an extrapolation from history and a pious hope for the future, not a law of nature. Yet few economists question it. Governments, businesses and institutions are now, and have been for several decades, effectively addicted to the presumption of perpetual and inevitable economic growth. Any suggestion that growth might not continue indefinitely (or that it might not be a good thing) is ignored or derided. Periods of recession are invariably regarded as exceptional. Analysts and pundits of all stripes speak of 'recovery' as though the economy were merely suffering from a cold, or perhaps, a mild case of the flu. We think, on the contrary, that the emperor probably has no clothes. In short, future GDP growth is not only not guaranteed, it is more than likely to end within a few decades. Indeed, we suspect that US national wealth has already peaked, and is now declining.

One of the more interesting digressions among economic theorists, especially since the *Limits to Growth* controversy in the early 1970s (Meadows et al. 1972, 1974), has been the attempt to demonstrate that perpetual growth is theoretically possible, even in a world characterized by exhaustible resources. The argument is reminiscent of Aesop's race between the tortoise and the hare. Growth can continue indefinitely as human-produced capital replaces natural capital, while the exhaustible resources are consumed at an ever-slower rate. In this context, one might cite influential papers by several leading economists, in the 1970s, including Solow (1973, 1974a, 1974b), Stiglitz (1974) and others. Assessments of the long-term implications of climate change also assume perpetual growth, at least for the next century (for example, Nordhaus 1993a, 1998, 2002; International Institute for Applied Systems Analysis (IIASA) and World Energy Council (WEC) 2000; Nakicenovic and Riahi 2002).

In contrast, as explained in Chapter 8, the REXS model developed in this book does not assume, nor does it predict, perpetual growth. It has a finite horizon only a few decades ahead. Indeed, a new growth impulse after the projected medium-term slowdown is not excluded, although it would require a new and different 'growth engine' – not part of the model – and probably a new source of *useful work* at costs significantly lower than current resources and conversion technologies appear to allow. In fact, we take this possibility seriously. But that is a subject for another book.

NOTES

1. Say really meant that a produced good represents demand for other goods, and not that every produced good will be sold (Say 1821 [1803]).
2. The best-known advocate is Amory Lovins (Lovins 1977; Lovins et al. 1981; Lovins and Lovins 1987; Lovins 1988; Lovins and Lovins 1991; Lovins 1998). See also Johansson et al. (1989), von Weizsaecker et al. (1998) and Jochem et al. (2000).
3. A good review of the evidence can be found in a special issue of *Energy Policy* (2000) edited by Lee Schipper. See also Jaccard (2005).
4. In the 1930s, the hereditary Nizam of Hyderabad (the largest and richest of the princely states of India) was reputed (in the press) to be 'the richest man in the world', on the strength of his possessions of this kind (*Time* magazine cover story, 22 February 1937). His wealth was estimated at one billion dollars in the 1940s. Much of it was from the fabled diamond mines of Golconda, in his realm. He used the 184-carat Jacob diamond as a paperweight. At one point in the 1930s, he was worried that he might be deposed by his subjects, so he loaded six lorries (trucks) with gold bullion in case he was forced to flee. They were found in the courtyard of his palace upon his death in 1967. It is rumored that six truckloads of treasures were removed from the palace on the night of his death. Another example of wealth derived from gold and gems is that of the Aga Khan, hereditary Imam of the Ismaili sect of Muslims. In 1936, his grandfather, Aga Khan III, celebrating his golden jubilee as Imam, was presented with his weight (220 lb) in gold by his followers; a decade later he received a gift of 243 lb of diamonds (Edwards 1996).
5. However, divorce-related property settlements often do reflect the value of pension rights.
6. This was possibly because his labor theory of value, which considered capital to be a sort of accumulation of past labor, could not be reconciled with the marginalist preference-based theory of value that was coming into vogue. Marx's book was published in 1867. The seminal marginalist contributions of Jevons, Menger and Walras appeared in 1871–4 (Marx 1867; Jevons 1871; Menger 1994 [1871]; Walras 1874).
7. The research in question was reported in *Monitoring Environmental Progress: A Report on Work in Progress* (also referred to as MEP) by the World Bank (ESD 1995). It was summarized in a draft monograph that was apparently never published in final form (Serageldin and Steer 1994).

Appendix A: Elasticities of production in neoclassical equilibrium

Neoclassical equilibrium in a system that produces a single output Y from the factors K, L, X is characterized by the maximum of profit $(Y - C)$ at fixed total factor cost $C(K, L, X)$. The cost C is given by

$$C(K, L, X) = P_K \cdot K + P_L \cdot L + P_X \cdot X \tag{A.1}$$

where P_K, P_L, P_X are the unit prices of capital K, labor L and a third factor X (which need not be specified, although it can be equated either to commercial energy, E, or to useful work U).

Neoclassical economics assumes that all combinations of factors that are consistent with fixed total cost C are accessible without any further constraints, that is, they are mutually substitutable. This implies that the profit maximum lies somewhere within the interior of accessible K, L, X space (that is, not on a boundary). According to the Lagrange multiplication rule, the necessary condition for a local extremum in K, L, X space is that, in equilibrium, for some real number λ, the gradient of $Y - \lambda C$ must vanish:

$$\nabla(Y - \lambda C) = \nabla Y - \lambda \nabla C = \left[\frac{\partial Y}{\partial K}, \frac{\partial Y}{\partial L}, \frac{\partial Y}{\partial X} \right] - \lambda \cdot [P_K, P_L, P_X] = (0,0,0)$$
$$\tag{A.2}$$

It follows from the equality of the individual vector components that the neoclassical condition for economic equilibrium is given by

$$\frac{\partial Y}{\partial K} = \lambda \cdot P_K$$

$$\frac{\partial Y}{\partial L} = \lambda \cdot P_L \tag{A.3}$$

$$\frac{\partial Y}{\partial X} = \lambda \cdot P_X$$

(The special case of zero profit, where all of the output is allocated to the factor owners, corresponds to $\lambda = 1$). Now multiply the first of these equations by K/Y; the second by L/Y and the third by X/Y, and introduce the elasticities α for K, β for L and γ for X, as follows:

$$
\alpha = \frac{K}{Y}\frac{\partial Y}{\partial K}
$$

$$
\beta = \frac{L}{Y}\frac{\partial Y}{\partial L} \tag{A.4}
$$

$$
\gamma = \frac{X}{Y}\frac{\partial Y}{\partial X}
$$

Then, in equilibrium,

$$
\alpha = \lambda \cdot P_K\frac{K}{Y}
$$

$$
\beta = \lambda \cdot P_L\frac{L}{Y} \tag{A.5}
$$

$$
\gamma = \lambda \cdot P_X\frac{X}{Y}
$$

Finally, given constant returns to scale ($\alpha + \beta + \gamma = 1$) we get

$$
Y = Y \cdot (\alpha + \beta + \gamma) = \lambda \cdot (P_K K + P_L L + P_X X) = \lambda \cdot C \tag{A.6}
$$

Substituting $Y = \lambda \cdot C$ in the equilibrium conditions for α, β, and γ, one obtains:

$$
\alpha = \frac{P_K K}{C}
$$

$$
\beta = \frac{P_L L}{C} \tag{A.7}
$$

$$
\gamma = \frac{P_X X}{C}
$$

which are the cost shares of the three factors.

Appendix B: Data

B.1 DERIVATION OF HUMAN/ANIMAL CONTRIBUTIONS TO EXERGY CONSUMPTION

Table B.1 Derivation of food/feed biomass consumption

Flows	Efficiencies (trade neutral values)	Definition	Notes
Human appropriated phytomass	Feed and Feedstock utilization efficiency *Values:* US: 0.64 JP: 0.65 EU: 0.62	Feed intake (for animal commodities) and feedstock use (for processed vegetable commodities) per corresponding phytomass appropriation	Factors having the largest impact include the harvest index, pasture utilization, and extent of use of by-products and residues as feed. Also reflects phytomass internal uses, losses in distribution and storage and feed processing losses See Wirsenius (2000, pp. 114–16)
	Product generation efficiency US: 0.16 JP: 0.20 EU: 0.24	Product generated per feed intake	Reflects efficiency of the conversion to commodity. For animal food systems equivalent to the *feed-equivalent* conversion efficiency
	Commodity utilization efficiency US: 0.55 JP: 0.77 EU: 0.58	Food eaten per food product generated	Takes account of losses in distribution and storage, losses in the food utilization process (i.e. non-eaten). Application of this efficiency to 'food end-use per capita' provides 'food intake per capita' (see below)
Food end-use per capita	Wirsenius (2000, p. 61, table 3.3)	Digestible energy – gas, feces and, urine losses = metabolizable energy	Estimates from wholesale supply (end-use supplied from FAO Food Balance Sheets). Note this is not the actual food intake

Food intake per capita	Wirsenius (2000, p. 62, table 3.4) *Values* US: 9.3 J JP: 9.0 EU: 9.3	Estimated using daily food energy requirements instead of data on true food intake. The driving variable in the FPD model (Wirsenius 2000) is end-use. End-use − intake = non-eaten food. The amount of feces and urine is estimated as the difference between GE and ME for each eaten flow. We have used data from 2000 (Wirsenius) and estimates of 1900 daily intake to fit a logistic curve, providing a time series of daily intake estimates
Workers' food intake	Employed * work-to-rest ratio	Time series of per-capita intake reconstructed from 10 year averages using a logistic function of time with start and end values: 2500 kcal per capita per day in 1900, 2900 kcal per capita per day in 2000
Muscle work (workers)	Food-to-work efficiency (human = 0.2)	Workers' food intake * food-to-work efficiency Approximation from Smil (1998, pp. 91–2)

B.2   US DATA SOURCES

The following were the principal data sources for the US (Tables B-2 and B-3):

(1)   Energy Information Administration Office of Energy Markets and End Use (1999), *Annual Energy Review 1998*, Washington, DC: United States Department of Energy, Energy Information Administration.

(2)   Energy Information Administration Office of Oil and Gas (1999), *Historical Natural Gas Annual 1930 Through 1998*, Washington, DC: United States Department of Energy, Energy Information Administration.

(3)   United States Bureau of the Census (1975), *Historical Statistics of the United States, Colonial Times to 1970*, Bicentennial edition, two volumes. Washington, DC: United States Government Printing Office.

(4)   Schurr, Sam H. and Bruce C. Netschert (1960), *Energy in the American Economy, 1850–1975*, Baltimore, MD: Johns Hopkins University Press.

(5)   Groningen Growth and Development Centre (2006), *Industry Growth Accounting Database* (internet website), September 2006 (cited October 2006), accessed at www.ggdc.net.

(6)   Groningen Growth and Development Centre (2007), *The Conference Board and Groningen Growth and Development Centre Total Economy Database*, Faculty of Economics, University of Groningen, January, accessed October at www.ggdc.net.

(7)   Maddison, Angus (1993), 'Standardized Estimates of Fixed Capital Stock', in R. Zoboli (ed.), *Essays on Innovation, Natural Resources and the International Economy*. Ravenna, Italy: Studio AGR.

(8)   Maddison, Angus (2003), *The World Economy: Historical Statistics*, Paris: Organisation for Economic Co-operation and Development.

(9)   Potter, Neal and Francis T. Christy Jr. (1968), *Trends in Natural Resource Commodities*, Baltimore, MD: Johns Hopkins University Press.

(10) United States Bureau of the Census annual, *Statistical Abstract of the United States*, Washington, DC: United States Government Printing Office.

(11) Smil, Vaclav (1998), *Energies: An Illustrated Guide to the Biosphere and Civilization*, Cambridge, MA: The MIT Press.

(12) Wirsenius, S. (2000), 'Human use of land and organic materials: modeling the turnover of biomass in the global food system'.

Ph.D. thesis, dissertation no. CPL 827, Chalmers University of Technology, Goteborg, Sweden.

Other data sources, all from the United States Department of Commerce Bureau of Economic Analysis, include

- 1973, *Long Term Economic Growth 1860–1970*, Washington, DC: United States Government Printing Office.
- 1992, *Business Statistics, 1963–1991*, Washington, DC: United States Department of Commerce.
- Monthly, *Survey of Current Business*, Washington, DC: United States Department of Commerce.

Table B.2a Data sources for US economic data

Title	Units	Period	Source
Population	million persons	1950–2006 1900–1949	(6) Groningen: *Total Economy Database* (8) Maddison: *The World Economy: Historical Statistics*
GDP	million 1990 International Geary Khamis dollars	1950–2006 1900–1949	(6) Groningen: *Total Economy Database* (8) Maddison: *The World Economy: Historical Statistics*
Capital	million 1990 International Geary Khamis dollars	1993–2006 1900–1992	(5) Groningen: *Industry Growth Accounting Database* TIMES 1.1935 conversion to 1990 from their 2007 data. (7) Maddison: Standardized Estimates of Fixed Capital Stock
Labor	million annual hours worked	1950–2006 1900–1949	(6) Groningen: *Total Economy Database* (3) *Historical Statistics of the United States* Tables I, D765, D803 (civilian employment * hours worked)

Table B.2b Data description and sources for US coal

Material	Title	Period	Source	Mass (1 short ton = 0.9071847 metric tons)		Heat content (1 Btu = 1055.056 joules)	
				Reference	Series name and/or formula	Reference	Formula
Coal Exergy = Heat* 1.088	Raw coal production	1949–2006	(1) *Annual Energy Review*	Table 7.1, Col. 1	Production	Table 7.1, Col. 1 Table A5, Col. 1	(7.1.1) * (A5.1) Production
		1850–1948	(3) *Historical Statistics* – volume 1	M93 + M123	Sum production of bituminous coal + Pennsylvania anthracite	M77 + M78	Same definition as for mass
	Raw coal apparent consumption	1949–2006	(1) *Annual Energy Review*	Table 7.1, Col. 6	Coal consumption = production + imports – exports – stock change – losses & unaccounted for	Table 7.1, Col. 6 Table A5, Col. 1	(7.1.6) * (A5.1, production)
		1880–1948	(3) *Historical Statistics* – volume 1	M84, M85 interpolated before 1900	(Bituminous consumption in Btus) /25.4 + (Anthracite consumption in Btus) /26.2	M84 + M85 interpolated before 1900	Sum 'Consumption in Btus': bituminous coal + Pennsylvania anthracite
		1850–1879	(3) *Historical Statistics* – volume 1	M93 + M123	Consumption assumed equal to production	M77 + M78	Consumption assumed equal to production

Table B.2b (continued)

Material	Title	Period	Source	Mass (1 short ton = 0.9071847 metric tons)		Heat content (1 Btu = 1055.056 joules)	
				Reference	Series name and/or formula	Reference	Formula
Coal, apparent consumption as finished fuel		1949–2006	(1) *Annual Energy Review*	Table 7.1, Col. 6 Table 7.3, Cols 2, 8 Table 7.7, Col. 5	Finished fuel = apparent consumption (7.1.6) – coal used in coke plants (7.3.2) – coal used in power plants (7.3.8) + coke consumption (7.7.5)	Table 7.1, Col. 6 Table 7.3, Cols 2, 8 Table 7.7, Col. 5 Table A5, Cols 1, 3, 7, 10	Same definition as for Mass (7.1.6) * (A5.1) – (7.3.2) * (A5.3) – (7.3.8) * (A5.7) + (7.7.5) * (A5.10)
		1916–1948	(3) *Historical Statistics –* volume 1	M85, M84, M116, M114, M122	Finished fuel = apparent consumption (M84/25.4 + M85/26.2) – coal used in coke plants (M116) – coal used in power plants (M114) + coke production (M122 = consumption)	M85, M84, M116, M114, M122	M84 + M85 – (26.8 * M116) – (25 * M114) + (24.8 * M122)

320

1890–1915	(3) *Historical Statistics* – volume 1	M85, M84, M114 extrapolated to zero in 1890, M122	Finished fuel = apparent consumption (M84/25.4 + M85/26.2) – coal used in coke plants (1.51 * M122) – coal used in power plants (M114) + coke production	M85, M84, M114 extrapolated to zero in 1890, M122	M84 + M85 – (1.51 * 26.8 * M122) (25 * M114) + (24.8 * M122)
1872–1889	(3) *Historical Statistics* – volume 1	M85, M84 interpolated, M122	Finished fuel = apparent consumption (M84/25.4 + M85/26.2) – coal used in coke plants (1.51*M122) + coke production (M122 = consumption)	M85, M84 interpolated, M122	M84 + M85 – (1.51 * 26.8 * M122) + (24.8 * M122)
1850–1871	(3) *Historical Statistics* – volume 1	M93 + M123	Finished fuel assumed equal to production	M77 + M78	Finished equal to production

Notes:

1. Multipliers (26.2, 25.4, 1.51) derived by exponential fits on years where both series were available.
2. The *Annual Energy Review* table numbers from 1999–2006 are different from those shown here. The newer numbered AER tables were used in updating 1999–2005.
3. From 1989 on, where available, data are computed separately for CHP and non-CHP.

Table B.2c   Data description and sources for US petroleum

Material	Title	Period	Source	Reference	Series name and/or formula	Reference	Formula	Heat content $(1\ Btu = 1055.056\ joules)$ Metric tons: M(product) = F(product) * B(product) F(P) = factor (lbs/gal) from Table X for product B(P) = value in bbls/day * 365 * 42(gals/bbl) /2204(lbs/tonne)
Petroleum Exergy = Heat* 1.088	Crude oil production	1949–2006	(1) *Annual Energy Review*	Table 5.2, Col. 8	M(crude oil production)	Table 1.2, Col. 3	Production	
		1859–1948	(4) Schurr and Netschert, Statistical appendices	Table A1:1, Col. 4	M(crude oil production)	Table A1:II, Col. 4	Production	
		1850–1858			zero			
	Crude oil apparent consumption	1949–2006	(1) *Annual Energy Review*	Table 5.2, Col. 8 Table 5.1, Cols 5, 10	M(crude oil production + crude oil imports – crude oil losses) with stock changes + net exports for crude oil *per se* assumed zero	Table 5.2, Col. 8 Table 5.1, Cols 5, 10 times Table A2, Cols 1–2	M(crude oil production + crude oil imports – crude oil losses) with stock changes + net exports for crude oil *per se* assumed zero	
		1859–1948	(4) Schurr and Netschert, Statistical appendices	Table A1: VI, Col. 4	M(crude oil apparent consumption)	Table A1:VII, Col. 4	Apparent crude oil consumption	
		1850–1858			zero			

322

Petroleum products consumption as finished fuel	1949–2006	(1) *Annual Energy Review*	Table 5.12a, Cols 1–5, 7–14 Table 5.12b, Cols 1, 7	Finished fuel = M(Asphalt/road) + M(Distillate) + M(Jet) + M(LPG total) + M(Gasoline) + M(Residual) + M(Other) for residential/ commercial, industrial and transport	Table 2.1, Cols 3, 9, 13	Finished fuel = consumption by residential, commercial, industrial and transport
	1920–1948	(4) Schurr and Netschert, Statistical appendices (3) *Historical Statistics*, volume II	Table A1:VI, Col. 4 Table 8.8, Col. 5 (EIA) Table II:S45 (HIST)	Finished fuel = apparent consumption (A1V1.4) – energy sector use (8.85 extrapolated to zero in 1876 using rates from II.S45)	Table A1:VII, Col. 4 Table 8.8, Col. 6 (EIA) Table II:S45 (HIST)	Finished fuel = apparent consumption (A1V1.4) – energy sector use (8.85 extrapolated to zero in 1876 using rates from II.S45)
	1850–1858	zero				

Notes:

1. Finished fuel calculation: comparison of values in *Annual Energy Review* from Table 5.12b (energy sector use) and Table 8.8 (electric utility use) in common units produce similar numbers for 1949–2006. This suggests that internal use by the petroleum industry of petroleum products has been excluded from apparent consumption. Hence it has not been subtracted twice.
2. The *Annual Energy Review* table numbers from 1999–2006 are different from those shown here. The newer numbered AER tables were used in updating 1999–2005.
3. From 1989 on, where available, data are computed separately for CHP and non-CHP.

Table B.2d Data description and sources for US natural gas

Material	Title	Period	Source	Mass (cubic feet = metric tons*50875.05)		Heat content (1 Btu = 1055.056 joules)	
				Reference	Series name and/or formula	Reference	Formula
Natural gas Base units = million cubic feet Exergy = Heat* 1.04	Natural gas production includes natural gas liquids (NGL)	1936–2006	(2) *Historical Natural Gas Annual*	Table 1, Col. 1	Gross withdrawals	Table 1, Col. 1, EIA. A4, Col. 1	Gross withdrawals (t7.1) * Dry production factor (A4.1)
		1930–1935	(2) *Historical Natural Gas Annual*	Table 1, Col. 5	1.25*marketed production (1.25*T1.5)	Table 1, Col. 5, EIA.A4, Col. 1	1.25 * marketed production * Dry production factor (A4.1)
		1882–1929	(4) Schurr & Netschert, Statistical appendix I	Table I, Col. 5	1.25*marketed production (1.25*T1.5)	Constant 1.035 from EIA.A4	1.035 * 1.25 * marketed production*
		1850–1881			zero		
	Natural gas apparent consumption includes natural gas liquids	1930–2006	(2) *Historical Natural Gas Annual*	Table 2, Col. 8, Table 1, Col. 6	Consumption (T2.8) + NGL (T1.6)	Table 2, Col. 8, Table 1, Col. 6 Table A4, Cols 1, 2	Dry consumption (t2.8*A4.1) + NGL (T1.6*A4.2)

Natural gas consumption	Period	Source	Method / Table reference	Consumption (natural gas + NGL) interpolated 1882–1890	Method / Table reference	Consumption (natural gas + NGL) interpolated 1882–1890
	1882–1930	(4) Schurr and Netschert, Statistical appendix I	Table VI, Cols 5 and 6		Table VII, Cols. 5 and 6 Statistical appendix I	
	1850–1881			zero		
Natural gas consumption as finished fuel (excludes NGL)	1930–2006	(2) *Historical Natural Gas Annual*	Table 3, Col. 8 Table 3, Col. 7	Finished fuel = total delivered to consumers (T3.8) – electric utility use (T3.7) (total deliveries excludes pipeline and plant use). Same as sum (residential, commercial, industrial and transport (T3.1 + T3.4 + T3.5 + T3.6)	Table 3, Col. 8 Table 3, Col. 7 EIA A4, Cols 3 and 4	Delivered to consumers (T3.8 * A4.4) – electric utility use (T3.7 * A4.3)
	1890–1929	(4) Schurr and Netschert (S&N), Statistical appendix I (2) *Historical Natural Gas Annual*	Table 3, Cols 7, 8 extrapolated to zero in 1882 using rates from S&N, Table VI, Cols 5, 6	Finished fuel = delivered to consumers (T3.8 via VI.6) – electric utility use (T3.7 via VI.7)	Table 3, Cols 7, 8 extrapolated Constant factor 1.035	Finished fuel = 1.035 * (Delivered to consumers (T3.8 via VI.6) – electric utility use (T3.7 via VI.7))
	1850–1881			zero		

Notes overleaf

Table B.2d (*continued*)

326

Table B.2e   Data description and sources for US fuelwood and biomass

Material	Title	Period	Source	Mass (million cubic feet roundwood equivalent*(0.017–0.022) = MMT. Multiplier time dependent)	
				Reference	Formula
Fuelwood Exergy = Heat* 1.152	Fuelwood production = consumption = consumption as finished fuel	1997–2006	(1) *Annual Energy Review*	Table 10.3, row 1	Wood energy (Btu)*1535
		1965–1996	(10) *Statistical Abstract*	Table 1152, last row	Fuelwood consumption (mcfre)*multiplier
		1958–1964	Interpolation		
		1900–1957	(9) Potter and Christy	Table FO-13, Col. B	New supply fuelwood*multiplier
		1850–1899	(4) Schurr and Netschert	Table 7, Col. 1	5-yr interpolations*multiplier

Heat Content (1 Btu = 1055.056 joules)

		Period	Source	Reference	Formula
		1981–2006	(1) *Annual Energy Review*	Table 10.3, Row 1	Wood energy
		1970–1980		Table 10.3, row 1 and Table 1.2, Col. 10	Wood energy and energy from biomass, adjusted and interpolated
		1949–1969		Table 1.2, Col. 10	Energy from biomass (= fuelwood only)
		1850–1949	(3) *Historical Statistics,* volume 1	M92, interpolated	Fuelwood consumption

Notes: The *Annual Energy Review* table numbers from 1999–2006 are different from those shown here. The newer numbered AER tables were used in updating 1999–2005.

B.3   JAPANESE DATA SOURCES

The following were the principal data sources for Japan:

(1)   1956, *Coal Historical Statistics*, in Japanese, Tokyo: Japan Coal Association.
(2)   1995, *History of Nihon Oil Corporation* [*Nihonsekiyu hyakunen-shi*], Tokyo.
(3)   1995, *Statistics of Coal* [*Sekitan toukei soukan*], Tokyo: Japan Coal Association (in Japanese).
(4)   2001, *Energy Statistics* [*Sougou energy toukei*], Tokyo.
(5)   2001, *Historical Statistics of Japan 1985–1998 Extension*, Tokyo: Japan Statistics Association.
(6)   2001, *Historical Statistics of Japan (1868–1984)* [*Nihon toukai souran*], Tokyo: Japan Statistics Association.

Other data sources include:

● EDMC (2001, 2006), *EDMC Handbook of Energy and Economic Statistics* [*Enerugii keizai toukei youran*], Japanese edn, Tokyo: The Energy Conservation Center (in Japanese).
● Japan Electric Power Civil Engineering Association (JEPOC) (1992), *100 Year History of Hydropower Technology*, Japanese edn, Tokyo: Japan Electric Power Civil Engineering Association (in Japanese).
● METI (2000), *Integrated Energy Statistics*, Tokyo: Ministry of Economics, Trade and Industry Publishing (in Japanese).
● Mori, N. (1999), *Energy Handbook for Residential Sector*, Japanese edn, Tokyo: Energy Conservation Center (in Japanese).

Table B.3a   Data sources for Japanese economic data

Title	Units	Period	Source
Population	Million persons	1950–2006 1900–1949	(6) Groningen: *Total Economy Database* (8) Maddison: *The World Economy: Historical Statistics*
GDP	Million 1990 International Geary Khamis dollars	1950–2006 1900–1949	(6) Groningen: *Total Economy Database* (8) Maddison: *The World Economy: Historical Statistics*
Capital	Million 1990 International Geary Khamis dollars	1993–2006 1900–1992	Authors' calculation – est from Maddison and extrapolation (7) Maddison: standardized estimates of fixed capital stock
Labor	Million annual hours worked	1950–2006 1900–1949	(6) Groningen: *Total Economy Database* Authors' calculation: employment * 365 days * 5.7 hours

Table B.3b *Description and sources of Japanese coal data*

	Title	Period	Series title	Source	Units
Coal	Production	1900–1988		1	1000 tons
		1988–1998		2	1000 tons
	Imports	1900–1988		1	1000 tons
	Consumption: residential	1900–1955	Supply and demand: non-industrial	3	1000 tons
		1955–1983	Fuel consumption: household use	1	1000 tons
		1983–1998	Coal – public welfare sector	2	1000 tons
	Consumption: industrial	1900–1955	Supply and demand: industrial	3	1000 tons
		1955–1998	Coal – industrial sector	2	1000 tons
	Consumption: gas cokes	1925–1956	Supply and demand: industrial	3	1000 tons
		1956–1998	Coal-gas cokes	2	1000 tons
	Consumption: steel cokes	1925–1956	Supply and demand: industrial	3	1000 tons
		1956–1998	Coal-steel cokes	2	1000 tons
	Consumption: cokes	1946–1955	Supply and demand: industrial	3	1000 tons
		1956–1998	Coal-cokes	2	1000 tons
	Consumption: electricity generation	1900–1998	Fuel consumption: power generation	1	1000 tons
	Consumption: other prime movers	1900–1910	Consumption: total railways	3	1000 tons
			Consumption: shipping	3	1000 tons
		1911–1925	Consumption: private railways	1	1000 tons
		1935–1998	Missing years interpolated		
			Consumption: national railways	1	1000 tons
			Consumption: shipping	3	1000 tons
		1926–1934	Consumption: transportation	3	1000 tons

Table B.3c Description and sources of Japanese petroleum data

Material	Title	Period	Series title	Source	Units
Petroleum Products	Consumption: gasoline	1900–1910	Gasoline imports	4	1000 kl
			Gasoline production	4	1000 kl
		1911–1923	Consumption: gasoline	4	1000 kl
		1924–1987	Supply: gasoline	4	1000 kl
		1988–1998	Consumption: gasoline	2	1000 kl
	Consumption: kerosine	1900–1910	Kerosine imports	4	1000 kl
			Production: kerosine	4	1000 kl
		1911–1923	Consumption: kerosine	4	1000 kl
		1924–1987	Supply: kerosine	4	1000 kl
		1988–1998	Consumption: kerosine	2	1000 kl
	Consumption: light oil	1900–1910	Light oil imports	4	1000 kl
			Production: light oil	4	1000 kl
		1911–1923	Consumption: light oil	4	1000 kl
		1924–1987	Supply: light oil	4	1000 kl
		1988–1998	Consumption: light oil	2	1000 kl
	Light oil: transportation	1955–1998	Light oil – transportation sector	2	1000 kl
	Light oil: power generation	1955–1998	Light oil – power generation	2	1000 kl
	Consumption: heavy oil	1900–1910	Heavy oil imports	4	1000 kl
			Production: heavy oil	4	1000 kl
		1911–1923	Consumption: heavy oil	4	1000 kl
		1924–1987	Supply: heavy oil	4	1000 kl
		1988–1998	Consumption: heavy oil	2	1000 kl
	Heavy oil: power generation	1924–1998	Heavy oil – power plant	2	1000 kl

Table B.3c *(continued)*

Material	Title	Period	Series title	Source	Units
	Heavy oil: industrial use	1924–1998	Heavy oil – industrial sector	2	1000 kl
	Heavy oil: transportation	1955–1998	Heavy oil – transportation sector	2	1000 kl
	Heavy oil: residential/commercial	1955–1998	Heavy oil – residential/commercial	2	1000 kl
	Consumption: machine oils and lubricants	1900–1910	Machine oils and lubricants: imports Production: machine oils and lubricants	4	1000 kl
		1911–1923	Consumption: machine oils and lubricants	4	1000 kl
		1924–1987	Supply: machine oils and lubricants	4	1000 kl
		1988–1998	Consumption: machine oils and lubricants	2	1000 kl
	Consumption: naphtha	1963–1985	Supply: naphtha	4	1000 kl
		1985–1998	Consumption: naphtha	2	1000 kl
	Jet oil	1960–1998	Consumption: jet oil	2	1000 kl
	Asphalt	1900–1998	Production: asphalt	1	1000 tons
	Liquid petroleum gas	1950–1998	Consumption: LPG	2	1000 kl

Table B.3d Description and sources of Japanese natural gas data, 1953 to present

Material	Title	Series title	Source	Units
Natural Gas	Consumption	Natural gas, LNG – total supply	2	quadrillion Joules
	Power generation	Natural gas, LNG – power plant	2	quadrillion Joules
	Residential/commercial	Natural gas, LNG – city gas	2	quadrillion Joules
	Industrial use	Natural gas, LNG – industrial sector	2	quadrillion Joules
	Transportation	Natural gas, LNG – transportation sector	2	quadrillion Joules

Table B.3e Description and sources of Japanese renewables and biomass data

Material	Title	Period	Series title	Source	Units
Renewables	Electricity output from renewable sources	1914–1998	Total electricity output from non-fossil fuel sources	1	million kwh
	Hydro-electric electricity output	1914–1998	Hydro-electric	1	million kwh
	Nuclear electricity output	1914–1998	Nuclear	1	million kwh
	Geo-thermal electricity output	1914–1998	Geo-thermal	1	million kwh
Forest Products	Charcoal	1900–1983	Production: minor forest products – charcoal	1	1000 tons
	Fuelwood	1900–1983	Production: minor forest products – charcoal	1	1000 bundles

B.4 US DATA

Table B.4 Basic US data, 1900–2006

	Population millions	GDP million 1990 International Geary-Khamis dollars	Capital million 1990 International Geary-Khamis dollars	Labor million annual hours worked	Exergy exajoules E = sum of individual resources	Useful work exajoules U = sum (each resource times its efficiency)	Aggregate efficiency percent U/E = ratio of two previous columns
	P	Y	K	L			
1900	76.391	312499	947156	74256	15.578	0.387	2.48%
1901	77.888	347681	990833	76597	16.475	0.417	2.53%
1902	79.469	351303	1043124	78414	17.038	0.483	2.83%
1903	80.946	368377	1104675	79733	18.842	0.519	2.76%
1904	82.485	363720	1164051	80147	18.812	0.537	2.86%
1905	84.147	390624	1218823	83294	20.246	0.587	2.90%
1906	85.770	435636	1276429	87318	20.821	0.621	2.98%
1907	87.339	442362	1341062	88923	23.138	0.694	3.00%
1908	89.055	406146	1401743	85225	21.450	0.652	3.04%
1909	90.845	455814	1455813	89895	23.069	0.741	3.21%
1910	92.767	460471	1514213	91328	24.667	0.749	3.03%
1911	94.234	475475	1574436	92061	24.565	0.786	3.20%
1912	95.703	497722	1636496	94268	25.900	0.867	3.35%
1913	97.606	517383	1702796	95572	27.168	0.909	3.34%
1914	99.505	477545	1761113	93199	25.921	0.898	3.46%
1915	100.941	490996	1807936	92713	26.624	0.966	3.63%

1916	102.364	558774	1856425	97120	28.639	1.106	3.86%
1917	103.817	544804	1908218	95952	30.791	1.211	3.93%
1918	104.958	593956	1958076	95095	31.816	1.279	4.02%
1919	105.473	599130	2004790	94258	28.518	1.219	4.27%
1920	106.881	593438	2049662	96640	31.509	1.330	4.22%
1921	108.964	579986	2087084	83061	27.660	1.111	4.02%
1922	110.484	612064	2130095	91102	28.585	1.261	4.41%
1923	112.387	692776	2196212	100527	33.817	1.517	4.49%
1924	114.558	713989	2270592	95543	32.549	1.570	4.82%
1925	116.284	730545	2347316	101159	33.120	1.709	5.16%
1926	117.857	778144	2426173	104898	35.050	1.799	5.13%
1927	119.502	785905	2501046	104963	34.430	1.824	5.30%
1928	120.971	794700	2577302	104180	35.153	1.934	5.50%
1929	122.245	843334	2660227	106204	36.469	2.044	5.60%
1930	123.668	768314	2736682	96725	34.851	1.944	5.58%
1931	124.633	709332	2784271	86988	30.733	1.711	5.57%
1932	125.436	615686	2796230	75756	27.889	1.430	5.13%
1933	126.180	602751	2789051	75389	28.564	1.445	5.06%
1934	126.978	649316	2785993	72526	29.807	1.530	5.13%
1935	127.859	698984	2794769	79312	31.145	1.656	5.32%
1936	128.681	798322	2819138	89667	33.828	1.892	5.59%
1937	129.464	832469	2851955	81716	35.481	2.073	5.84%
1938	130.476	799357	2877383	89665	32.312	1.895	5.87%
1939	131.539	862995	2899456	106299	34.343	2.106	6.13%
1940	132.637	929737	2923258	126828	36.692	2.259	6.16%
1941	133.922	1098921	2957092	119479	39.802	2.635	6.62%
1942	135.386	1318809	3004823	115782	41.506	2.821	6.80%
1943	137.272	1581122	3050086	122185	44.457	3.100	6.97%

Table B.4 (*continued*)

	Population millions	GDP million 1990 International Geary-Khamis dollars	Capital million 1990 International Geary-Khamis dollars	Labor million annual hours worked	Exergy exajoules E = sum of individual resources	Useful work exajoules U = sum (each resource times its efficiency)	Aggregate efficiency percent U/E = ratio of two previous columns
	P	Y	K	L			
1944	138.937	1713572	3088216	116242	46.463	3.373	7.26%
1945	140.474	1644761	3133168	120465	46.083	3.419	7.42%
1946	141.940	1305357	3195452	92468	44.579	3.412	7.65%
1947	144.688	1285697	3279660	94147	47.577	3.703	7.78%
1948	147.203	1334331	3378052	127460	48.513	3.647	7.52%
1949	149.770	1339505	3467477	121451	45.022	3.503	7.78%
1950	152.271	1455916	3551081	122515	48.128	3.845	7.99%
1951	154.878	1566784	3643855	129554	51.001	4.127	8.09%
1952	157.553	1625245	3750173	130878	50.840	4.202	8.27%
1953	160.184	1699970	3875991	132347	52.016	4.465	8.58%
1954	163.026	1688804	4011186	128479	50.990	4.306	8.44%
1955	165.931	1808126	4144295	132695	55.214	4.899	8.87%
1956	168.903	1843455	4278085	134902	57.141	5.101	8.93%
1957	171.984	1878063	4408092	133695	57.356	5.284	9.21%
1958	174.882	1859088	4523220	129044	57.367	5.188	9.04%
1959	177.830	1997061	4628872	133739	59.615	5.522	9.26%
1960	180.671	2046727	4749400	134706	61.645	5.743	9.32%
1961	183.691	2094396	4874169	133818	62.587	5.916	9.45%

Year							
1962	186.538	2220732	4990050	137198	65.138	6.219	9.55%
1963	189.242	2316765	5122629	138294	67.397	6.586	9.77%
1964	191.889	2450915	5280482	141884	70.026	7.088	10.12%
1965	194.303	2607294	5463511	146769	72.702	7.515	10.34%
1966	196.560	2778086	5672606	151936	76.249	8.102	10.63%
1967	198.712	2847549	5889860	153653	78.519	8.359	10.65%
1968	200.706	2983081	6112499	156444	82.638	8.927	10.80%
1969	202.677	3076517	6347846	160245	86.362	9.412	10.90%
1970	205.052	3081900	6588664	157446	89.049	9.868	11.08%
1971	207.661	3178106	6839325	156748	90.862	10.145	11.17%
1972	209.896	3346554	7121745	161060	94.924	10.689	11.26%
1973	211.909	3536622	7443691	166189	98.509	11.397	11.57%
1974	213.854	3526724	7868669	166805	96.752	11.263	11.64%
1975	215.973	3516825	8077663	162073	94.756	10.907	11.51%
1976	218.035	3701163	8340215	166745	99.527	11.562	11.62%
1977	220.239	3868829	8614306	172598	102.011	11.886	11.65%
1978	222.585	4089548	8919285	180711	104.440	12.348	11.82%
1979	225.055	4228647	9249389	185577	105.756	12.804	12.11%
1980	227.726	4230558	9568320	185077	103.101	12.701	12.32%
1981	229.966	4336141	9873454	185436	101.130	12.153	12.02%
1982	232.188	4254870	10178342	182691	97.932	11.260	11.50%
1983	234.307	4433129	10467685	185967	98.034	11.522	11.75%
1984	236.348	4755958	10784472	195323	102.353	12.108	11.83%
1985	238.466	4940383	11152728	199787	102.379	12.087	11.81%
1986	240.651	5110480	11514747	202134	102.930	12.218	11.87%
1987	242.804	5290129	11830664	207592	105.838	12.716	12.01%
1988	245.021	5512845	12127793	213794	110.244	13.396	12.15%
1989	247.342	5703521	12460097	219700	112.933	13.929	12.33%

Table B.4 (continued)

	Population millions	GDP million 1990 International Geary-Khamis dollars	Capital million 1990 International Geary-Khamis dollars	Labor million annual hours worked	Exergy exajoules E = sum of individual resources	Useful work exajoules U = sum (each resource times its efficiency)	Aggregate efficiency percent U/E = ratio of two previous columns
	P	Y	K	L			
1990	250.132	5803200	12814617	220079	112.884	14.359	12.72%
1991	253.493	5791931	13122665	217226	113.066	14.271	12.62%
1992	256.894	5985152	13377454	217661	114.950	14.625	12.72%
1993	260.255	6146210	13633366.991	223011	117.243	14.880	12.69%
1994	263.436	6395859	13917293.559	230256	119.393	15.291	12.81%
1995	266.557	6558151	14244404.499	236155	121.850	15.691	12.88%
1996	269.667	6803769	14628489.548	239377	125.568	16.388	13.05%
1997	272.912	7109775	15070100.058	246651	126.673	16.642	13.14%
1998	276.115	7406631	15571614.474	252245	127.538	16.848	13.21%
1999	279.295	7736163	16134446.975	257486	129.722	17.105	13.19%
2000	282.339	8019378	16746902.242	257972	132.521	17.359	13.10%
2001	285.024	8079583	17312634.706	255046	130.152	16.953	13.03%
2002	287.676	8208732	17734647.2	251725	132.137	17.296	13.09%
2003	290.343	8414751	18097823.882	249431	133.007	17.372	13.06%
2004	293.028	8743548	18546678.329	252901	135.846	17.879	13.16%
2005	295.734	9025456		256375	135.624	17.860	13.17%
2006	298.444			261043			

B.5 JAPANESE DATA

Table B.5 Basic Japanese data, 1900–2005

	Population millions	GDP million 1990 International Geary-Khamis dollars	Capital million 1990 International Geary-Khamis dollars	Labor million annual hours worked	Exergy exajoules E = sum of individual resources	Useful work exajoules U = sum (each resource times its efficiency)	Aggregate efficiency percent U/E = ratio of two previous columns
	P	Y	K	L			
1900	44.103	52020	37968	51534	1.253	0.049	3.890%
1901	44.662	53883	38850	51929	1.288	0.053	4.092%
1902	45.255	51089	39704	52262	1.306	0.052	3.984%
1903	45.841	54671	40385	52637	1.334	0.054	4.029%
1904	46.378	55101	41102	52928	1.357	0.052	3.834%
1905	46.829	54170	42410	53261	1.401	0.054	3.819%
1906	47.227	61263	44242	53531	1.450	0.056	3.878%
1907	47.691	63198	46427	53802	1.496	0.060	4.022%
1908	48.260	63628	48450	54031	1.513	0.060	3.990%
1909	48.869	63556	50634	54280	1.551	0.062	4.008%
1910	49.518	64559	52705	54447	1.561	0.064	4.098%
1911	50.215	68070	55183	54634	1.629	0.071	4.342%
1912	50.941	70507	58061	54821	1.696	0.074	4.373%
1913	51.672	71653	60989	54967	1.758	0.080	4.578%
1914	52.396	69503	63888	55071	1.794	0.084	4.683%
1915	53.124	75952	66556	55196	1.757	0.082	4.684%

Table B.5 *(continued)*

	Population millions	GDP million 1990 International Geary-Khamis dollars	Capital million 1990 International Geary-Khamis dollars	Labor million annual hours worked	Exergy exajoules E = sum of individual resources	Useful work exajoules U = sum (each resource times its efficiency)	Aggregate efficiency percent U/E = ratio of two previous columns
	P	Y	K	L			
1916	53.815	87703	69308	55258	1.836	0.092	5.026%
1917	54.437	90641	73409	55320	1.938	0.102	5.246%
1918	54.886	91573	78811	55383	1.985	0.108	5.452%
1919	55.253	100959	85443	55383	2.073	0.113	5.473%
1920	55.818	94654	92781	56714	2.040	0.113	5.535%
1921	56.490	105043	99121	57214	1.972	0.110	5.579%
1922	57.209	104757	104635	57692	2.038	0.112	5.512%
1923	57.937	104828	108892	58192	2.102	0.116	5.526%
1924	58.686	107766	112905	58691	2.157	0.123	5.723%
1925	59.522	112209	117492	58254	2.218	0.125	5.651%
1926	60.490	113212	123609	59669	2.317	0.121	5.226%
1927	61.430	114860	130216	60147	2.376	0.129	5.445%
1928	62.361	124246	136842	60655	2.423	0.136	5.618%
1929	63.244	128116	143760	61125	2.487	0.148	5.935%
1930	64.203	118801	150662	61624	2.438	0.152	6.216%
1931	65.205	119804	155767	60314	2.356	0.140	5.938%
1932	66.189	129835	158439	60709	2.423	0.152	6.289%
1933	67.182	142589	160389	61957	2.617	0.181	6.933%
1934	68.090	142876	163600	64059	2.768	0.200	7.239%

Year							
1935	69.238	146817	169336	65328	2.674	0.217	8.118%
1936	70.171	157493	177417	64204	2.783	0.237	8.524%
1937	71.278	165017	186789	65473	2.908	0.255	8.760%
1938	71.879	176051	198052	66118	2.984	0.257	8.613%
1939	72.364	203781	213101	67783	3.124	0.264	8.442%
1940	72.967	209728	230111	69480	3.303	0.279	8.440%
1941	74.005	212594	247087	70613	3.200	0.258	8.052%
1942	75.029	211448	263144	71670	3.112	0.238	7.645%
1943	76.005	214457	279771	72672	3.084	0.240	7.789%
1944	77.178	205214	298517	75148	2.819	0.213	7.562%
1945	76.224	102607	271214	67824	2.155	0.125	5.786%
1946	77.199	111492	238687	64828	2.260	0.142	6.294%
1947	78.119	120377	248613	67575	2.444	0.159	6.505%
1948	80.155	138290	259846	68681	2.625	0.190	7.220%
1949	81.971	147534	269779	72110	2.694	0.204	7.568%
1950	83.805	160966	276632	74095	2.954	0.252	8.525%
1951	85.164	181025	282714	75107	3.201	0.288	8.985%
1952	86.459	202005	290340	76096	3.218	0.310	9.627%
1953	87.655	216889	299164	77063	3.433	0.346	10.077%
1954	88.754	229151	308629	79889	3.467	0.363	10.481%
1955	89.815	248855	318209	82571	3.725	0.406	10.897%
1956	90.766	267567	330971	86326	3.999	0.451	11.283%
1957	91.563	287130	347702	89007	4.129	0.469	11.363%
1958	92.389	303857	366508	91812	4.205	0.474	11.259%
1959	93.297	331570	362418	94572	4.554	0.546	11.987%
1960	94.092	375090	431786	98577	5.241	0.688	13.129%
1961	94.943	420246	485426	100066	5.435	0.738	13.570%

Table B.5 (continued)

	Population millions	GDP million 1990 International Geary-Khamis dollars	Capital million 1990 International Geary-Khamis dollars	Labor million annual hours worked	Exergy exajoules E = sum of individual resources	Useful work exajoules U = sum (each resource times its efficiency)	Aggregate efficiency percent U/E = ratio of two previous columns
	P	Y	K	L			
1962	95.832	457742	550160	100302	5.813	0.765	13.152%
1963	96.812	496514	622871	100861	5.964	0.850	14.253%
1964	97.826	554449	704342	102521	6.850	1.061	15.496%
1965	98.883	586744	790772	103283	7.135	1.150	16.111%
1966	99.790	649189	881615	105787	7.857	1.302	16.575%
1967	100.825	721132	995398	108511	8.876	1.554	17.502%
1968	101.961	813984	1131661	110512	9.819	1.757	17.889%
1969	103.172	915556	1286191	110665	11.107	2.030	18.281%
1970	104.345	1013602	1466124	111340	11.759	2.201	18.715%
1971	105.697	1061230	1660155	111515	11.987	2.247	18.743%
1972	107.188	1150516	1864415	111748	12.846	2.562	19.941%
1973	108.707	1242932	2087259	113888	13.652	2.801	20.519%
1974	110.162	1227706	2309053	110261	13.417	2.753	20.516%
1975	111.573	1265661	2513598	108447	13.378	2.658	19.864%
1976	112.775	1315966	2713055	110911	13.832	2.817	20.367%
1977	113.872	1373741	2914942	112761	14.070	2.803	19.918%
1978	114.913	1446165	3127130	114374	14.927	3.001	20.104%
1979	115.890	1525477	3359322	116140	15.279	3.106	20.326%

1980	116.807	1568457	3606127	117419	15.753	3.198	20.304%
1981	117.648	1618185	3856766	117536	15.003	2.930	19.529%
1982	118.455	1667653	4102061	118624	14.685	2.869	19.540%
1983	119.270	1706380	4334008	120106	15.705	3.062	19.495%
1984	120.035	1773223	4503656	121547	16.130	3.124	19.367%
1985	120.754	1851315	4812631	121541	16.477	3.241	19.672%
1986	121.492	1904918	5067987	122737	16.825	3.293	19.574%
1987	122.091	1984142	5332066	123895	17.326	3.353	19.351%
1988	122.613	2107060	5630441	125750	17.809	3.506	19.686%
1989	123.108	2208858	5986053	126850	18.326	3.603	19.659%
1990	123.537	2321153	6390909	126917	18.925	3.739	19.757%
1991	123.946	2398928	6827654	127253	19.371	3.834	19.794%
1992	124.329	2422245	7245540	126467	19.562	3.734	19.087%
1993	124.668	2428242	7645705	122873	19.977	3.806	19.053%
1994	125.014	2454919	8030889	122478	20.629	3.917	18.988%
1995	125.341	2501530	8401334	121650	21.289	4.051	19.029%
1996	125.645	2565848	8784300	122715	21.589	4.039	18.708%
1997	125.957	2601475	9162918	122222	21.759	4.125	18.957%
1998	126.246	2555786	9521957	119988	21.878	4.061	18.563%
1999	126.494	2550158	9870844	116993	22.331	4.164	18.647%
2000	126.700	2625106	10216197	117403	22.929	4.260	18.581%
2001	126.892	2635207		115993	22.680	4.218	18.597%
2002	127.066	2638731		113813	22.757	4.306	18.922%
2003	127.215	2685608		113751	22.416	4.275	19.073%
2004	127.333	2747430		113237	22.892	4.405	19.241%
2005	127.417	2819584		112830			
2006	127.464	2898171		113185			

Appendix C: Details of the simplified REXSF model

C.1 ELECTRIFICATION AND URBANIZATION

It is tempting to test two variables that are highly correlated with technology improvement and economic growth, namely electrification (Ele) and urbanization (Urb).

Figure C.1 plots the relationship between GDP fraction and electrification, expressed as electricity consumption per capita, as a fraction of the US level. The data used in this figure are from 1997 to 2001 for 130 countries. We can see that for relatively low income countries (GDP below 40 percent) the relationship is almost linear and the variance is smaller. Beyond that, the data are much more scattered. There is an obvious divergence among countries with a GDP fraction above 80 percent.

Figure C.2 shows the relationship between urbanization (Urb) and GDP fraction. The trend relationship is almost exponential, but the variance among countries is extremely large. The correlation between Ele and Urb over time for nine major countries is exhibited in Figure C.1 and Figures C.3a–e. The indices in each graph are defined as dividing the variables by their values of the first year. The countries are France, Japan, Sweden, UK, US, Brazil, India, Indonesia and China. The correlations of these two variables for developing countries and late developed countries shown in Figure C.1 are so high (almost unity) that they cannot be regarded as independent. Hence we select electrification as the more reliable choice, and more directly related to the output of useful work, U.

The urbanization data used in this Appendix C are from the UN population database issued annually by the UN Statistical Office, New York (United Nations Statistical Office annual). However, the urbanization data appear to be less reliable than the electrification data, probably due to inconsistent definitions of what constitutes an urban area. The peculiar data for France (Figure C.3a) between 1980 and 1995, the UK before 1972 (Figure C.3d) and for the US between 1970 and 1980 (Figure C.3e) illustrate the problems. N.B., according to this UN data, the urbanization index for the UK decreased between 1960 and 1972, which is not credible. Table C.1 shows the correlations of electrification and urbanization.

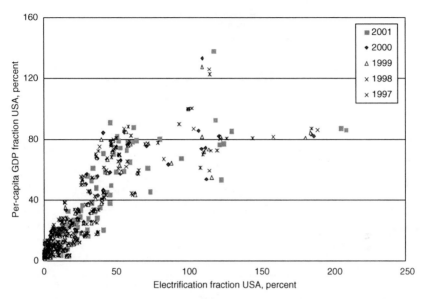

Figure C.1   Relationship between GDP and electrification for 1997–2001

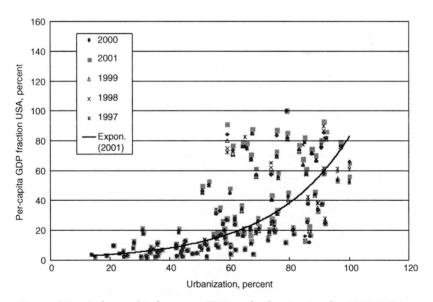

Figure C.2   Relationship between GDP and urbanization for 1997–2001

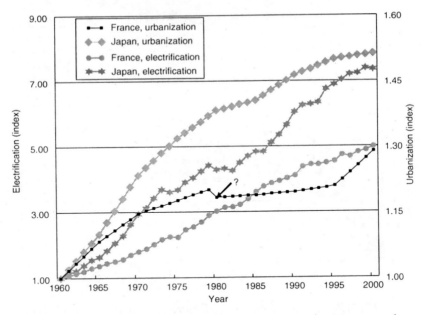

Figure C.3a   Processes of urbanization and electrification (France and Japan, 1960–2001)

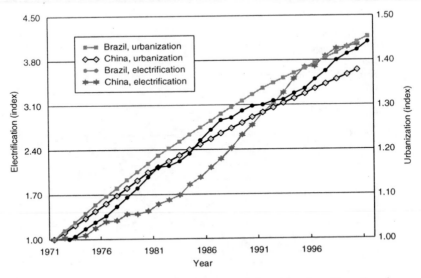

Figure C.3b   Processes of urbanization and electrification (Brazil and China, 1971–2001)

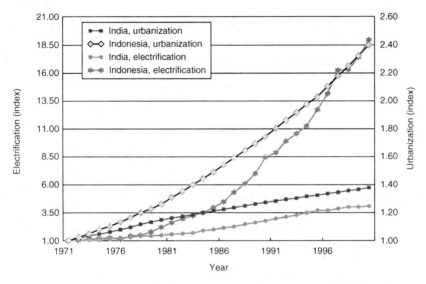

Figure C.3c   Processes of urbanization and electrification (India and Indonesia, 1971–2001)

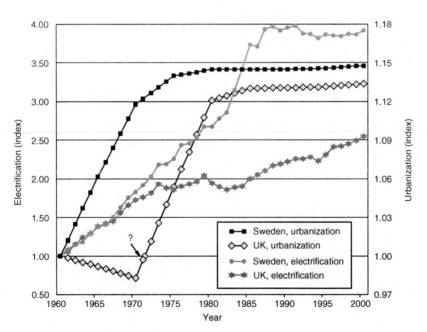

Figure C.3d   Processes of urbanization and electrification (Sweden and UK, 1960–2001)

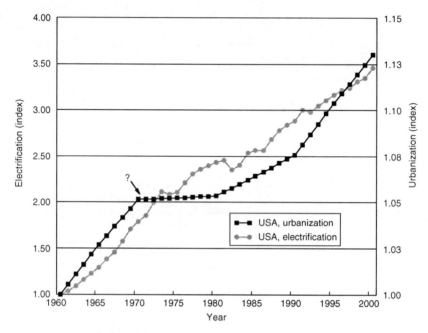

*Figure C.3e   Processes of urbanization and electrification (USA,
1960–2001)*

*Table C.1   Correlations of electrification (E) and urbanization (U) for
nine countries*

Country	Correlation of E to U
France	0.8778
Japan	0.9702
Sweden	0.812
UK	0.8428
USA	0.9544
Brazil	0.9963
India	0.9614
Indonesia	0.9818
China	0.9897

C.2 MODEL DEFINITIONS

Table C.2   Group 4 and group 8

Countries in group 4		Countries in group 8	
4	Argentina	6	Australia
10	Bangladesh	12	Belgium
13	Benin	14	Bolivia
25	Côte d'Ivoire	40	France
27	Cuba	43	Germany
28	Cyprus	45	Gibraltar
32	Dominican Rep.	46	Greece
47	Guatemala	55	Ireland
52	India	58	Italy
59	Jamaica	60	Japan
61	Jordan	64	Korea
73	Malaysia	65	Korea, DPR
74	Malta	72	Luxembourg
76	Morocco	81	Netherlands
78	Myanmar	91	P.R. China
82	Netherlands Antilles	95	Portugal
88	Pakistan	106	South Africa
93	Philippines	107	Spain
101	Senegal	118	Turkey
103	Singapore	122	UK
114	Thailand	124	USA
115	Togo		
128	Vietnam		
129	Yemen		

Table C.3 Full country list

No.	Country	No.	Country	No.	Country	No.	Country
1	Albania	34	Egypt	67	Kyrgyzstan	100	Saudi Arabia
2	Algeria	35	El Salvador	68	Latvia	101	Senegal
3	Angola	36	Eritrea	69	Lebanon	102	Serbia-Montenegro
4	Argentina	37	Estonia	70	Libya	103	Singapore
5	Armenia	38	Ethiopia	71	Lithuania	104	Slovak Republic
6	Australia	39	Finland	72	Luxembourg	105	Slovenia
7	Austria	40	France	73	Malaysia	106	South Africa
8	Azerbaijan	41	Gabon	74	Malta	107	Spain
9	Bahrain	42	Georgia	75	Mexico	108	Sri Lanka
10	Bangladesh	43	Germany	76	Morocco	109	Sudan
11	Belarus	44	Ghana	77	Mozambique	110	Sweden
12	Belgium	45	Gibraltar	78	Myanmar	111	Switzerland
13	Benin	46	Greece	79	Namibia	112	Syria
14	Bolivia	47	Guatemala	80	Nepal	113	Tajikistan
15	Bosnia-Herzegovina	48	Haiti	81	Netherlands	114	Thailand
16	Brazil	49	Honduras	82	Netherlands Antilles	115	Togo
17	Brunei	50	Hungary	83	New Zealand	116	Trinidad-Tobago
18	Bulgaria	51	Iceland	84	Nicaragua	117	Tunisia
19	Cameroon	52	India	85	Nigeria	118	Turkey
20	Canada	53	Indonesia	86	Norway	119	Turkmenistan
21	Chile	54	Iraq	87	Oman	120	Ukraine
22	Colombia	55	Ireland	88	Pakistan	121	United Arab Emirates
23	Congo	56	Iran	89	Panama	122	United Kingdom
24	Costa Rica	57	Israel	90	Paraguay	123	Tanzania

25 Côte d'Ivoire	58 Italy	91 P.R. of China	124 United States
26 Croatia	59 Jamaica	92 Peru	125 Uruguay
27 Cuba	60 Japan	93 Philippines	126 Uzbekistan
28 Cyprus	61 Jordan	94 Poland	127 Venezuela
29 Czech Republic	62 Kazakhstan	95 Portugal	128 Vietnam
30 D.R. of Congo	63 Kenya	96 Qatar	129 Yemen
31 Denmark	64 Korea	97 Rep. of Moldova	130 Zambia
32 Dominican Republic	65 Korea, DPR	98 Romania	131 Zimbabwe
33 Ecuador	66 Kuwait	99 Russia	

C.3   GLOSSARY

Ele	Electrification, per capita electricity consumption
Electrification fraction	One country electricity consumption per capita fraction of that of the USA in the same year
EP	Energy Proxy, electricity consumption plus oil fraction = Ele + Oil
EP (Ele + Oil) fraction (X)	One country EP fraction of that of the USA in the same year
EP Index	Index of EP = EP/(EP of the first year)
GDP	Gross domestic product (purchase power parity) in 1995 US$
GDP fraction (Y)	One country GDP-PPP per capita fraction of that of the USA in the same year
GDP index	Index of per-capita GDP = per-capita GDP/ (per-capita GDP of the first year)
Index of electrification	Electrification/(Electrification of the first year)
Index of Urbanization	Urbanization/(Urbanization of the first year)
K	Capital
L	Labor
Urb	Urbanization, percentage of population at mid-year residing in urban areas by country

References

Abernathy, William J. and James M. Utterback (1975), 'A dynamic model of process and product innovation', *Omega*, **3** (6).

Abernathy, William J. and James M. Utterback (1978), 'Patterns of industrial innovation', *Technology Review* **80**: 40–47.

Abramovitz, Moses (1952), 'Economics of growth', in Haley (ed.), *A Survey of Contemporary Economics*, New York: Richard D. Irwin, Inc.

Abramovitz, Moses (1956), 'Resources and output trends in the United States since 1870', *American Economic Review*, **46**.

Adams, Henry (1918), *The Education of Henry Adams*, Boston, MA: Houghton-Mifflin.

Adriaanse, Albert, Stefan Bringezu, Allen Hammond, Yuichi Moriguchi, Eric Rodenburg, Donald Rogich and Helmut Schuetz (1997), *Resource Flows: The Material Basis of Industrial Economies*, Washington, DC: World Resources Institute.

Aghion, Philippe and Peter Howitt (1992), 'A model of growth through creative destruction', *Econometrica*, **60** (2): 323–51.

Aghion, Philippe and Peter Howitt (1998), *Endogenous Growth Theory*, Cambridge, MA: The MIT Press.

Alchian, A.A. (1950), 'Uncertainty, evolution and economic theory', *Journal of Political Economy*, **58**: 211–22.

Allais, Maurice (1962), 'The influence of the capital-output ratio on the real national income', *Econometrica*, **30**: 700–28.

Allen, Edward L. et al. (1976), *US Energy and Economic Growth, 1975–2010*, Oak Ridge, TN: Oak Ridge Associated Universities Institute for Energy Analysis.

American Physical Society; Walter Carnahan, Kenneth W. Ford, Andrea Prosperetti, Gene I. Rochlin, Arthur H. Rosenfeld, Marc H. Ross, Joseph E. Rothberg, George M. Seidel and Robert H. Socolow (1975), *Efficient Use of Energy: A Physics Perspective*, New York: American Physical Society.

Andress, F.J. (1954), 'The learning curve as a production tool', *Harvard Business Review*, **32**: 87–97.

Anonymous (1956), *Coal Historical Statistics*, Japanese edn, Tokyo: Japan Coal Association.

Anonymous (1995a), *History of Nihon Oil Corporation* [*Nihonsekiyu hyakunen-shi*], Tokyo.

Anonymous (1995b), *Statistics of Coal* [*Sekitan toukei soukan*], Tokyo: Japan Coal Association (in Japanese).

Anonymous (2001a), *Energy Statistics* [*Sougou energy toukei*], Tokyo.

Anonymous (2001b), *Historical Statistics of Japan 1985–1998 Extension*, Tokyo: Japan Statistics Association.

Anonymous (2001c), *Historical Statistics of Japan (1868–1984)* [*Nihon toukai souran*], Tokyo: Japan Statistics Association.

Anonymous (2003), 'Paradox lost', *The Economist*, September 13, 13–14.

Argote, Linda and Dennis Epple (1990), 'Learning curves and manufacturing', *Science*, **247**: 920–24.

Arrow, Kenneth J. (1962), 'The economic implications of learning by doing', *Review of Economic Studies*, **29**: 155–73.

Arrow, Kenneth J., H.B. Chenery, B.S. Minhas and Robert M. Solow (1961), 'Capital-labor substitution and economic efficiency', *Review of Economics and Statistics*, **43**: 225–50.

Arrow, Kenneth J. and Gerard Debreu (1954), 'Existence of an equilibrium for a competitive economy', *Econometrica*, **22** (3).

Arthur, W. Brian (1994), 'Increasing returns and path dependence in the economy', in T. Kuran (ed.), *Economics, Cognition and Society*, Ann Arbor, MI: University of Michigan Press.

Arthur, W. Brian (1983), *Competing Technologies and Lock-in by Historical Small Events: The Dynamics of Allocation under Increasing Returns*, Palo Alto, CA: Committee for Economic Policy Research, Stanford University.

Arthur, W. Brian (1988), 'Competing technologies: an overview', in G. Dosi, C. Freeman, R. Nelson, G. Silverberg, and L. Soete (eds), *Technical Change and Economic Theory*. London: Pinter.

Atkeson, Andrew and Patrick K. Kehoe (1999), 'Models of Energy Use: putty-putty vs. Putty-clay', *American Economic Review*, **89** (4): 1028–43.

Atkins, Patrick R., Don Willoughby and Herman J. Hittner (1991), 'Some energy and environmental impacts of aluminum usage', in J.W. Tester, D.O. Wood, and N.A. Ferrari (eds), *Energy and the Environment in the 21st Century*. Cambridge, MA: MIT Press.

Ayres, Clarence E. (1944), *The Theory of Economic Progress*, Chapel Hill, NC: The University of North Carolina Press.

Ayres, Eugene E. and Charles A. Scarlott (1952), *Energy Sources: The Wealth of the World*, New York: McGraw-Hill.

Ayres, Robert U. (1969), *Technological Forecasting and Long-range Planning*, New York: McGraw-Hill.

Ayres, Robert U. (1978), *Resources, Environment and Economics: Applications of the Materials/Energy Balance Principle*, New York: John Wiley and Sons.

Ayres, Robert U. (1987), *The Industry-technology Life Cycle: An Integrating Meta-Model?*, Laxenburg, Austria: International Institute for Applied Systems Analysis.

Ayres, Robert U. (1988a), 'Barriers and breakthroughs: an expanding frontiers model of the technology industry life cycle', *Technovation*, 7: 87–115.

Ayres, Robert U. (1988b), 'Optimal growth paths with exhaustible resources: an information-based model', *Journal of Environmental Economics and Management*.

Ayres, Robert U. (1989a), 'The barrier-breakthrough model of innovation and the life-cycle model of industrial evolution as applied to the US electrical industry', in Andersson, Batten and Karlsson (eds), *Knowledge and Industrial Organization*, Berlin: Springer-Verlag.

Ayres, Robert U. (1989b), Energy Inefficiency in the US Economy: A New Case for Conservatism, Laxenburg, Austria: International Institute for Applied Systems Analysis.

Ayres, Robert U. (1989c), 'Technological transformations and long waves', *Journal of Technological Forecasting and Social Change*, 36 (3).

Ayres, Robert U. (1992), 'The energy policy debate: a case of conflicting paradigms', *World Energy Council Journal*, 29–44.

Ayres, Robert U. (1994a), *Information, Entropy and Progress*, New York: American Institute of Physics.

Ayres, Robert U. (1994b), 'Towards a nonlinear dynamics of technological progress', *Journal of Economic Behavior and Organization*, 24: 35–69.

Ayres, Robert U. (1995), 'Life cycle analysis: a critique', *Resources, Conservation and Recycling*, 14: 199–223.

Ayres, Robert U. (1996), 'The economics of Factor Four', in *Would a Sustainable Development be Feasible without Fundamental Changes in Economic Structure?*, The Hague, the Netherlands: Dutch Council for the Environment.

Ayres, Robert U. (1998a), 'Eco-thermodynamics: economics and the second law', *Ecological Economics*, 26 (2): 189–209.

Ayres, Robert U. (1998b), 'The rationale for a physical account of economic activities', in P. Vellinga, F. Berhout and J. Gupta (eds), *Managing a Material*, Dordrecht, the Netherlands: Kluwer Academic Publishers.

Ayres, Robert U. (1998c), *Turning Point: An End to the Growth Paradigm*, London: Earthscan Publications Ltd.

Ayres, Robert U. (1999), 'The second law, the fourth law, recycling and limits to growth', *Ecological Economics*, **29** (3): 473–83.

Ayres, Robert U. (2002), 'Exergy flows in the economy: efficiency and dematerialization', in R.U. Ayres and L.W. Ayres (eds), *A Handbook of Industrial Ecology*, Cheltenham, UK and Northampton, MA, USA: Edward Elgar.

Ayres, Robert U. (2005), 'Resources, scarcity, technology and growth', in D.S. Simpson, M.A. Toman and R.U. Ayres (eds), *Scarcity and Growth in the New Millennium*, Baltimore, MD: Johns Hopkins University Press.

Ayres, Robert U. (2006), 'On the practical limits to substitution', *Ecological Economics*, **61** (1): 115–28.

Ayres, Robert U. and Leslie W. Ayres (1998), *Accounting for Resources 1: Economy-wide Applications of Mass-balance Principles to Materials and Waste*, Cheltenham, UK and Lyme, MA, USA: Edward Elgar.

Ayres, Robert U. and Leslie W. Ayres (1999), *Accounting for Resources 2: The Life Cycle of Materials*, Cheltenham, UK and Northampton, MA, USA: Edward Elgar.

Ayres, Robert U., Leslie W. Ayres and Vladimir Pokrovski (2005), 'On the efficiency of US electricity usage since 1900', *Energy*, **30**: 1092–145.

Ayres, Robert U., Leslie W. Ayres and Benjamin Warr (2003), 'Exergy, power and work in the US economy, 1900–1998', *Energy*, **28** (3): 219–73.

Ayres, Robert U. and James Cummings-Saxton (1975), 'The materials-process-product model: theory and applications', in W. Vogeley (ed.), *Mineral Materials Modeling – A State-of-the-art Review*. Baltimore, MD: Johns Hopkins University Press.

Ayres, Robert U., Ralph C. d'Arge and Allen V. Kneese (1970), *Aspects of Environmental Economics: A Materials Balance–General Equilibrium Approach*, Baltimore, MD: Johns Hopkins University Press.

Ayres, Robert U. and Ike Ezekoye (1991), 'Competition and complementarity in diffusion: the case of octane', *Journal of Technological Forecasting and Social Change*, **39** (1–2): 145–58.

Ayres, Robert U. and Allen V. Kneese (1969), 'Production, consumption and externalities', *American Economic Review*, **59**: 282–97.

Ayres, Robert U. and Allen V. Kneese (1989), 'Externalities: economics and thermodynamics', in Archibugi and Nijkamp (eds), *Economy and Ecology: Towards Sustainable Development*. Dordrecht, the Netherlands: Kluwer Academic Publishers.

Ayres, Robert U. and Katalin Martinás (1990), *A Computable Economic Progress Function*, Laxenburg, Austria: International Institute for Applied Systems Analysis.

Ayres, Robert U. and Katalin Martinás (1992), 'Learning from experience and the life cycle: some analytic implications', *Technovation*, **12** (7): 465–86.

Ayres, Robert U., Jukka-Pekka Ranta and H.-J. Warnecke (1991), 'Flexible metalworking technologies', in R.U. Ayres, W. Haywood, M.E. Merchant, J.-P. Ranta, and H.-J. Warnecke (eds), *Computer Integrated Manufacturing: The Past, the Present and the Future*, London: Chapman and Hall.

Ayres, Robert U., Friedrich B. Schmidt-Bleek and Katalin Martinás (1993), Is there a Universal Measure of Environmental Disturbance?, Fontainebleau, France: INSEAD.

Ayres, Robert U. and Udo E. Simonis (1999), 'Organismus industriesystem', *Oekologie*, **62**.

Ayres, Robert U., Hal Turton and Tom Casten (2007), 'Energy efficiency, sustainability and economic growth', *Energy*, **32**: 634–48.

Ayres, Robert U. and Benjamin Warr (2002), 'Economic growth models and the role of physical resources', in P. Bartelmus (ed.), *Unveiling Wealth: On Money, Quality of Life, and Sustainability*, Dordrecht, Boston and London: Kluwer Academic Publishers. Original edition in German, 2001.

Ayres, Robert U. and Benjamin Warr (2003), *Useful Work and Information as Drivers of Growth*, Fontainebleau, France: INSEAD.

Ayres, Robert U. and Benjamin Warr (2005), 'Accounting for growth: the role of physical work', *Structural Change & Economic Dynamics*, **16** (2): 181–209.

Bagnoli, Philip, Warwick J. McKibben and Peter J. Wilcoxen (1996), 'Future Projections and Structural Change', paper read at Climate Change: Integrating Science, Economics and Policy, December, at Laxenburg, Austria.

Bailey, N.T.J. (1957), *Mathematical Theory of Epidemics*, New York: Hafner.

Baily, Martin Neal (2003), 'The sources of economic growth in OECD countries: a review article', *International Productivity Monitor*, **7** (Fall): 1–5.

Baily, Martin Neal, Robert J. Gordon and Robert M. Solow (1981), 'Productivity and the services of capital and labor', *Brookings Papers on Economic Activity*, (1): 1–65.

Baloff, N. (1966), 'The learning curve: some controversial issues', *Journal of Industrial Economics*, **14**: 275–82.

Barnett, Harold J. (1979), 'Scarcity and growth revisited', in V.K. Smith (ed.), *Scarcity and Growth Reconsidered*, Baltimore, MD: Johns Hopkins University Press.

Barnett, Harold J. and Chandler Morse (1963), *Scarcity and Growth: The Economics of Resource Scarcity*, edited by H. Jarrett, Baltimore, MD: Johns Hopkins University Press.

Barro, Robert J. (1991), 'Economic growth in a cross-section of countries', *Quarterly Journal of Economics*, **106** (2): 407–43.

Barro, Robert J. and Xavier Sala-I-Martin (1992), 'Convergence', *Journal of Political Economy*, **100** (2): 223–51.

Barro, Robert J. and Xavier Sala-I-Martin (1995), *Economic Growth*, New York: McGraw-Hill.

Barsky, Robert B. and Lutz Kilian (2004), 'Oil and the Macroeconomy since the 1970s', *Journal of Economic Perspectives*, **18** (4): 115–34.

Bastiat, M. Frederic (2006), *That which is Seen and that which is Not Seen; The Unintended Consequences of Government Spending*, original edition, 1850, translated by F.T. French paperback edition. West Valley City, UT: Waking Lion Press.

Bauer, Peter T. (1957), *Economic Analysis and Policy in Underdeveloped Countries*, Durham, NC: Duke University Press.

Baumol, William J. (1986), 'Productivity growth, convergence, and welfare: what the long run data show', *American Economic Review*, **76** (5): 1072–85.

Baumol, William J., Sue Blackman, Anne Batey and Edward N. Wolff (1989), *Productivity and American Leadership: The Long View*, Cambridge, MA: MIT Press.

Ben-David, Dan (1994), *Convergence Clubs and Diverging Economies*, London: CEPR.

Benkard, C.L. (1999), *Learning and Forgetting: The Dynamics of Aircraft Production*, Cambridge, MA: National Bureau of Economic Research.

Bernard, A. and M. Vielle (2003), 'Measuring the welfare cost of climate change policies: a comparative assessment based on the computable general equilibrium model GEMINI E3', *Environmental Modeling and Assessment*, **8** (3).

Berndt, Ernst R., M. Manove and David O. Wood (1981), *A Review of the Energy Productivity Center's Least-cost Energy Strategy Study*, Cambridge, MA: Massachusetts Institute of Technology.

Berndt, Ernst R. and David O. Wood (1975), 'Technology, prices, and the derived demand for energy', *Review of Economics and Statistics*, **56** (3).

Berry, R.S., Geoffrey Heal and Peter Salamon (1978), 'On a relation between economic and thermodynamic optima', *Resources and Energy*, **1**: 125–7.

Berry, Stephen (1972), 'Recycling, thermodynamics and environmental thrift', *Bulletin of Atomic Scientists*, **27** (5): 8–15.

Best, Ben (2007), 'Say's Law and economic growth 2007', accessed 20 July at www.benbest.com/polecon/sayslaw.html.

Binswanger, Hans P. and Vernon Ruttan (1978), *Induced Innovation: Technology, Institutions and Development*, Baltimore, MD: Johns Hopkins University Press.

Blackman, A. Wade (1972), 'A mathematical model for trend forecasts', *Journal of Technological Forecasting and Social Change*, 3 (3).

Blades, D.W. (1991), 'Capital measurement in the OECD countries: an overview', in G. Bell, F. Chesnais, and H. Weinert (eds), *Technology and Productivity: The Challenge for Economic Policy*, Paris: OECD.

Blair, Peter D. (1986), 'Electricity use and economic productivity: coincidence, correlation or causal relationship?' paper read at IIASA roundtable on energy use and economic productivity, October 27-9, at Laxenburg, Austria.

Bleviss, Debore (1988a), *Energy Efficiency: The Key to Reducing the Vulnerability of the Nation's Transportation Sector*, Washington, DC: International Institute for Energy Conservation.

Bleviss, Debore (1988b), *The New Oil Crisis and Fuel Economy Technology*. Quorum Books.

Boadway, R. (1974), 'The welfare foundations of cost-benefit analysis', *The Economic Journal*, 84 (December): 926–39.

Bohi, Douglas R. (1991), 'On the macroeconomic effects of energy price shocks', *Resources and Energy*, 13: 145–62.

Boulding, Kenneth E. (1966), 'The economics of the coming spaceship Earth', in H. Jarrett (ed.), *Environmental Quality in a Growing Economy: Essays from the Sixth RFF Forum*, Baltimore MD: Johns Hopkins University Press.

Boulding, Kenneth E. (1981), *Evolutionary Economics*, Beverly Hills, CA: Sage Publications.

Bridges, Jack (1973), *Understanding the national energy dilemma (1973)*, Washington, DC: United States Congress Joint Committee on Atomic Energy.

Brookes, Len (1979), 'A low-energy strategy for the UK by G. Leach et al: a review and reply', *Atom*, (269): 3–8.

Brookes, Len (1990), 'Energy efficiency and economic fallacies', *Energy Policy*, 18 (2): 199–201.

Brookes, Len (1992), 'Energy efficiency and economic fallacies: a reply', *Energy Policy*, 20 (5): 390–92.

Brookes, Len (1993), 'Energy efficiency fallacies: the debate concluded', *Energy Policy*, 21 (4): 346–7.

Brooks, Daniel R. and E.O. Wiley (1986), *Evolution as Entropy: Towards a Unified Theory of Biology*, Chicago: University of Chicago Press.

Bryant, Lynwood (1967), 'The beginnings of the internal combustion engine', in M. Kranzberg and C.J. Pursell (eds), *Technology in Western Civilization*, New York, London and Toronto: Oxford University Press.

Burbridge, J. and A. Harrison (1984), 'Testing for the effects of oil price rises using vector autoregressions', *International Economics Review*, **25**: 459–84.

Burwell, C.C. and D.B. Reister (1985), *Electricity Use Trends in the Production of Chemicals*, Oak Ridge, TN: Institute for Energy Analysis, Oak Ridge Associated Universities.

Cairncross, Frances (1997), *The Death of Distance*, Cambridge, MA: Harvard Business School Press.

Campbell, Colin J. (1997), *The Coming Oil Crisis*, Brentwood, UK: Multiscience Publishing and Petroconsultants.

Campbell, Colin J. (2003), *The Essence of Oil and Gas Depletion: Collected Papers and Excerpts*, Brentwood, UK: Multi-Science Publishing Co.

Campbell, Colin J. (2004), *The Coming Oil Crisis*, Brentwood, UK: Multi-Science Publishing Co.

Campbell, Colin J. and Jean H. Laherrère (1998), 'The End of Cheap Oil', *Scientific American*, **278** (3): 60–65.

Carhart, Steven C. (1979), *The Least-cost Energy Strategy-technical Appendix*, Pittsburgh, PA: Carnegie-Mellon University Press.

Carlsson, B. (1984), 'The development and use of machine tools in historical perspective', *Economic Behavior and Organization*, **5**: 91–114.

Carnot, N.L.S. (1826), *Réflexions sur la puissance motrice du feu*, publisher unknown.

Cass, David (1965), 'Optimum growth in an aggregative model of capital accumulation', *Review of Economic Studies*, **32**: 233–40.

Cass, David (1966), 'Optimum growth in an aggregative model of capital accumulation: a turnpike theorem', *Econometrica*, **34**: 833–50.

Cassel, Gustav (1932), *The Theory of Social Economy*, first German edn 1918, New York: Harcourt-Brace.

Casten, Thomas R. and Robert U. Ayres (2007), 'Energy myth #8: the US energy system is environmentally and economically optimal', in B. Sovacool and M. Brown (eds), *Energy and Society: Twelve Myths*, Dordrecht, the Netherlands: Kluwer.

Casten, Thomas R. and Martin J. Collins (2002), 'Co-generation and on-site power production: optimizing future heat and power generation', *Technological Forecasting and Social Change*, **6** (3): 71–7.

Casten, Thomas R. and Martin J. Collins (2003), 'Optimizing future heat and power generation', accessed at www.primaryenergy.com.

Casten, Thomas R. and Brennan Downes (2004), 'Economic growth and the central generation paradigm', *Dialogue* at the (International Association of Energy Economists IAEE), **12** (2): 7–13.

Christensen, Lauritz R., Diane Cummings and Dale W. Jorgenson (1983), 'An international comparison of growth in productivity, 1947–1973', in J.W. Kendrick and B.N. Vaccara (eds), *New Developments in Productivity Measurement*. New York: National Bureau of Economic Research.

Christensen, Lauritz R., Dale W. Jorgenson and Lawrence J. Lau (1971), 'Conjugate duality and the transcendental logarithmic production function', *Econometrica*, **39** (3): 225–56.

Christensen, Lauritz R., Dale W. Jorgenson and Lawrence J. Lau (1973), 'Transcendental logarithmic utility functions', *American Economic Review*, **65**: 367–83.

Clarke, Arthur C. (1958), *Profiles of the Future*, New York: Harper and Row.

Cleveland, Cutler J. (1991), 'Natural resource scarcity and economic growth revisited: economic and biophysical perspectives', in R. Costanza (ed.), *Ecological Economics: The Science and Management of Sustainability*, New York: Columbia University Press.

Cleveland, Cutler J., Robert Costanza, C.A.S. Hall and Robert K. Kaufmann (1984), 'Energy and the US economy: a biophysical perspective', *Science*, **255**: 890–97.

Cline, W.R. (1992), *Optimal Carbon Emissions over Time: Experiments with the Nordhaus DICE Model*, Washington DC: Institute for International Economics.

Cobb, Clifford, Ted Halstead and Jonathan Rowe (1995), 'If the GDP is up, why is America down?', *Atlantic Monthly*, 59–78.

Congressional Research Service (CRS) (1973), 'Energy facts', Washington, DC: Subcommittee on Energy, Committee on Science and Astronautics, House of Representatives, United States Congress.

Conlisk, John (1996), 'Why bounded rationality?', *Journal of Economic Literature*, **34**: 669–700.

Conway, R.W. and A. Schultz (1959), 'The manufacturing progress functions', *The Journal of Industrial Engineering*, **10**: 39–54.

Costanza, Robert (1980), 'Embodied energy and economic valuation', *Science*, **210**: 1219–24.

Costanza, Robert (1982), 'Economic values and embodied energy', *Science*, **216**: 1143.

Costanza, Robert and Herman E. Daly (1992), 'Natural capital and sustainable development', *Conservation Biology*, **6**: 37–46.

Cunningham, James A. (1980), 'Using the learning curve as a management tool', *IEEE Spectrum*, 45–8.

Dalby, William Ernest (1911), 'Railways: locomotive power', in *Encyclopedia Britannica*, Cambridge, UK: Cambridge University Press.

Daly, Herman E. (1973), *Toward a Steady State Economy*, San Francisco: W.H. Freeman and Company.

Daly, Herman E. (1986), 'Thermodynamic and economic concepts as related to resource-use policies: comment', *Land Economics*, **62**: 319–22.

Daly, Herman E. (1989), 'Towards an environmental macroeconomics', *Ecological Economics*, **1** (1).

Daly, Herman E. (1992), 'Is the entropy law relevant to the economics of natural resource scarcity? Yes, of course it is!', *Journal of Environmental Economics and Management*, **23**: 91–5.

Daly, Herman E. (2000), 'When smart people make dumb mistakes', *Ecological Economics*, **34** (1): 1–3.

Daly, Herman E. and John Cobb (1989), *For the Common Good*, Boston, MA: Beacon Press.

Darby, M.R. (1982), 'The price of oil and world inflation and recession', *American Economic Review*, **72**: 738–51.

Darrat, Ali F. and Otis W. Gilley (1996), 'US oil consumption, oil prices and the macroeconomy', *Empirical Economics*, **21**: 317–34.

Dasgupta, Partha and Geoffrey Heal (1974), 'The optimal depletion of exhaustible resources', paper read at symposium on the Economics of Exhaustible Resources.

David, Paul A. (1970), 'Learning-by-doing and tariff protection: a reconsideration of the case of the ante-bellum United States cotton textile industry', *Journal of Economic History*, **30**: 521–601.

David, Paul A. (1975), *Technical Choice, Innovation and Economic Growth*, London: Cambridge University Press.

David, Paul A. (1985), 'CLIO and the economics of QWERTY', *American Economic Review (Papers and Proceedings)*, **75**: 332–7.

David, Paul A. (1991), 'Computer and dynamo', in *Technology and Productivity: The Challenge of Economic Policy*, Paris: OECD.

David, Paul A. (2003), 'General purpose technologies and surges in productivity: historical reflections on the future of the ICT revolution', in P.A.D.a.M. Thomas (ed.), *The Economic Future in Historical Perspective*. Oxford: Oxford University Press.

Davies, S. (1979), *The Diffusion of Process Innovations*, Cambridge, UK: Cambridge University Press.

Day, Richard H. (1984), 'Disequilibrium economic dynamics: a post-Schumpeterian contribution', *Journal of Economic Behavior and Organization*, **5** (1): 57–76.

Day, Richard H. (1987), 'The general theory of disequilibrium economics and of economic evolution', in D. Batten et al. (eds), *Economic Evolution and Structural Change*, New York: Springer-Verlag.

Day, Richard H. (1989), 'Dynamical systems, adaptation and economic evolution: on the foundation of evolutionary economics', paper read at International Symposium on Evolutionary Dynamics and Nonlinear Economics, April, Austin, TX.

Day, Richard H. and Gunnar Eliason (eds) (1986), *The Dynamics of Market Economies*, Amsterdam: North-Holland.

de Beer, Jeroen (1998), 'Potential for industrial energy efficiency improvements in the long term', Ph.D. thesis, University of Utrecht, Utrecht, the Netherlands.

Deffeyes, Kenneth S. (2001), *Hubbert's Peak*, Princeton, NJ: Princeton University Press.

Deffeyes, Kenneth S. (2005), *The View from Hubbert's Peak*, Hill and Wang.

Denison, Edward F. (1962), *The Sources of Economic Growth in the United States and the Alternatives before Us*, New York: Committee for Economic Development.

Denison, Edward F. (1967), *Why Growth Rates Differ*, Washington, DC: Brookings Institution Press.

Denison, Edward F. (1974), *Accounting for US Economic Growth, 1929–1969*, Washington, DC: Brookings Institution Press.

Denison, Edward F. (1979), *Accounting for Slower Growth*, Washington, DC: Brookings Institution Press.

Denison, Edward F. (1979), 'Explanations of declining productivity growth', *Survey of Current Business*, **59** (part II): 1–24.

Denison, Edward F. (1985), *Trends in American Economic Growth, 1929–1982*, Washington, DC: Brookings Institution Press.

Desrousseaux, J. (1961), 'Expansion table et taux d'interêt optimal', *Annales de Mines*: 31–6.

Devine, W.D., Jr. (1982), *An Historical Perspective on the Value of Electricity in American Manufacturing*, Oak Ridge, TN: Oak Ridge Associated Universities Institute for Energy Analysis.

Dewhurst, J.F. Associates (1955), *America's Needs and Resources: A New Survey*, New York: Twentieth Century Fund.

Dewhurst, J. Frederick (1947), *America's Needs and Resources*, New York: Twentieth Century Fund.

Dickey, D.A. and W.A. Fuller (1981), 'Likelihood ratio statistics for an autoregressive time series with a unit root', *Econometrica*, **49**: 1057–72.

Diewart, W.E. (1974), 'Applications of duality theory', in M. Intriligator and D. Kendrick (eds), *Frontiers of Quantitative Economics, Volume II*, Amsterdam: North-Holland.

Domar, Evsey D. (1946), 'Capital expansion, rate of growth and employment', *Econometrica*, **14**: 137–47.

Dosi, Giovanni (1982), 'Technological paradigms and technological trajectories: a suggested interpretation of the determinants and directions of technical change', *Research Policy*, **11** (3): 147–62.

Dosi, Giovanni (1988), 'Sources, procedures and microeconomic effects of innovation', *Journal of Economic Literature*, **26** (3): 1120–71.

Dosi, Giovanni, Christopher Freeman, Richard Nelson, Gerald Silverberg and Luc Soete (eds) (1988), *Technical Change and Economic Theory*, New York: Francis Pinter.

Douglas, Paul H. (1948), 'Are there laws of production?', *American Economic Review*, **38**: 1–42.

Durbin, James and Geoffrey S. Watson (1950), 'Testing for serial correlation in least-squares regression, I', *Biometrika*, **37**: 409–28.

Durbin, James and Geoffrey S. Watson (1951), 'Testing for serial correlation in least squares regression, II', *Biometrika*, **38**: 159–79.

Easingwood, C.J., Vijay Mahajan and E. Muller (1983), 'A non-symmetric responding logistic model for technological substitution', *Journal of Technological Forecasting and Social Change*, **20**: 199–213.

Easterly, William and Ross Levine (2001), 'It's not factor accumulation: stylized facts and growth models', *The World Bank Economic Review*, **15** (2): 177–219.

Ecobilan (1998), *Worldwide LCI Database for Steel Industry Products*, Brussels: International Iron and Steel Institute.

EDMC (2001, 2006), *EDMC Handbook of Energy and Economic Statistics* [*Enerugii keizai toukei youran*], Japanese edn, Tokyo: The Energy Conservation Center.

Edwards, Anne (1996), *Throne of Gold*.

Eichengreen, Barry (1989), 'The political economy of the Smoot-Hawley tariff', *Research in Economic History*, **12**: 1–43.

Eldredge, Niles and Steven Jay Gould (1972), 'Punctuated equilibria: an alternative to phyletic gradualism', in T.J.M. Schopf (ed.), *Models in Paleobiology*, San Francisco, CA: Freeman, Cooper and Co.

Elliott, John F. (1991), 'Energy, the environment and iron and steel technology', in J.W. Tester, D.O. Wood, and N.A. Ferrari (eds), *Energy and the Environment in the 21st Century*, Cambridge, MA: MIT Press.

Energy Information Administration (EIA) (2004), *World Energy Outlook 2003*, Washington, DC: United States Department of Energy, Energy Information Administration.

Energy Information Administration Office of Oil and Gas (1999), *Historical Natural Gas Annual 1930 through 1998*, Washington, DC: United States Department of Energy, Energy Information Administration.

Engle, R.F. and Clive W.J. Granger (1987), 'Cointegration and error correction: representation, estimation and testing', *Econometrica*, **55**: 251–76.

Enos, J.L. (1962), *Petroleum Progress and Profits, a History of Process Innovation*, Cambridge, MA: MIT Press.

EPRI (1993), Unknown title, Palo Alto, CA: Electric Power Research Institute.

ESD (1995), *Monitoring Environmental Progress: A Report on Work in Progress*, Washington, DC: World Bank.

Evans, C. (1979), *The Micro-millennium*, New York: Viking Press.

Faber, Malte (1985), 'A Biophysical Approach to the Economy, Entropy, Environment and Resources', in W. van Gool and J.J.C. Bruggink (eds), *Energy and Time in the Economic and Physical Sciences*, Amsterdam: North-Holland.

Faber, Malte, H. Niemes and Gunter Stephan (1995), *Entropy, Environment and Resources*, 2nd edn, Berlin: Springer Verlag.

Faber, Malte, Horst Niemes and Gunter Stephan (1987), *Entropy, Environment and Resources*, Berlin: Springer-Verlag.

Faber, Malte and John L.R. Proops (1986), 'Time irreversibilities in economics', in M. Faber (ed.), *Studies in Austrian Capital Theory, Investment and Time; Lecture Notes in Economics and Mathematical Systems*, Berlin: Springer-Verlag.

Faber, Malte and John L.R. Proops (1989), *Evolution in Biology, Physics and Economics: A Conceptual Analysis*, Heidelberg, Germany: University of Heidelberg Department of Economics.

Fabricant, Solomon (1954), 'Economic progress and economic change', in *34th Annual Report*, New York: National Bureau of Economic Research.

Factor Ten Club (1994 and 1997), *Carnoules Declaration*, Wuppertal, Germany: Wuppertal Institute.

Faere, Rolf, Shawna Grosskopf and C.A.K. Lovell (1988), 'An indirect approach to the evaluation of producer performance', *Journal of Public Economics*, **37**(1): 71–89.

Faere, Rolf and Shawna Grosskopf (1993), 'Derivation of shadow prices for undesirable outputs: a distance function approach', *Review of Economics and Statistics*, (75): 374–81.

Faere, Rolf and Shawna Grosskopf (1994), *Production Frontiers*, Cambridge, UK: Cambridge University Press.

Faere, Rolf, Shawna Grosskopf, Mary Norris and Zhongyang Zhang (1994), 'Productivity growth, technical progress and efficiency change in industrialized countries', *The American Economic Review*, **84**: 66–83.

Faith, William, Lawrence Keyes and R.C. Clark (1950), *Industrial Chemicals*, 1st edn, New York: Wiley-Interscience.

Fel'dman, G.A. (1928), 'On the theory of the rates of growth of national income', *Planovoe Khozyaistvo*, (11/12).

Fel'dman, G.A. (1964), 'On the theory of the rates of growth of national income', in N. Spulber (ed.), *Foundations of Soviet Strategy for Economic Growth*, Bloomington, IN: Indiana University Press.

Felipe, Jesus and Franklin M. Fisher (2003), 'Aggregation in production functions: what applied economists should know', *Metroeconomica*, **54** (2–3): 208–62.

Fiddaman, Thomas (1998), 'A feedback rich climate-economy model', paper read at 16th International Conference of the Systems Dynamics Society, Quebec, at Quebec, Canada.

Field, D.C. (1958), 'Internal combustion engines', in C.E. Singer, J. Holmyard, J.R. Hall, and T.I. Williams (eds), *History of Technology: The Late 19th Century c. 1850-c.1900*, New York and London: Oxford University Press.

Fisher, Franklin M. (1965), 'Embodied technology and the existence of an aggregate capital stock', *Review of Economic Studies*, **32**: 263–88.

Fisher, Franklin M. (1968), 'Embodied technology and the existence of labor and capital aggregates', *Review of Economic Studies*, **35**: 391–412.

Fisher, Franklin M. (1969a), 'Approximate aggregation and the Leontief conditions', *Econometrica*, **37** (4): 457–69.

Fisher, Franklin M. (1969b), 'The existence of aggregate production functions', *Econometrica*, **37** (4): 553–77.

Fisher, Franklin M. (1987), 'Aggregation problem', in J. Eatwell, M. Millgate, and P. Newman (eds), *The New Palgrave: A Dictionary of Economics*, London: Macmillan.

Fisher, Franklin M. (1993), *Aggregation, Aggregate Production Functions and Related Topics*, Cambridge, MA: MIT Press.

Fisher, John C. and Robert H. Pry (1971), 'A simple substitution model of technological change', *Journal of Technological Forecasting and Social Change*, **3** (1).

Forbes, R.J. and E.J. Dijksterhuis (1963), *A History of Science and Technology 2: The 18th and 19th Centuries*, 2 vols. vol 2, Harmondsworth, Middlesex, UK and Baltimore, MD: Penguin Books.

Ford Foundation Energy Policy Study (1974), 'Exploring energy choices', in *Energy Policy Project*, Washington, DC: Ford Foundation.

Foster, Richard N. (1986), *Innovation: The Attackers' Advantage*, New York: McKinsey and Company, Inc.

Frankhauser, S. (1995), unknown title, in *Valuing Climate Change*, London: Earthscan.

Freeman, Christopher (1989), 'The nature of innovation and the evolution of the productive system', paper read at Seminar on Contributions of Science and Technology to Economic Growth, June 5.

Friedman, Milton (1953), 'The methodology of positive economics', in M. Friedman (ed.), *Essays in Positive Economics*, Chicago, IL: University of Chicago Press.

Fuss, Melvin (1977), 'The structure of technology over time: a model for testing the "putty-clay" hypothesis', *Econometrica*, **45** (8): 1797–821.

Georgescu-Roegen, Nicholas (1966), *Analytic Economics*, Cambridge, MA: Harvard University Press.

Georgescu-Roegen, Nicholas (1971), *The Entropy Law and the Economic Process*, Cambridge, MA: Harvard University Press.

Georgescu-Roegen, Nicholas (1977), 'The steady state and ecological salvation: a thermodynamic analysis', *Bioscience*, **27** (4).

Georgescu-Roegen, Nicholas (1984), 'Feasible recipes and viable technologies', *Atlantic Economic Journal*, **12**: 21–30.

Gerlagh, Reyer (2000), 'Discounting and sustainability in applied IAMs', in C. Carraro (ed.), *Efficiency and Equity of Climate Change Policy*, Dordrecht, the Netherlands: Kluwer.

Gerlagh, R. and B.C.C. van der Zwaan (2003), 'Gross World Product in a global warming model with endogenous technological change', *Resource & Energy Economics*, **25**: 35–57.

Ghali, Khalifa H. and M.I.T. El-Sakka (2004), 'Energy use and output growth in Canada: a multivariate cointegration analysis', *Energy Economics*, **26**: 225–38.

Ghosh, A. (1958), 'Input-output approach in an allocation system', *Economica*, **25** (97): 58–64.

Giarratani, F. (1976), 'Application of an interindustry supply model to energy issues', *Environment and Planning A*, **8** (4): 447–54.

Goeller, Harold and Alvin Weinberg (1976), 'The age of substitutability', *Science*, 191.

Goldemberg, Jose et al. (1987a), *Energy for a Sustainable World*, Washington, DC: World Resources Institute.

Goldemberg, Jose et al. (1987b), *Energy for Development*, Washington, DC: World Resources Institute.

Gollop, Frank M. and Dale W. Jorgenson (1980), 'US productivity growth by industry, 1948–1973', in J.W. Kendrick and B.N. Vaccara (eds), *New Developments in Productivity Measurement and Analysis*, Chicago: National Bureau of Economic Research.

Gollop, Frank M. and Dale W. Jorgenson (1983), 'Sectoral measures of labor cost for the United States, 1948–1978', in J.E. Triplett (ed.), *The Measurement of Labor Cost*, Chicago, IL: Chicago University Press.

Gompertz, B. (1832), 'On the nature of the function expressive of the awe of human mortality and on the mode of determining the value of life contingencies', *Philosophical Transactions of the Royal Society of London*, **123**: 513–85.

Goodwin, Richard M. (1961), 'The optimal growth path for an underdeveloped economy', *Economic Journal*, **71**: 756–74.

Gould, Steven J. (1982), 'The meaning of punctuated equilibrium and its role in validating a hierarchical approach to macroevolution', in R. Milkman (ed.), *Perspectives on Evolution*, Sunderland, MA: Sinauer.

Granger, Clive W.J. and P. Newbold (1974), 'Spurious regressions in econometrics', *Journal of Econometrics*, **35**: 143–59.

Greene, David L. (1994), 'Alternative fuels and vehicle choice model', Oak Ridge National Laboratory report no. ORNL/TM-12738, Oak Ridge, TN.

Griliches, Zvi (1957), 'Hybrid corn: an exploration of the economies of technological change', *Econometrica*, **25** (4).

Griliches, Zvi (1958), 'Research costs and social return: hybrid corn and related innovations', *Journal of Political Economy*, 419–32.

Griliches, Zvi and Jacques Mairesse (1998), 'Production functions: the search for identification', in *Econometrics and Economic Theory in the Twentieth Century: The Ragnar Frisch Centennial Symposium*, Cambridge, UK: Cambridge University Press.

Groningen Growth and Development Centre (2006), 'Industry growth accounting database' accessed October at www.ggdc.net.

Groningen Growth and Development Centre (2007), 'The Conference Board and Groningen Growth and Development Centre Total Economy Database', Faculty of Economics, University of Groningen, accessed October at www.ggdc.net.

Gruebler, Arnulf (1998), *Technology and Global Change*, Cambridge: Cambridge University Press.

Gruver, G.W. (1989), 'On the plausibility of the supply-driven input-output model – a theoretical basis for input-coefficient change', *Journal of Regional Science*, **29** (3): 441–50.

Guo, Hui and Kelvin L. Kliesen (2005), 'Oil price volatility and US macroeconomic activity', *Federal Reserve Bank of St. Louis Review*, (November/December 2005): 669–83.

Guyol, Nathaniel B. (1984), 'Energy and work in the United States: a new approach to the analysis and understanding of the American energy economy', paper read at IAEE conference, April 11, San Francisco, CA.

Gyftopoulos, E.P., L.J. Lazaridis and T.F. Widmer (1974), *Potential Fuel Effectiveness in Industry*, Cambridge, MA: Ballinger Publishing Company.

Hall, Charles A.S., Cutler J. Cleveland and Robert K. Kaufmann (1986), *Energy and Resource Quality: The Ecology of the Economic Process*, New York: Wiley-Interscience.

Hall, E.H., W.H. Hanna, L.D. Reed, J. Varga Jr., D.N. Williams, K.E. Wilkes, B.E. Johnson, W.J. Mueller, E.J. Bradbury and W.J. Frederick (1975), Evaluation of the Theoretical Potential for Energy Conservation in Seven Basic Industries, Columbus, OH: Battelle Columbus Laboratories.

Hamilton, James Douglas (1983), 'Oil and the macroeconomy since World War II', *Journal of Political Economy*, **91**: 228–48.

Hamilton, James Douglas (1989), 'A new approach to the economic analysis of non-stationary time series and business cycles', *Econometrica*, **57**: 357–84.

Hamilton, James Douglas (1996), 'Specification testing in Markov-switching time series models', *Journal of Econometrics*, **70**: 127–57.

Hamilton, James D. (2003), 'What is an oil shock?', *Journal of Econometrics*, **113**: 363–98.

Hamilton, James D. (2005), 'Oil and the macroeconomy', in J. Eatwell, M. Millgate, and P. Newman (eds), *The New Palgrave: A Dictionary of Economics*, London: Macmillan.

Hanke, Steve H. and James B. Anwyll (1980), 'On the discount rate controversy', *Public Policy*, **28** (2).

Hannon, Bruce M. (1973), 'The structure of ecosystems', *Journal of Theoretical Biology*, **41**: 535–46.

Hannon, Bruce M. and John Joyce (1981), 'Energy and technical progress', *Energy*, **6**: 187–95.

Hanusch, Horst (ed.) (1988), *Evolutionary Economics: Applications of Schumpeter's Ideas*, New York: Cambridge University Press.

Harcourt, G.C. (1972), *Some Cambridge Controversies in the Theory of Capital*, Cambridge, UK: Cambridge University Press.

Harrod, Roy F. (1939), 'An essay in dynamic theory', *Economic Journal*, **49**.

Harrod, Roy F. (1948), *Towards a Dynamic Economics*, London: Macmillan.

Heertje, A. (1983), 'Can we explain technical change?' in Lamberton et al. (eds), *The Trouble With Technology: Explorations in the Process of Technological Change*, New York: St. Martin's Press.

Helmer, Olaf (1967), 'Science', *Science Journal*, 46–53.

Henderson, David R. (2002), 'Japan and the myth of MITI', Liberty Fund Inc., accessed August 2006 at www.econlib.org.

Herfindahl, Orris C. and Allen V. Kneese (1973), 'Measuring social and economic change: benefits and costs of environmental pollution', in M.

Moss (ed.), *The Measurement of Economic and Social Performance*, New York: Columbia University Press.

Herman, Robert, Simiak Ardekani and Jesse H. Ausubel (eds) (1989), 'Dematerialization', in J. Ausubel and H.E. Sladovich, *Technology and Environment*, Washington, DC: National Academy Press.

Herman, Robert, Simiak Ardekani and Jesse H. Ausubel (1990), 'Dematerialization', *Journal of Technological Forecasting and Social Change*, **38** (4): 333–48.

Herring, Horace (1996), 'Is energy efficiency good for the environment? Some conflicts and confusions', in G. MacKerron and P. Pearson (eds), *The UK Energy Experience; A Model or a Warning*, London: Imperial College Press.

Herring, Horace (1999), 'Does energy efficiency save energy? The debate and its consequences', *Applied Energy*, **63**: 209–26.

Herzog, Howard J. and Jefferson W. Tester (1991), 'Energy management and conservation in the pulp and paper industry', in J.W. Tester, D.O. Wood and N.A. Ferrari (eds), *Energy and the Environment in the 21st Century*, Cambridge, MA: MIT Press.

Heston, Alan, Robert Summers and Bettina Aten (2006), Penn World Tables Version 6.1 accessed at http://pwt.econ.upenn.edu/php_site/pwt61_form.php.

Hinterberger, Friedrich and Friedrich Schmidt-Bleek (1999), 'Dematerialization, MIPS and Factor 10: physical sustainability indicators as a social device', *Ecological Economics*, **29** (1): 53–6.

Hirsch, Werner (1956), 'Firm Progress Ratios', *Econometrica*.

Hogan, W.W. and Dale W. Jorgenson (1991), 'Productivity trends and the costs of reducing carbon dioxide emissions', *The Energy Journal*, **12**: 67–85.

Hogan, Warren P. (1958), 'Technical progress and production functions', *The Review of Economics and Statistics*, **40** (4): 407–11.

Holton, Gerald (1962), 'Scientific research and scholarship: notes toward the design of proper scales', *Daedelus*.

Hotelling, H. (1931), 'The economics of exhaustible resource', *Journal of Political Economy*, **39**: 137–75.

Hounshell, David A. (1984), *From the American System to Mass Production, 1800–1932: The Development of Manufacturing Technology in the United States*, vol 4, Baltimore, MD: Johns Hopkins University Press.

Hubacek, Klaus and L. Sun (2001), 'A scenario analysis of China's land use and land-cover change: incorporating biophysical information into input-output modeling', *Structural Change & Economic Dynamics*, **12** (4): 367–97.

Huntington, Samuel (1993), 'The clash of civilizations', *Foreign Affairs*, summer.

Inada, Ken-Ichi (1963), 'On a two sector model of economic growth: comments and a generalization', *Review of Economic Studies*, **30**: 119–27.

International Energy Agency (2004), *World Energy Outlook 2004*, Paris: OECD/IEA.

International Institute for Applied Systems Analysis (IIASA) and World Energy Council (WEC) (2000), *Global Energy Perspectives: Interactive Database*, Laxenburg, Austria: IIASA.

Iwai, K. (1984a), 'Schumpeterian dynamics I: an evolutionary model of innovation and imitation', *Journal of Economic Behavior and Organization*, **5**: 159–90.

Iwai, K. (1984b), 'Schumpeterian dynamics II: technological progress and economic selection', *Journal of Economic Behavior & Organization*, **5**: 321–51.

Jaccard, Mark (2005), *Sustainable Fossil Fuels*, Cambridge, UK: Cambridge University Press.

Jackson, Tim and Nick Marks (1994), *Measuring Sustainable Economic Welfare: A Pilot Index: 1950–1990*, Stockholm: Stockholm Environmental Institute.

Jantsch, Erich (1975), *Self-organization and Planning in the Life of Human Systems*, New York: Braziller.

Jantsch, Erich (1980), *The Self-organizing Universe: Scientific and Human Implications of the Emerging Paradigm of Evolution*, Oxford, UK: Pergamon Press.

Japan Electric Power Civil Engineering Association (JEPOC) (1992), *100 Year History of Hydropower Technology*, Japanese edn, Tokyo: JEPOC.

Jevons, William Stanley (1871), *The Theory of Political Economy*, 5th edn, New York: Kelley.

Jevons, William Stanley (1974), 'The coal question: can Britain survive?', extracts from 1865 original, *Environment and Change*.

Jewkes, John, David Sawers and Richard Stillerman (1958), *The Sources of Invention*, London: Macmillan.

Jochem, E., J. Sathaye and D. Bouille (eds) (2000), *Societal Behavior and Climate Change Mitigation*, Dordrecht: Kluwer Academic Press.

Johansen, S. (1988), 'Statistical analysis of cointegration vectors', *Journal of Economic Dynamics and Control*, **12**: 231–54.

Johansen, S. (1995), *Likelihood-based Inference in Cointegrated Vector Auto-regressive Models*, Oxford: Oxford University Press.

Johansson, Thomas B., Birgit Bodlund and Robert H. Williams (eds) (1989), *Electricity: Efficient End-use and New Generation Technologies, and their Planning Implications*, Lund, Sweden: Lund University Press.

Jones, L. and R. Manuelli (1990), 'A convex model of equilibrium growth: theory and policy implications', *Journal of Political Economy*, **98**: 1008–38.

Jorgenson, Dale W. (1983), 'Energy, prices and productivity growth', in S.H. Schurr, S. Sonenblum and D.O. Woods (eds), *Energy, Productivity and Economic Growth*, Cambridge, MA: Oelgeschlager, Gunn and Hain.

Jorgenson, Dale W. (1984), 'The role of energy in productivity growth', *The Energy Journal*, **5** (3): 11–26.

Jorgenson, Dale W. (1996), 'Empirical studies of depreciation', *Economic Inquiry*, **34**: 24–42.

Jorgenson, Dale W., Lauritz R. Christensen and Lawrence J. Lau (1973), 'Transcendental logarithmic production frontiers', *Review of Economics and Statistics*, **55** (1): 28–45.

Jorgenson, Dale W., Frank M. Gollop and Barbara M. Fraumeni (1987), *Productivity and US Economic Growth*, Cambridge, MA: Harvard University Press.

Jorgenson, Dale W. and Hendrik S. Houthakker (eds) (1973), *US Energy Resources and Economic Growth*, Washington, DC: Energy Policy Project.

Jorgenson, Dale W., Lawrence J. Lau and T.M. Stoker (1982), 'The transcendental logarithmic model of aggregate consumer behavior', in R.L. Basmann and G. Rhodes (eds), *Advances in Econometrics*, Greenwich, CT: JAI Press.

Joyce, William H. (1991), 'Energy consumption spirals downwards in the polyolefins industry', in J.W. Tester, D.O. Wood, and N.A. Ferrari (eds), *Energy and the Environment in the 21st Century*, Cambridge, MA: MIT Press.

Kaldor, Nicholas (1961), 'Capital accumulation and economic growth', in Lutz and Hague (eds), *The Theory of Capital*, New York: St. Martin's Press.

Kaldor, Nicholas (1972), 'The irrelevance of equilibrium economics', *Economic Journal*, **82**.

Kaldor, Nicholas (1979), 'Equilibrium theory and growth theory', in M.J. Boskin (ed.), *Economics and Human Welfare*, Academic Press.

Kaldor, Niko (1966), *Causes of the Slow Rate of Growth of the United Kingdom*, New York: Cambridge University Press.

Kaldor, Niko (1971), *Economics without Equilibrium*, Armonk, NY: M. E. Sharpe Inc.

Kander, Astrid (2002), *Economic Growth, Energy Consumption and CO2 Emissions, 1800–2000, Lund Studies in Economic History*, vol 19, Lund, Sweden: Almquist & Wiksell Intl.

Kaufmann, Robert K. (1994), 'The relation between marginal product and price in US energy markets: implications for climate change policy', *Energy Economics*, **16** (2): 145–58.

Kay, J.J. and E.D. Schneider (1992), 'Thermodynamics and measures of ecosystem integrity', paper read at International Symposium on Ecological Indicators, Fort Lauderdale, FL.

Kendrick, John W. (1956), 'Productivity trends: capital and labor', *Review of Economics and Statistics*.

Kendrick, John W. (1961), *Productivity Trends in the United States*, Princeton, NJ: Princeton University Press.

Kendrick, John W. (1973), *Postwar Productivity Trends in the United States, 1948–1969*, New York: National Bureau of Economic Research.

Kendrick, John W. (1991), 'Total factor productivity: what it does and does not measure', in G. Bell, F. Chesnais, and H. Weinert (eds), *Technology and Productivity: The Challenge for Economic Policy*, Paris: OECD.

Kendrick, John W. and Elliot S. Grossman (1980), *Productivity in the United States: Trends and Cycles*, Baltimore, MD: Johns Hopkins University Press.

Kenney, J.F. and E.S. Keeping (1962), *Mathematics of Statistics*, 3rd edn, Princeton, NJ: Van Nostrand.

Keynes, John Maynard (1936), *The General Theory of Employment, Interest and Money*, London: Macmillan.

Khazzoom, J. Daniel (1980), 'Economic implications of mandated efficiency standards for household appliances', *Energy Journal*, **1** (4): 21–39.

Khazzoom, J. Daniel (1987), 'Energy savings resulting from the adoption of more efficient appliances', *Energy Journal*, **8** (4): 85–9.

Kimura, Motoo (1979), 'The neutral theory of molecular evolution', *Scientific American*.

King, R.G. and S. Rebelo (1990), 'Public policy and economic growth: developing neoclassical implications', *Journal of Political Economy*, **98**: 126–50.

Klein, Lawrence R. (1946), 'Remarks on the theory of aggregation', *Econometrica*, **14**: 303–12.

Koopmans, Tjalling C. (ed.) (1951), *Activity Analysis of Production and Allocation*, monograph 13, New York: John Wiley and Sons.

Koopmans, Tjalling C. (1960), 'Stationary ordinal utility and impatience', *Econometrica*, **28**: 287–309.

Koopmans, Tjalling C. (1965), 'On the concept of optimal economic growth', *Pontificae Academiae Scientiarum Scripta Varia*, **28**: 225–88.

Koopmans, Tjalling C., P.A. Diamond and R.E. Williamson (1964), 'Stationary utility and time perspective', *Econometrica*, **32**: 82–100.

Kornai, Janos (1973), *Anti-equilibrium*, New York: North-Holland.

Krugman, Paul R. (1995), *Development Geography and Economic Theory: The Ohlin Lectures*, Cambridge, MA: MIT Press.

Kuczynski, M. (1971), *Quesnay oekonomische Schriften*, Berlin: Akademia Verlag.

Kümmel, Reiner (1980), 'Growth dynamics in the energy dependent economy', in W. Eichhorn and R. Henn (eds), vol 54, *Mathematical Systems in Economics*, Cambridge, MA: Oeigeschlager, Gunn & Hain.

Kümmel, Reiner, Dietmar Lindenberger and Wolfgang Eichhorn (2000), 'The productive power of energy and economic evolution', *Indian Journal of Applied Economics*, special issue on Macro and Micro Economics.

Kümmel, Reiner, Wolfgang Strassl, Alfred Gossner and Wolfgang Eichhorn (1985), 'Technical progress and energy dependent production functions', *Journal of Economics*, **45** (3): 285–311.

Kummer, J.T. (1974), *The Automobile and the Energy Crisis*, Dearborn, MI: Ford Motor Company.

Kuznets, Simon (1940), 'Schumpeter's business cycles', *American Economic Review*, **30**: 152 ff.

Kuznets, Simon (1963), 'Quantitative aspects of the economic growth of nations', *Economic Development and Cultural Change*, **11** (2/II): 1–80.

Kwasnicki, Witold (1996), 'Technological development: an evolutionary model and case study', *Technological Forecasting and Social Change*, **52**: 31–57.

Lakhani, H. (1976), *Diffusion of Environment-saving Technology Change: A Petroleum Refining Case-study*, Elsevier.

Landes, David S. (1969), *The Unbound Prometheus: Technological Change and Industrial Development in Western Europe from 1750 to the Present*, Cambridge, UK: Cambridge University Press.

Landsberg, Hans H., Leonard L. Fischman and Joseph L. Fisher (1963), *Resources in America's Future*, Baltimore, MD: Johns Hopkins University Press.

Larson, Eric D., H. Marc and Robert H. Williams (1986), 'Beyond the era of materials', *Scientific American*, **254** (6): 24–31.

Leibig, Justus (1876), 'Die Chimie in ihrer Anwendung auf Agriculture und Physiologie', *Annalen der Chemie und Pharmazie*.

Leontief, Wassily (1936), 'Quantitative input output relations in the economic system of the US', *Review of Economics and Statistics*, **18**: 105–25.

Leontief, Wassily W. (1941), *The Structure of the American Economy 1919–1839*, New York: Oxford University Press.

Levine, Herbert (1960), 'A small problem in the theory of growth', *Review of Economic Statistics*, **42**: 225–8.

Levitt, Theodore (1965), 'Exploit the product life cycle', *Harvard Business Review*.

Lewis, W. Arthur (1955), *Theory of Economic Development*, London: Allen and Unwin.

Li, Jie and Robert U. Ayres (2007), 'Economic growth and development: towards a catchup model', *Environmental & Resource Economics*, **40**(1).

Lindenberger, Dietmar, Robert Stresing, Joerg Schmid and Reiner Kuemmel (2007), 'Growth, elasticities of production and structural change', Wuerzburg Institute of Theoretical Physics, University of Wuerzburg.

Linstone, Hal and Devandra Sahal (eds) (1976), *Technological Substitution*, Amsterdam: Elsevier.

Loch, C.S. and B.A. Huberman (1999), 'A punctuated-equilibrium model of technology diffusion', *Management Science*, **45**: 455–65.

Locke, John (1998), *An Essay concerning Human Understanding*, original edition 1689, Penguin Classics edn, New York: Penguin USA.

Lotka, Alfred J. (ed.) (1939), *Proceedings of the American Philosophical Society*, **80**.

Lotka, Alfred J. (1956), *Elements of Mathematical Biology*, second reprint, original edition 1924, New York: Dover Publications.

Lovins, Amory B. (1977), *Soft Energy Paths: Towards a Durable Peace*, Cambridge, MA: Ballinger Publishing Company.

Lovins, Amory B. (1988), 'Negawatts for Arkansas: Saving Electricity, Gas and Dollars to Resolve the Grand Gulf Problem', Snowmass, CO: Rocky Mountain Institute.

Lovins, Amory B. (1996), 'Hypercars: the next industrial revolution', paper read at 13th International Electric Vehicle Symposium (EVS 13), October 14, Osaka, Japan.

Lovins, Amory B. (1996), 'Negawatts: twelve transitions, eight improvements and one distraction', *Energy Policy*, **24** (4).

Lovins, Amory (1998), 'Energy efficiencies resulting from the adoption of more efficient appliances: another view', *Energy Journal*, **9** (2): 155–62.

Lovins, Amory B., Michael M. Brylawski, David R. Cramer and Timothy C. Moore (1996), *Hypercars: Materials, Manufacturing, and Policy Implications*, Snowmass, CO: The Hypercar Center, Rocky Mountain Institute.

Lovins, Amory B. and L. Hunter Lovins (1981), *Energy/War: Breaking the Nuclear Link*, New York: Harper and Row.

Lovins, Amory B. and L. Hunter Lovins (1987), 'Energy: the avoidable oil crisis', *Atlantic Monthly*, **260** (6): 22–9.

Lovins, Amory B. and L. Hunter Lovins (1991), 'Least-cost climatic stabilization', *Annual Review of Energy*, **25** (X).

Lovins, Amory B., L. Hunter Lovins, Florentin Krause and Wilfred Bach (1981), *Least-cost Energy: Solving the CO2 Problem*, Andover, MA: Brickhouse Publication Co.

Lucas, Robert E. Jr. (1988), 'On the mechanics of economic development', *Journal of Monetary Economics*, 22 (1): 2–42.

Lucas, Robert E. and Nancy L. Stokey (1984), 'Optimal growth with many consumers', *Journal of Economic Theory*, 32: 139–71.

Maddison, Angus (1982), *Phases of Capitalist Development*, Oxford: Oxford University Press.

Maddison, Angus (1987), 'Growth and slowdown in advanced capitalist economies: techniques and quantitative assessment', *Journal of Economic Literature*, 25: 649–98.

Maddison, Angus (1995a), *Explaining the Economic Performance of Nations*, Cambridge: Cambridge University Press.

Maddison, Angus (1995b), *Monitoring the World Economy 1820–1992*, Paris: Organisation for Economic Co-operation and Development.

Maddison, Angus (2003), *The World Economy: Historical Statistics*, Paris: Organisation for Economic Co-operation and Development.

Mahajan, Vijay and R.A. Peterson (1985), *Models for Innovation Diffusion*, Beverly Hills, CA: Sage Publications.

Mahajan, Vijay and M.E.F. Schoeman (1977), 'Generalized model for the time pattern of the diffusion process', *IEEE Transactions on Engineering Management*, 1: 12–18.

Mahajan, Vijay and Yoram Wind (1986), *Innovation Diffusion Models of New Product Acceptance*, Cambridge, MA: Ballinger.

Malinvaud, Edmond (1965), 'Croissance optimale dans une modèle macroeconomique', *Pontificae Academiae Scientiarum Scripta Varia*, 28: 301–84.

Malthus, Thomas Robert (1946), 'An essay on the principle of population as it affects the future improvement of society', original edition, 1798, in L.D. Abbott (ed.), *Masterworks of Economics: Digest of Ten Great Classics*. New York: Doubleday and Company.

Mankiw, N. Gregory (1995), 'The growth of nations', *Brookings Papers on Economic Activity*, (1995:1): 275–326.

Mankiw, N. Gregory (1997), *Macroeconomics*, Worth Publishing.

Mankiw, N. Gregory, David Romer and David Weil (1992), 'A Contribution to the empirics of economic growth', *Quarterly Journal of Economics*, 107 (May): 407–37.

Mann, Charles C. (2000), 'The end of Moore's Law?', *Technology Review*: 43–8.

Manne, Alan S. and Richard G. Richels (2004), 'The impact of learning-by-doing on the timing and costs of CO2 abatement', *Energy Economics*, 26 (4): 603–19.

Manne, Alan S. and Clas-Otto Wene (1994), 'MARKAL/MACRO: a linked model for energy economy analysis', in *Advances in Systems Analysis: Modeling Energy-Related Emissions on a National and Global Level*, Juelich, Germany: Forschungszentrum Juelich GMBH.

Mansfield, Edwin (1961), 'Technical change and the rate of imitation', *Econometrica*, **29** (4): 741–66.

Mansfield, Edwin (1963), 'Intra-firm rates of diffusion of an innovation', *Review of Economics and Statistics*.

Mansfield, Edwin (1965), 'Rates of return from industrial R and D', *American Economic Review*, **55** (2): 310–22.

Mansfield, Edwin et al. (1977), 'Social and private rates of return from industrial innovation', *Quarterly Journal of Economics*, **91** (2): 221–40.

Marchetti, Cesare (1981), *Society as a Learning System: Discovery, Invention and Innovation Cycles Revisited*, Laxenburg, Austria: International Institute for Applied Systems Analysis.

Marchetti, Cesare and Nebojsa Nakicenovic (1979), *The Dynamics of Energy Systems and the Logistic Substitution Model*, Laxenburg, Austria: International Institute for Applied Systems Analysis.

Mark, Herman F. (1984), 'The development of plastics', *American Scientist*, **72** (March–April): 156–62.

Markandya, Anil and David Pearce (1988), *Environmental Considerations and the Choice of Discount Rate in Developing Countries*, Washington, DC: World Bank.

Martinás, Katalin and Robert U. Ayres (1993), *Entropy, Information and Evolutionary Selection*, Fontainebleau, France: INSEAD.

Martino, Joseph P. (1983), *Technological Forecasting for Decision Making*, New York: North-Holland.

Marx, Karl (1867), *Das Kapital*, German edn, 2 vols.

Massell, Benton (1962), 'Another small problem in the analysis of growth', *Review of Economic Statistics*, **44**: 330–2.

May, K. (1947), 'Technological change and aggregation', *Econometrica*, **15**: 51–63.

Mayumi, Kozo (1993), 'Georgescu-Roegen's fourth law of thermodynamics, the modern energetic dogma and ecological salvation', in L. Bonati, U. Consentino, M. Lagsagni, G. Moro, D. Pitea and A. Schiraldi (eds), *Trends in Ecological Physical Chemistry*, Amsterdam: Elsevier.

McCombie, J.S.L. (1982), 'Economic growth, Kaldor's laws and the static-dynamic Verdoorn law paradox', *Applied Economics*, **14**: 279–94.

McCombie, J.S.L. and J.R. de Ridder (1984), 'The Verdoorn law controversy: some new empirical evidence using US state data', *Oxford Economic Papers*, **36**: 268–84.

McKibben, W.J. and P.J. Wilcoxen (1994), 'The Global Costs of Policies to Reduce Greenhouse Gas Emissions III', Washington, DC: The Brookings Institution.

McKibben, W.J. and P.J. Wilcoxen (1995), 'The theoretical and empirical structure of the G-cubed model', in *Brookings Discussion Papers on International Economics*, Washington, DC.

McMahon, James E. (1991), 'National appliance efficiency regulations and their impact', in J.W. Tester, D.O. Wood, and N.A. Ferrari (eds), *Energy and the Environment in the 21st Century*. Cambridge, MA: MIT Press.

Meade, James E. (1961), *A Neoclassical Theory of Economic Growth*, London: Allen and Unwin.

Meadows, Dennis L., Donella H. Meadows, Jorgen Randers and William Behrens III (1972), *The Limits to Growth, Club of Rome Reports*, New York: Universe Books.

Meadows, Donella H., Dennis L. Meadows, Jorgen Randers and William W. Behrens III (1974), *Dynamics of Growth in a Finite World*, Cambridge, MA: Wright-Allen Press.

Mendershausen, Horst [1938]. 'On the significance of Professor Douglas' production function', *Econometrica*, **6** (2): 143–53.

Menger, Carl (1994) [1871], *Grundsaetze der Volkswirtschaftslehre* [*Principles of Economics*], original edition, 1871, Institute for Humane Studies Series in Economic Theory, Vienna: Libertarian Press.

Messner, Sabine and M. Strubegger (1994), 'The energy model MESSAGE III', in J.F. Hake et al. (eds), *Advances in Systems Analysis: Modeling Energy-Related Emissions on a National and Global Level.* Juelich, Germany: Forschungszentrum Juelich GMBH.

Metcalfe, J.S. and P.H. Hall (1983), 'The Verdoorn law and the Salter mechanism: a note on the Australian Manufacturing Industry', *Australian Economic Papers*, **22**: 364–73.

Metcalfe, Stanley (1992), 'Variety, structure and change: an evolutionary perspective on the competitive process', *Revue d'Economie Industrielle*, (59): 46–61.

METI (2000), *Integrated Energy Statistics*, Tokyo: Ministry of Economics, Trade and Industry Publishing.

Meyer, P.S. and Jesse H. Ausubel (1999), 'Carrying capacity: a model with logistically varying limits', *Technological Forecasting and Social Change*, **61** (3): 209–14.

Meyer, P.S., J.W. Jung and Jesse H. Ausubel (1999), 'A primer on logistic growth and substitution', *Technological Forecasting and Social Change*, **61**: 247–71.

Miller, R.E. and Peter D. Blair (1985), *Input-output Analysis: Foundations and Extensions*, Englewood Cliffs, NJ: Prentice-Hall Inc.

Mirowski, Philip (1989), *More Heat than Light: Economics as Social Physics; Physics as Nature's Economics*, edited by C.D. Goodwin, paperback edition, *Historical Perspectives on Modern Economics*, Cambridge: Cambridge University Press.

Mirrlees, James A. (1967), 'Optimal growth when technology is changing', *Review of Economic Studies*, **34** (1): 95–124.

Mori, N. (1999), *Energy Handbook for Residential Sector*, Japanese edn, Tokyo: Energy Conservation Center.

Moroney, John R. (1992), 'Energy, capital and technological change in the United States', *Resource & Energy Economics*, **14**: 363–80.

Morris, Samuel C., Barry D. Solomon, Douglas Hill, John Lee and Gary Goldstein (1990), 'A least cost energy analysis of US CO_2 reduction options', in J.W. Tester, D.O. Wood and N.A. Ferrari (eds), *Energy and the Environment in the 21st Century*, Cambridge, MA: MIT Press.

Morrison, Elting E. (1966), *Men, Machines and Modern Times*, Cambridge, MA: MIT Press.

Mulder, Peter (2004), A New Framework for Economic Projections, Laxenburg, Austria: International Institute for Applied Systems Analysis.

Mulder, Peter, H.L.F. de Groot and Marjan W. Hofkes (2001), 'Economic growth and technological change: a comparison of insights from a neoclassical and an evolutionary perspective', *Technological Forecasting and Social Change*, **68**: 151–71.

Murray, Francis Xavier (1976), *Energy: A National Issue*, Washington, DC: Center for Strategic and International Studies.

Nabseth, L. and G.F. Ray (eds) (1974), *The Diffusion of New Industrial Processes*, Cambridge: Cambridge University Press.

Nakicenovic, Nebojsa, ed (1993), 'Long-term strategies for mitigating global warming', *Energy – The International Journal*, **18** (5): 401–609.

Nakicenovic, Nebosja and K. Riahi (2002), *An Assessment of Technological Change across Selected Energy Scenarios*, Vienna, Austria: International Institute for Applied Systems Analysis.

National Petroleum Council Committee on US Energy Outlook (1972), *US Energy Outlook*, Washington, DC: National Petroleum Council (NPC).

National Research Council National Academy of Sciences (1989), *Materials Science and Engineering for the 1990s*, Washington, DC: National Academy Press.

Nelson, Kenneth E. (1989), 'Are there any energy savings left?', *Chemical Processing*.

Nelson, Richard P. (ed.) (1962), *The Rate and Direction of Inventive Activity*, Princeton, NJ: Princeton University Press.

Nelson, Richard R. (1973), 'Recent exercises in growth accounting: new understanding or dead end?', *American Economic Review*, **63** (3): 462–8.

Nelson, Richard R. (1982), 'The role of knowledge in R and D efficiency', *Quarterly Journal of Economics*, **97**: 453–70.

Nelson, Richard R. and Sidney G. Winter (1974), 'Neoclassical vs. evolutionary theories of economic growth: critique and prospectus', *Economic Journal*, **84** (336): 886–905.

Nelson, Richard R. and Sidney G. Winter (1977), 'In search of a useful theory of innovation', *Research Policy*, **6** (1): 36–76.

Nelson, Richard R. and Sidney G. Winter (1982), *An Evolutionary Theory of Economic Change*, Cambridge, MA: Harvard University Press.

Nelson, Richard R. and Sidney G. Winter (1982), 'The Schumpeterian tradeoff revisited', *American Economic Review*, **72** (1): 114–32.

Nordhaus, William D. (1992), *The DICE Model: Background and Structure of a Dynamic Integrated Climate Economy Model of the Economics of Global Warming*, New Haven, CN: Cowles Foundation.

Nordhaus, William D. (1993), 'Optimal greenhouse gas reductions and tax policy in the "DICE" model', *American Economic Review, Papers and Proceedings*, **83** (2): 313–17.

Nordhaus, William D. (1993a), 'Pondering greenhouse policy', *Science*, 259: 1383.

Nordhaus, William D. (1993b), 'Rolling the "DICE": an optimal transition path for controlling greenhouse gases', *Resources and Energy Economics*, **15** (1): 27–50.

Nordhaus, William D. (1994), '*Do Real Output and Real Wage Measures Capture Reality? The History of Lighting Suggests Not*, New Haven, CT: Cowles Foundation for Research in Economics at Yale University.

Nordhaus, William D. (1998), Roll the DICE Again: The Economics of Global Warming, New Haven, CN: Yale University.

Nordhaus, William D. (2001), *Productivity Growth and the New Economy*, Cambridge, MA: National Bureau of Economic Research.

Nordhaus, William D. (2004), 'Schumpeterian profits in the American economy: theory and measurement', in *Cowles Foundation Discussion Papers*, New Haven, CN: Yale University; Cowles Foundation for Research in Economics.

Nriagu, Jerome O. and Cliff I. Davidson (eds) (1986), *Toxic Metals in the Atmosphere*, New York: John Wiley and Sons.

Nriagu, Jerome O. and Jösef M. Pacyna (1988), 'Quantitative assessment of worldwide contamination of air, water and soils by trace metals', *Nature*, **33**: 134–9.

Odum, Howard T. (1971), *Environment, Power and Society*, New York: Wiley.

Odum, Howard T. (1973), 'Energy, ecology and economics', *Ambio*, **2** (6): 220–27.

OECD (2003), *The Sources of Economic Growth in OECD Countries*, Paris: OECD.

Okada, Toshihiro (2006), 'What does the Solow model tell us about economic growth?', *Contributions to Macroeconomics*, **6** (1): 1–30.

Olivier, David and Hugh Miall (1983), *Energy Efficient Futures: Opening the Solar Option*, London: Earth Resources Research.

Oosterhaven, Jan (1988), *On the Plausibility of the Supply-driven Input-Output Model*.

Organisation for Economic Co-operation and Development (1995), *OECD Environment Data Compendium 1995*, Paris: OECD.

Organisation for Economic Co-operation and Development, and International Energy Agency (2005), *Energy Balances of Non-OECD Countries 1971–2003*, Paris: OECD.

Organisation for Economic Co-operation and Development, and International Energy Agency (2005), *Energy Balances of OECD Countries 1960–2003*, Paris: OECD.

Organisation for Economic Co-operation and Development, and International Energy Agency (2005), *Energy Statistics of non-OECD Countries 1971–2003*, Paris: OECD.

Organisation for Economic Co-operation and Development, and International Energy Agency (2005), *Energy Statistics of OECD Countries 1960–2003*, Paris: OECD.

Oyi, W.Y. (1967), 'The neoclassical foundations of progress functions', *Economic Journal*, **77**: 579–94.

Paley, William (Chairman) (1952), Resources for Freedom, Washington, DC: President's Materials Policy Commission.

Pasinetti, L.L. (1959), 'On concepts and measures of changes in productivity', *Review of Economics and Statistics*, **41** (3): 270–86.

Pearl, Raymond (1925), *The Biology of Population Growth*, New York: Alfred Knopf, Inc.

Perez-Perez, Carlotta (1983), 'Structural change and assimilation of new technologies in economic and social systems', *Futures*: 357 ff.

Perry, G.L. (1977), 'Potential output and productivity', *Brookings Papers on Economic Activity*, 1.

Phelps, Edmund S. (1961), 'The golden rule of accumulation: a fable for growthmen', *American Economic Review*, **51**: 638–43.

Phelps Brown, E.H. (1957), 'The meaning of the fitted Cobb-Douglas production function', *Quarterly Journal of Economics*, **71** (4): 546–60.

Phillips, P.C.B. and Pierre Perron (1988), 'Testing for a unit root in time series regression', *Biometrika*, **75** (2): 335–46.

Pigou, A.C. (1920), *The Economics of Welfare*, 1st edn, London: Macmillan.

Polli, Rolando and Victor Cook (1969), 'Validity of the product life cycle', *Journal of Business*, **42** (4): 385.

Potter, Neal and Francis T. Christy Jr. (1968), *Trends in Natural Resource Commodities*, Baltimore, MD: Johns Hopkins University Press.

Preston, L.E. and E.C. Keachie (1964), 'Cost functions and progress functions: an integration', *American Economic Review*, **54**: 100–6.

Price, Derek de Solla (1963), *Little Science, Big Science*, New York: Columbia University Press.

Prigogine, Ilya (1976), 'Order through fluctuation: Self-organization and social system', in E. Jantsch and Waddington (eds), *Evolution and Consciousness*. New York: Addison-Wesley.

Prigogine, Ilya, Gregoire Nicolis and A. Babloyantz (1972), 'Thermodynamics of evolution', *Physics Today*, **23** (11/12): 23–8(N) and 38–44(D).

Prigogine, Ilya and I. Stengers (1984), *Order out of Chaos: Man's New Dialogue with Nature*, London: Bantam Books.

Quah, Danny (1996), 'Empirics for economic growth and convergence', *European Economic Review*, **40**: 1353–75.

Ramsey, Frank P. (1928), 'A mathematical theory of saving', *Economic Journal*, **38** (152): 543–59.

Rapping, Leonard (1965), 'Learning and World War II production functions', *Review of Economics and Statistics*, **47**: 81.

Ray, Dixie Lee (Chairperson) (1973), *The Nation's Energy Future*, Washington, DC: United States Atomic Energy Commission.

Rayment, P.B.W. (1981), 'Structural change in manufacturing industry and the stability of the Verdoorn law', *L'Economia Internationale*, **34** (1): 104–23.

Rebelo, S. (1991), 'Long-run policy analysis and long-run growth', *Journal of Political Economy*, **99** (3): 500–21.

Reid, T.R. (1985), *The Chip: The Micro-electronic Revolution and the Men who Made it*, New York: Simon and Schuster.

Repetto, Robert (1985), 'Natural resource accounting in a resource-based economy: an Indonesian case study', paper read at 3rd Environmental Accounting Workshop, October, at Paris.

Repetto, Robert (1988), *The Forest for the Trees?*, Washington, DC: World Resources Institute.

Repetto, Robert (1992), 'Accounting for environmental assets', *Scientific American*: 64–70.

Repetto, Robert, William Macgrath, Michael Wells, Christine Beer and Fabrizio Rossini (1989), *Wasting Assets: Natural Resources in the National Income Accounts*, Washington, DC: World Resources Institute.

Resources for the Future (1954), *A Nation Looks at its Resources*, Baltimore, MD: Resources for the Future Inc. and Johns Hopkins University Press.

Rhodes, F.H.T. (1983), 'Gradualism, punctuated equilibrium and the origin of species', *Nature*, **305**: 269–72.

Rhodes, Richard (1988), *The Making of the Atomic Bomb*, original edition 1986, New York: Touchstone.

Ridenour, Louis (1951), *Bibliography in an Age of Science Annual Windsor Lectures*, vol. 2, Urbana, IL: University of Illinois Press.

Robinson, Arthur L. (1980), 'Are VLSI microcircuits too hard to design?', *Science*, **209**: 258–62.

Robinson, Joan (1953–4), 'The production function and the theory of capital', *Review of Economic Studies*, **21** (1): 81–106.

Robinson, Joan (1962), 'A neoclassical theorem', *Review of Economic Studies*, **29**: 219–26.

Robinson, Joan (1971), 'The measure of capital: the end of the controversy', *The Economic Journal*, **81**: 597–602.

Romer, Paul M. (1986), 'Increasing returns and long-run growth', *Journal of Political Economy*, **94** (5): 1002–37.

Romer, Paul M. (1987a), 'Crazy explanations for the productivity slowdown', *Macroeconomic Annual, NBER*: 163–210.

Romer, Paul M. (1987b), 'Growth based on increasing returns due to specialization', *American Economic Review*, **77** (2): 56–62.

Romer, Paul M. (1990), 'Endogenous technological change', *Journal of Political Economy*, **98** (5): S71–S102.

Romer, Paul M. (1994), 'The origins of endogenous growth', *Journal of Economic Perspectives*, **8** (1): 3–22.

Romer, Paul M. (2006), 'Economic growth', Liberty Fund Inc, accessed June 2006 at http://econlib.org.

Romm, Joseph J. (1993), 'Lean-and-clean management: how to increase profits and productivity by reducing pollution: a systems approach', unpublished.

Romer, Joseph J. (2004), *The Hype about Hydrogen: Fact and Fiction about the Race to Save the Climate*, Island Press.

Rosenberg, Nathan (1969a), 'The direction of technological change: inducement mechanisms and focusing devices', *Economic Development and Cultural Change*, **18**: 1–24.

Rosenberg, Nathan (ed.) (1969b), *The American System of Manufacturing*, Edinburgh: Edinburgh University Press.

Rosenberg, Nathan (1976), *Perspectives in Technology*, New York: Cambridge University Press.

Rosenberg, Nathan (1982a), *Inside the Black Box: Technology and Economics*, New York: Cambridge University Press.

Rosenberg, Nathan (1982b), 'US technological leadership and foreign competition: de te fabual narratur?', in Nathan Rosenberg, *Inside the Black Box: Technology and Economics*, New York: Cambridge University Press.

Rostow, W.W. (1960), *The Stages of Economic Growth*, Cambridge: Cambridge University Press.

Rowthorn, R.E. (1975), 'What remains of Kaldor's law', *Economic Journal*, **85**: 10–19.

Ruth, Matthias (1993), *Integrating Economics, Ecology and Thermodynamics*, Dordrecht, The Netherlands: Kluwer Academic Publishers.

Rutledge, David (2007), 'The coal question and climate change', The Oil Drum, accessed June 20, at www.theoildrum.com/node/2697.

Ruttan, Vernon (1959), 'Usher and Schumpeter on invention, innovation and technological change', *Quarterly Journal of Economics*.

Sachs, Wolfgang (1992), 'The economists' prejudice', in P. Ekins and M. Max-Neef (eds), *Real-Life Economics*, London: Routledge.

Sahal, Devandra (1979), 'A theory of progress functions', *AIIE Transactions*, **11** (1): 23–9.

Sahal, Devendra (1981), *Patterns of Technological Innovation*, Reading, MA: Addison-Wesley.

Sala-I-Martin, Xavier (1996), 'Regional cohesion: evidence and theories of regional growth and convergence', *European Economic Review*, **40**: 1325–52.

Sala-I-Martin, Xavier (1997), 'I just ran two million regressions', *American Economic Review*, **87** (2): 178–83.

Salter, W.E.G. (1960), *Productivity and Technical Change*, New York: Cambridge University Press.

Samuelson, Paul A. (1966), *The Foundations of Economic Analysis*, Cambridge, MA: Harvard University Press.

Samuelson, Paul A. and Robert M. Solow (1956), 'A complete capital model involving heterogeneous capital goods', *Quarterly Journal of Economics*, **70** (4): 537–62.

Sanderson, Warren (2006), *The Impact of Population Cohort Shifts on Savings and Investment*, Laxenburg, Austria: International Institute for Applied Systems Analysis.

Sant, Roger W. (1979), *The Least-cost Energy Strategy: Minimizing Consumer Costs through Competition*, Virginia: Mellon Institute Energy Productivity Center.

Sant, Roger W. and Steven C. Carhart (1981), *8 Great Energy Myths: The Least Cost Energy Strategy, 1978–2000*, Pittsburgh, PA: Carnegie-Mellon University Press.

Saunders, Harry (1992), 'The Khazzoom-Brookes postulate and neoclassical growth', *Energy Journal*, **13** (4): 131–48.

Say, Jean Baptiste (1821), *A Treatise on Political Economy*, translated by Prinsep, 4th 1821 edn, original edition, 1803, Paris.

Schelling, Thomas C. (2002), 'Greenhouse effect', Liberty Fund Inc., accessed 26 June 2006 at www.econlib.org.

Schirmer, Wolfgang (1986), *The Influence of Chemical Technology on Energy Use for Chemical Processes*, Laxenburg, Austria: International Institute for Applied Systems Analysis.

Schmidt-Bleek, Friedrich B. (1992), 'Ecorestructuring economies: operationalizing the sustainability concept', *Fresenius Environmental Bulletin*, **1** (46).

Schmidt-Bleek, Friedrich B. (1993), 'MIPS – a universal ecological measure?', *Fresenius Environmental Bulletin*, **2** (6): 306–11.

Schubert, H.R. (1958), 'Extraction and production of metals: iron and steel', in Singer et al. (eds), *The Industrial Revolution*, London: Oxford University Press.

Schumpeter, Joseph A. (1912), *Theorie der Wirtschaftlichen Entwicklungen*, Leipzig, Germany: Duncker and Humboldt.

Schumpeter, Joseph A. (1934), *Theory of Economic Development*, Cambridge, MA: Harvard University Press.

Schumpeter, Joseph A. (1939), *Business Cycles: A Theoretical, Historical and Statistical Analysis of the Capitalist Process*, 2 vols, New York: McGraw-Hill.

Schurr, Sam H. and Bruce C. Netschert (1960), *Energy in the American Economy, 1850–1975*, Baltimore, MD: Johns Hopkins University Press.

Serageldin, Ismael and Andrew Steer (eds) (1994), 'Making Development Sustainable: From Concepts to Action', Washington, DC: World Bank.

Shaikh, A. (1974), 'Laws of production and laws of algebra: the "humbug" production function', *Review of Economics and Statistics*, **56** (61): 115–20.

Shaikh, A. (1980), 'Laws of production and laws of algebra: humbug II', in E.J. Nell (ed.), *Growth, Profits and Property: Essays in the Revival of Political Economy*, Cambridge: Cambridge University Press.

Shannon, Claude E. (1948), 'A mathematical theory of communication', *Bell System Technical Journal*, **27**.

Shell, Karl (1967), 'Optimal programs of capital accumulation in an economy in which there is exogenous technical change', in K. Shell (ed.),

Essays on the Theory of Optimal Economic Growth, Cambridge, MA: MIT Press.

Silverberg, Gerald (1988), 'Modeling economic dynamics and technical change: mathematical approaches to self-organization and evolution', in G. Dosi, C. Freeman, R. Nelson, G. Silverberg and L. Soete (eds), *Technical Change and Economic Theory*, London: Pinter Publishers.

Silverberg, Gerald, Giovanni Dosi and Luigi Orsenigo (1988), 'Innovation, diversity and diffusion: a self-organizing model', *Economic Journal*, **98** (393): 1032–54.

Silverberg, Gerald and D. Lehnert (1993), 'Long waves and evolutionary chaos in a simple Schumpeterian model of embodied technological change', *Structural Change & Economic Dynamics*, **4**: 9–37.

Silverberg, Gerald and B. Verspagen (1994), 'Collective learning, innovation and growth in a boundedly rational, evolutionary world', *Journal of Evolutionary Economics*, **4**: 207–26.

Silverberg, Gerald and B. Verspagen (1996), 'From the artificial to the endogenous: modeling evolutionary adaptation and economic growth', in E. Helmstaedter and M. Perlman (eds), *Behavioral Norms, Technological Progress and Economic Dynamics: Studies in Schumpeterian Economics*, Ann Arbor, MI: University of Michigan Press.

Silverberg, Gerald and B. Verspagen (1994), 'Learning, innovation and economic growth: a long-run model of industrial dynamics', *Industrial and Corporate Change*, **3**: 199–223.

Simon, Herbert A. (1955), 'A behavioral model of rational choice', *Quarterly Journal of Economics*, **69**: 99–118.

Simon, Herbert A. (1959), 'Theories of decision-making in economics', *American Economic Review*, **49**: 253–83.

Simon, Herbert A. (1979), 'On parsimonious explanations of production relations', *The Scandinavian Journal of Economics*, **81** (4): 459–74.

Singer, Charles, E.J. Holmyard, A.R. Hall and Trevor I. Williams (eds) (1958), *A History of Technology: The Industrial Revolution; c 1750 to c 1850*, vol. IV, New York and London: Oxford University Press.

Skiadas, Christos (1985), 'Two generalized rational models for forecasting innovation diffusion', *Journal of Technological Forecasting and Social Change*, **27**: 39–61.

Smil, Vaclav (1998), *Energies: An Illustrated Guide to the Biosphere and Civilization*, Cambridge, MA: The MIT Press.

Smil, Vaclav (1999), *Energies: An Illustrated Guide to the Biosphere and Civilization*, Cambridge, MA: MIT Press.

Smil, Vaclav (2001), 'Enriching the earth: Fritz Haber, Carl Bosch and the transformation of world food production', to be published.

Smil, Vaclav (2003), *Energy at the Crossroads: Global Perspectives and Uncertainties*, Cambridge, MA: MIT Press.

Smith, Adam (1976), *An Inquiry into the Nature and Causes of the Wealth of Nations*, original edition 1776, in *Collected works of Adam Smith*. Oxford: Clarendon Press.

Smith, V. Kerry and John Krutilla (eds) (1979), *Scarcity and Growth Reconsidered*, Baltimore, MD: Johns Hopkins University Press.

Sobel, Dava (1996), *Longitude: The True Story of a Lone Genius who Solved the Greatest Scientific Problem of his Time*, London: Fourth Estate.

Söllner, Fritz (1997), 'A reexamination of the role of thermodynamics for environmental economics', *Ecological Economics*, **22** (3): 175–202.

Solorzano, Raul, Ronnie de Camino, Richard Woodward, Joseph Tosi, Vicente Watson, Alexis Vasquez, Carlos Villabos, Jorge Jimenez, Robert Repetto and Wilfrido Cruz (1991), *Accounts Overdue: Natural Resource Depreciation in Costa Rica*, Washington, DC: World Resources Institute.

Solow, Robert M. (1956), 'A contribution to the theory of economic growth', *Quarterly Journal of Economics*, **70**: 65–94.

Solow, Robert M. (1957), 'Technical change and the aggregate production function', *Review of Economics and Statistics*, **39**: 312–20.

Solow, Robert M. (1970), 'Foreword', in E. Burmeister and A.R. Dobell (eds), *Mathematical Theories of Economic Growth*, New York: Macmillan.

Solow, Robert M. (1973), 'Is the end of the world at hand?' in A. Weintraub et al. (eds), *The Economic Growth Controversy*, White Plains, NY: International Arts and Science Press.

Solow, Robert M. (1974a), 'The economics of resources or the resources of economics', *American Economic Review*, **64**.

Solow, Robert M. (1974b), 'Intergenerational equity and exhaustible resources', *Review of Economic Studies*, **41**: 29–45.

Solow, Robert M. (1978), 'Resources and economic growth', *American Economist*, **22**: 5–11.

Solow, Robert M. (1986), 'On the intergenerational allocation of natural resources', *Scandinavian Journal of Economics*, **88**: 141–9.

Solow, Robert M. (1987), 'We'd better watch out', *New York Review of Books*, July 12, 36.

Solow, Robert M. (1992), *An Almost Practical Step towards Sustainability*, Washington, DC: Resources for the Future.

Solow, Robert M. (1994), 'Perspectives on growth theory', *Journal of Economic Perspectives*, **8** (1): 45–54.

Solow, Robert, James Tobin, C.C. von Weizsacker and M. Yaari (1966), 'Neoclassical growth with fixed proportions', *Review of Economic Studies*, **33**: 79–116.

Sorokin, Pitirim A. (1957), *Social and Cultural Dynamics*, 2nd revised and abridged edn, 4 vols, original edition, 1937, Cambridge, MA: Harvard University Press.

Spreng, Daniel T. (1988), *Net Energy Requirements and the Energy Requirements of Energy Systems*, New York: Praeger Press.

Sraffa, Piero (1960), *Production of Commodities by Means of Commodities: Prelude to a Critique of Economic Theory*, Cambridge, UK: Cambridge University Press.

Stanford Research Institute (1972), *Patterns of Energy Consumption in the United States*, Washington, DC: Office of Science and Technology, Executive Office of the President.

Stern, David I. (1993), 'Energy use and economic growth in the USA: A multivariate approach', *Energy Economics*, **15**: 137–50.

Stern, David I. (2000), 'A multivariate cointegration analysis of the role of energy in the US macroeconomy', *Energy Economics*, **22** (2): 267–83.

Stiglitz, Joseph (1974), 'Growth with exhaustible natural resources: efficient and optimal growth paths', *Review of Economic Studies*.

Stone, Richard A. (1961), *Input-output and National Accounts*, Paris: OECD.

Stoneman, Paul (1976), *Technological Diffusion and the Computer Revolution*, Cambridge: Cambridge University Press.

Strahan, David (2007), *The Last Oil Shock*, London: John Murray Ltd.

Summers, Claude M. (1971), 'The conversion of energy', *Scientific American*.

Swan, Trevor (1956), 'Economic growth and capital accumulation', *The Economic Record*, **32** (68): 334–61.

Swan, Trevor W. (1963), 'Of golden ages and production functions', in K. Berrill (ed.), *Economic Development with Special Reference to East Asia*, London: Macmillan.

Sylos Labini, Paulo (1995), 'Why the interpretation of the Cobb-Douglas production function must be radically changed', *Structural Change and Economic Dynamics*, **6**: 485–504.

Szargut, Jan, David R. Morris II and Frank R. Steward (1988), *Exergy Analysis of Thermal, Chemical, and Metallurgical Processes*, New York: Hemisphere Publishing Corporation.

Tatom, J.A. (1981), 'Energy prices and short-run economic performance', *Federal Reserve Bank of St. Louis Review*, **63**: 3–17.

Tinbergen, Jan (1956), 'The optimum rate of saving', *Economic Journal*, **66**: 603–9.

Tinbergen, Jan (1960), 'Optimal savings and utility maximization over time', *Econometrica*, **28**: 481–9.

Tobin, James and William Nordhaus (1972), 'Is growth obsolete?', in *Economic Growth*, New York: Columbia University Press.

Tol, Richard S.J. (1994), 'The damage costs of climate change: a note on tangibles and intangibles, applied to DICE', *Energy Policy*, **22** (4): 436–8.

Tversky, A. and D. Kahneman (1974), 'Judgment under uncertainty: heuristics and biases', *Science*, **185**: 1124–31.

United Nations Industrial Development Organization (UNIDO) (2003), *Productivity Enhancement for Social Advance*, Vienna: UNIDO.

United Nations Statistical Office (Annual), *Statistical Yearbook*, various years, New York: United Nations.

United States Bureau of the Census (1975), *Historical Statistics of the United States, Colonial Times to 1970*, Bicentennial edn, 2 vols, Washington, DC: United States Government Printing Office.

United States Bureau of the Census (Annual), *Statistical Abstract of the United States*, Washington, DC: United States Government Printing Office.

United States Congress Office of Technology Assessment (1983), *Industrial Energy Use*, Washington, DC: United States Congress Office of Technology Assessment.

United States Department of Commerce Bureau of Economic Analysis (1973), *Long Term Economic Growth 1860–1970*, Washington, DC: United States Government Printing Office.

United States Department of Commerce Bureau of Economic Analysis (1992), *Business Statistics, 1963–1991*, Washington, DC: United States Department of Commerce.

United States Department of Commerce Bureau of Economic Analysis (Monthly), *Survey of Current Business*, Washington, DC: United States Department of Commerce.

United States Department of Energy, Energy Information Administration (Annual), *EIA Annual Energy Review*, Washington, DC: United States Government Printing Office.

United States Department of Highway Statistics Bureau of Transportation Statistics (1994), *Transportation Statistics: Annual Report 1994*, Washington, DC: United States Government Printing Office.

United States Energy Information Agency (2002a), 'Manufacturers Energy Consumption Survey 1991', (PDF or Lotus 123), accessed at www.eia.doe.gov/emeu/mecs.

United States Energy Information Agency (2002b), 'Manufacturers Energy Consumption Survey 1994', (PDF and Lotus 123), accessed at www.eia.doe.gov/emeu/mecs.

United States Energy Information Agency (2002c), 'Electricity Consumption in Buildings 1995', (PDF or Lotus 123), accessed at www.eia.doe.gov/emeu/consumption/reports.

United States Energy Information Agency (2002d), 'Residential Energy Consumption Survey 1997', (PDF or Lotus 123), accessed at www.eia. doe.gov/emeu/recs.

United States Energy Information Agency (2002e), 'Manufacturers Energy Consumption Survey 1998', (PDF or Lotus 123), accessed at www.eia. doe.gov/emeu/mecs.

United States Office of Emergency Preparedness (OEP), Executive Office of the President (1972), *The Potential for Energy Conservation*, Washington, DC: United States Office of Emergency Preparedness (OEP), Executive Office of the President.

United States Office of Science and Technology (OST), Executive Office of the President (1972), *Patterns of Energy Consumption in the United States*, Washington, DC: United States Office of Science and Technology (OST), Executive Office of the President.

Usher, Albert Payson (1929), *A History of Mechanical Inventions*, Cambridge, MA: Harvard University Press.

Uzawa, H. (1962), 'On the stability of Edgeworth's barter process', *International Economic Review*, **3**: 218–32.

Van den Bergh, Jeroen C.J.M. (2003), 'Evolutionary analysis of economic growth, environment and resources', in D. Simpson, M.A. Toman, and R.U. Ayres (eds), *Scarcity and Growth in the New Millennium*, Baltimore, MD: Johns Hopkins University Press for Resources for the Future Inc.

Van den Bergh, Jeroen C.J.M., Ada Ferrer-i-Carbonell and Giuseppe Munda (2000), 'Alternative models of individual behavior and implications for environmental policy', *Ecological Economics*, **32**: 43–61.

Verdoorn, P.J. (1951), 'On an empirical law governing the productivity of labor', *Econometrica*, **19**: 209–10.

Verdoorn, P.J. (1956), 'Complementarity and long range projections', *Econometrica*, **24**: 429–50.

Vernon, Raymond (1966), 'International investment and international trade in the product cycle', *Quarterly Journal of Economics*: 290–307.

von Bertalanffy, Ludwig (1957), 'Quantitative laws in metabolism and growth', *Quarterly Review of Biology*, **32**: 217–31.

von Neumann, John (1945), 'A model of general economic equilibrium', originally published in 1932, *Review of Economic Studies*, **13**: 1–9.

von Weizsaecker, C.C. (1962), *Wachstum, Zins und Optimale Investifionsquote*, Basel, Switzerland: Kyklos-Verlag.

von Weizsaecker, Ernst Ulrich, Amory B. Lovins and L. Hunter Lovins (1998), *Factor Four: Doubling Wealth, Halving Resource Use*, London: Earthscan Publications Ltd.

Wald, Abraham (1936), 'Uber einige Gleichungssysteme der mathematischen Oekonomie', *Zeitschrift für Nationalkonomie*, 7: 637–70.

Walker, Susan (2002), *U.S. Consumer Credit Card Debt May Crash Economy*, 2004 (cited 25 April 2006).

Wall, Goran (1977), Exergy: A Useful Concept within Resource Accounting, Goteborg, Sweden: Institute of Theoretical Physics, Chalmers University of Technology and University of Goteborg.

Walras, Leon (1874), *Elements d'économie politique pure*, Lausanne, Switzerland: Corbaz.

Warr, Benjamin and Robert U. Ayres (2006), 'The MEET-REXS model', *Structural Change & Economic Dynamics*, 17: 329–78.

Williams, Eric, Robert Ayres and Benjamin Warr (2008), 'Efficiency dilution: long-term exergy conversion trends in Japan', *Environmental Science and Technology*, 42: 4964–70.

Watanabe, Chihiro, Bing Zhu and T. Miyazawa (2001), 'Hierarchical impacts of the length of technology waves: an analysis of technolabor homeostasis', *Technological Forecasting and Social Change*, 68: 81–104.

Weissmahr, Joseph A. (2000), 'The elimination of the factor land and its consequences to economic theory', paper read at Conference on Physics and Economics, October, Bad Honnef, Germany.

Wene, Clas-Otto (2000), *Experience Curves for Energy Technology Policy*, Paris: International Energy Agency (OECD).

Wernick, I.K. (1994), 'Dematerialization and secondary materials recovery: a long-run perspective', *Journal of the Minerals, Metals and Materials Society*, 46: 39–42.

Wertime, Theodore A. (1962), *The Coming of the Age of Steel*, Chicago, IL: The University of Chicago Press.

Weyant, J.P.E. (1999), 'The costs of the Kyoto Protocol', *Energy*, (special issue).

Wikipedia (2006), 'Japanese Postwar Economic Miracle', accessed 13 September at http://en.wikipedia.org/wiki/Japanese_post-war_economic_miracle.

Williams, E.J., A. Guenther and F.C. Fehsenfeld (1992), 'An inventory of nitric oxide emissions from soils in the United States', *Journal of Geophysical Research*, 97 (D7): 7511–19.

Williams, Eric, Benjamin Warr and Robert U. Ayres (2008), 'Efficiency dilution: long-term exergy conversion trends in Japan', *Environmental Science and Technology*, 42(13): 4964–70.

Williamson, Harold F. and Arnold R. Daum (1959), *The American Petroleum Industry*, Evanston, IL: Northwestern University Press.

Winter, Sidney G. (1964), 'Economic "natural selection" and the theory of the firm', *Yale Economic Essays*, **4** (1): 225–72.

Winter, Sidney G. (1984), 'Schumpeterian competition in alternative technological regimes', *Journal of Economic Behavior and Organization*, **5** (3–4): 287–320.

Wirsenius, S. (2000), 'Human use of land and organic materials: modeling the turnover of biomass in the global food system', Ph.D. thesis, dissertation no. CPL 827, Chalmers University of Technology, Goteborg, Sweden.

Woodbury, Robert (1972), *Studies in the History of Machine Tools*, Cambridge, MA: MIT Press.

World Bank (2005), 'World Development Indicators (2005)', World Bank, accessed at http://web.worldbank.org/wbsite/external/datastatistics/.

World Resources Institute (WRI) (2000), *Weight of Nations: Materials Outflows from Industrial Economies*, Washington, DC: World Resources Institute.

Wright, T.P. (1936), 'Factors affecting the cost of airplanes', *Journal of Aeronautical Sciences*, **3**: 122–8.

Yelle, L.E. (1979), 'The learning curve: historical review and comprehensive survey', *Decision Sciences*, **10** (2): 302–28.

Yergin, Daniel (1991), *The Prize: The Epic Quest for Oil, Money and Power*, New York: Simon and Schuster.

Young, Allyn (1928), 'Increasing Returns and Economic Progress', *The Economic Journal*, **38**: 527–42.

Young, Alwyn (1995), 'The tyranny of numbers: confronting the statistical realities of the east Asian experience', *Quarterly Journal of Economics*: 641–80.

Yu, E.S.H. and J.C. Jin (1992), 'Cointegration tests of energy consumption, income and employment', *Resource & Energy Economics*, **14**: 259–66.

Zivot, E. and Donald W.K. Andrews (1992), 'Further evidence on the Great Crash, the Oil Shock and the unit root hypothesis', *Journal of Business and Economic Statistics*, **10** (3): 251–70.

Zwicky, Fritz (1951), 'Tasks we face', *Journal of the American Rocket Society*, **84**: 3–20.

Index